THE AUSTRADE STORY

Export and Investment Facilitation under
the Microscope

THE AUSTRADE STORY

Export and Investment Facilitation under the Microscope

Edited by Bruno Mascitelli

Connor Court Publishing

Connor Court Publishing Pty Ltd

Copyright © Bruno Mascitelli 2015

PO Box 224W
Ballarat VIC 3350
sales@connorcourt.com
www.connorcourt.com

ISBN: 9781925138894 (pbk.)

Cover design by Ian James

Printed in Australia

CONTENTS

Section One: Setting the scene for the establishment of the Australian Trade Commission

Section Two: The formative years of Austrade

Section Three: Consolidation of Austrade

Section Four: Austrade Today and Tomorrow

Appendices

Foreword

Minister for Trade and Investment Andrew Robb

The history of the Australian Trade Commission (Austrade), and the earlier Australian Trade Commissioner Service, is one of dedication to advancing Australia's economic interests.

Austrade's great strength is in seeking out new market opportunities abroad for our goods and services. It helps our businesses identify and take advantage of commercial openings, promotes Australia's areas of competitive advantage and pursues investment.

The *Austrade Story* is an important collection of essays and interviews which focuses on Austrade after its formation in 1986; it builds on the earlier work of Boris Schedvin in his book *Emissaries of Trade: A History of the Australian Trade Commissioner Service.*

This publication provides a revealing insight into an organisation that has, for the most part, sat comfortably between government and business. While documenting the successes, it also offers some frank assessments of the organisation at different periods over the past three decades.

It includes the reflections of former trade ministers, current and former senior executives, trade commissioners and Austrade's locally engaged staff abroad.

It is apparent that the fundamentals of trade promotion have remained much the same over the years; identifying new opportunities, building strong relationships with our customers, providing accurate information to business and marketing our brands.

The markets themselves and our priorities have however changed and evolved over the decades since the formation of the Trade Commissioner Service. Austrade has adapted along the way.

Today for example, Austrade is actively involved in the promotion of our two biggest services exports, international education and tourism. There has also been a rebalance of strategic purpose since

2011 with a shift towards growth and emerging markets, especially those in the Asia Pacific which offer so much promise.

While it is business that is the primary driver of growth and job creation for Australia, two recent examples of trade promotion illustrate how the badge of government can be so important to opening doors in overseas markets.

Australia Week in China in April 2014 and *Australia Business Week in India* in January 2015 involved some 1,150 of our business leaders in the biggest ever Australian business missions to these most important markets. Austrade was absolutely instrumental to these commercially successful visits.

It also has a major role to play in assisting business to capitalise on the landmark free trade agreements we have recently concluded with Korea, Japan and China.

Efforts to attract new investment into Australia have also intensified and we have a keener eye on investment opportunities for Australian businesses in overseas markets.

An important part of my job when overseas is to promote Australia as open for business. Essentially, this is what Austrade does on a day-to-day basis in its posts around the world, from Bangalore to Bogota and from London to Lima.

The Austrade Story will contribute to a broader understanding of this work. I commend Bruno Mascitelli for his efforts as project editor and thank all contributors.

The Hon Andrew Robb AO MP
Minister for Trade and Investment
11 February 2015

Acknowledgements

This book is the work of a number of people some of whom appear in this volume and others that do not. They both need acknowledgement. I am especially thankful to the contributors to the book for their diligence in completing their manuscripts for the love of the project and doing so in a timely manner. There is an army of former (and current) Austraders and protagonists of the Austrade story who have all assisted me and other contributors in this endeavour. Each has provided a piece of the picture which appears in this book. They include in alphabetical order:

Michael Abrahams, Mike Adams, Roger and Julie Bayliss, Hazel Bennett, Nicholas Brown, Peter Collens, David Crook, John Dawkins, Lloyd Downey, Pat Evans, Ralph Evans, Ted Exell, Bill Ferris, Tim Fischer, Mark Gwizdalla, Tim Harcourt, Kym Hewett, Prue Holstein, Shelley Jackson, Greg Joffe, Richard Johns, Michael Johnson, Roger James, Terry Goss, Peter Langhorne, Peter McNamara, Alan McDonald, Lindsay MacAlister, Ross Maddock, Elizabeth Masamune, Michael Moignard, Bruce Nicholls, Peter O'Byrne, Charles O'Hanlon, David Oliver, Diane Robinson, Bill Scales, Boris Schedvin, Jim Scully, Julia Selby, Laurie Smith, Geoff Spears, Ashley Stevenson, Penny Styles, Petr Vodvarka, Des Walsh, Frank Walsh, Ashley White, Leigh Wilmott, Ian Wing, Hayden Williams.

It is an honour and privilege to have the foreword from Minister Robb. Most importantly the Minister clearly acknowledges the importance of a study of this kind. I wish to also acknowledge the support received from the current Austrade management including Bruce Gosper, Laurie Smith and Tim Beresford who all accepted to be interviewed for this project. Michael Lindquist has provided all the photographic expertise required for the photos that appear in the book. I also wish to acknowledge the heroic efforts made by Geoff Spears supported by Michael Abrahams to assist the writing of more than one chapter.

Connor Court Publishers have yet again shown their trust in me and have supported this project from the outset. Special recognition within Connor Court goes to Michael Gilchrist for his editing guidance and to Anthony Cappello for accepting to publish this book. The inspirers of his book have turned out to be three mentors who engaged with me on a daily basis helping, criticising and encouraging me to pursue this project. With little prompting they would guide me through the meanderings of Austrade dealing with each and every turn in this project. Many of key decisions taken on this book belong to them. Their presence in the book is a pale reflection of the contribution they have made to this project. Most importantly unbeknownst to them they provided me with the balance and approach which only I can appreciate. I wish to warmly acknowledge Greg Dodds, Leith Doody and John Tinney. Without their support the sceptics of the project would have won. Thank you.

Biographies of Contributors

Mike Adams is a former DFAT economist with extensive experience on trade-related aspects of e-commerce, free trade agreements, climate change and agricultural protectionism. Mike was Australia's economic counsellor in Beijing from 2000 to 2004 and commercial counsellor in Wellington from 1989 to 1992. He holds a PhD in economic history from the University of Hull. A recent book covers the experience of British prisoners of war on the Thailand-Burma railway during and after the Second World War. Mike is also joint author, with Nicolas Brown and Ron Wickes, of *Trading Nation: Advancing Australia's interests in world markets*, published by UNSW Press in 2013. They are also partners in the trade policy consulting firm, Trading Nation Consulting.

Nicolas Brown headed DFAT's branch responsible for analysis and strategic advice about trade and economic issues for five years to 2008. He also headed the Canada and Latin America Branch over 2009 and 2010 and was Australia's Deputy High Commissioner to Malaysia from 2000 to 2003. Nic joined DFAT in 1996 from the Department of the Prime Minister and Cabinet and worked in the Australian Bureau of Statistics in the early part of his career. He holds a Masters degree from the London School of Economics. Nicolas along with Mike Adams are joint authors, along with Ron Wickes, of *Trading Nation: Advancing Australia's interests in world markets,* published by UNSW Press in 2013. They are also partners in the trade policy consulting firm, Trading Nation Consulting.

Peter Collens retired from Austrade in 2012 in the role of Head of Investment Division. His early professional background was in banking with extensive experience in commercial, international and merchant banking, holding positions both in Australia and offshore. Peter returned to Australia in the early 90's to take up a position on the Royal Commission into Tricontinental. In 1992 he joined Austrade in Melbourne and had a key role in the early development of the Investment Promotion in Australia. As Senior Investment Commissioner (Australian Projects) he was instrumental in attracting investors to a number of major projects around Australia. Following a secondment to Business Victoria in 1999, Peter held a number of key roles with the Victorian department including acting Deputy Secretary Industry and Trade and CEO of Invest Victoria, the Victorian Government's investment promotion agency. In April 2010 Peter returned to Austrade in the investment leadership role to continue the integration of investment promotion into Austrade. Peter championed professional training for investment promotion in Australia, and strongly supported collaboration across investment attraction agencies. He continues to mentor and contribute to training and strategic planning for agencies in Australia and overseas.

John Dawkins, was born in Perth and was educated the University of Western Australia, where he graduated in economics. In 1974, Dawkins was elected to the House of Representatives for the marginal seat of Tangney, but lost the seat in the 1975 election following the dismissal of the Whitlam government. In 1977 Dawkins returned to the House as member for the safe Labor seat of Fremantle, succeeding Kim Beazley (senior), and defeating his son, Kim Beazley, for the Labor pre-selection. He became Minister for Finance following the election of the first Hawke government in 1983. In the second Hawke Ministry (1984–1987) he was Minister for Trade. From 1987 to 1991 he was Minister for Employment, Education and Training. He moved to the Treasury in the Keating Labor government from December 1991 to December 1993. In that month of December 1993 Dawkins, announced his resignation, and quit politics altogether soon after.

Greg Dodds was born in Perth in 1947 and did his secondary schooling at St Louis Jesuit School in Claremont. He graduated into the Intelligence Corps from the Royal Military College Duntroon in 1968. After several appointments including active service in Vietnam, he was trained as a Japanese linguist at Point Cook and left the Army in 1979 to open the office of the Australia-Japan Foundation in Tokyo.

After being Senior Private Secretary to the Special Minister of State in Canberra, he was the Commissioner General for Australia at the Tsukuba Expo in 1985. He became Senior Trade Commissioner for Austrade in Tokyo in 1986 and then the Minister and Charge d'Affaires in the Embassy in 1990. In 1992, he left DFAT to become the Austrade Executive General Manager for Japan/Korea and then for all of North East Asia in 1996. He retired in 2004 and now lives in Perth.

Leith Doody FAICD is an International Business Advisor. He has four decades of experience in general management of international organisations, including sitting on a number of Boards, in both the public and private sector, living and working in Australia, the UK, RO Korea, Hong Kong, New Zealand, Germany and Indonesia. Leith is a Fellow of the Australian Institute of Company Directors and a member of the Chairman's Circle at Asialink and Chancellor's Circle at the University of Melbourne. In the 20 years he was with the Australian Trade Commission (Austrade), Leith held various State, National & International positions, including: Regional Senior Trade & Investment Commissioner–ASEAN & Minister (Commercial) to Indonesia Jakarta, Regional Director – Europe, Middle East & Africa based in Frankfurt, Acting Executive Director – Corporate & Government Services Canberra, State Manager – Victoria/Tasmania; National Leader – Corporate Partnerships Melbourne ; Consul-General for Australia & Senior Trade Commissioner – Pacific Auckland, New Zealand; General Manager – Marketing & Promotions Group, Product & Services Group & Major Opportunities Group Melbourne, Australia.

Pat Evans was an Executive Director with Austrade from 2003-2011. During this time she was the Executive Director for Export and Investment Services (2003-10) and Executive Director for International Education (2010-11). With responsibility for the operational onshore division, she led successful change management and integration programs over a number of years. Prior to joining Austrade Pat held the following senior roles over a 25 year career in educational publishing: Managing Director of Pearson Education Australia, the largest education publisher in Australia; CEO of Prentice Hall Australia, and Managing Director of CBS Publishing. She has a Bachelor of Commerce from the University of Alberta, Canada and has also worked in Canada, Turkey, Sweden, and been responsible for businesses in South Africa and New Zealand. In retirement Pat is a Director of, and active volunteer for a women's charity, Dress for Success Sydney.

Ralph Evans began his career as a chemical engineer at the CSR Company Distillery Division in Sydney. Looking for larger horizons, he went to California for an MBA at Stanford, class of 1971. From there he joined management consultants McKinsey and Company, Inc., in London. After several years in Europe and long assignments in east and north Africa, Ralph transferred home to Sydney. In 1979, Ralph joined three other consultants to form the Australian-based business strategy consulting partnership Pappas Carter Evans and Koop. The firm grew and eventually was acquired by the global leader in its field, the Boston Consulting Group, where Ralph became a vice-president. His work continued to include periods in a number of overseas countries as well as Australia and New Zealand. Ralph was introduced to government through his work on a major study of the future of Australian manufacturing. In 1991, following the review of Austrade by McKinsey, Ralph joined as Managing Director. His brief was to complete the implementing of McKinsey's recommendations and continue adding commercial edge to Austrade's work. An important Austrade program during his tenure was the International Trade Enhancement Scheme, or ITES, which was recommended by the manufacturing review. It lent up to $5 million to fast-growing exporters to expand their overseas activities.

Tim Fischer served as an Australian Army Officer in Australia and Vietnam (1966-69). He served in the New South Wales Parliament (1971-84) and the Australian Federal Parliament (1984-2001) including as Leader of the National Party, Minister for Trade and Deputy Prime

Minister (1996-99). Tim was the Shadow Minister for Energy and Resources, Shadow Minister for Veterans' Affairs and the Federal Parliamentary National Party Liaison Officer for Western Australia. Tim also led the Official Australian Delegation which oversaw the East Timor Referendum on 30 August 1999. He was Chairman of Tourism Australia 2004-07, and of the Australia Thailand Institute 2005-08. In 2005 Tim Fischer was appointed Companion of the Order of Australia. In 2008 Tim Fischer became the first Rome resident Australian Ambassador to the Holy See and for a period Special Envoy to Bhutan, Eritrea and South Sudan. He is the author of several books on Trains, also one on Rome and most recently he wrote "Maestro John Monash: Australia's greatest Citizen General".

Richard Fletcher PhD was a Trade Commissioner for twenty five years – a period that began with the Menzies-McEwen era and concluded with the first three years of Austrade. Following completion of a three year marketing cadetship with Unilever (Australia) Ltd, he joined the second intake of Trainee Trade Commissioners in 1964 and his postings included New Delhi 1965-66; Bombay, 1966-67; New Delhi 1967-68; San Francisco, 1968-72; Jakarta 1972-74; 1974-76; Market Advisory Services, Sydney 1976-78; Tripoli 1979-80; Los Angeles, 1882-86 and Bangkok, 1986-89. In 1989 he embarked on a new career as an international marketing academic. During the next 21 years he moved from senior tutor to Professor. In retirement he continues involvement in international marketing as Adjunct Professor of Marketing at the University of Western Sydney. He is the principal author of the largest selling international marketing textbook in Australia, now in its sixth edition, "International Marketing – an Asia-Pacific Perspective".

Bruce Gosper is CEO of Austrade, the Australian Government agency responsible for promoting trade, investment and international education, and tourism policy, programs and research. Prior to Austrade, Mr Gosper was Deputy Secretary with the Department of Foreign Affairs and Trade as Australia's Senior Trade Policy Official, responsible for all trade negotiations. His career also includes roles as Ambassador and Permanent Representative to the World Trade Organization, where he was also Chair of the General Council and Chair of the Dispute Settlement Body. He was previously Minister (Commercial) at the Australian Embassy in Washington, and Counsellor Agriculture at the Australian Embassy in Tokyo. Mr Gosper has represented the government on the Export Finance and Insurance Corporation, the Australia Japan Foundation, the Australia Korea Foundation, the Australian Pork Corporation and Tourism Australia.

Terry Goss has had a long and varied career in international trade promotion and facilitation with Austrade and its antecedent organisations. He served as a Senior Trade Commissioner in posts in North America, Africa and Europe and was Executive Manager of Austrade's Business Club Australia at the 2000 Sydney Olympics. He has subsequently consulted to state, federal and foreign governments in projects involving best practice in international trade facilitation. This included a period as internal consultant on Trade Support Institutions with the International Trade Centre in Geneva. He is an Honorary Life Member of the Australian Institute of Export. Terry is currently based in Sydney.

Tim Harcourt is the J.W.Nevile Fellow in Economics at the UNSW Business School, Sydney, Australia. Tim also teaches International Business strategy in Asia and Latin America at the Australian Graduate School of Management (AGSM) and is a visiting Professor at the Pontificia Universidad Catolica (PUC) in Chile. A prolific author and globetrotter, Tim has visited over 58 countries in the past five years alone. Tim was Chief Economist of the Australian Trade Commission (Austrade) for over a decade and also worked for the Reserve Bank of Australia (RBA) and the Australian Council of Trade Unions (ACTU) and in the corporate sector internationally. Tim is also the Adviser – International Engagement to the Premier of South Australia, Hon Jay Weatherill, MP and Expert Panel Member – Minimum Wage and Superannuation Funds review, for the Fair Work Commission. Tim was educated at the University of Adelaide, the University of Minnesota and Harvard University (and by his own students!) Tim is the author of seven books on the international economy including: *Beyond Our Shores*, *Going the Distance*, *Great Southern Lands – building ties between Australia & Brazil*, *Latin Lessons* and his best known book *The Airport Economist His new book is Trading Places – The Airport Economist's guide to International Business*.

Roger James was Austrade's Senior Trade Commissioner in Moscow from 1992 to 1995. He joined the Australian Trade Commissioner Service in 1980 following a career in international marketing in the steel and coal industries in the United Kingdom, France and Australia. His early postings were to Chicago (1981-84) and Beijing (1985-88), the latter being during the emergence of China after the Cultural Revolution, which was a useful introduction to life at a hardship post. His domestic assignments for Austrade included Manager, Japan/Korea (1991) and member of the Workflows team (1996/7). His final posting was as STC Paris (1997-99). Since retiring from Austrade in 2004, he has undertaken a range of consultancies and advisory positions and has lectured in International Business at universities in Melbourne and Beijing, China. He now retired and lives on the Mornington Peninsula in Victoria.

Greg Joffe is a Principal at Nous Group. He works across Nous' strategy, public policy, digital strategy and organisation capability practices. He has been a Principal at Nous since leaving Austrade in 2003. At Austrade, Greg was head of strategic development and also Chief Information Officer in his last year. Prior to Austrade, Greg worked as a management consultant at McKinsey & Company, traded equity options and physical oil and derivatives in London and Monaco. He has a BA (Hons) and MA from Stanford University and an LLB from UNSW, where he is an adjunct Associate Professor with the AGSM.

Peter Langhorne occupied the position of Principal Private Secretary to Prime Minister John Howard until 17 December 2007.

Prior to that he was Senior Adviser to the Senate Leader, and Chief of Staff and Principal Adviser to the Deputy Prime Minister. In 1992 he joined Austrade as Executive General Manager Corporate Affairs. In August 1996, the then Minister for Trade appointed him to the Office of Deputy Managing Director of Austrade, a position he occupied until 2001. Prior to joining the Australian Trade Commission, Mr Langhorne occupied senior management and policy positions in the CSIRO, Departments of Primary Industry, Defence and National Resources and Energy. He is a graduate of the Royal Melbourne Institute of Technology in Spatial Science and holds post graduate qualifications in corporate management. Mr Langhorne is a Director of The Page Research Centre and a Director of John McEwen House Ltd. He recently retired as Chair of the Nationals Standing Policy Committee and as a member of the Federal Management Committee. Mr Langhorne has served as an office bearer of the National Party of Australia, holding the elected positions of Campaign Chairman, Chairman of the Monaro Electorate Council, Secretary, Queanbeyan Branch and Delegate to Central Council.

Lucy Luo is an Australian Chinese, who came to Australia as a student in 1990s with a Chinese bachelor degree in engineering. She graduated from Monash University with a masters degree in accounting and RMIT with a diploma in International Trade. She has been dedicated to the facilitation and promotion of two-way collaboration, trade and investment opportunities between Australia and China. She joined Austrade Beijing office as a locally engaged staff and served between 2001 and 2010 as Office Manager and Senior Business Development Manager. In 2010 she returned to Australia and continued to work with Austrade Melbourne until 2011 as an Industry Advisor. Lucy is currently based in Melbourne working with City of Melbourne as a China specialist Trade Advisor.

Bruno Mascitelli is an Associate Professor at Swinburne University of Technology. He was a local employed staff with the Australian Trade Commission for 16 years based in Milan (Italy) between 1982 and 1997. On returning to Australia he joined the US Foreign Commercial Service based in Melbourne from 1998 until 2000. Since joining Swinburne University in 2000 he completed his PhD in 2005 and has taught in areas such as international business, Australian trade and European Union matters. His publications cover numerous journal articles and book chapters as well as 12 books on themes such as Australian trade and investment, migration, expatriate voting and international business.

Elizabeth Masamune joined the Tokyo office of Austrade locally in 1987 as an overseas engaged employee. She was posted to Jakarta as an A-based officer in 1996, to serve as the Japan Trade Commissioner in Asia. She went on to serve from 1999-2011 as Senior Trade Commissioner Hanoi, Senior Trade Commissioner Seoul, and Senior Trade Commissioner Tokyo/Country Manager Japan. In 2006 she was awarded the Public Service Medal for advancing the interests of Australian business in Asian markets. Elizabeth worked onshore as General Manager East Asian Growth Markets and General Manager Trade, retiring from Austrade in 2014. She is now Managing Director of @Asia Associates. Elizabeth holds a Bachelor of Arts (Hons) from Monash University, and a Master of Literary Studies from Queensland University. She is also a Graduate of the Australian Institute of Company Directors.

Bruce Nicholls (B.Commerce/Diploma of Business, FFAICD) joined the TC Service from CSR in 1972, aged 24. He was posted to India, Germany, China and Hong Kong and was the inaugural TC – "China Action Plan". He then served on the boards of three listed public companies, on Goulburn Valley Water Corporation and as Chairman of the RACA. He was President of the Australia China Chamber of Commerce & Industry and a Trustee of the Committee for Economic Development of Australia. He is currently on the boards of the Port of Melbourne Corporation and Norcen Financial Services (Bendigo Community Banks). In 2012 he published *A Briefcase in Transit – Undiplomatic Reflections of a Trade Commissioner*.

Phil Ruthven is the founder and Chairman of IBISWorld, an international corporation providing online business information, forecasting and strategic services. In 2014, Phil became a Member of the Order of Australia, in recognition of his significant service to business and commerce, and to the community. Phil contributes regularly to radio, TV, newspapers, magazines and documentaries on business, economic and social issues. He continues to be one of Australia's most frequent and prolific commentators in demand by the media, and is widely considered the nation's most respected strategist and futurist on business, social and economic matters. He addresses about 70 congresses, seminars and conferences each year and has done so for three decades. His involvement as a communicator takes him around Australia and occasionally overseas. Phil is a science graduate with further studies in management and economics at various universities and institutes, and was a Rotary awardee to the United States in the late 1960s. He spent over 10 years in the food industry, including executive positions in research, production and marketing, before establishing IBIS in 1971. Phil is currently an Adjunct Professor at The University of Technology (Sydney), and a member of the ANU College of Business & Economics Advisory Board. He is a recent past board member of the Melbourne Institute, CEDA and a past Director of Open Family Australia (the charitable foundation aiding street children) where he continues to help as an Ambassador for Whitelion/ Open Family.

Laurie Smith has been Executive Director, International Operations since 2011. In this role, he is responsible for a network of 82 offices in 48 markets and also leads teams in Australia responsible for marketing, advice to Australian exporters and liaison across government in Canberra. He is based in Sydney. From 2004 to 2011, Laurie was Austrade's Regional Director, North East Asia, leading teams in over 20 locations across Japan, Korea, Greater China, Mongolia and Vietnam. Laurie previously held a number of senior roles with a major multinational corporation in Hong Kong and Beijing. He led China business development for multiple divisions of the company, overseeing a range of direct and portfolio investments in China. Earlier, as Executive Director of a Sydney-based, Asian markets strategy consultancy, Laurie worked on projects across India, Thailand, Laos, Vietnam, China, Taiwan, Hong Kong, Japan, Korea, Indonesia and South Africa for a client base that spanned Australia, Europe, the USA and Asia. Laurie's early career was with the Department of Trade and the Department of Foreign Affairs and Trade in Canberra and Taipei. Laurie has a Bachelor of Science from Melbourne University, and undertook post-graduate study at Peking University. He is fluent in Mandarin.

Geoff Spears - Prior to his retirement at the end of 2009, Geoff Spears had an extensive career with the Australian Public Service promoting Australia's exports and assisting companies achieve international business success. He served with the Australian Trade Commission (Austrade) in Sydney and Canberra and also in offshore postings at Australian Embassies in New Zealand, Italy and Britain (short term). Key onshore roles included: secretary of the then Austrade Board; executive officer of the Austmine industry export network for mining services; and general manager, overseeing the development of industry strategies and networks across Austrade to deliver on Australia's trade and investment objectives. Geoff has a Bachelor of Economics Degree from the Australian National University, Canberra.

John Tinney - After university studies in France, John worked in the Australian trade commissioner's office in Paris. He later became a trade commissioner and then a senior executive with the Australian Trade Commission (Austrade), spending a total of twenty years in Geneva, Moscow, Paris, Rome and Frankfurt. He also undertook short-term assignments in many other countries and territories in north Africa, Asia, eastern and western Europe, the Americas and the South Pacific. Since then he has taught various undergraduate and post-graduate international business courses at the Swinburne University of Technology and has contributed to two books on Australia's international business.

Petr Vodvarka was born in 1956 in industrial city Ostrava, Czechoslovakia (from 1993 Czech Republic). Elementary and high school was focused on humanities and languages. Due of political reasons, he was not allowed to study at university as per his choice (humanities) but only technical subjects. He finally decided for Chemical-Technological University in Pardubice, which he passed in 1980. His first job (after compulsory military service) was in a foreign trading company and was lost soon based on his refusal to join communist party. His next job at the Ore Research Institute brought new opportunities (e.g. visiting North Korea) but also possibilities to develop two patents. After the "velvet revolution" in 1989 he spent a year in Milwaukee, USA, working for M&A company Einhorm Associates. After returning back to the Czech Republic, he worked for consulting companies (Arthur D. Little and PA Consulting Group) focusing on strategic management of reformed companies. Finally, in 1998 he became the Austrade country manager (Czech Republic and Slovakia) focusing on education, biotechnology and innovative materials. At the same time, he was appointed as Australian Honorary Consul in the Czech Republic. Petr has two children and two grandchildren. His hobbies cover history and Prague architecture, numismatic and music.

Dr. Peter Wilton teaches strategy, marketing, and international management in the Haas School of Business at the Haas School of Business, University of California, Berkeley. Dr. Wilton has published widely in numerous leading journals, including the *Journal of Marketing Research, Management Science,* the *Journal of Consumer Research,* the *Journal of Retailing,* the *Journal of Business & Economic Statistics, European Research,* and elsewhere. In addition to his teaching activities, through his private consulting company known as ORBIS Associates, Dr. Wilton also has a long-standing relationship with Austrade, having collaborated on a variety of strategic and operational matters, including: Senior Executive Strategic Planning Session (2000); Review of Austrade's client value-creation and delivery strategy ("Journey to Export & International

Business", 2007); Review of Austrade's international partner and ally strategy ("Strategic Partnering for Global Success: The Customer/Ally Perspective", 2008); Review of Austrade's on-shore operations ("A Strategic Review of Austrade's On-Shore Operations: The Stakeholder Value Perspective", 2011) and Continuing member of a standing panel for "Building Austrade Capability".

Ian Wing is an independent business consultant based in Old Chatham, New York. He had 32 years service with the Australian Government's Department of Trade and its successor organisation, the Australian Trade Commission. Based in Frankfurt, Germany from 2008 until 2011 he was Regional Director, Europe, Middle East and Africa and from 2003 until 2007 he was Regional Director, Americas based in Los Angeles. He also served as Acting Executive General Manager, Middle East/Indian Ocean Region and was Senior Trade Commissioner in Moscow, Tokyo, Washington and Atlanta. In prior years he was Trade Commissioner in Moscow and Tokyo. In 2013 he returned to Austrade on contract to act as Senior Trade Commissioner in Moscow for 5 months. He has an honours degree in Economics from the University of Adelaide and a Diploma in Japanese Studies from the Osaka University of Foreign Studies.

Acronyms and Abbreviations

AAP	Austrade Advancement Program
ABS	Australian Bureau of Statistics
A-Based	Australian based staff
ACTU	Australian Council of Trade Unions
ANAO	Australian National Audit Office
AOPL	Austrade overseas performance level
APEC	Asia–Pacific Economic Cooperation
APL	Austrade performance level
APS	Australian Public Service
ASEAN	Association of Southeast Asian Nations
ATO	Australian Taxation Office
APS	Australian Public Service
Austrade	Australian Trade Commission
AWN	Austrade Women's Network
BRICS	Brazil, Russia, India, China and South Africa
CEO	Chief Executive Officer
DFAT	Department of Foreign Affairs and Trade
DITAC	Department of Industry, Technology and Commerce
EFIC	Export Finance and Insurance Corporation
EMDG	Export Market Development Grants
FDI	Foreign Direct Investment
FIRB	Foreign Investment Review Board
FOI	Freedom of Information
FTA	Free Trade Agreement
G20	WTO group of 20 major economies
GE	General Electric
GDP	Gross domestic product
GFC	Global financial crisis
GST	Goods and Services Tax
IMF	International Monetary Fund
IP	Intellectual Property

KPI	Key Performance Indicator
LES	Local Employed Staff
MIP	Market Information Package
NAFTA	North American Free Trade Agreement
OECD	Organisation for Economic Cooperation and Development
OEE	Overseas Engaged Employees
PRC	People's Republic of China
RBA	Reserve Bank of Australia
SES	Senior Executive Service
SME	Small medium enterprise
SOE	State Owned Enterprise
STC	Senior Trade Commissioner
UAE	United Arab Emirates
UNCTAD	United Nations Conference on Trade and Development
USTR	United States Trade Representative
WB	World Bank
WIGB	Women in global business
WTO	World Trade Organization

SECTION ONE

Setting the scene for the establishment of the Australian Trade Commission

1

How we arrived at a book
on the Australian Trade Commission

Bruno Mascitelli

This is a book about the Australian Trade Commission (Austrade). The story contained in this volume emerges at a special moment for Austrade as it inches closer to its 30th anniversary and hence a timely moment to provide some reflections and observations on its three decades of performance. It is also a critical juncture in its history, considering the Abbott government initiated National Commission of Audit recommendation for a total absorption of Austrade into DFAT. It is worth noting that the story of the Australian Trade Commission would be difficult and incomplete to recount without reference to the epic history of the Trade Commissioner Service completed by Boris Schedvin in 2008. While the scope of this current book does not allow us to restate the fascinating historic journey of trade promotion in the early decades of the 20th century in Australia as explored by Schedvin, the Austrade story seeks to sit firmly on the shoulders of this monumental work *Emissaries of Trade: A History of the Trade Commissioner Service*. There is however one significant difference between these two books. It is the contribution of 25 plus authors who have addressed different and significant aspects of the Austrade story.

This book is partly a history of Austrade, partly a recollection of personal stories, interviews with prominent managers and representatives of Austrade about their work and impressions of responsibility they may have had in Austrade. Clearly the list of themes tackled in the book is not an exhaustive or complete one. We make no apologies for this. We acknowledge there is an eclectic quality to the contents of this book in terms of what is tackled and what is not. This project has taken 12 months to bring to fruition and was from day one based on seeking out volunteers within and outside Austrade to relive and recount the themes that were in their minds and which defined their experience in this organisation. This project was not entirely a planned and carefully crafted set of themes. The reader will agree that the chapters cover an exceptional range of topics over this short 30 year span. Moreover this book was produced at almost zero cost, with no seed funding or key sponsor. Passion, fascination and other non-monetary values can sometimes still produce a worthy output as we trust you will agree, has been achieved with this volume.

This was a study undertaken with Austrade's awareness and the themes, content and observations within this book are those of its authors with only gentle prompting from its editor. Editorial independence was a priority for this project and was respected by the subject of this book: Austrade. The CEO of Austrade, Bruce Gosper, has supported and participated in this project from the beginning. To his credit he supported the project without necessarily knowing exactly what the book would say. I am sure he like others in Austrade will not be disappointed.

Every project has its high points as well as its limitations and this book is no exception. Many aspects recounted by the authors are indeed fascinating, credible but also arguable. Each chapter has been reviewed by other experts and colleagues and the recommended changes suggested to the authors have on the whole been integrated into the final manuscript. Some who read this book may be in strong disagreement with the views of the authors and this is to be expected. With such a raw subject as Austrade, "there is no final word" on most themes addressed in this book. Clearly there maybe bias and subjectivity in the views expressed. This book is not classical history where the subjects have disappeared and where the rawness of the subject has worn off and historians apply their instruments of examination and analysis on the basis of available evidence. Austrade is a living entity with a very short history, where its actors remain engaged and attached to their subject, even after retirement from the Service.

The methodology for this book has been to call on the past and present actors within Austrade and ask them to recount their story, where possible with evidence and build a constructive narrative. Authors of this volume approached their subject with awareness that they would be the subject of public scrutiny. In all cases authors have sought to address their theme with fact-based evidence. This was not always possible for reasons of access to available data and the methodology used by the author. This limitation does not detract from the work presented in this volume. In many cases the authors are offering what in effect is primary data. While most authors retain their inner loyalty to Austrade it has not made their analysis any less critical of Austrade and the activity they are analysing. While not wishing to use the euphemism of "frank and fearless", the substance of each author's approach has been to seek to provide critique in a constructive manner.

Why this book?

The idea of pulling together a book on Austrade has been communicated to me as a project to avoid. "It was not possible", there were too many "legal nuances" and other such concerns. I knew from the outset that the Austrade story could be told in a holistic way, by those that made it and on the whole would be a positive one. Whatever the verdict may be on the quality of this book, the pages of discourse on Austrade can only be an addition to what has been a major gap in our knowledge. The content of this book will be important reading for the future, for government, policy makers, civil servants, business, academia and students. Part of the skepticism about completing a book on a government agency is precisely because it is government – often media shy and wary of scholarly scrutiny. This is understandable but is not an excuse. Putting one's head in the sand is a fine escape but not a constructive one. Austrade deserved more. Fortunately most actors of Austrade cooperated with this study. The few that did not may see from this work that there is much to be gained and little to be concerned about.

A government organisation like Austrade needs to have a story, a history, a consciousness, a narrative presence in the annals of this country. With limited exceptions Austrade has generally not sought attention. This organisational culture of avoiding attention along with lost historic files and records gives us the horrible scenario that all could easily disappear. In some cases it is already too late and sad to contemplate for an organisation that is barely 30 years old. As its 30th birthday approaches much of what has defined this organisation has remained the domain of former employees who still argue through the pro and cons of certain directions, activities, programs and effectiveness of leaders. Little of this has been put on the table of public scrutiny. Much information about Austrade has in fact been lost or resides in personal archives of former staff. This makes the task of recounting the events in an objective mode more difficult. It would be an error to think that Austrade has avoided *all* scrutiny. Not so. It has been the subject of countless reviews and audits many of which have changed the course of the organisation (like the 1990 McKinsey Review). The work produced in this volume might well be a starting point for a constructive discussion on trade promotion organisations like Austrade.

This book is not an analysis of an administrative kind and in fact it is not even a criticism of the organisation. To the contrary, it is an examination of how an organisation of this kind operated, what strategies it put in place, what activities worked and did not work, what role leadership plays in being successful and a host of other important themes. In some cases there is critical commentary on what they felt they were doing and how they did it. It is not a hagiography or some kind of publicity statement on how good Austrade is or was. That is best left to others. Readers will find that the authors have been constructive in their observations of their organisation and what their organisation achieved. Their comments are made in good faith on what were the expectations of an organisation of this kind. Readers will find that behind much of what is said throughout the 25 chapters is a positive reflection and analysis for government and others to consider. Moreover it is the desire by many of us behind this book that this be a first treatment of Austrade in a broader sense with the expectation that others who follow will have more information at their disposal and even greater hindsight on which to make even deeper observations.

Literature review on the subject

Commentary on Austrade as a subject has primarily originated from the media. Very little besides tabloid or financial press coverage mentions Austrade. This is not for any lack of commentary on the Hawke/ Keating governments and the economic reforms of that period. There is no lack of account of the glorious 1980s or of the Hawke and Keating governments and the Labor government policies and achievements of the period, but little or nothing on the establishment of Austrade.

From a scholarly standpoint the literature analysis of Austrade is scarce and fragmentary. Schedvin (2008) is by far the most thorough coverage of the predecessor of Austrade going back to the founding of the Trade Commissioner Service in 1933. But it did not go beyond the establishment of Austrade. Academically there have been limited and clumsy attempts at analysing Austrade. Jones (1994) made scant reference to Austrade and did so with little or no evidence. Its findings were superficial and not serious. Trade analysts including Capling (2001) and Stutchbury (1991) are both commentary and judgments on the Australian trading system and only in limited ways to the role played by Austrade. Ferris (1993) former chair of the Austrade Board in his *Really Making a Difference* provides a glimpse of the thinking of the early 1980s and how Austrade could make a difference. This would become a slogan in the early Austrade Annual Reports. Brewer (2009) makes an excellent attempt to discuss the effectiveness of trade facilitators including the role of Austrade and has important pieces on performance management indicators. An exception to the literature on Austrade is the commendable work by Barrett and Wilkinson

(1990) who dissect Austrade and its tasks from a business perspective. Moreover they report for the first time the good standing of Austrade as a trade promotion organisation internationally. For example in a British study of 1986 Austrade was ranked in sixth place of 19 countries. Another important contribution comes from Adams, Brown & Wickes (2013) in their work entitled *Trading Nation* (they are participants in this volume also). There are numerous personal anecdotal accounts: Tallboys (2009) *Encounters of a Diplomatic Kind*, Molloy (2011) *Colossus Unsung*, and Nicholls (2012) *A Briefcase in Transit*. All provide personal material on experiences lived as trade commissioners. Then there are the many nostalgic reviews of the Hawke/Keating period from biographies of prime ministers to ministers taking up the writing profession. Interestingly almost without exception, Austrade barely gets a mention. The exception is John Button (1994) who in his *Flying the Kite* provides observations on the trade environment and indirectly discusses Austrade and tasks facing Austrade. Little can be said of the plethora of political biographies from the Howard/Rudd/ Gillard period. There is a long queue of former politicians recording their ministerial or political experience which litter the airport bookshops. None of these stories mention Austrade, so low was it in their recollection of government.

What is in the book?

The book is opened under a section entitled "Setting the scene for the establishment of the Australian Trade Commission." This chapter sets the broad brush scene for the reader to better comprehend the themes which are more articulated in the chapters that follow. The remainder of the book is divided into three other sections including "The formative years of Austrade" followed by the "Consolidation of Austrade" and closing with "Austrade today and tomorrow". Chapters which are included in these sections include a historical reflection of the immediate period prior to and immediately after the establishment of Austrade by Richard Fletcher. The chapters that follow do so in a chronological manner from the 1986 establishment of Austrade until the last section on Austrade's future and the questions it faces today and tomorrow. Two prominent former Ministers, John Dawkins the initiator of Austrade and Tim Fischer the first Conservative Coalition Minister to assume responsibility for Austrade are interviewed in this book. Three of the six Managing Directors (now called CEOs) are also interviewed and they provide a firsthand view of their organisation seen from its pinnacle. Peter Langhorne, Deputy Managing Director of Austrade during much of the Charles Jamieson stewardship of Austrade seeks to fill the void of Jamieson's sad and untimely death in 2013. The other chapters cover a range of periods, activities and campaigns which defined Austrade. These include Austrade's response to the turbulent period of the fall of the Berlin Wall and the end of the USSR, the McKinsey Review in 1990, key performance indicators, "doubling the exporters", the Special Markets, investment promotion and Austrade and the media. A special effort is undertaken to examine some of the special sides of Austrade including how it has opened up to female leadership and the role of Overseas Engaged Employees (OEE) in Austrade posts. The closing segment of the book examines the future of Austrade and trade and whether there is a better model for an export facilitator. It includes a chapter on Austrade's role in future and changing trading scenarios and an interview with the current Austrade CEO. A further closing chapter is provided by former DFAT Trade Analysts Mike Adams and Nicolas Brown on the DFAT view of Austrade and where and how they have and can work more closely together. The concluding chapter seeks to address the thorny issue of Austrade's future direction.

What is missing in this book?

One of the key stakeholders for Austrade is the business community which has not participated in this project and was beyond the scope of this study. The first priority of this project was to get Austrade staff, past and present to explain their organisation and how it worked. This book is therefore primarily an inward looking examination of Austrade and Australian trade and investment trends. This might be seen as a weakness but it is a story that needed telling. A further weakness of this study was not all the Managing Directors participated in this project. Of the six three appear in this volume (Lindsay MacAlister, Ralph Evans and Bruce Gosper). Charles Jamieson died prematurely in 2013 and the two other CEOs preferred to not participate actively in this study. A further missing element in this book is a lack of treatment of the role of the Board which was active from 1986 until 2006, when as a result of the Uhrig Review commissioned by the Howard Government, many government agency Boards were abolished. The Austrade Board, like many others was removed as a consequence of this review.

2

Setting the scene for the Austrade story

Bruno Mascitelli

Background and context for an Australian Trade Commission

Trade activity has, in the short life of this country, been generally a strong agenda item. The official government approach towards trade from the outset of colonial Australia was defined in the very first political election in post-Federation Australia (1901). It was a political battle between the Free Traders concentrated in NSW and the Protectionist Party based in Victoria. The Protectionist Party (along with State Labor) became Australia's first government and under the leadership of Andrew Barton would embark on a protectionist (trade) regime for Australian products against incoming goods. While these distant beginnings towards an official trade approach might seem no longer relevant to the thinking and comportment of any modern economy today, what is evident in these political beginnings is the importance that trade had on the political psyche of this country and since then rarely has the issue of protection versus free trade been distant from government thinking and policy making.

The Australian trade and export scenario throughout the 20th century was a story of episodic booms and busts. As Australia was and is predominantly an exporter of commodities and an importer of manufactured goods it was a victim of frequent fluctuations. The domination of wool ended in the 1970s while the 1980s was a kind of "line in the sand" for Australian trade. At that time the value of exports on the trade balance sheet was close to $A19 billion. This would grow to $A52 billion in the early 1990s to a staggering $A318 billion in 2013 (DFAT 2014: DFAT 2012). One of the key indicators was the importance of China to the Australian economy. In the mid-1980s China's share of Australian exports was less than three per cent ($A467 million). In 2014 it reached over 24 per cent (DFAT Fact Sheet 2014).

The 1980s are considered by economic scholars as the decade of significant economic reform and globalisation of the Australian economy (Eslake 2007). John Button, the then Minister for Industry, Technology and Commerce in the Hawke-Keating governments, was even more conscious of its significance describing it thus:

> The period of real economic change in Australia began in the early
> 1980s. The need was dramatised by Treasurer Paul Keating's
> "Banana Republic" reference in 1985. But Ministers in the
> Hawke government elected in 1983 had a strong commitment to
> internationalising the Australian economy (Button 1994: 7).

It was the decade of the Australian currency float, smaller government, the (trade union) Accord, freeing up the labour market, tax reform, lowering inflation and tackling high levels of unemployment. During the early 1980s the Australian economy was running on levels of inflation almost in double digits and at interest rates close to 19 per cent (December 1985). The terms of trade (the ratio of the average price of Australia's exports to the average price of Australian imports) between 1949-50 and 1986-87 fell by 40 per cent (Eslake 2007). In 1985 Australian exports were riding the wave of a historically favorable export dollar (US 57c). There was also concern about "buying Australian" and a fear that the economy and its trade reflection was simply not performing (Capling 2001). The culmination of this worrying picture was that in the early 1980s exports accounted for less than 14 per cent of the Australian Gross Domestic Product (GDP). Bill Ferris noted:

> ...[there was an] appalling decline in Australia's position as an

exporter over the last two decades. Australia has between 1963 and 1986 dropped from 8th to 23rd as a world exporter" (Ferris 1987:36).

It is not difficult to conclude that these were not auspicious times for Austrade to be established and play its hand at turning these negative trends around.

The making of an organisation: Austrade

The Australian Trade Commission, or Austrade as it is generally called, came into existence in January 1986 as a statutory government agency initially tasked with coordinating and facilitating the country's export promotion schemes. The then Minister for Trade, John Dawkins, was the architect of the new to be Australian Trade Commission. It was one of the most ambitious changes on the government trade promotion landscape since the creation of the Trade Commissioner Service in 1933. This transition from the Trade Commissioner Service along with four smaller export schemes (Department of Trade, Trade Commissioner Service, Export Finance Insurance Corporation and the Export Market Development Grant scheme) into a "one-stop-shop", was visionary and exhilarating all at the same time. It was, in the words of future Managing Director of Austrade, Ralph Evans, "a bold step" (Evans 1993). More importantly it was typical of the Hawke-Keating period of the 1980s and 1990s – a Labor government aggressively pursuing a reform agenda as it had in other areas of economic policy.

Austrade was tasked with helping exporters get into global markets, with being the nation's eyes and ears to better the chances of exports sales. More importantly from the Trade Minister's standpoint Austrade needed to harness the disparate segments of export promotion and better focus and direct the attention to markets that needed assistance. It was also seeking to drive a manufacturing agenda initially by better promoting and developing Australian manufacturing exports which were flagging and which needed to overturn the worrying export dilemma in Australia of reliance on exports of agriculture, resources and primary industries (Ferris 1985).

Austrade's beginnings were closely bound with the legacy of the previous Trade Commissioner Service, defined by Schedvin as the *"Emissaries of Trade"* (2008). This new organisation emerging in the 1980s did so in an economically challenging climate but with the advantage of an invigorated government ready for economic reform. It was a Labor government prepared to turn the tables economically and ironically do what was more expected of a conservative government.

After a double dissolution confirming a second Hawke government in 1984, the Trade portfolio was allocated to John Dawkins who according to Schedvin "... turned his attention to what was perceived to be a fragmented set of institutions concerned with export promotion" (2008: 312). At the time it appeared to Dawkins that the Trade Commissioner Service, was conflicted between trade policy duties and the task of active trade promotion a conflict that led "... to the deterioration in export performance" (Schedvin 2008: 328). Dawkins saw these conflicts within the Trade Commissioner Service as issues at the forefront of Australian export performance and to be tackled – he did so with little delay and with determination earning himself the name of the "Minister for Austrade" (Ferris 2014).

The justification for Austrade as Dawkins saw it was for an organisation which needed to get on with trade promotion as a single entity and at the same time not be shackled with trade policy work. Behind much of the strategy which would provide content to the aims and objectives of this new organisation would be the report produced by a government appointed Export Marketing Strategy Panel in December 1984 entitled "Lifting Australia's performance as an exporter of manufactures and services". It became commonly known by many as the Ferris Report, named after its author Bill Ferris, then Manager of Barlow Marine Limited, a successful exporter of boat fittings. Dawkins refers to this report as the defining document which would convince the Labor government of the need for this new organisation. As Dawkins stated himself: "I tabled the report in Parliament as Minister of Trade in 1985, the Labor Government set about implementing virtually all of the report's 65 recommendations" (Dawkins 1993: 6).

The public notification of this new entity (Austrade) was in April 1985. It still needed to be passed in Parliament and there was still need for it to be more properly presented to its new staff members who were unaware what awaited them. As Ferris reminds us:

> What the Act and Austrade initiative was all about was the bringing together of all of those activities and efforts by government into a single organisation with the objective of providing these efforts with a more market-driven and commercial set of disciplines (Ferris 1993:14).

The formal establishment Austrade as a statutory agency was for 1 January 1986. It would operate with an external Board (predominantly of business leaders) along with a Managing Director who would report to the Board and thence to the Minister. The key feature of this organisation would be its ability to concentrate on trade promotion. This would lead to a smaller Department of Trade as primarily a trade policy entity, having lost its trade promotion staff to the newly created Australian Trade Commission. It was in no way a "business as usual" change and most insiders knew this.

Alongside the new commercial emphasis lay an unprecedented blueprint of a government organisation needing to be proactive and working with business. Its prime change and new approach was eloquently summarised by Ralph Evans:

> The Australian Trade Commission Act 1986 provides for a Board of Directors and a management structure under a chief executive, just as one finds in a large commercial company. The Board was given the task of making this entity market-driven while pursing the basic goal of lifting Australia's export performance. Bill Ferris was the inaugural Deputy Chairman, and then Chairman from 1987 to the end of 1993 (Evans 1993:10).

Austrade began with great expectations and behind it an effective and experienced Trade Commissioner Service. Its international footprint was exceptional for a small nation like Australia. It had no sprawling bureaucracy and was able to operate with a minimum of resources and personnel (which has remained to this day). The staffing level of the Australian Trade Commission at the time of its formation was 1,327 of which 137 were actual trade commissioners. The rest of the staff were Australian based or skilled overseas locally engaged.

The early beginnings of Austrade were far from smooth sailing despite the exciting and exhilarating way in which it came about. There was little in the way of a blueprint and the Austrade merger of disparate divisions of the export area was equally testing for all. This newly merged organisation in its early days found itself a source of political power play between the two sides of Australian politics, a position Austrade did not relish. From the days in which its predecessor the Trade Commissioner Service (as well as the Department of Trade) was often considered the play thing of the Country/National Party (Schedvin 2008: 314) to the cold shower of the incoming Howard government in 1996, Austrade became a victim of the political partisan identification which only added to its extraordinary difficulty in establishing itself as an export facilitator. This political identification changed with the arrival of Minister Tim Fischer who was both a leader of the National Party (hence Deputy Prime Minister as well) and at the same time a big believer in the importance of Austrade. What Fischer provided was a continuation of that closeness to government and political clout that Austrade needed for presence and survival.

While the Trade Commissioner Service was strongly endowed with business savvy exponents not all of Austrade was of the same ilk. Much of the staff were still in the main civil servants with limited or no business acumen. This would change with the first appointments and the new structures established. As a first step, Minister Dawkins appointed Lindsay MacAlister who was known as having a strong commercial and mining background as Managing Director of Austrade.

Austrade takes shape – New directions and new managers

Lindsay MacAlister arrived with a unique industry pedigree. He was the Chairman and Managing Director of the Australian General Electric Group with hard–nosed commercial principles and was a geologist by training. Austrade Board Secretary Geoff Spears in that period considered that "Lindsay MacAlister's background as CEO of GE Australia was ideally suited to his appointment as Managing Director of the new commercially focused trade promotion organisation in 1986. He was well connected and well regarded by the business community" (Spears 2014). The new structure awaiting him would include a new Austrade Board, initially chaired by Commonwealth Bank Managing Director Vern Christie along with Deputy Chairman Bill Ferris. The first Austrade board included David Asimus, a grazier who was Chairman of the Australian Wool Corporation, Kevan Gosper AO, not only Chairman and Chief Executive of Shell Australia but also Vice President of the International Olympic Committee (IOC) and President of the Australian Olympic Committee (AOC) and Nicholas Whitlam, Managing Director of the State Bank of NSW (*The Canberra Times*, 10 January 1986).

The early MacAlister period was characterised by vibrancy, excitement but also great uncertainty. There was an attempt to redefine Austrade's work and priorities but the period was also objectively a difficult one. MacAlister in his first few months was keen to be on the job. He planned visits to posts and regional centres from the start and wanted to familiarise himself with the markets, the issues and the needs of Australian businesses (Thornhill 1986).

The new management was looking for market opportunities and possibly some quick successes as the spotlight was shining on this new organisation and how it would perform. Export success would also inevitably require "picking [export] winners" – a view supported by Austrade Board Chair, Bill Ferris, but not necessarily the view of all export commentators (Stutchbury 1991:69). The new Austrade management seemed comfortable with this approach which fell in line with Labor government thinking at the time. The Liberal/National party view seemed more inclined to leave the exporters to their own devices. Having the right machinery in place to help Australian exporters was one thing. Having the right trading environment was another. Despite all good intentions, Australia and Austrade had to contend with what appeared to be a global non-level playing field. As Button realised himself a few years later as Minister of the Department of Industry, Technology and Commerce:

> ... selling the place [Australia] promoting investment and trade ... In the 1980s it was hard work; largely because of fixed, frequently outdated and strongly held negative perceptions about Australia. It was said that it was too far away to think about seriously. The market was too small. The country was unsophisticated producer of raw materials: nothing else. Unions provoked a constant climate of industrial unrest. The people were lazy. Inflation was too high (Button 1994: 10).

Button's candid summary highlighted but one of the obstacles Austrade needed to address in the difficult road of selling Australian products around the world. The new Austrade management team was aware that in order for this new commercial focus to take root, it would need to remove some of the "tired" public servants from the organisation and bring in new blood. MacAlister had the unpleasant task of proposing staff cuts (mostly in the Australian operations).

Part of the new Austrade included EFIC (the Export Finance and Insurance Corporation). However EFIC was quite different from Austrade, with different functions and tasks and in effect preferred to remain separate. Despite attempts at merger EFIC kept its separate existence until its formal establishment and separation in 1991. The role and activities of EFIC are treated in greater detail in the chapter on the MacAlister years.

Throughout 1987 and 1988 Austrade with its new Department (Industry, Technology and Commerce) began implementing a new investment attraction portfolio and strategy. As part of this process Austrade recruited a number of special investment commissioners. These included Walter Roso formerly from Nissan Australia for

Frankfurt and Richard Seddon a former solicitor for New York. This is treated in great detail by Peter Collens in a later chapter in this book. In a media release Austrade declared:

> Dr. Roso and Mr. Seddon are the first trade commissioners appointed by the Australian Trade Commission (Austrade) with the sole function of attracting investment and promoting industrial collaboration between Australia and foreign firms (*The Canberra Times*, 31 March 1988: 6).

Some years later new investment commissioners' offices were set up in other locations such as London, Paris, Milan, New York and Tokyo.

The merger of Foreign Affairs and Trade

In July 1987, the two Departments of Foreign Affairs and Trade were merged creating a single large department. However this merger of portfolios, curiously did not include Austrade which went to the Ministry of Industry and Commerce under Minister John Button. Only in 1991 did Austrade return to Foreign Affairs and Trade. This merger ended some of the old separation of foreign policy and economic activities and of course some interdepartmental turf warfare. According to Capling the move by the Hawke government however created a "broader desire to cut costs and enhance ministerial control of departments" (Capling 2001:111). The merger saw a significant reduction in the number of Departments from 28 to 18 and specifically put trade policy and trade development in the same ministry. This saw some improvements in relations and operations but the reporting lines remained as they had and trade commissioners at posts would still need to ensure a smooth relationship with the ambassadors who were ultimately Head of Mission. The merger also made inroads towards greater collaboration. According to Bartos:

> In many respects the amalgamation was a success. Trade officials had been inclined to despise or resent diplomats as effete cocktail-party-goers and foreign affairs officials tended to look down on

trade officials as déclassé menials. After the merger they could
no longer take these attitudes, and the potential existed for much
better communications between the two sets of interests (Bartos
2006 : 62).

However not all was as simple as it seemed. Bartos reveals:

> But the divide [between DFAT and Austrade] remains at an
> operational level, not least because much of the trade function is
> still organisationally separate in Austrade, a statutory authority
> within DFAT portfolio with the primary role of providing
> assistance to Australian exporters. Some foreign affairs officials
> still look down on Austrade ("they are all cowboys" a senior
> diplomat told me) because of the applied, operational nature of
> its business (Bartos 2006: 62).

Soon after the DFAT merger in 1988, Richard Woolcott AC became
the new Secretary of the Department of Foreign Affairs and Trade,
which would also include a place on the Austrade Board.

Identifying what exporters need

In 1989 the then Manager of Austrade's Market Intelligence Task
Force, Lloyd Downey, produced a "Bart Simpsons version" of the
state of Austrade and the intelligence needs of business to better export
their products abroad. This comic format message was sent to every
staff member of Austrade around the world, entitled "The MARIS
Massage(!)", provided an astonishing list of tasks, facts and figures
on the market intelligence needed by business and what Austrade
needed to do to better respond. In pursuing this market intelligence
the report provided a snap shot of Austrade's prospective clients. It
acknowledged that it could locate 10,000 actual exporters, a further
50,000 would be exporters, around 76,000 overseas buyers (MARIS
Massage 1989). This highlighted all of Austrade's clientele, reach and
the range of its penetration in the export area. It then identified the "Top
twenty tasks" of changes to be undertaken which would shift Austrade
to becoming an "organisation which has moved more towards a

professional consultancy role with our clients. Providing tailor-made export marketing strategies usually for a fee (Maris Massage 1989: 68). The report was clearly pre-empting what would become a couple of years later the recommendations of the McKinsey Review.

In that same year the government called for another review (Hughes Review) to examine the government's financial support for Australian export industries and in particular the use of the Export Market Development Grant (EMDG) scheme. Besides acknowledging that exports were lagging behind imports, the Review urged stronger use of schemes such as EMDG and other financial instruments to enhance exports.

The McKinsey Review and the MacAlister downfall

Austrade's lack of performance was beginning to become evident. In one case an exporter from Melbourne met with Austrade executives in 1990 reporting that "he came away from the meeting aghast at what he believed was their inability to comprehend the size of the shakeup needed to make the [trade] commission more responsive to the export industry" (Hooper 1991: 29). There was a distinct sense that Austrade had lost its way with exporters and their export needs. While initially ambitious in its direction, it would appear the management of Austrade soon lost touch with the business community, the organisation and its objectives. The imposition of strong commercial practices and cultural change was only slowly occurring. Many in Austrade especially in the Australian operations were still functioning in "civil servant" mode, unfamiliar with the commercial needs of companies. This made them even easier targets for removal.

Making Austrade's position even more untenable was its handling of its principal stakeholder: the Minister (Button). MacAlister had little experience working with government and in Austrade which was in effect part of government. He was strongly convinced this organisation needed to take on commercial practices and distance itself from government. According to anecdotal communication, Dawkins had made his directives very clear to MacAlister and it would seem MacAlister embraced them to their full extent. MacAlister assumed he had *carte blanche* to do as he saw fit for Austrade. When in 1987 Hawke carried out his third Ministerial reshuffle putting Dawkins in Education, Austrade went to Button's Ministry of Industry, Technology and Commerce. Within a short space of time in this new Ministry, Button's understanding of Austrade's performance and the role of the Managing Director troubled him and became an immediate source of tension.[1]

A defining aspect of the MacAlister era was his misreading of where government counted. Given the encouragement from Dawkins at the outset to commercialise Austrade, MacAlister assumed he did not need to advise government of what the organisation was doing and what was its intentions. That Austrade would be above politics and ignore the role of the government and the minister. This was a fatal error and Button and MacAlister were headed for confrontation.

In the Austrade Board, plans were afoot to tackle the troubling loss of direction of Austrade and to do so in an overarching manner. There were concerns that MacAlister was out of his depth but what was more concerning to the Board was his inability to balance the government protocol required of a government agency with the new business ethos. On 30 May 1990, Bill Ferris, Chairman of the Board, announced an independent review of Austrade indicating that this request had been "welcomed by Minister Button" (*The Canberra Times*, 31 May 1990). In July 1990 the so-called "independent review" was announced by Ferris in these words: "McKinsey and Co. will undertake a review of Austrade ... the board and management of Austrade look forward to working with McKinsey & Co." [!] (*The Canberra Times*, 16 July 1990).

As part of the review integration, Austrade established its own working party to assist and oversee its preparation largely to provide the

---

1 This frustration which Minister Button had with Austrade and its Managing Director has been communicated to the author by numerous people in senior level management and close to the Minister.

bridge between McKinsey and the realities of Austrade. This committee included senior Austrade figures including: Terry Goss, Michael Johnson, Julia Selby, Kym Hewett and in a lesser way representatives from EFIC. Whatever personnel intentions this review may have been designed to undertake it was clearly high profile and by the end of the review there were estimations that the cost of such a review reached $1.3million (Nicholls 2012: 494). The report which was never officially public but is known and cited by all stated the obvious (in hindsight) and provided the biggest push towards commercialisation of a government statutory agency. Almost at the same time as the release of McKinsey Review, The Australian Manufacturing Council released a report produced by business consultants Pappas, Carter, Evans and Koop/Telesis on *The Global Challenge: Australian manufacturing in the 1990s*. The report concluded:

> The international competitiveness of Australia's manufacturing industry is not strong. Further it has been revealed that significant issues, often ones which have been around for some time, still exist and are placing exigencies upon the manufacturing sector's ability to adapt to change to the new international trading world (Pappas et al 1990).

The McKinsey recommendations

The McKinsey Review was a watershed of positive and negative dimensions for Austrade. In hindsight it appears very logical and clear in its direction. Because of its commercial astuteness, some protagonists of Austrade claim some kind of ownership to the ideas of this report. In effect the McKinsey Review provided the context in which the current Austrade senior management, especially Lindsay MacAlister would step aside. When the review was presented to the Board in late 1990, MacAlister had already resigned from Austrade. It was clear to MacAlister as "the review team's regular briefings revealed the depth of Austrade's troubles" (Hooper 1991: 30) that defending his management was a lost cause. But McKinsey was more than the resignation of the Managing Director. The review made significant recommendations which would reconstruct the very foundations of Austrade. Under the title of: *"Organising to deliver export impact: The Australian Trade Commission"* the report offered six significant recommendations. They included:

1. Adopt a market-driven approach, based on yielding better access to overseas customers through utilising government clout and in-depth market know-how and relationships.
2. Restructure the organisation to push more resources and responsibility to the field.
3. Revitalise and re-engineer the international and domestic network to improve service delivery and impact.
4. Change the leadership direction to increase "initiative taking' and change the culture of the organisation.
5. Reconfigure its relationship with Government, other trade development bodies (allies) and business.
6. Initiate and manage a major program of organisational change (McKinsey Review 1990: 1-2).

Some markets were defined as making "less impact" and therefore the review recommended Austrade withdraw from them. These included some locations in Europe as well as in the US. It was also the moment when greater recognition was given to Asian markets. Most importantly it set in motion the need for performance measurement and key performance indicators (KPIs) which had been missing in Austrade (*McKinsey Review* 1990). One of the key outcomes of the review was a realisation that resources and authority were overly concentrated in Australia at the expense of overseas operations. Amongst other things the review also encouraged Austrade move its base more to the commercial centre of Sydney and away from Canberra to cut down on bureaucracy! Ironically some of MacAlister's initiatives, including moving much of Austrade activities to Sydney had already been initiated but re-proposed by McKinsey. In any event a new era was afoot.

The McKinsey watershed and the arrival of Ralph Evans

With MacAlister resigning on 12 December 1990, and no immediate replacement for the Managing Director, Bill Ferris began the task of implementing the McKinsey recommendations. Some media speculation indicated that this crisis might have seen Ferris follow MacAlister and resign but this was not to be (Hooper 1991:29). In actual fact "he [Ferris] has stepped up his involvement by working full time in the Sydney office without any increase in what he was paid as part time chairman" (Hooper 1991:29). In a public gathering of Austrade staff in Canberra in February 1991, the findings of the McKinsey report were presented to staff (McKinsey Staff Presentation 1991), and Ferris, clearly in charge, sought to bring order to a troubled and confused organisation. The message was that McKinsey needed to be implemented and implemented fast. Ferris continued to chair the Board and acted as Managing Director for almost seven months while the Egon Zehnder recruitment agency went about looking for a replacement for MacAlister and a new senior executive team.

Along with the task of finding a replacement to Lindsay MacAlister, there was the question of the salary offered for such a position which "would be a package of up to $260,000, well at the top end of government salaries" (Hooper 1991: 30). The thinking according to Ferris was that there needed to be relativity to private commercial salaries in order to attract the right person. This of course did not sit well with equivalent public servants in comparable ministries and especially Foreign Affairs.

The implementation of McKinsey recommendations which Austrade accepted in total was not without its pain and sacrifice. In the Australian operations there were many who feared losing their jobs and in a media release of 14 February 1991 it was reported that "200 jobs to go in Austrade shake-up" (*The Canberra Times*, 14 February 1991: 11). On the whole overseas operations were less affected in terms of losses and would be the major beneficiaries in terms of the new management structure which would come into being. The selection process through the executive recruiters took its course and in mid-

1991 Ralph Evans was selected as the new Managing Director. Evans was formerly Vice President of the Boston Consulting Group, which had absorbed the firm where he was a Partner/Director (Pappas Carter & Evans & Coop). Ironically, he had also worked with McKinsey & Company in both the UK and Australia.

Evans was quick to implement the McKinsey recommendations with the new proposed structure of so-called G10 (meaning the 10 executive general managers) occupying key geographic and strategic positions, going ahead and top managers were selected one after the other. The Corporate Plan for 1992-93, not surprisingly called "Really making a difference ..." (Austrade 1992), showed that the organisation had certainly set in motion the organisational change starting with major global decentralisation. Its new motto was "We help win business overseas, and we bring investment to Australia" (Austrade 1992). At the time it had a Board membership chaired by Bill Ferris, but supported by Roger Allen AM as Deputy Chairman, Ralph Evans Managing Director, Michael Costello Secretary of the Department of Foreign Affairs and Trade, Graeme Lawless Managing Director of EFIC, Neville Stevens Secretary of the Department of Industry, Nixon Apple national research officer of the Amalgamated Metal Workers' Union, Lorraine Martin, Paul Salteri, Rodney Unsworth, John Down and David Asimus. It was again powerful representation from business as well as government.

With a more confident Austrade pushing ahead, also came a greater level of interference and attacks from political quarters. In the early 1990s as part of it's stepped up opposition to the incumbent Labor government, the then Opposition Foreign Affairs and Trade spokesman, Alexander Downer, intensified his attacks against Austrade primarily through its targeting of Minister Button. According to one report:

> Mr. Downer launched an attack on Austrade, saying despite its
> $130 million annual budget, it had failed since its establishment
> in 1986 to increase Australian trade and was regarded by large
> companies as a "big dud" (Connors 1991).

The Liberal government's apparent hostility towards Austrade continued throughout 1992 and came mostly from Downer and Peacock. In another report in March 1992, Downer alleged: "Austrade is responsible for promoting Australian exports, yet it has been exposed time and again as one of the most rort-ridden government organisations" (*The Canberra Times*, 28 March 1992). Besides being unsubstantiated, the comments were hurtful to the recovering Austrade as it tried to compose itself for the McKinsey reforms it wanted to undertake. Downer came across the McKinsey Review and their criticism of Austrade's functioning. Downer used some of the content of this report to attack the Hawke government with Button as its main target. Ralph Evans recalls meeting Downer for lunch "to take him through how these issues were all in the past and how we had plans well under way to realise Austrade's potential as a dynamic force for Australian exports".[2]

Downer continued to hold anti-Austrade views into the mid-1990s and in early 1996 Evans met with Downer to smooth the waters. In that conversation Downer stated "that if elected he intended to make very deep cuts to Austrade" which he did. However after Evan's departure from Austrade, Downer became quite supportive of Austrade during most of his time as Foreign Minister.[3]

Bob McMullan assumed the Ministerial portfolio for Austrade in the last years of the Keating period and was very supportive of Austrade, emphasising that it was part of the government's economic pillar which was called at the time – "Winning Markets". In this strategy the task for Austrade was "providing services to assist the efforts of exporters". The statement indicated that "Austrade has been reshaping its international and Australian networks ... it would be providing more free services to new and potential exporters, practical assistance for new market entrants including generous subsidies and revised charging practices for experienced exporters" (McMullan 1995). Major technological advances emerged in this period including website access, internet

2 From an exchange of emails with Ralph Evans, January 2014.
3 From an exchange of emails with Ralph Evans, January 2014.

access, email communication for posts catapulting export servicing to a new height and changing the whole basis of service provision to exporters. The Minister also announced the launching of TradeBlazer – Austrade's new on-line information and marketing service. In that same speech McMullan also appreciated the limitations on the impact that an Austrade could have on the export scenario. He acknowledged that especially for small and medium enterprises:

> The Government and Austrade are committed to assisting you make the most of the opportunities which are out there and assisting you to overcome the obstacles in the path of your success. According to the best estimates, there are some 4,500 Australian SMEs regularly engaged in exporting activity, generating around $6.5 billion in international turnover which is growing at $500 million per annum. However, it is estimated that these firms represent only 7 per cent of all SMEs engaged in manufacturing and around 1 per cent of service SMEs (McMullan 1995).

Downer continued his diatribe against Austrade including against McMullan, though on the whole it was more an attack against the government of the day rather than Austrade. Interestingly when the Howard government came to power in 1996, Downer's vindictiveness towards Austrade disappeared. What also took the heat off Austrade was the ministerial appointments within the new Howard government with Austrade coming under the jurisdiction of the new Trade Minister, and Deputy Prime Minister, Tim Fischer. Matters however were touch and go between the two and Fischer's biographer Peter Rees notes the sensitivity of the relationship between Downer and Fischer as a matter of concern:

> At senior levels of the Coalition, there was concern about how the working relationship between Fischer and Downer would evolve. Fischer, as Deputy Prime Minister, was the senior minister in protocol, but Downer was the portfolio minister in administration. Some members of the government feared it would be a difficult relationship (Rees 2001: 249).

1996 – The change of government and a new approach towards Austrade

In 1996 John Howard led a decisive victory against Keating to put a Liberal-National Party Coalition government back in power after 13 years of Labor rule. The ripple effects of this victory would be felt across the land, in business and government. Significant changes were afoot including the removal of longstanding loyal Labor public servants. The Howard government removed six of the 18 Departmental Secretaries ramping up the politicisation of the public service to new heights. It also shone the light towards Austrade. Ralph Evans, after initial budget cuts to Austrade in his tenure as Managing Director felt betrayed by the new conservative government recognising that his plans for Austrade would not be allowed to be implemented. He saw no other option but to resign. The search for his replacement produced the nomination of an experienced former Trade Commissioner and G10 member, Charles Jamieson, who was well known and respected by most key stakeholders. The period of Jamieson's directorship (1996-2002) saw significant internal stabilisation and much needed regrouping. Amongst the many challenges however was that which saw Austrade make a most effective export enhancement campaign with the important 2000 Sydney Olympic Games. Austrade placed itself in a solid position to use the event to boost international business. Utilising the Business Club Australia brand, this event allowed show-casing to a global audience like never before. According to Austrade:

> The Federal Government's "Australia Open for Business" campaign generated over $1.2bn worth of export & investment opportunities during the Sydney 2000 Olympic Games. In 2005, five years after the completion of the Sydney Olympics, the on-going success of the BCA program around other sporting events was officially recognised by the Australian Marketing Institute who awarded Austrade the Australian Award for Innovation in Marketing Excellence (Austrade ND).

It was common for Austrade to face ongoing public scrutiny and review of its activities. In 2001 the Productivity Commission undertook a review of Austrade and found a third of its $350 million budget failed to achieve anything. The report said the nation's trade broker, which also supplies grants and information to exporters, was largely unused by its target businesses who were put off by Austrade red tape. It found that exporters were likely to fail or succeed no matter what Austrade did for them (Wright 2001). The Federal Government, a little embarrassed by these findings went quickly to the aid of Austrade and while there were red faces for some months, no action was taken by the government and the Commission's recommendations were largely ignored.

During the Jamieson period, Austrade made a rather astute appointment by bringing on board as Chief Economist, the Australian Council of Trade Unions (ACTU) Research Officer, Tim Harcourt who brought high public profiling and media engagement to Austrade – something Austrade badly needed. For the duration of Harcourt's stay in Austrade, he pounded the media with upbeat stories on the need for exports and the role of Austrade in helping this process. While occasionally irritating more sedate colleagues, his *chutzpah* made a world of difference to the perception not only of the benefits of export and investment, but also to engage Austrade in society as well as with business.

Changing management – a trying time for Austrade

Peter O'Byrne took over from Charles Jamieson in 2002 and remained at the helm until 2009. O'Byrne came from running the government enterprise, Australian Hearing Service and prior to that a large pharmaceutical firm Reckitt and Colman, where he was head of Asia operations. The O'Byrne management period was the most challenging and in some respects the least fortunate. One of the first tasks was to implement the government's ambitious goal of "Doubling the number of exporters" a theme expanded on in this book by Greg Joffe. The proposal posited the ambition to double the number of exporters from 25,000 in 2001 to 50,000 in 2006 (O'Byrne 2004). While grounded in good intentions, at the very least a strong rallying call to action, it was a recipe for potentially playing with numbers and for some, became an end in itself. Some eventually came to the realisation that the expectation was not reachable. However as the chapter in this book on "doubling the exporters" will reveal, there was much misunderstanding of the activity and an equivalent amount of misinformed gossip.

Strategically, O'Byrne also needed to reduce the Executive General Managers positions including in the normally protected sanctuary of overseas operations. While McKinsey had recommended greater breadth to the management overseas, some of these recommendations were becoming unsustainable. One included the extensive array of Executive General Managers (EGMs) overseas. O'Byrne proposed in a submission to the Trade Sub Committee of the Joint Standing Committee on Foreign Affairs, Defence and Trade that Austrade would establish four regions from the five that had been re-organised in 2002 (Lyons 2004). This would now include Europe, Middle East and Africa (EMEA); North East Asia; South East Asia, South Asia and Pacific; and the Americas. Another important development which would impact Austrade was the Howard government's Uhrig review. As a result, and not limited solely to Austrade, the Uhrig Review, as noted by Schedvin "transitioned from a statutory authority with a board of directors to a statutory agency with an executive management structure reporting directly to the Minister for Trade" (Schedvin 2008: 341). This meant there would be no board and instead of a Managing Director, there would be a Chief Executive Officer reporting directly to the Minister. This was another of the old Austrade "commercial" style structures of 1986 being undone.

Throughout the 2000s Austrade found itself caught up in some ethical and governance incidents which was a reminder to Austrade of the potential pitfalls of international business, notwithstanding the retention of one of the Board's subcommittees, the Audit and Risk Committee, after the Austrade Board was abolished. This committee continued to be chaired up until 2013, by David Morgan, Chancellor of Deakin University and former President of Ford Motor Company of Australia.

The first of these "incidents" was that of the Australian Wheat Board and the kickbacks to the Saddam Hussein regime. Labor parliamentarian Kelvin Thomson reported through Hansard unfairly points the finger at Austrade's behaviour in a speech to the House of Representatives:

> The recent AWB scandal has raised several serious governance and accountability questions for the Australian Trade Commission and, so far, we are yet to hear answers to these questions. Austrade has been peculiarly silent about AWB providing hundreds of millions of dollars in kickbacks to Saddam Hussein. The fact is that Austrade, the Australian Trade Commission, was one of many government agencies that were aware of substantive information about the link between Alia, AWB, Saddam Hussein and the coordinated subversion of the UN's oil for food program (Thomson 2006).

The subsequent Royal Commission found that other government agencies had played very prominent roles indeed but it's instructive that Thomson chose Austrade as a soft target for his attacks against the conservative Howard government. (Ironically Kelvin Thomson subsequently became the Parliamentary Secretary for Trade in the second Gillard ministry.)

Alongside the troubles with AWB, throughout the 2000s a new corporate scam was emerging in the name of Firepower. It had the ability to draw in and dupe many across the high end of Australia – corporates and politicians alike. However its ability to achieve acceptance and corporate legitimacy came unstuck with "an unlikely saviour in the form of the Australian Trade Commission" in the person of John Finnin, the Frankfurt-based head of Austrade's Europe-Middle-East &-Africa Region (Ryle 2009: 93). The Firepower episode achieved significant notoriety and even received the noteworthiness of being dubbed: "The most spectacular fraud in Australian history" (Ryle 2009). Between 2004 and 2006 Austrade reportedly granted special access privileges and funds totaling $394,009 in export development grants to Firepower International. Finnin along with another senior Austrade officer in

Moscow subsequently joined Firepower, which later failed in one of the country's biggest corporate collapses (Pearlman 2009).

Finally, there was the Securency issue with unsubstantiated allegations of Austrade involvement in corrupt payments to foreign officials in several countries to "facilitate" the sale of Australian polymer banknote technology. The tradecraft for dealing with corruption in foreign markets is a lively topic of conversation and the idea of Austrade itself actually facilitating such corrupt payments is difficult to believe. Tabloid charges against Austrade were thick and thin. After extensive investigations by the Australian Federal Police no charges were laid at any Austrade personnel and the matter as it relates to Austrade is closed. What did these three episodes mean for Austrade? As an organisation it needed to ensure its staff were well briefed and educated on global and business obligations under Australian law and bribery rulings around the world. The following period would see important education programs implemented and addressed to meet these new challenges.

In 2008 the long awaited history of the Trade Commissioner Service, entitled *Emissaries of trade: A history of the Trade Commissioner Service*, commissioned earlier by Charles Jamieson and authored by Professor Boris Schedvin, was launched. This filled a much needed gap in the trade promotion history of Australia. Sadly in July 2009 Austrade was rocked by the untimely death of Trade Commissioner Craig Senger, killed in Jakarta at the J. W. Marriott Hotel, along with two other Australians as a result of a Jemaah Islamiyah bomb planted in the hotel.[4] The death of Craig Senger was an event that shook staff in Austrade and especially the Australian Embassy community in Jakarta to the core. Subsequently Austrade established a scholarship at Monash University to honour Craig Senger's to an outstanding student studying Engineering and Commerce.

---

4 The first diplomat to be killed in the line of duty was Vivian Bowden, also a Trade Commissioner, who was executed by the Japanese after the fall of Singapore during WWII. Charles Bowden, grandson of Vivian was a Trade Commissioner for many years.

The O'Byrne era was the longest of any CEO to date and not without its successes. The public face of Austrade, assisted by Harcourt's media astuteness took on levels never seen before all of which seemed very positive. More women were being appointed in senior management roles and the Business Club Australia experience for the Sydney Olympics in 2000 was rebadged for the Rugby World Cup, the Melbourne Commonwealth Games and the Beijing Olympics in 2008. The number of companies that Austrade worked with to achieve export and international business success grew to 16,000. To achieve this, Austrade widened and deepened its reach onshore with a presence in some 70 locations across Australia, many in collaboration with allies, through the TradeStart program and corporate partners in the professional service community. After the re-integration of Invest Australia and towards the end of the O'Byrne tenure in 2009, 60 international investors were assisted – investing $A13.4 billion in Australia and some 150 Australian companies made investments abroad totaling $A700 million. In that same year (2009) over 4,000 Australian companies availed themselves of $185m in grants for promotional purposes overseas, under the Export Market Development Grant Scheme.

Peter O'Byrne completed his term at the end of 2009 and within a few months a senior Foreign Affairs and Trade diplomat Peter Grey emerged as the new CEO. One of Grey's early tasks (May 2011) was the implementation of a major re-examination of Austrade. The "Rationale for the Review" was:

> Despite the changes in Austrade's functions, responsibilities, governance and operating environment, there has been no whole-of-organisation review of Austrade's operational model and organisational structure since one by the McKinsey and Company in 1990 (Austrade Annual Report 2010-2011).

It was without doubt one of the more far-reaching reviews in more than two decades which provided for, amongst other things, a smaller international executive group (Austrade Annual Report 2010-11). The Annual report summarised the changes:

... [the review] strengthened executive management of the organisation through a smaller executive group, meeting on a weekly rather than monthly basis; a global rather than regional management structure with strategic management and oversight of the international network based in Austrade's headquarters: clearer lines of responsibility for Austrade's core functions – trade, investment and education – and for the EMDG scheme; and renewal of indicators of organisational effectiveness during 2011-12 to better reflect the organisation's strategy and directions, including incorporation of governance considerations (Austrade Annual Report 2010-11).

During Grey's leadership education as a services export had acquired critical importance and provided Austrade a new portfolio of significant importance. By 2010 education services as an export had become Australia's fourth largest export (after iron ore, coal and gold). The promotion of International education shifted from the Department of Education, Employment and Workplace Relations to Austrade. Austrade took the challenge with gusto and in many markets it elevated the responsibility to senior management. As part of enhancing the Education portfolio, Austrade introduced a new education brand, Future Unlimited in June 2011.

In the meantime Austrade continued the rollout of the Australian Government's Brand Australia program both in Australia and internationally. The Australia Unlimited nation brand was implemented at a range of major events, including the China International Small and Medium Enterprises Fair, business events in New Delhi during the Commonwealth Games, and at the Forbes Global CEO Conference in Sydney. In Australia, the brand has been used across a range of sectors, including clean energy, ICT, biotechnology, film, visual arts and publishing.

In late 2011 the Grey leadership instigated a governance review of Austrade which was taken up by former public servants turned academics at the University of Canberra. The purpose of the review as stated in the Annual Report (2011-12) was to ensure "that the organisation operates with the highest ethical standards" (Annual Report 2011-12: iv) and to ascertain whether the structures put in place to actively manage the integrity of the organisation were working. One of the recommendations from the report was the recommendation that:

> Austrade ethics committee be assigned responsibility for providing assurance to the executive, on a regular basis, that the adopted integrity indicators and related monitoring strategies are effective in detecting and responding to challenges to the organisation's integrity, including ethical conduct of Austrade officials and agents (Burmester et al 2011:3).

The Austrade Annual Report (2011-12) stated that its findings "concluded that Austrade's corporate governance structures were of a high quality, particularly in the area of anti-corruption training, which represented international best practice" (Austrade Annual Report 2011-12: iv). There was a sense of satisfaction that the cases of AWB, Firepower and Securency had been addressed and that Austrade was better prepared for any future similar occurrence. In conversations with the University of Canberra team, their only concern about their review was to ensure that Austrade's ethics structure had an agenda and the power to probe into Austrade activities and not just be reactive to situations as they emerged (Burmester 2014).

By June 2012 Austrade operated in 90 locations in 50 countries, including 17 consulates abroad and 12 Austrade locations and a network of 31 Trade Start advisers throughout Australia. It "employed 985 staff, 76 per cent of whom were employed in overseas locations and client-focused operations in Australia (Austrade Annual report 2011-12: 7). These figures manifested a clear resource decline which was making operations in Austrade more difficult and more reactive. In late 2012 Grey resigned after what was a relatively short mandate and one dominated by a series of reviews of Austrade. Nonetheless his leadership was appreciated by the Labor Minister Emerson who accredited Grey's leadership with important achievements. He stated:

Austrade's resources ... [were] more keenly focused on helping Australian businesses break into frontier and emerging markets, particularly in Asia ... This shift in focus fits with the vision set out in the Government's Asian Century White Paper (Trade Minister media release 2012).

Replacing Peter Grey at the helm of Austrade saw the arrival of Bruce Gosper in early 2013. Formerly Deputy Secretary with the Department of Foreign Affairs and Trade, he was known as being knowledgeable about trade and Austrade as well as having extensive trade and diplomatic experience. The challenges facing Gosper, whom many think highly of, remain as large as they were for his predecessor. While there was recognition that the Grey reform *Maximising Our Value* was important, Gosper will not see this as a lasting reform in a constantly changing and challenging environment for Austrade. After one year at the helm Gosper faced his first serious hiccup with the National Commission of Audit recommendation which he tackled with a cool head and firm direction. He is at the same time compensated by the plethora of free trade agreements and a pro-active no-nonsense Minister who has embraced Austrade in quite positive similar terms as did Fischer in his period. These are interesting times for Gosper and for Austrade.

Bibliography

Austrade (ND), major sporting events, https://www.austrade.gov.au/Buy/Australian-Industry-Capability/Major-sporting-events/Business-Club-Australia/BCA-Sydney-2000, accessed 15 May 2014.

Austrade (1992), Really making a difference ..., Corporate Review 1992-93, Austrade, Sydney.

Austrade, (2010), Annual Report 2010-2011, Australian Trade Commission, Sydney.

Austrade, (2011), Annual Report 2011-2012, Australian Trade Commission, Sydney.

Bartos S., (2006), *Against the Grain: The AWB Scandal and Why it Happened*, UNSW Press, Sydney.

Burmester B., Evans M. & Whitton H., (2011), Governance Review for the Australian Trade Commission (Austrade) by the ANZSOG Institute for Governance (ANZIG) at the University of Canberra, Canberra.

Burmester B., (2014), personal communication and phone discussion with the author, 14 May 2014.

Button J., (1994), *Flying the Kite: Travels of an Australian Politician*, Random House, NSW.

Capling A., (2001), *Australia and the Global Trade System*, Cambridge University Press, UK.

Connors T., (1991), Opposition goes for Button over Austrade, *The Canberra Times*, 24 September 1991, p. 2, http://nla.gov.au/nla.news-article122386194, accessed 15 March 2014.

Dawkins J., (1993), Foreword to B. Ferris, *Really Making a Difference: The Essential Anthology of Australian Export Activity 1983-1993*, Gore & Osment Publications, Sydney.

DFAT (2002), *Direction of Trade Time series – 2000-01, One hundred years of trade*, Market Information and Analysis Unit, DFAT, February 2002, Canberra.

DFAT 2014, Trade at a glance – 2014, Department of Foreign Affairs and Trade, http://www.dfat.gov.au/publications/trade/trade-at-a-glance-2014/trade-performance-at-a-glance/part01_profile_of_australias_trade_in_2013.html, accessed 24 January 2015.

DFAT Fact Sheet, (2014), *China Fact Sheet*, DFAT, Canberra, http://www.dfat.gov.au/geo/fs/chin.pdf, accessed 17 January 2015.

Eslake S., (2007), An introduction to the Australian economy, http://www.anz.com.au/resources/e/6/e6742e804e472aae9633b66672659df2/CO-Article-An-Introduction-to-the-Australian-Economy-Jan2007.pdf?MOD=AJPERES, accessed 17 February 2014.

Evans R., (1993), Introduction to B. Ferris, *Really Making a Difference: The Essential Anthology on Australian Export Activity 1983-1993*, Gore & Osment Publications, Sydney.

Ferris B., (2014), Personal communication with the author, Sydney, 21 February 2014.

Ferris B., (1993), *Really Making a Difference: The Essential Anthology of Australian Export Activity 1983-1993*, Gore & Osment Publications, Sydney.

Ferris B., (1987), Export: Your country needs you, in 1993, *Really Making a Difference: The Essential Anthology of Australian Export Activity 1983-1993*, Gore & Osment Publications, Sydney.

Ferris B., (1985), Implications of the Ferris Report, in Ferris B., 1993, *Really Making a Difference: The Essential Anthology of Australian Export Activity 1983-1993*, Gore & Osment Publications, Sydney.

Hooper N., (1991), Will Austrade take the McKinsey cure? *Business Review Weekly*, 22 February 1991.

Lyons M., (2004), Letter to Pierre Huetter, Trade Sub-Committee, Joint Standing Committee on Foreign Affairs, Defence and Trade, by Austrade's Margaret Lyons, 6 August 2004.

MARIS Massage (1988), The Maris Massage: All will be revealed inside, Austrade, Lloyd Downey, Maris Task Force, Canberra 1988.

McKinsey Review (1990), Organising to deliver export impact: Australian Trade Commission, 20 December 1990, Sydney.

McKinsey Staff Presentation (1991), McKinsey Review of Austrade, Staff Presentation, Canberra, 14 February 1991.

McMullan B., (1995), Top exporters dinner, Speech by the Minister for Trade, senator Bob McMullan at the Top exporters Dinner, Melbourne, 15 August 1995.

Nicholls B., (2012), *A Briefcase in Transit: Undiplomatic Reflections of a Trade Commissioner*, Xlibris Corporation, USA.

O'Byrne P., (2002), Austrade and the New Australian Trade Imperative: A speech to the 4th World Conference of 4th World Conference of Trade Promotion Organizations, China.

Pappas G, Carter C, Evans R. and Koop/Telesis, (1990), The global challenge: Australian Manufacturing in the 1990s, report commissioned by the Australian Manufacturing Council, December 1990, Sydney.

Pearlman J., (2009), Austrade denies tip-off on child sex: Diplomat was not warned, it says, *The Age*, 4 August 2009, Fairfax Press, Melbourne, EbscoHost.

Rees P., (2001), *The Boy from Boree Creek: The Tim Fischer Story*, Allen & Unwin, Crows Nest, NSW.

Ryle G., (2009), *Firepower: The Most Spectacular Fraud in Australian History*, Allen & Unwin, Crows Nest, NSW.

Schedvin C.B., (2008), *Emissaries of Trade: A History of the Australian Trade Commissioner Service*, DFAT, Canberra.

Spears G., (2014), Email interview conducted with the author in April 2014.

Stutchbury M., (1991), *The Competitors: Overseas and Undersold*, David Flatman productions, NSW.

The Canberra Times, (1986), Austrade talents, 10 January 1986, p. 13, National Library of Australia, http://nla.gov.au/nla.news-article122420135, accessed 13 April 2014.

The Canberra Times, (1988), New Trade positions to attract investment, 31 March 1988, p. 6, The Canberra Times, http://trove.nla.gov.au/ndp/del/article/101985724?, accessed 13 April 2014.

The Canberra Times, (1988), Recommendation on trade body shelved, 12 December 1988, p. 3, National library of Australia, http://nla.gov.au/nla.news-article102037290, accessed 13 April 2014.

The Canberra Times, (1990), Austrade review, 31 May 1990, p. 17, National Library of Australia, http://nla.gov.au/nla.news-article122250664, accessed 13 April 2014.

The Canberra Times, (1990), Austrade review, 16 July 1990, p. 18, National Library of Australia, http://nla.gov.au/nla.news-article122297838, accessed 13 April 2014.

The Canberra Times, (1991), 200 jobs to go in Austrade shake-up, 14 February 1991, p. 11, National Library of Australia, http://nla.gov.au/nla.news-article129096218, accessed 13 April 2014.

The Canberra Times, (1992), Opposition calls for explanation of Austrade, 28 March 1992, p. 4, National Library of Australia, http://nla.gov.au/nla.news-article122406367, accessed 13 April 2014.

Thomson K., 2006, Australian Trade Commission legislation Amendment Bill, Second Reading, Intervention by Labor MP, Kelvin Thomson, 30

May 2006, http://parlinfo.aph-.gov.au/parlInfo/search/display/display.w 3p;db=CHAMBER;id=chamber%2Fhansardr%2F2006-05-30%2F0070; query=Id%3Achamber%2Fhansardr%2F2006-05-30%2F0000, accessed 15 January 2015.

Thornhill A., (1986), Austrade chief's plan to improve business, *The Canberra Times*, 12 March 1986, p. 36.

Wright S., (2001), Government Exporters back Austrade against the Productivity Commission report, *AAP General News*, 20 November 2001, EBSCO Host.

3

The Australian trade and investment big picture over the past decades

Phil Ruthven

The 20th century for Australia was a dramatic one as it was for most nations. Whilst involvement in wars in eight decades of the century, a Great Depression and 12 recessions tested our resolve and strengthened us in the process, our capabilities and courage in trade and investment took place only very late in the century. The first chart shows the importance of exports as a share of our GDP from Federation in 1901 to 2014.

Australia's Export Performance 1900-2014

Protectionism, adopted in Federal Parliament in 1908, led to a deterioration in our exports from a quarter of our GDP to a low point of 13.5 per cent in 1969, punctuated only by the artificial boom of the post-World War II and Korean War period. Australia's fall from having the world's highest standard of living at Federation to lower than 20th by the early 1980s was partly due to this fearfulness.

The substantive recovery began in the mid-1980s with the freeing of trade by two successive Labor federal governments in the 1970s and 1980s; and now continued with our present government via FTAs with China and other Asian nations. It has been coincidental with the formation of Austrade in 1985, an organisation that provided outstanding assistance to existing and budding new exporters.

Our exports are now consistently over 20 per cent of GDP, and it is gratifying to know Australia now has the word's eighth highest standard of living; fourth if we ignore countries with a population under a million persons such as Lichtenstein, Luxemburg, Brunei and Iceland.

Our governments and businesses now see the world, and especially the Asian region, as opportunistic rather than threatening. Over two thirds of our immigrants and inbound tourists emanate from Asia, and over 80 per cent of our merchandise exports as the second chart

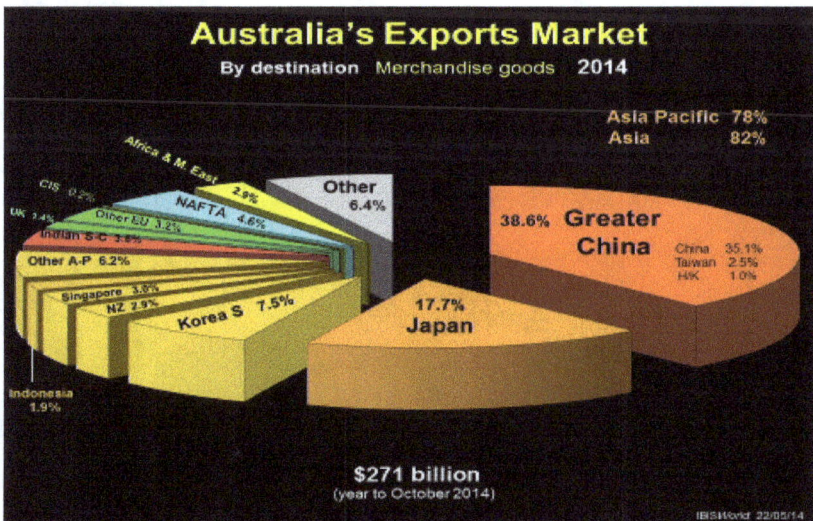

Australia's Exports Market
By destination Merchandise goods 2014

Asia Pacific 78%
Asia 82%

Other 6.4%

38.6% Greater China
China 35.1%
Taiwan 2.5%
H/K 1.0%

17.7% Japan

Korea S 7.5%
NZ 2.9%
Singapore 3.0%
Other A-P 6.2%
Indian S-C 1.8%
UK 1.4%
Other EU 3.2%
CIS 0.2%
NAFTA 4.6%
Africa & M East 2.9%
Indonesia 1.9%

$271 billion
(year to October 2014)

IBISWorld 22/05/14

reveals. China is the new Japan in this regard, and with a population of 1.4 billion and a GDP growing at eight per cent over the past 55 years, it is likely to remain a huge trading partner through this century.

At the time of the formation of Austrade, Japan was our biggest export destination absorbing around a quarter of the total. NAFTA was nearly three times the current share and Europe much bigger than its current share of 4.6 per cent. So Asia is the place to be, heading as its GDP is: twice the size of the EU or NAFTA, and bigger than both in the early 2020s.

But what are we exporting? The third chart reveals the significant changes over more than a century. Mining and agriculture have battled for line honours over this long period, with mining winning during its cyclical booms, as is the case in the mid-2010s. Yet services, especially in the form of tourism, may well make the front-running by the end of the next decade as mining weakens on the downside of its current cycle which began in the early 2000s. Again the potential from Asia for inbound tourists, especially China (now the world's biggest tourists) is exciting and very prospective.

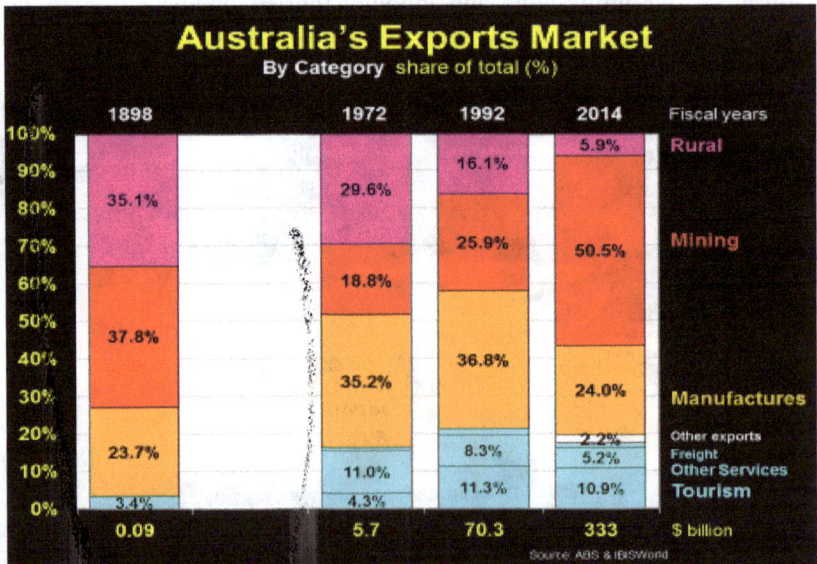

Australia's Exports Market
By Category share of total (%)

	1898	1972	1992	2014	Fiscal years
				5.9%	Rural
	35.1%	29.6%	16.1%		
			25.9%	50.5%	Mining
	37.8%	18.8%			
		35.2%	36.8%	24.0%	Manufactures
	23.7%		8.3%	2.2%	Other exports
		11.0%		5.2%	Freight / Other Services
	3.4%	4.3%	11.3%	10.9%	Tourism
$ billion	0.09	5.7	70.3	333	

Source: ABS & IBISWorld

These constant changes present big challenges to Austrade as it enters its fourth decade of help to our exporters, importers, and inward and outward investors. Which leads to the investment picture. The following chart traces recent dispositions of foreign and abroad investment.

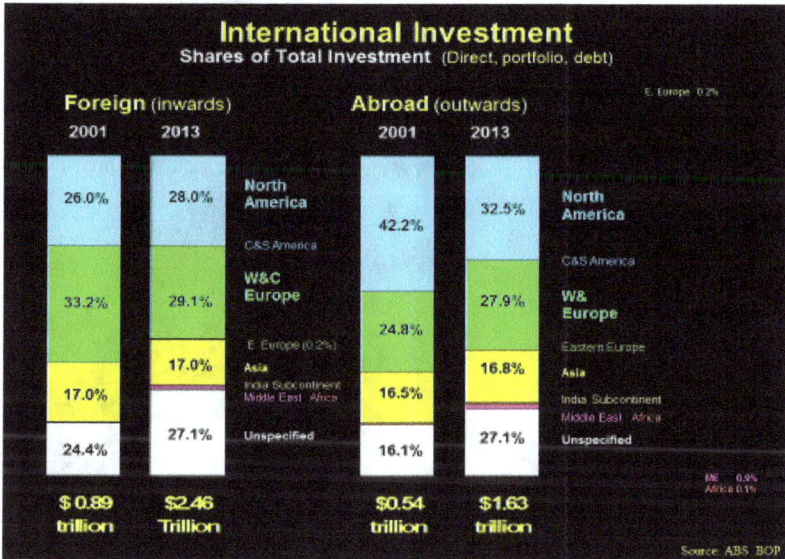

Clearly in terms of total sunk investments, North America and Europe still dominate, unlike our trade which favours Asia (the Asia Pacific and the Indian sub-continent). Interestingly we have yet to see investment to and from Asia follow our trade direction. It almost certainly will over the decades to come; and that too offers challenges to Austrade.

The fifth chart shows what sort of investment makes up Australia's inward and outward sunk investments in 2014. The dominance of portfolio is patent; explaining in large measure why Asian investment – foreign and abroad – has remained low compared with our trade. Portfolio money is not yet convinced that it is as "safe" or profitable as Europe and North America. That perception ad actuality will change as the 21st century unfolds.

And Austrade will almost certainly play a part in this changing investment journey as well as the changing trade journey.

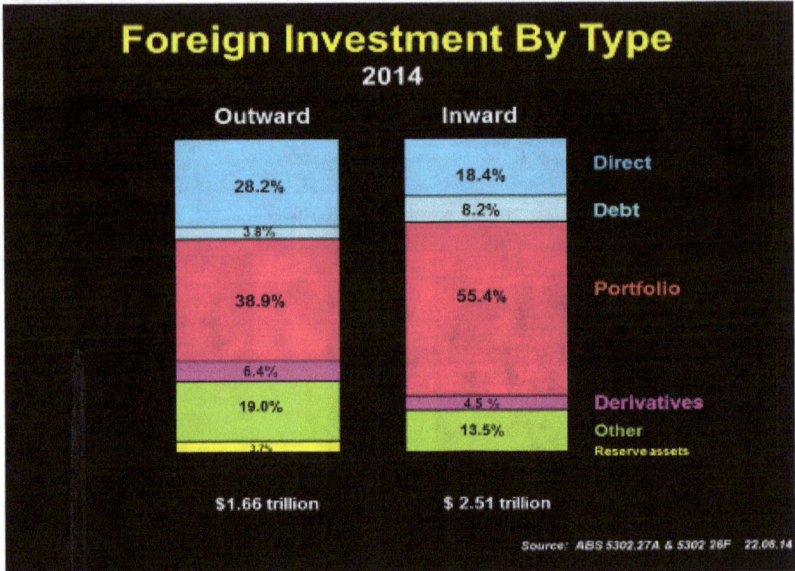

Foreign Investment By Type
2014

Outward	Inward	
28.2%	18.4%	Direct
3.8%	8.2%	Debt
38.9%	55.4%	Portfolio
6.4%	4.5%	Derivatives
19.0%	13.5%	Other
3.7%		Reserve assets
$1.66 trillion	$ 2.51 trillion	

Source: ABS 5302.27A & 5302 26F   22.06.14

SECTION TWO

The formative years of Austrade

4

The Australian Trade Commissioner Service – the impact of its ethos on its operation and its reputation

Richard Fletcher

Introduction

Any evaluation of Austrade over the 25 years or so since its creation in 1986 needs to take into account the body from which it sprang, the Australian Trade Commissioner Service whose operations extend back to the 1920s and whose modus operandi was prescribed in the *Trade Commissioners Act* of 1933.

This is particularly the case as since its formation, Austrade has frequently identified itself with the high esteem in which the Trade Commissioner Service was held by the community, especially those in the business sector. The only former Trade Commissioner to head up Austrade (the late Charles Jamieson), commissioned Professor Boris Schedvin to write a history of the Australian Commissioner Service titled "Emissaries of Trade" as few "contemporary trade commissioners knew much about the organisation's history" (Schedvin 2008, p. vii).

Schedvin wrote about the Trade Commissioner Service mostly in the context of the Australian political scene, balance of payments concerns and bureaucratic jostling for influence – i.e., in terms of domestic political expediency. However, government and the bureaucracy are only two of the major stakeholders involved and any evaluation of Austrade needs to consider as background how its performance compares with the Trade Commissioner Service in terms

of the assistance it provides to its two other major stakeholders – the
Australian exporter and the overseas importer.[1]

The difference in the titles of the two bodies that suggests a possible
difference in orientation. Austrade was an acronym for the Australian
Trade Commission (Schedvin, 2008 p. 332) and its title differs from
that of the Australian Trade Commissioner Service in the omission
of the word "service". It will be argued in this chapter that it was
the concept of "service" that underpinned the ethos of the Australian
Trade Commissioner Service. The omission of this word from the
body for which Austrade is an acronym, implies a potential change
in orientation away from directly serving the needs of its commercial
stakeholders to doing so indirectly as an instrument of government
and political will.

Ethos

Although the trade commissioners date back to the 1920s and the *Trade
Commissioner Act* to 1933, it was in the post-war Menzies-McEwen
era that the ethos underpinning the Trade Commissioner Service was
forged.

Critical to this was the concept of providing a service to exporters
via locating persons with business experience overseas to assist
Australian firms earn foreign exchange from undertaking activities in
overseas markets. It was during this period that there was a change in
the composition of Australia's exports away from primary products
towards manufactures and these required a greater degree of marketing
effort. It was also during this period that there was a broadening in the
range of Australia's export markets with an additional focus towards
Asia and a reduced focus on Europe. Coping with these changes
required trade commissioners who were flexible, proactive and
commercially experienced.

---

1 The terms "exporter" and "importer" are used loosely throughout this chapter and
relate to those involved in international trade in goods, services, investment, projects
and intellectual property.

These trade commissioners were to be given sufficient autonomy to achieve such an objective, were to be provided with the necessary support and were to be exempt from a number of public service constraints. Because they were expected to relate to businessmen, they were to forego public service conditions such as overtime and be available 24/7 to provide assistance as and when required. Security of tenure paralleled that of the business community and not the public service. Under the *Trade Commissioner Act*, trade commissioners were appointed for three year terms and unsatisfactory performance resulted in the contract not being renewed.

They were to be offered the prospect of a career largely spent overseas. The high percentage of the career being spent overseas was the result of trade commissioners being employed under the *Trade Commissioner Act* and not the *Public Service Act*. This meant there were limited roles for trade commissioners back in Australia as they could not readily be employed in the Department of Trade in Australia nor compete with public servants for established positions in the Department as was the case with those in the diplomatic service of the Department of Foreign Affairs. Even the occasional public servant posted as a trade commissioner overseas had to take leave of absence from the public service. Such public servants had the right to return to the public service but only at the level they had previously occupied prior to becoming a Trade Commissioner.

The career structure consisted of three levels of Assistant Trade Commissioner (Grades 3, 2 and 1) and three levels of Trade Commissioner (Grades C, B and A). Recruitment was principally from the business community with junior executives being mostly recruited as Assistant Trade Commissioners Grades 2 or 1, middle level executives being recruited as Trade Commissioners Grade C and the occasional senior executive as Trade Commissioner Grade B. Rarely were there any recruits at the Trade Commissioner Grade A level as most of these positions were reserved for senior departmental officers occupying policy positions in posts such as Washington, Geneva etc.

In 1963, an additional form of recruitment was introduced. This was the Trainee Trade Commissioner Scheme. Foreign Affairs for many years had a cadetship scheme whereby they recruited direct from university promising graduates for the diplomatic service. Such graduates usually had honours degrees, double degrees or masters degrees but little if any work experience. After a training period in Australia of 12 to 18 months, these recruits were sent to their first posting overseas. Trainee trade commissioners on the other hand were recruited on the basis of holding a university degree and a minimum of three year's work experience preferably as a trainee for a major Australian commercial organisation. Two other selection criteria were personality and ability to learn a foreign language. The trainees were recruited initially into the public service and those who successfully completed the 18 month training, were then appointed to their first posting under the *Trade Commissioner Act* as Assistant Trade Commissioners Grade 3. It was anticipated that the career for trade commissioners spent mostly overseas would contain a mix of developing country (hardship) postings and developed country postings. It was the ability to be sufficiently flexible to be able to operate in a variety of different overseas environments that was required rather than a focus on a specific region and it was expected that trade commissioners would become expert in the effective representation of Australian commercial interests overseas, regardless of where they were sent.

Trade commissioner responsibilities overseas involved not only a marketing function but also involvement in representation and reporting on trade relations, trade policy and commodity policy issues as they related to the countries for which the trade commissioner was responsible. In posts where the total or majority of issues involved policy rather than marketing issues, the trade commissioner was usually from the Department of Trade. These cases were few in number and in most posts trade commissioners performed both trade relations and marketing functions. The trade relations activity was a useful vehicle for trade commissioners to develop contacts at senior government and ministerial levels in the overseas country.

For most trade commissioners, the role as envisaged was primarily a marketing one. They were to act as a catalyst between the Australian exporter and the importer in the territory covered by the post. They were expected to be proactive in searching out new business opportunities and in bringing them to the attention of the Australian business community as well as effectively reacting to requests for assistance from Australian exporters. In order to be effective, they had to become experts in each country to which they were posted in relationship creation and network formation. In this, they were assisted by locally engaged marketing staff. Relationship creation and network formation required significant levels of entertainment by trade commissioners. This requirement was recognised and funds were provided for this purpose. As these funds would go further if entertainment was in the home instead of restaurants, crockery, cutlery, glassware and napery were provided to facilitate this. As a consequence, the partners of trade commissioners were expected to be heavily involved in entertaining.

Career trade commissioners faced considerable family stress. This was due to the nature of the overseas life, the uncertainties associated with it, the fact that the majority of time was spent overseas, remoteness from family and friends in Australia and issues with the education of children. These latter included the frequent changing of schools due to postings being for only two or three years. Another education issue was the need to send children to boarding school in Australia, and having to 'bludge' on one's friends to mind children at boarding school during boarders' weekends and in those vacations when they were not eligible for a reunion visit to parents overseas. Keeping children at the post during secondary education was not an option for most trade commissioners due frequent changes in overseas postings, different curricula in schools overseas and lack of the acceptability of different education systems for matriculation to Australian universities.

The nature of the work, the sense of pride in the job and the difficult personal circumstances faced by trade commissioners created a bond between trade commissioners as manifested in their looking out for each other, helping family members and children when transiting the post and keeping each other informed of developments in their territory that could impact on potential in other areas. Bonds formed out of adversity and shared experiences, facilitated the professionalism of the Trade Commissioner Service and were part of its ethos. These bonds, the high regard in which trade commissioners were held by the Australian business community coupled with the selective recruitment and operational independence (Schedvin 2008, p. 287) created an image of elitism which was reinforced by the fact that trade commissioners by and large did not consider themselves to be typical public servants (Schedvin 2008, p. 287). The Department encouraged this elitism in a number of ways and established a special branch in the personnel division to manage the Trade Commissioner Service. Each week a newsletter would be published known as the "yellow peril" which focused not only on matters that affected trade commissioners but also on the doings of various trade commissioners so one knew what one's colleagues were doing and the experiences they encountered.

Reputation

The Australian Trade Commissioner Service over the years developed an enviable reputation amongst the export community specifically and the business community in general. In addition, it developed a strong reputation with governments overseas and with multinational agencies such as the International Trade Centre (ITC) in Geneva. It was held up as a model for other countries of how to structure and operate an overseas government commercial service. A former senior executive of the ITC, Claude Cellich (now a professor of International Business at the International University of Geneva) often recommended to developing countries that they adopt a similar model of overseas commercial representation to that of Australia. While posted to Geneva, John Tinney was seconded to Algiers at ITC's request to assist Algerian officials tasked with planning a national foreign trade service.

Another example of this international recognition was a request made of Keith Le Rossignol, a very experienced Trade Commissioner who in the early 1960s was Director of the Trade Commissioner Service, by the United Nation's International Trade Centre to write a manual for them to publish on how to organise an overseas trade commissioner service. Titled "Entering new markets: a guide to trade representatives", it was first issued in 1973 and in 2013 the third edition was released principally written by another Trade Commissioner, Lloyd Downey.

Peter O'Byrne, a former managing director of Austrade, writing the afterword to Schedvin's book, captures both the reputation and ethos of the Trade Commissioner Service as follows:

> There is a sense of adventure in the way in which Australia's trade commissioners sought out new markets and opportunities for the nation's exports. To engage in this sometimes hazardous pursuit they were people of great character with flair and dynamism. The difficulties they faced were offset by the satisfaction that was derived by these men and women from promoting our nation's economic interests, both abroad and at home (Schedvin 2008 p. 335).

Operation

Trade commissioners in general were a catalyst between the two poles of the dyad between the Australian exporter and the overseas importer. Prior to the formation of Austrade, trade commissioners were heavily involved in both promotional activities overseas supporting Australian firms and in undertaking basic market research for Australian exporters.

Promotion

During the time before the creation of Austrade, the Department to which trade commissioners were responsible supported both elements of the dyad with a wide ranging program of promotional activities intended to improve the *Country of Origin Image* of Australia in the overseas market on the one hand and promote specific Australian

products and services to importers and distributors in the overseas
market on the other. These activities were either initiated at the 'post'
level or at the Australian end.

The former included:

> A monthly publication *Australian Trading News* which was
> mailed to a wide range of commercial contacts in the overseas
> market. The publication was primarily devoted to featuring
> Australian products and services relevant to the specific market
> as well as highlighting commercial developments in Australia
> of likely interest and profiling trade commissioners as contact
> points for more information.

> The *Trade* Promotion *Visits Fund.* This was a program by which
> significant potential buyers and decision makers from both
> the private and government sectors were provided with an 'all
> expenses paid' visit to Australia to expose them at first hand to
> the products and services of Australian firms and to government
> officials of relevance. The latter included:

> *General Australian Trade Displays* in the overseas market
> featuring a wide range of products and services from Australia
> (e.g., San Francisco 1969; Jakarta 1973). Often used at a stage
> when the problem to be addressed was creating overall awareness
> and open up the market, these general displays were usually
> intended to assist firms appoint agents and for those already in
> the market, to expand their distribution network.

> *Specialised Trade Displays.* These usually involved having
> an Australian stand at an industry specific trade display in
> the overseas market (e.g., California Sailboat Show, 1984).
> Participation was based on selecting Australian industries
> perceived as having good prospects in the market.

> *Australian Trade Missions* to the country/market overseas.
> These missions could be general (as when opening up a market
> e.g., Trade Mission to Vietnam, 1986) or specific (industry based
> or problem based e.g., Australian Offsets Mission to the US,
> 1985). They were usually led by a leading figure from Australian

industry and managed by an official from the Department in Australia or by the local Trade Commissioner.

Trade Commissioner Showroom Displays. In a number of posts, display rooms were established and equipped with display units etc. (e.g., San Francisco 1970, Jakarta 1973, Bangkok 1986). These could be used for mounting small specialised displays of Australian products or for displays, technical seminars or other promotional activities by individual Australian companies.

The monthly magazine *Overseas Trading.* Distributed to Australian exporters and decision makers, this magazine was mootly booed on information oupplied by trade commissioners on developments in their areas of responsibility and opportunities that existed as a consequence.

Supporting this promotional program were:

A Trade Publicity Branch in Melbourne staffed by journalists, publicity professionals and personnel expert in the creation and management of displays in overseas markets and the accompanying logistics.

A network of regional offices in each state tasked with assisting Australian exporters. They were largely responsible for recruiting Australian firms as participants in trade displays trade missions and other overseas promotional activities.

There were no charges levied on firms for participating in overseas trade activities such as displays and missions leaving the only expense for firms to meet being fares and staffing costs. Even these could be claimed under export incentive schemes in vogue at the time. These promotional activities were scheduled on an annual basis and publicised well in advance to Australian firms so participation could become an element of their annual export activities.

With the formation of Austrade there appears to have been a reduction in promotional activities designed to support Australian exporters. Most of the above measures no longer exist. The Trade Publicity Branch was closed and firms now pay up front the full costs of any promotional activity they undertake in overseas markets. However, exporters in the early years of their international activity continue to have access to export incentives through the Export Markets Development Grants Scheme now administered by Austrade.

Market research

Traditionally trade commissioners, as an extension of their role in bring market opportunities to the attention of Australian firms, would undertake basic market research for firms. This was normally based on secondary data available in the market, office records and experience and limited primary research based on showing products to interested major buyers and/or agents. They would also undertake research on prospects for a specific industry category deemed to have potential in the market. Until the creation of Austrade, no charge was made for provision of such research. If detailed primary research was required such as mass surveys, focus groups, mall intercept studies, ethnographic research and the like, a commercial research provider in the market would be recommended to the Australian firm. With the formation of Austrade, the 'user pays' principle was introduced and firms charged for a range of services, particularly market research, provided by trade commissioners. Only readily available basic market information continued to be provided free of charge, mainly to new or small exporters. Little thought appears to have been given to the 'user pays' concept prior to its introduction at Trade Commissioner posts. It was assumed that posts had the resources and skills to undertake all kinds of market research – this was not the case. Also, initially fees were set back in Australia on a basis that took no account of different costs of research in specific markets. The fee set for Bangkok was higher than commercial rates prevailing in the market. In cases where the post could not undertake the requested research, it was required to commission research by an external provider and add a service fee. As a consequence, it was cheaper for Australian firms wishing to research prospects in Thailand to commission research through a commercial research organisation than through the Austrade office. Moves of this kind placed trade commissioners in a difficult position as far as relationships with Australian exporters were concerned.

The Foreign Affairs-Trade power struggle

In the McEwen-Anthony era the Trade Commissioner Service was viewed and supported as an overseas service to assist the business community operating parallel to and relatively autonomous from overseas representation by Foreign Affairs. This was resented by Foreign Affairs who pressed for its incorporation into Foreign Affairs with trade commissioners being responsible to and reporting through the Head of Mission/Head of Post. Although there were moves in this direction during the Whitlam years, these were successfully resisted and a separate Trade Commissioner Service continued to operate until the formation of Austrade.

Some Ambassadors and Consuls General (Heads of Mission/ Heads of Post) challenged this autonomy and Schedvin has used my unfortunate experience in Iran as an example (pp. 254-5). Overall, it was my experience that the more senior Ambassadors (e.g., Bob Furlonger in Jakarta and Dick Smith in Bangkok) accepted the situation and made it work for both parties and to the overall benefit of the Australian taxpayer. This was achieved through a co-operative relationship with the Senior Trade Commissioner whereby Ambassadors used their influence to secure access to ministers and high level public sector decision makers for trade commissioners and Australian business groups whilst the trade commissioners involved the Ambassadors in trade promotion activities thereby broadening their involvement with the local business community. It was the more junior occupants of Head of Mission/Head of Post positions who challenged the relative autonomy of the trade commissioner's operation in overseas locations, often because the main relationship between Australia and the overseas country was a commercial one which they wished to manage.

One irritant in the above relationship was the progressive introduction of "common services" at overseas posts whereby rather than resources being directly provided by the Department of Trade to the trade post, these were to be provided through the Foreign Affairs operation overseas. At first glance such a cost cutting measure appeared sensible but its implementation created problems and interfered with the operational efficiency of trade commissioners. Motor vehicles were a particular source of irritation. Initially a vehicle was reserved for exclusive use by the Trade Office and requirements for additional vehicles by trade staff met from the pool of vehicles at the mission/post. However, dating from the Whitlam years, this situation deteriorated and heads of mission/post withdrew allocated vehicles and trade commissioners had to take their chances of a pool vehicle being available or use cabs. One of the initial attractions of the formation of Austrade from a trade commissioner perspective was the hope that the common services irritant would be eliminated or at least significantly reduced. In the early days of Austrade the practice common in the private sector commenced of supplying a vehicle to the Senior Trade Commissioner and deducting from the salary a specific amount to cover estimated savings of being able to use the vehicle for private purposes.

Politics and the Australian Trade Commissioner Service

Schedvin (2008) documents this in detail from a macro perspective. From the perspective of the serving Trade Commissioner, the following describes the political situation during the period 1964 to 2009 (including the early years of Austrade). In the Menzies-McEwen era, the Trade Commissioner Service was seen as a counterpart to the diplomatic service of the Department Foreign Affairs with its relative autonomy being implicitly underwritten by the fact that the department to which it was responsible was headed by the leader of the Country Party, who was also the Deputy Prime Minister. This was at a time when the Country Party was a very significant partner in the coalition government of the day. It also reflected the fact that in most cases, Australia's principal relationship with overseas countries was trade driven. This situation continued when Doug Anthony replaced Jack

McEwen as Trade Minister[2] and Deputy Prime Minister. Although trade commissioners were cognisant of the views of the minister of the day, they were able to offer opinions (provided they were well supported by evidence) that may have diverged from those of the Minister and advisors as this was an environment where public servants were more encouraged to offer unbiased advice than is currently the case.

With the advent of the Whitlam government in 1972, there was suspicion that the Trade Commissioner Service had been a tool of the Country Party (National Party as from 1971). However, as Schedvin (2008) documents, the Trade Commissioner Service emerged relatively unscathed from the turbulence of the Whitlam era and continued to serve the needs of its major stakeholder, the Australian exporter, due in part to the Deputy Prime Minister continuing to be the Trade Minister and thus having clout within the cabinet of the Whitlam government.

With the fall of the Whitlam government in 1975, National Party leader Doug Anthony resumed his former role as both Trade Minister and Deputy Prime Minister. This situation continued until the election of the Hawke government in 1983. For a year the tradition continued of the trade minister also being Deputy Prime Minister with the appointment of Lionel Bowen. However, thereafter, the Trade Minister was no longer the Deputy Prime Minister and a more junior minister, John Dawkins, was appointed to the Trade Ministry. He was the architect of Austrade. Anecdotal comment at the time credits Dawkins with having early in his career worked in the regional office of the Department of Trade in Perth. Allegedly, he was disillusioned that under the situation that existed at the time, he could not as a public servant become a Trade Commissioner. With the formation of Austrade, he was said to have proclaimed that every member of Austrade "had a Trade Commissioner's baton in their briefcase".

---

2 The terms Trade Minister and Department of Trade are used to refer to Departments to which trade commissioners were responsible. These varied during the period of time covered by this chapter as follows: 1956-63 Department of Trade; 1963-72 Department of Trade and Industry; 1972-77 Department of Overseas Trade; 1977-83 Department of Trade and Resources; 1983-87 Department of Trade; 1987 Department of Foreign Affairs and Trade.

Another development having implications for Trade Commissioners in the field was the creation of a parallel and often competitive
source of advice to the Minister on trade matters in addition to the
Department of Trade. Prior to the Whitlam Government in 1972,
ministers had had private secretaries and possibly an expert advisor in
their parliamentary office. The number of these advisors increased in
the Whitlam era because of distrust by that government of the public
service. In the Hawke era commencing 1983, this distrust increased
and the number of advisors in each minister's office increased
exponentially.

Traditionally when ministers visited overseas posts and trade
matters were involved, they would discuss the brief they had
received with the Trade Commissioner in charge so as to get a 'feel
on the ground'. This was the case with ministers regardless of political
persuasion. Unlike his ministerial colleagues at the time having
portfolios with a trade interest such as Kerin (Primary Industries,
Beasley (Defence/Offsets) and Button (Industry), in my experience
in Bangkok when Dawkins held the education portfolio and the trade
post was responsible for marketing Australia as a location for Thai
students, he tended to rely on the brief from his office and was not that
interested in seeking the views of trade commissioners.

The departure of Tom Walton, the Senior Trade Commissioner
in Milan,[3] also raises questions as to his underlying attitude towards
trade commissioners. Walton, who joined the Trade Commissioner
Service as a Senior Trade Commissioner in 1968, became involved
in a disagreement with the minister in 1986. Presumably, based on
information gleaned in Australia, the minister publically announced
that a very large number of Italian tourists would visit Fremantle
(the minister's electorate) for the America's Cup. Walton was not
consulted before this announcement was made and as the claim was
surprising, the press questioned Walton who allegedly claimed he was

---

3 Editorial footnote: It would appear there was a common belief that Tom Walton
was sacked soon after this confrontation with the Minister. According to Austrade
management sources of the time he was not sacked but resigned a few days later.

unaware of the size of this anticipated tourist influx. The minister then attempted to have Walton recalled on the basis that he was 'unsuitable for pursuing recent trade initiatives by Dawkins' (Humphries, January 30, 1986). The dispute escalated with defamation writs, prime-time media attention and an opposition censure motion (Hartcher 1986b). The Minister's office then claimed Walton's past performance was unsatisfactory citing as evidence an issue some eight years old when it was alleged that whilst Senior Trade Commissioner in Jakarta, he took unreasonable advantage of a provision in the custom's regulations whereby residents who had owned and used vehicles overseas could on return, bring them into Australia free of duty and sales tax. Subsequently there was a leak to the press of a confidential performance appraisal on Walton's performance in Milan written by the acting director of the new Australian Trade Commission (Hartcher 1986b). It was counter-claimed that Walton's recall was prompted by the Minister's desire to appoint a "political crony" (Emanuel Klein, Senior Private Secretary to the Minister for Sports, Recreation and Tourism) to the post (Hartcher 1986a).

There were three developments in staffing of trade commissioner posts heralded with the arrival of the Hawke government that had implications for the continuation of a professional career Trade Commissioner Service. These were the posting of career public servants as trade commissioners, the appointment of trade commissioners based on expertise in a particular market due to linguistic abilities or ethnic affiliations and the posting of political appointees.

Posting of public servants as trade commissioners. For the most part, these appointments were as deputy to the senior Trade Commissioner in charge of the post – a level at which a professional trade commissioner would be able 'to hit the ground running' as far as relationship formation and network creation were concerned. Unlike professional trade commissioners who mostly had had several overseas postings before reaching this level, those appointed usually had no commercial experience or experience of how to act as a commercial representative of the Australian Government overseas. In some cases they brought their public service work habits with them. Because of lack of prior overseas experience they often shied away from entertaining local business persons and officials preferring the easier task of entertaining members of the local expatriate community. Often they were reluctant to entertain in the home so as to make their representation allowances go further despite the fact that housing standards overseas allowed for entertaining in the home and representation kits of glassware, cutlery, crockery and napery were provided for this purpose.

Appointment of trade commissioners based on linguistic abilities on ethnic affiliations. Described by Schedvin (2008, p. 314) as "a large number of appointments to the trade commissioner service of people with unconventional backgrounds ... who were not appropriately qualified", those recruited in this way also were at a senior level and also were "not able to hit the ground running". Whilst such persons may become effective in the first post for which they were selected on the grounds of linguistic competence or ethnic affiliation, a problem presented itself should they wish for a subsequent posting in a different market. These appointments could create morale problems by distorting the accepted balance between hardship and non-hardship postings accepted as the norm by career trade commissioners. This method of recruitment could also result in an increase in the percentage of 'one-off' single postings which could undermine the continuity of the ethos of the Trade Commissioner Service.

Political appointees. Whilst political appointees to the role of Ambassador, High Commissioner or Consul-General had always been a fact of life for the Department of Foreign Affairs, with one or two rare exceptions this had not been the case with the Trade Commissioner Service prior to 1983. This is not to say that there were not cases where politicians had not influenced appointments of career trade commissioners and occasionally their local staff, but even these cases were rare. Commencing in 1983, there was an increase in the number of political appointments to the Trade Commissioner Service including those with "unconventional backgrounds" referred to above. One of the more extreme examples was the appointment of

David Combe as Senior Trade Commissioner and Consul-General to Vancouver following the Combe-Ivanov affair in which it was alleged that Combe as National Secretary of the Labor Party had, through his relationship with Ivanov at the Russian Embassy in Canberra, created a significant security threat.

Another example of political involvement in activities of trade commissioners was the policy to include a senior trade union official in any trade mission sent overseas. This created difficulty in a mission of business persons who wanted to be able to assure potential importers and investors that Australia was a reliable country with which to do business and that industrial disputes were not likely to interfere with the flow of goods or the operation of investment in Australia should business be placed with the Australian firm. As an example, when I was based in Los Angeles, I was heavily involved in a policy (the Offsets Policy) that with all defence and civil aircraft purchases by Australia, compensating work of equivalent technology had to be placed in Australia to partially offset the foreign exchange cost of the purchase. US firms were very nervous of this requirement as they did not wish to import components from Australia that would cause their aircraft to fall out of the sky or their vessels to sink to the bottom of the ocean. In an endeavour to address these concerns and reassure the US defence and aerospace sector, an Offsets Trade Mission was sent to the US in 1985 of which I was the manager. The trade union member of the mission was John Halfpenny who had a reputation amongst the business community of being somewhat militant. He was in a very difficult position as other mission members wanted him to assure their US counterparts that should they award offsets business to their companies in Australia, there would be no interruption to production or the shipping of the finished product due to industrial disputes. On the other hand, the trade union movement in general and John Halfpenny's union in particular could not abrogate the right to strike which if mentioned would have undermined the purpose of the mission. This conundrum necessitated a negotiation session between John Halfpenny, the trade mission leader and myself

at which we rehearsed scenarios he was likely to encounter and came
up with suggested responses on his part which would not undermine
the purpose of the Trade Mission on the one hand nor place him in a
position where "my members would bloody well crucify me if they
knew I said that" on the other.

The Trade Commissioner Service and Austrade

Since inception, the Trade Commissioner Service operated in an
environment where there were changes in the Australian market
environment, changes in the global market environment and
changes in individual markets overseas. Not only did this require
trade commissioners to adopt a flexible approach and react speedily
to change but it also required the Department of Trade to adjust its
priorities, its support mechanisms to assist exporters and its allocation
of resources to individual posts. At the Australian end, this was
reflected in various campaigns to boost export performance and varied
from an emphasis to getting new firms involved in export (e.g., Export
Now) to picking winners to focussing on specific countries or regions
(e.g., North American Special Exercise). At the overseas level this was
reflected in varying between posts the extent of promotional activities
(e.g., Trade Displays, Trade Missions, publicity campaigns, etc.) and
at the post level in the strengthening of some posts, the reduction in
others, the closing of some posts and in the opening of new posts.
Until the formation of Austrade, the one constant was that no minister
or bureaucrat attempted to interfere with the ethos, the recruitment
basis or the general operation of Trade Commissioner posts overseas.

There is an old adage – "If it ain't broke, don't fix it." What was
broke about the Trade Commissioner Service that required the new
Trade Minister John Dawkins to fix it? Schedvin (2008) documents
a number of inquiries into Australia's overseas trade and its overseas
representation. None of these inquiries recommended tinkering
with the ethos, the recruitment basis or the general operation of the
Trade Commissioner Service. In 1983, the Department of Trade set
up its own task force, followed by an external review of the Trade

Commissioner Service by a panel of four senior business executives. Although these inquiries found a number of areas for improvement, the overall conclusion of the external review was:

> The need for a strong and independent Trade Commissioner Service is as evident now as it was 50 years ago when the Service was formally established through the passage of the *Trade Commissioners Act* (Schedvin, 2008 p.318).

However, some trade commissioners welcomed the creation of Austrade, believing it meant an enhanced commercial focus and more distance from bureaucracy. This was to be achieved by its head office being moved from Canberra to Sydney, by its managing director reporting directly to a business-oriented board and by a reduction in the demands of "policy" work being greatly reduced, enabling trade commissioners to concentrate on the core business of helping exporters.

Nature of the research underpinning the creation of Austrade

Given the fact that the ethos, the recruitment and the operation of the Trade Commissioner Service had operated satisfactorily under a separate act for over 50 years, it would have been thought that any tinkering with it, let alone radical change, would only occur following widespread consultation with stakeholders, in particular the Australian export community. As the creation of Austrade involved changing the ethos, the recruitment basis and the general operation of the Trade Commissioner Service, it is reasonable to ask whether rigorous market research, either by survey, focus groups or other vehicle for primary research, was undertaken amongst Australian exporters. This did not occur. Nor did it seem that basic analysis of its effectiveness in terms of its strengths, weaknesses, threats and/or opportunities took place. Schedvin (2008 p.317) comments that individual trade commissioners were given the opportunity to comment on the Report of the 1983 Department of Trade Task Force and implies that seeking the opinion of trade commissioners in matters of this kind was unusual. However, trade commissioners were not asked to comment on the proposal to establish Austrade in 1986, nor on the changes that would result to the ethos, the recruitment basis and the general operation of the Trade Commissioner Service. The hype surrounding the creation of Austrade was that it would provide a 'one-stop-shop' for Australian exporters by bringing together the Trade Commissioner Service, the Export Development Grants Board, the Export Finance and Insurance Corporation (EFIC) and the Overseas Projects Corporation (AOPC). It appears that no research was undertaken as to whether these four bodies would fit well together and within a short space time EFIC was separated from Austrade and the AOPC withered on the vine.

The birth of Austrade in January 1986 was followed by the appointment of its first Managing Director, Lindsay MacAlister, who was a geologist by training and managing Director of the General Electric Group in Australia. This was a surprising appointment as it would have been expected that the appointee would have been a person active in export (and therefore known to trade commissioners), drawn from the manufacturing or services sector, experienced in dealing with both ministers and the bureaucracy and familiar with the Trade Commissioner Service and its culture. The selection process appears to have been a hurried one.

The above points to Austrade having been conceived in haste without adequate consideration being given to the opinions of its principal group of stakeholders – Australian exporters. The structural change required was achieved at breakneck speed according to Schedvin (2008, p. 332) and for the person responsible, "Austrade was the centrepiece" of his relatively brief tenure as Minister for Trade (John Dawkins – December 1984 to July, 1987).

From the foregoing, there is evidence that the operation of the Trade Commissioner Service under the Hawke government was influenced by political expediency to a greater extent than had been the case with previous governments and that political expediency had a role in the creation of Austrade.

Issues for consideration in evaluating the performance of Austrade arising from the foregoing discussion:

- Was the architect of Austrade, John Dawkins, driven more by personal views concerning the Trade Commissioner Service and trade commissioners than by what was needed to assist Australian exporters improve their export performance?

- Would the subsequent performance of Austrade have been improved had wider consultation with its major stakeholders, particularly the export community, occurred before its creation.

- Did the overall service offered to the export community improve or suffer as a consequence of changes to the method for the appointment of trade commissioners?

- Was Austrade able to fulfil the promise of greater autonomy for trade commissioner operations at overseas posts?

- Considering that the current and previous managing directors of Austrade were both drawn from very senior levels of the Senior Executive Service of the Department of Foreign Affairs and Trade, did trade commissioners in practise experience greater autonomy in their operations overseas following the creation of Austrade?

- Were the relationship formation and network creation roles of trade commissioners constrained by the shifting of responsibility for trade policy and trade relations to foreign affairs officers at overseas posts?

- Has Australian export performance, especially in labour intensive sectors, suffered as a result of the "user pays" principle introduced by Austrade?

- Were decisions by Austrade to either eliminate or charge for promotional assistance measures based on:

  Rigorous research into their continued usefulness to Australian firms?

  Change in the international market environment?

  A philosophical view that firms should not be subsidised in this way?

  Financial exigencies resulting in cost cutting measures?

Bibliography

Downey, L. (2013) "Entering new markets: a guide for Trade Representatives", International Trade Centre, Geneva.

Hartcher, P. (1986a) "Dawkins in new row over Milan job", *Sydney Morning Herald*, 18 April 1986, p. 3.

Hartcher, P. (1986b) "Dawkins bout goes another round", *Sydney Morning Herald*, 30 April 1986, p. 3.

Humphries, D. (1986) "Dawkins accused of bid to punish trade envoy", *The Age*, 30 January 1986, p. 3.

Le Rossignol, K. (1973) "Official commercial representation abroad: a handbook for officers of developing countries", International Trade Centre, Geneva.

Schedvin, B. (2008) "Emissaries of Trade: A History of the Australian Trade Commissioner Service", Commonwealth of Australia.

5

The Ministerial architect of Austrade:
Extracts of an interview with John Dawkins

Introduction

The establishment of the Australian Trade Commission (Austrade) in 1986 in the big scheme of economic reforms of the Hawke/Keating governments of the 1980s and 1990s was, often and unfairly, overlooked. The reforms in trade received no mention in Bob Hawke's memoirs (Hawke 1994) nor does it get any treatment in the recollections of the Keating period in government (Watson 2002). While there were other significant and even greater economic achievements which defined this period, the establishment of Austrade was not simply a reshuffling of chairs or departments. It was the culminations of reforms giving a new look and task to the government export provision which it had lacked prior. When John Dawkins was appointed Minister for Trade it was in a portfolio which prior to the Hawke period had not been given too much attention by Labor. In the 1983 first Hawke government, Lionel Bowen had acquired the Trade portfolio and according to Capling was known as: "an old style protectionist from the Whitlam era" (Capling 2001: 106).

In export terms, the establishment of Austrade was the most significant reform since the enactment of the Trade Commissioner Service in 1933. Moreover as will become evident, it was the most significant step in the consolidation of a single export promotion body as well as the separation of Trade Promotion from Trade Policy – a division of labor considered at the time, vital to going beyond the policy enactment. Today this division of responsibilities and the location of these tasks are questioned. Not surprisingly much of that questioning is as a result of rationalising resources and seeking to get more for less from government outlays. John Dawkins, as will be seen, became better known for his achievements in budget control and in education, and only his initiative in the establishment of the Cairns Group in 1986 gets some kind of public acknowledgement in the trade field. Nor was it due to any timidness by Dawkins as fellow former Minister Walsh observed "Dawkins was often the incubator of ideas ... And whatever his faults may be, sycophancy or cowardice are not among them" (Walsh 1995: 153).

Not only is there little acknowledgement but also scant reference in the literature on the establishment of Austrade in government business of the day, the exception here being the Schedvin treatment of the Australian Trade Commissioner Service (Schedvin 2008). This chapter explores the journey of the creation and development of Austrade seen from the viewpoint of the then Minister of Trade John Dawkins. His comments (in quotations) are provided from an interview conducted in August 2014.

The beginnings

The background to the creation of Austrade has its origins in the period of economic reform and to the nature of the government in power in that period. The Australian economy in the mid-1980s was at one of its lowest points in the post war period but ironically with one of the strongest reform-minded governments of the post war era. The poorer economic performance of the 1980s was not limited to macroeconomic indicators. It was equally evident in the trading conditions and performance of the Australian economy. Not only was it a dire period of double digit unemployment, double digit interest rates, but the terms of trade was at one of its lowest in the previous decade with an Australian dollar at exceptionally low levels. Australia had declined in the rankings as an exporter nation and the export agenda was suffering from catch up and a need to modernise.

John Dawkins entered the parliament in 1974 and was shaken by the dismissal of the Whitlam government in November 1975 losing his seat and re-entering parliament again in 1977. For the following six years he remained in the upper echelons of the Labor opposition and when victory came to a Hawke government in 1983 he was nominated as Finance Minister. In December 1984 he became Minister for Trade, a Department which today almost ceases to exist after the merger with Foreign Affairs in 1987. For decades, according to Capling, "... the ALP tended to regard the Trade Department as something of a National Party secretariat that looked after pastoralists and mining companies, not exactly Labor's core support base. The Dawkins appointment [which followed] was one of the new generation economic reformers of the new Labor Government ... and a bit of a maverick" (Capling 2001: 106). Dawkins was not oblivious to this existing prejudice within the Department of Trade. His reasoning on this matter follows:

> I think the explanation for [The Department of Trade being considered as a National Party Secretariat] is because the Deputy Prime Minister had always come from the Country/ National Party and the leader of the National/Country Party had always been either Trade Minister or Trade and Industry. McEwen was the latter, Anthony was the former. So in a sense the Trade Department had become the Department of the Deputy Prime Minister. It had a huge second division for the size of the department and that was because the Deputy Prime Minister wanted advice over a whole range of issues. The National Party never trusted Treasury. They always wanted to have a separate source of economic advice. So the Trade Department, from the days of McEwen, had this internal contradiction within it. On the one hand it was interested in trade – on the other hand it was interested in protection. So it had agriculture and mining, unsubsidised and exposed to the international markets. On the other hand manufacturing industry was hiding behind various kinds of trade protection, tariffs

and quantitative quotas for example. There is no doubt that the tradition of the department was influenced by that association with the National Party.

The Department of Trade, at the time, was essentially separated along two lines. One was the trade policy area responsible for trade negotiations, agreements and membership of multilateral associations and the other was the Trade Commissioner Service which undertook the get out there and do the trade marketing and flanking of business to get to market. Today this is called trade promotion. Dawkins elaborated:

> ... when I was appointed as Minister for Trade in 1984 there were really two aspects to this responsibility. One was trade negotiations and the other was trade promotion. In relation to trade negotiations, we were heavily involved in activities such as setting up the Cairns Group and it was Australia's role which saw that agriculture was included in the world trade negotiations for the first time. We were very keen to ensure that from Australia's standpoint, we did something about subsidies for agricultural products particularly from Europe and also from the US and Japan. Because we wanted our agricultural exporters to have a fairer go in the world and not be confronted by subsidised products being dumped into our markets. From an economic point of view, while important, trade negotiations was considered more long term as it takes a long time to get agreement on reduction in subsidies and opening markets. On the other hand, there was the trade promotion activity. I was interested in knowing what the Department of Trade thought about Australia's challenge in terms of improving the balance of payments through either exports or income replacements. There was a lot of emphasis on the exported product. The government didn't have to do much about promoting mining exports, and given the fact

that they were mostly large companies they were able to do it themselves. So at the time there was an emphasis on exports of manufactured goods, some of which were doing well however poor productivity improvement risked pricing ourselves out of the market.

The Trade Commissioner Service and its new home: Austrade

As the new Minister for Trade, Dawkins inherited the Trade Commissioner Service which had been in existence since 1933. However he was not entirely enamoured by what he saw. He explained:

> The Trade Commissioner Service was large and it had a focus which had grown over time. It was heavily concentrated in Europe. There wasn't enough going on in other countries. Of course, China was just sort a glint in the eye at that time. I couldn't understand why they were so many trade commissioners in Europe. So in 1984 I convened a meeting in Dublin of all trade commissioners based in Europe. I was astounded at the dislocation of most of the trade commissioners from the task we had in Australia. Many of them had enjoyed cross postings and had not been back to Australia for years and moreover some had been in the service for too long and had become very comfortable.

Measuring the performance of trade commissioners and the service overall became a requirement and it concerned the new Minister how this would be undertaken in this traditional Department:

> I thought that the Trade Commissioner Service was a very confused outreach of this confused Department. I don't think any of the trade commissioners had KPIs. So they set their own priorities and they might need to report to their ambassadors though the ambassadors largely left

them alone. So we were trying to overcome, what I call an almost moribund and directionless organisation. There was no great strategy as to what this huge and costly resource was actually trying to do. It was often the case that trade commissioners would find an excuse for never returning back to Australia. So the old trick of being cross posted from one post to another was well utilised. There were a couple of old characters and one comes to mind whom we named the Flying Dutchman because he had circumnavigated the world through cross postings and never actually landed in Australia. He wasn't alone. Thirty years of cross posting around the world and never coming back to Australia – he had no clue what was going on, and how can you know about Australia if you are never there.

Prior to assuming the role of Trade Minister, Dawkins had been Finance Minister and remained throughout the period of his tenure in Cabinet a member of the Expenditure Review Committee (ERC) where the Trade Commissioner Service as part of the overall Department of Trade budget came under financial scrutiny. Dawkins remembered clearly:

> One of the big components of Department of Trade's budget was the Trade Commissioner Service. We looked at ways we could get greater contribution from industry into the cost of managing the Trade Commissioner Service. This would also make it more responsive if people are paying for it and less so if it was free. Would some of the big companies take advantage of it? Many did. So we had that challenge of trying to do something about the cost of the service.

The establishment of Austrade

Setting up this new organisation was pre-empted by a number of considerations. One of them was how the Trade Commissioner Service interacted with exporters and how it should be best structured to meet the challenges of the day. Therefore the need for a special statutory structure with a business Board. Dawkins elaborates:

> I thought that the Trade Commissioner Service was not very responsive to industry. I thought it was expensive. I thought it had resources in the wrong places. And so we decided that the best way to improve its performance was rather than leaving it to the Minister and Secretary of the Department to set-up a management structure which could seriously look at where resources are allocated, find the most cost-effective way of delivering the service. This led to the creation of a statutory body with a Board to determine strategy and deliver a business plan. The Board was first chaired by Vern Christie, and later by Bill Ferris.

As the concept of Austrade was developed, it required a structure put in place and to provide a fee for service. As Dawkins notes this concept had some primitive beginnings:

> Prior to Austrade there was an attempt to set up an exporter's club. This exporter's club would ensure that to get access to Austrade, exporters would have to join the exporter's club and pay for the service. None of this was terribly well thought out. Moreover it was hard to implement in a departmental structure. The other big part of trade promotion was role of the EMDG [Export Market Development Grants] scheme which was a large and generous subsidy scheme for exporters. Australia's trade promotion activity was EMDG, EFIC and the Trade Commissioner Service which all became Austrade.

During the early Hawke years, the government made major inroads into economic reform including cutting tariffs, floating the dollar and exposing Australia to greater competition to the rest of the world. But as Dawkins reminds us:

As we were opening up the Australian economy, many would say, "Well that's all very well. That also means that over time we can lose a lot of manufacturing activity if you take the tariffs down, the textile, clothing, and footwear industries will go out the backdoor. Where are the new jobs coming from?" So we started looking around for new opportunities. And that partly focused on the export of education services. We sent a group to look around for opportunities in international education which at that stage was prohibited as universities in Australia were prohibited from charging tuition fees.

New export industries: education

The development of international education as part of Australia's new export profile had humble beginnings. Despite the rumblings from certain cabinet colleagues at the time, international education would undergo radical transformation from a scenario of almost none to an almost complete open market. Dawkins outlines the beginning of these developments:

> Universities weren't allowed to accept fee paying overseas students. And there were other restrictions because the immigration department was reluctant to issue student visas. The Federal Police were concerned that students might engage in criminal activity and so on.

An exploratory trade mission was arranged to evaluate the feasibility of promoting education and on the completion of the study it was judged to have good prospects for the export. This prompted Dawkins to approach cabinet with policies for the development of international education. Here is his account of this development:

> I put forward a Cabinet submission which argued that if we want to allow, let alone encourage, international students into Australian universities we have to change a number of laws and policies. The issuance of student visas needed

to be freed up. Police checks needed to be rationalised and the policy in relation to our universities accepting fee paying overseas students needed to change. I was opposed at every point by the Police Minister, the Immigration Minister, and the Education Minister. Fortunately I had the Prime Minister on my side and a few other Ministers who could see that this was a great export opportunity.

The rise of China and Asia

On the trade horizon emerged the powerhouse of China. The Hawke government was starting to take some interest in China and the appointment of Ross Garnaut as the Ambassador to China indicated this growing interest. The awareness of the importance of China within the Hawke government prompted Dawkins to act:

We were exploring cooperation opportunities in relation to wool, iron ore, chemicals, other minerals and metals with a view to not only selling our product but possibly greater industrial cooperation between Australia and China. This would manifested itself in Chinese investment in Australia and some of China's earliest investments were, outside of China were in Australia – they invested in the aluminium plant in Victoria and made their first investment into iron ore mining in Australia during my time. We thought if we could get China investing in the mining industry, not only will we get more mines more quickly, we would have a market for the product. Austrade activity in China and North Asia was beefed up and through North Asia and Paul Barratt was appointed as a roving Senior Trade Commissioner for North Asia. As far as South East Asia was concerned, I was very concerned about the poor trade performance in the region. By way of example when I went to Thailand, I was the first Australian Trade Minister to visit Thailand in seven or eight years. I went to Indonesia and exactly the same thing. All the Trade Ministers had flown over Asia to get to Europe and America and hadn't focused on these markets. Trade was soon improving though out the ASEAN region.

The limitations of the Austrade one-stop-shop and EFIC

The establishment of a combined one-stop-shop was an evident way to proceed but possibly easier said than done. EFIC was a loner and preferred to be that way. Dawkins saw the need to allow EFIC to operate separately even if this upset the initial one-stop-shop arrangements. Here he explains it in the following way:

> It seemed sensible to wrap up these organisations into one. However EFIC, because of its role in the provision of export finance and particularly when it came to the exercise of the national interest provisions, it probably needed a separate focus. EFIC was transferred to the Industry Department under Button. I thought that EFIC had been a pretty good organisation and I had exercised the national interest facility on a few occasions such as selling wheat to Iraq and trams in Hong Kong. When a deal that was too big and too risky, EFIC would approach the Trade Minister to ask government to invoke the national interest provision which allowed EFIC to support the deal with The Government providing cover for the additional risk involved.

The new portfolio of Investment

One of the additional areas which Austrade eventually took command of was investment attraction inwards and later investment holistically. It was a more complex activity with loaded issues embodied and a homeland view which was not entirely convinced. However at first with Dawkins and later expanded with Button, investment became a mainstay of Austrade activity. Dawkins gives us a glimpse of its origins and evolution over time:

When I was still Trade Minister, Button and I had an agreement to set-up an investment promotion activity. The Foreign Investment Review Board (FIRB) in Treasury was seen as a door that might be open but it might not. We wanted something which promoted Australia as an investment destination. As such we set up an investment promotion program called "Invest Australia". There was a question about where it should be located and we agreed that the policy aspect of it should be within the Department of Industry, but the promotion and its attraction would be through Austrade and its offices. I myself returned to that area after I left the government as a special investment representative. We thought that in order to promote investment there needed to be higher level capability to attract big companies from around the world. I spent a couple of years doing that. That investment facilitation program was a new function and I thought it was an important addition to the armoury of business promotion. It is fine to be exporting product but you have to have the capability to produce the product, and that was always going to require foreign investment. Australia at the time had a pretty indifferent reputation. We had industrial relations problems, which a lot of people did not understand, we appeared to be a high cost country, all the promotion of Australia particularly through tourism was about people sunbathing on the beach rather than being a vibrant country actually producing products. This was an attempt to let people know that we had achieved some important economic reform in terms of floating the dollar, and by that stage through the Wages Accord the rate of growth of wages had slowed. So there was a story to tell which we thought needed to be told more effectively.

One of the unique aspects of the new Austrade establishment was the role of the business Board. Dawkins was very mindful of the role played by the Board. He remarked:

> In establishing the Austrade Board we knew it would incorporate the functions of the EFIC Board and as such Austrade would be in part a financial organisation which needed skills from outside. As well I wanted to ensure was that there were better linkages with business and that there was a better understanding of what business wanted from Government. The danger always with sucking Austrade into DFAT was that foreign affairs priorities might overwhelm trade priorities. That's always a risk. Sometimes a fairly aggressive role is needed in order to promote Australia's economic interests. That might upset some of the foreign affairs people who loved things being nice and cheerful with all of the countries in which they were based.

Progressing the building of Austrade needed with some urgency the role of a Managing Director. The search for such a position started in earnest in 1985 and eventually locating General Electric (GE) Australia Manager Lindsay MacAlister. He was up and running by March 1986. Dawkins was convinced they had chosen the right person. He explains it in the following manner:

> Lindsay's background was in mining. His deputy was John Saunders. Saunders later ran the Department of State Development in New South Wales and he's now running a mining company in West Australia. I think the idea of recruiting those two was to move away from just having government officials running the organisation and get a new look at the organisation and how best to run it. It's always difficult to recruit people from the business sector into a public sector organisation, particularly one which had a history of such bureaucracy as this one did. The salaries were not great. So the combination of Lindsay and John Saunders together with a more diverse and experienced

Board was designed to give the whole organisation a bit more power, a bit more direction and most importantly a bit more efficiency as well.

The Austrade management while Dawkins was Minister of Trade (1984-7) seemed to work relatively smoothly despite everything being so new and not all understanding the nuances of this new organisation. In 1987 Austrade was shifted to the Department of Industry, Technology and Commerce under John Button. It did not take too long before cracks started to be felt in the relationships between MacAlister and the Board and later between MacAlister and the Minister. Dawkins moved on to Employment Education and Training and lost the closeness to the Trade portfolio. He explains he was unsure what actually caused the rift in the Austrade management. His new portfolio created new challenges and caused him to lose contact with that environment (Dawkins 2014).

Especially during the early 1990s Austrade was subjected to heavy criticism and judgement by the Conservative coalition especially from Alexander Downer and Andrew Peacock. Button and Labor were used to this vitriolic behaviour but some of it was over the top. Though Dawkins was no longer at the helm of Trade he was conscious of its occurrence and advanced suspicions of its provenance. He advises:

I think it was DFAT's resentment at having lost Austrade ... I think there were probably two factors at work. One was DFAT wanting to shaft Austrade because they no longer owned it. DFAT wanted an excuse to say when the government changed this all had to be cleaned up and the only way to clean it up was to send it all back to DFAT. There could also have been some of the old trade commissioner brigade who were still around who might have been getting to the Opposition as well.

Conclusion

The architect of Austrade moved on to a new Ministry in the then Hawke government which would also see the merger of Department of Foreign Affairs with Trade in 1987. From 1987 to 1991 Dawkins became the Minister for Employment, Education and Training and introduced a range of radical changes to Higher Education some referred to as the "Dawkins Revolution". Following Keating's challenge to Hawke in December 1991, and as a result becoming the Prime Minister, Dawkins became Keating's Treasurer until December 1993. Following the Keating 1993 Labor re-election, Dawkins brought down a budget which contained a series of highly-unpopular revenue measures. In December 1993 Dawkins, frustrated, announced his resignation, and quit politics altogether soon after.

Dawkins was known in all three ministerial portfolios to have wanted change and to have gone about it methodically. It can be argued that he was equally innovative in the Trade portfolio. The changes which brought about Austrade were groundbreaking and remain mostly in place to this day. It was with Dawkins that Labor assumed greater interest in Trade, which until his arrival, was seen as a portfolio that normally resided with the conservative side of politics. Looking back at the Austrade of 1986, the questions which defined the need for an Austrade are not too different from those same questions posed today. There is little doubt that the trade environment, the global economy, the ways in which international business is conducted has changed significantly. But more importantly it is the changed political context and the greater questioning of the role of government in the economy that has changed. It is possible that herein lie the real differences.

Interview conducted August 2014

Bibliography

Capling, A., 2001, *Australia and the Global Trade System: From Havana to Seattle*, Cambridge University Press, Cambridge, UK.

Dawkins, J., 2014, Interview with the author in Melbourne on 14 August 2014.

Hawke, R.J.L., 1994, *The Hawke Memoirs*, William Heinemann Australia, Melbourne.

Schedvin, B., 2008, *Emissaries of Trade: A History of the Australian Trade Commissioner Service*, Department of Foreign Affairs and Trade, Canberra.

Walsh, P., 1995, *Confessions of a Failed Finance Minister*, Random House, Sydney.

Watson, D., 2002, *Recollections of a Bleeding Heart: A Portrait of Paul Keating PM*, Knopf Books, Random House, Sydney.

6

Getting the Show on the Road:
the MacAlister years 1986-90[1]

Geoff Spears and Bruno Mascitelli

Introduction

The arrival of Lindsay MacAlister at Austrade in early February 1986 was a watershed moment in Austrade's establishment. The new Board and all the executive appointments were now in place and the 'go' button was pressed. Headhunted through human resource consultants Egon Zehnder, MacAlister came from being Chief Executive Officer of General Electric Australia (1978-86). His earlier background was in mining/geology including with Mt Isa Mines and the Kennecott Copper Corporation. One of the projects at Mt Isa Mines involved him being the geologist in charge of the Northern Territory exploration which resulted in the discovery of the McArthur River, the biggest concentration of zinc found anywhere at that time. Educated with a degree in science/geology and engineering/ metallurgy he also went on to complete executive and advanced management programs at Harvard University in the US.

Egon Zehnder was given the task of providing a short list of eligible Managing Directors for the newly established Austrade. MacAlister was invited to a selection panel interview which included Bill Ferris and Ted Exell.[2] After his selection as Managing Director,

1 We were assisted in writing this chapter by Michael Abrahams, Peter Cripps, Julia Selby and Lyndel Jack, among others.
2 Personal conversation between Bruno Mascitelli and Ted Exell, former Austrade Deputy Managing Director, Melbourne, May 2014.

the then Trade Minister John Dawkins invited MacAlister to meet with Prime Minister Bob Hawke to discuss his appointment and prospects for greater Australian trade. MacAlister was thrilled and sensed the responsibility and expectations that were placed on him.

The expectations for this new organisation along with its new Managing Director were pretty well laid out in the second reading speech of the Bill for the Australian Trade Commission. Besides addressing the serious deterioration of Australia's trading performance the Bill provided an elaborate and detailed road map of the tasks and objectives of this new organisation. These included:[3]

- Austrade will have prime responsibility for the development and implementation of programs for the encouragement, facilitation and promotion of the export of Australian goods and services.

  Austrade would act as a 'one-stop-Trade-shop' for exporters by assuming the powers, functions and responsibilities of the Export and Finance Insurance Corporation (EFIC), the Australian Overseas Projects Corporation (AOPC), the Export Development Grants Board (EDGB), the Trade Commissioner Service and the marketing and promotion areas of the Department of Trade including the regional offices.

  The new Austrade Board will seek overall guidance and direction from the Minister for Trade on major issues but on most matters of policy and day to day matters the Board will have a free hand. Austrade will have sufficient flexibility and independence of management to respond quickly to changes in international market conditions.

  Under Section 10 of the Austrade Act, the Minister may give the Commission in writing such directions with respect to the performance of its functions and the exercise of powers under the Act as appear to the Minister to be necessary.

---

3 The second reading speech for the Australian Trade Commission Bill 1985 says "As a world exporter, Australia's ranking has slipped from 8th to 23rd over the last 30 years. Our share of the world export market has dropped from 2.6 per cent to 1.2 per cent."

The Minister indicated that he would be requesting Austrade
to:

Develop specific proposals for assisting small new exporters
and exporters of high technology products.

Build on the work already done in identifying those industries
in Australia which have export capability or export potential
and also those markets requiring and justifying special
efforts.

Continue to develop marketing strategies aimed at improving
the export performance of the services sector, specifically
tourism, education, professional consulting and contracting
services, finance, insurance, entertainment and information
industries.

- Austrade to be a source of valuable advice for the Government
and provide an early warning mechanism on international
changes and trends affecting Australia's trade.

Austrade will report annually to Parliament and a three year
Corporate Plan is to be presented annually to the Minister for
Trade for approval; as well as an annual Operational Plan to
the Board.

Austrade given the power to charge for some services which
were at the time free. The budgeted revenue was set at $2.5
million for the period ending 30 June 1986.

Initial staff positions will total 1,400 and the estimated budget
allocation to Austrade for a full financial year would be of the
order of $200 million.

The Government had decided that the headquarters of Austrade
will be in Canberra and EFIC and Overseas Projects Groups
in Sydney.

MacAlister's early management of Austrade was well documented
in the media. *The Canberra Times* reported widely on the new
developments in Austrade and the activism of MacAlister. According
to Castle (1986) of *The Canberra Times*, MacAlister created a heavy
personal schedule designed to get to know this organisation, visiting

all State Offices trying to get a measure of the organisation. As much as possible this also included visiting international posts.[4]

Not surprisingly MacAlister's first observation of his new organisation was a need for a greater level of commercial business culture. Overall the organisation needed to adopt a stronger services perspective and many aspects of export delivery were very unclear. His GE experience came handy in terms of a stronger business culture but inculcating this into a government organisation would prove to be a very difficult assignment.

MacAlister was a good communicator and kept his message through this simple mantra. "The business and purpose of Austrade is to improve Australia's export performance by: *Advocating* for an improved environment for export; *Motivating* industry to become more export oriented; and *Facilitating* export marketing".

Along with the Board, MacAlister set about developing plans to meet the government's objectives and to meld its new entities into a commercially oriented organisation with a strategy-driven culture. It was not long before the new body was drawn into controversy but not of its own making. Political ructions in Canberra spilled over into Austrade in early 1986.

Vancouver and Milan appointments

Just prior to the establishment of Austrade, Minister Dawkins appointed David Combe to the position of Senior Trade Commissioner Vancouver, responsible for Western Canada. This was a controversial appointment given Combe's position as a former federal secretary of the ALP (1973-81), and the adverse findings of the Hope Royal Commission in 1985 relating to Combe's involvement with a Soviet Diplomat, which the Commission said had "serious implications for national security".[5]

---

4 Castle P., 1986, Now is the time to export, Austrade director says, 5 August 1986, *The Canberra Times*, Canberra.
5 Paul Kelly, How a former judge helped the Hawke government survive Ivanov Affair, *The Age*, 12 July 2010.

The Opposition condemned the appointment as 'jobs for the boys' and claimed it would be an international embarrassment for the Australian export community. Dawkins rejected these claims saying that the government had been advised that there were no security impediments against Combe having the job and that the matter had been run passed the Prime Minister.[6]

Combe took up the Vancouver position in November 1985 and went on to a second posting with Austrade as Senior Trade Commissioner Hong Kong 1990-91 before resigning to take up senior positions in the Australian wine industry. Despite all the controversy, the consensus of opinion within the organisation was that Combe was a highly effective operator and successful in his Austrade role.

The dust had hardly settled on the Combe appointment when a further posting controversy arose for the newly established Commission. Tom Walton, Senior Trade Commissioner in Milan stormed onto the front pages with allegations by the Federal Opposition that the Trade Minister, John Dawkins, had tried to remove him prematurely in favour of a political appointment, Emanuel Klein,[7] who was employed at the time as the senior private secretary to the Minister for Sport, Recreation and Tourism, John Brown.[8] The Opposition branded it as cronyism and a censure motion was moved against Dawkins. Walton and Dawkins had previously clashed at a meeting in Rome in October 1985 where Dawkins had allegedly wanted some papers from the meeting destroyed "because they were political dynamite" but Walton refused. Dawkins has denied this.[9]

Klein had reportedly initially applied for the Milan position at Dawkins suggestion but withdrew it, also at Dawkins suggestion,

6 Anthony Nagy, Combe gets the all clear for Vancouver position, *The Age*, 18 July1985,

7 Kevin Childs, Trouble can be a stock in Trade, *The Age*, 10 July 1986.

8 Rod Frail, Almost our man in Milan, *Sydney Morning Herald*, 30 April 1986.

9 Peter Hartcher, Tom, John and the Public Row, *Sydney Morning Herald*, 23 April 1986.

when the issue became too hot.[10] Material began circulating to the detriment of Tom Walton and legal action was threatened. The ensuing mess eventually quietened down following Klein's withdrawal of his application. Walton was left in place to complete his posting in Milan and retired soon after. It was a bruising affair for all parties involved.

Commercially driven culture

A key government objective was to put the activities of Austrade on more commercially oriented footing. To do so the appointment of a suitably qualified and commercially experienced Board was seen by the Trade Minister as crucial to the success of the Commission. Under the Austrade Act, the Managing Director reported to the Board and the Board reported to the Minister for Trade.

The first Business Board was a powerful group. It was high level, very supportive of Austrade activities and commanded significant authority in the business community. Dawkins is quoted as saying "Austrade has what is arguably the most talented and accomplished group of businessmen ever to come together in the service of a single government authority."[11] Besides having Vernon Christie AO, managing director of the Commonwealth Bank as Chairman, Bill Ferris, managing director of Panfida[12] as Deputy Chair and Lindsay MacAlister, managing director of Austrade, the rest of the board was no less talented and business savvy. They included: Nicholas Whitlam, managing director of the then State Bank of New South Wales; Kevan Gosper AO, chairman and chief executive of the Shell Ltd and executive member of the Australian Mining Industry Council; David Asimus AO, chairman of the Australian Wool Corporation, a grazier and chairman of the International Wool Secretariat; Alan Crompton AO, chairman of the Crompton Hannaford Group, a successful

---

10 Peter Hartcher, Tom, John and the Public Row, *Sydney Morning Herald*, 23 April 1986.
11 *Overseas Trading*, Vol. 38, No. 2, 2 February 1986.
12 Bill Ferris was previously Managing Director of Barlow Marine, a marine equipment exporter and Chairman of the National Export Strategy Panel.

exporter of hides, skins various agricultural products, and seed and grain cleaning machinery; Dick Verboon, chairman and managing director, Australian Shipbuilding Industries Pty Ltd with 30 years' experience in the marine engineering field; Diane Gribble, director of McPhee Gribble Publishers Pty Ltd a significant exporter of books and publishing rights; and Nixon Apple, national research officer of the Amalgamated Metal Workers' Union who was recognised for his contributions to the development of the trade union movement's approach to trade and industry policy.[13]

The Board's membership was subsequently expanded in the late 1980s to include the Secretary of the Department of Foreign Affairs and Trade, in addition to the Secretary of the Department of Industry, Technology and Commerce. The EFIC Managing Director also joined the Board November 1991 following EFIC's split from Austrade.

Many of the past Austrade personnel approached acknowledged that the successive Boards made good and positive contributions to Austrade's strategic direction, provided access to the business community and contributed to enhanced corporate governance. Some have argued however that the Board's role started to decline from the time that EFIC was separated from Austrade in 1991 possibly because the big commercial decisions regarding EFIC finance and guarantees were taken away from them. While Austrade introduced other funding programs in the early 1990s the relevance and effectiveness the Board was seen to have progressively declined until its abolition in 2006 as a result of the Uhrig Review. From that point forward the Managing Director of Austrade reported directly to the Minister for Trade.

Austrade in 1986 embarked on a strategy of recruiting key executives and staff from the private sector to contribute to and drive new programs and processes which were being developed. A substantial effort was made to increase the existing staff skills in marketing and client interaction. This also involved enhancing links with industry and exporters. By 1990-91 Austrade was spending in the order of seven percent of its budget on staff training.

---

13 The Australian Trade Commission, Australia – The future is export, 1986.

The Austrade Board including MacAlister was also strongly of the view that, if Austrade were to have a greater commercial orientation, its headquarters needed to be in a major commercial centre near businesses and organisations. Sydney was favoured. This issue was taken up with the new Minister, Senator Button, who agreed, on the understanding that some central functions such as Finance, Information Technology (IT) and Human Resources (HR) remain in Canberra as well as a government liaison unit. The executive move from Canberra to Sydney took place in mid-1988.

While Austrade was given the power to charge for its services, it was recognised by the Government that the nature of most of the Commission's functions would prevent the recovery of a significant proportion of its costs, outside the EFIC insurance area. Nevertheless the introduction of fee for service was initially a major challenge for staff that had, for most of their public sector careers, provided these services free to exporters and potential exporters. Many would now argue however that the introduction of a fee for service served the purpose of identifying those services valued by exporters and weeding out those who were not serious about exporting. The concept was disliked by exporters, particularly small exporters, who felt the Government should continue to support them with free services. State Government Departments were also unhappy about being charged for offshore work by Austrade. The amount raised from the fee for service rose from two per cent of budget at the commencement of Austrade to around five per cent in more recent times.

Strategic approach

Most of the strategic development in the early years was carried out by the Export Development Group, led initially by Ron Maxwell, a former senior executive from the resources area of the former Department of Trade and Resources and then subsequently by Dr Bob Webb who was recruited from CSR Ltd where he held the position of General Manager. This was the 'engine room' of Austrade, which under MacAlister's guidance, developed proactive strategies and industry based programs in contrast to the more reactive approach of the former Trade departments. This involved taking a top down approach to get a better understanding of industry, potential clients in those industries and understanding their needs to achieve export success.

Prior to Austrade's formation the Trade Commissioner Service had, with the support of Regional support offices (located in Canberra), developed and implemented marketing strategies for each market, referred to as the *market approach* to export development. On the formation of Austrade however the principal objectives were: to increase the export orientation of the manufacturing and service sectors, leading to increased proportional contribution to export revenue from these sectors, to assist the commodities sector to maintain its share of world trade, and to retain existing markets and penetrate new ones.[14] In pursuit of these objectives Austrade allocated resources in Canberra to develop a greater understanding of industry sectors and potential exporters in those sectors.

Austrade's industry specialists with both industry and client knowledge and active input from the industry, developed overarching industry export strategies that prioritised markets for export development. They were referred to as the *industry approach* to export development. Funding was made available to help implement these export development strategies with industry. With this industry strategy approach to export development, trade commissioners were required to work closely with industry specialists when developing their marketing plans though the different approaches to export development were to create some tensions within Austrade.

In a number of cases formal industry export networks were set up with the support of Austrade and these networks were tasked to not only increase their own exports but to grow the number of exporters via mentoring of potential new exporters. Such networks were set up to cover areas where there was no existing or relevant industry association, for example mining goods and services (under

14 Austrade Corporate Plan 1986/87 – Internal document.

the Austmine brand), energy goods and services (Austenergy brand), and railway goods and services (ARIC brand) and so on.

Other industry networks were established with existing industry associations, though less formal, but still supported the industry approach to export development. For example, export strategies with significant export growth potential included automotive parts and accessories, coal mining equipment and services, scientific and medical equipment, communication equipment, aerospace equipment and services, processed foods, horticulture, education and professional consultancy services. Later strategies were developed for materials handling equipment and services, the fasteners industry, computer software, wine, books, film industry, music industry, and air freight and freight handling.[15]

Thus, over the early years of Austrade, Canberra's export development group became the driving force of Austrade's export facilitation service. The actual activities however were devolved to the State offices, based in relevant industry concentrations e.g. automotive in Melbourne and marine in Perth. Minister Button was reportedly very interested in Austrade's work in this area as it fitted with the industry plans he was developing for the automotive and other industries.

The initiation of these industry groupings during the MacAlister period formed the building blocks of Austrade's major push on industry groups in the 1990's following McKinsey and again in the years following the "Doubling the Number of Exporters" period in 2006. There has long been a debate in Austrade as to whether to focus on industry or market strategies, but in the end analysis, most would agree that both are required.

Some of the new programs, schemes and services introduced by Austrade in the first five years included:

- **The Company Export Planning Program (CEP)** provided detailed export plans for large and small organisations across all industries. The plans were drawn

---

15 Austrade Corporate Plan 1986/87 – Internal document.

from market intelligence provided by Austrade's overseas offices and input provided by external consultants in Australia.

- **The Trade Opportunities Package (TOP)** which provided exporters each month with the details of international business opportunities identified by Austrade's overseas offices. Again this initiative was further developed and was enhanced by later Austrade management.

- **The Innovative Agricultural Marketing Program**, designed to encourage innovation in the marketing of new agricultural products and to encourage increased agricultural export performance. The program was concluded in 1995-6.

- **The International Business Development Scheme**, a discretionary program aimed at helping businesses establish in, or expand into, overseas markets for certain goods and services identified by Austrade as showing strong growth prospects.

- **The International Trade Enhancement Scheme (ITES)** provided concessional loans to assist exporters with marketing activities. This successful scheme was subsequently extended in 1993-4 to include smaller exporters who could not pass the previous eligibility criteria regarding export earnings thresholds. The scheme concluded in 1995-6.

- **Strategic Market Assessments (SMA)** – a research tool designed to expand Austrade's ability to meet the needs of clients with broad export potential. It documented export market attractiveness and Australia's competitiveness for a wide range of products and services.

International Operations

MacAlister laid the ground rules for overseas posts when he addressed the Trade Commissioner conferences in San Francisco and Jakarta in April 1986.[16] Pointing out that Austrade's International Operations were its most expensive and complex operational activity, costing $50m per year for some 50 posts, he foreshadowed a review of all overseas posts to look at how they fit with the operational plan priorities, how they were performing, costs and alternative forms of overseas representation. He said staff allocation to posts would depend on performance potential.

MacAlister also made it clear that while the planning process was based centrally in Canberra, operations would be field driven. He said he was looking for managers who could meet the organisation's planned tasks, effectively exploit the opportunities from location and who could direct head office's attention to new opportunities.

Reviews were subsequently undertaken later in 1986 covering the Middle East by John Hemphill and Glenn Bellchambers[17] and in Europe and the Americas by Frank Anderson and Michael Abrahams.[18] Further reviews of the remaining regions of North Asia and South East Asia were undertaken in the subsequent year. MacAlister was thinking about where to put his resources to best match the needs of the clients. Arising out of the *European Review*, A-based officers were withdrawn from some posts and numbers of smaller offices were closed. Trade commissioners were withdrawn from Stockholm, The Hague, Brussels and Madrid. In exchange resources were transferred to strengthen Frankfurt as a regional 'Hub' for Northern Europe. Other reporting lines also changed. For example, Paris was given responsibility for Spain and Portugal. Rome became the 'Hub' for Italy and the Eastern Mediterranean including Greece, Turkey, Libya and Israel.

In North America, Los Angeles (Western States) and New York (Eastern States) divided responsibilities along geographic lines.

---

16 Internal Austrade documents.
17 Senior Austrade executives.
18 Senior Austrade executives.

Houston was closed and the A-based position was transferred to a new office in Miami, which was recognised as the major gateway to South America. In a controversial decision, all A-based representation was removed from South America due to the lack of opportunities at the time. This latter decision, which MacAlister strenuously defended, drew considerable grief from the exporting community.

In Asia, where the introduction of the "Hubs and Spokes" approach was more problematic, country managers were introduced and some of the larger posts were strengthened including Tokyo, Beijing and New Delhi. Understandably there was little appetite to reduce resources given the growing importance of Asia for Australian companies. This did not stop criticism being leveled at MacAlister for not doing enough in these markets.

On other matters, MacAlister over time introduced a range of measures designed to improve life in overseas posts. These included new Head of Post packages for A-based staff (cars, annual leave and consultations etc.) and improved terms and conditions of employment for other staff – which were welcomed by the offshore network. New Regional IT training centres were established in Paris, Singapore and Los Angeles along with extensive systems upgrades across the globe.

National operations

Austrade took over the state offices of the Department of Trade, with offices in the capital cities providing a source of information and advice for new exporters, a channel for requests to the overseas offices and, importantly from the exporters point of view, the administration of the Export Market Development Grants Scheme. When charging for services was introduced, it was often left to the staff in the State offices to explain the rationale for the fee for service to exporters and potential exporters and to the State Governments.

Export finance and insurance

The export finance and insurance functions assumed by Austrade from EFIC were considered to be among the most potent instruments available to Austrade to improve export performance. EFIC engages in specialist export support activities through the provision of insurance, finance and guarantee facilities to both Australian exporters and overseas buyers of Australian goods and services. It also operates in a highly competitive international trading environment competing principally with similar services provided by overseas government backed export credit agencies. As the new Export Finance and Insurance Group within Austrade, the Government provided for it to continue to operate under the EFIC name for conducting business. Separate accounts and reserves were maintained for export finance and insurance functions and liabilities.[19] It was headed by Dr. David Fisher who had been recruited from the European Bank. EFIC was expected to write almost $3 billion in business in the first year.[20]

A key challenge was how to best incorporate EFIC within the Austrade framework. Austrade's objectives at the outset were to integrate the provision of finance and insurance services with its industry, market and state planning approaches and to ensure that the export sector obtained services that it needed to compete effectively in the international market place. For example Australian exporters required more flexibility in assembling mixed credit packages, a commitment of funding to the concessional export finance facility, development of co-financing opportunities from the World Bank and the Asian Development Bank funded projects, development of a direct performance bonding facility to supplement the existing bond indemnity facility and so on.

EFIC never sat all that comfortably within the Austrade framework. Its staff were mainly from a banking and insurance sector and as such were seen as different to the bulk of Austrade staff engaged

---

19 Second Reading Speech for the Australian Trade Commission Bill 1985.
20 Address by Lindsay MacAlister to the Australian Mining Industry Council, 1 May 1986.

in marketing activities and the nature of its work was of a highly commercial and confidential nature which made it difficult to share within the wider Austrade context. The Export Finance and Insurance Corporation (EFIC) was re-established as an independent corporation in November 1991 but the linkages with Austrade remained strong with representation on each other's board up until the abolition of the Austrade board in 2006.

Export Market Development Grants

Austrade was given the responsibility for administering the Export Market Development Grants Scheme on behalf of the Government, a role previously performed by the Export Development Grants Board since June 1974. Under this scheme exporters were eligible to receive taxable grants to assist in offsetting a range of export development and promotional expenditure. The scheme was highly valued by exporters and in 1986-7 provided export market development assistance for a total of $5.1 billion of Australia's exports representing 3,500 claimants.[21] The scheme in 1986 was projected to cost some $330 million over the following three years.[22]

Austrade was also charged with responsibility of monitoring the effectiveness of the Scheme and to recommend the introduction of new schemes consistent with Australia's international obligations to encourage Australian exporters to investigate and develop overseas markets. The Government specifically requested that Austrade develop proposals for export market development schemes tailored to assisting small new exporters and exporters of high technology products.

In 1989 the government established a review of trade and investment (Hughes Review) to examine the government's financial support for Australian export industries. Presided by Professor Helen Hughes, its intention was to examine support schemes especially in the light

21 Mr. Ian Sinclair MP, EMDG Amendment Bill 1988. Hansard, 23 August 1988, p. 176.
22 Austrade Corporate Plan 1986/87 – internal document.

of Australia's balance of payment deficit.[23] The report was released in July 1989 and sought to put Austrade's underestimated – and underutilised – Export Market Development Grant (EMDG) scheme in the front line of necessary changes. One of the Hughes Review objectives was to find ways to get greater leverage from EMDG and have it as a front line tool in export enhancement. The report's opening remarks however did little to hide the challenge ahead:

> Most Australians are now aware that our exports are lagging behind imports ... It is less well understood that our lagging economic performance is closely linked to our poor export growth. Australia is the only industrial country that has not increased its proportion of merchandise exports to GDP during the last 30 years.[24]

The Austrade executive and the Board had been effectively put on notice that Austrade needed to deliver improved outcomes in this area.

Overseas Projects

Austrade also assumed the functions of the previous Australian Overseas Projects Corporation (AOPC) which had initially been established in 1978. Its role was to assist Australian organisations compete for overseas development contracts. Against the background of the AOPC's limited success, the Government removed previous constraints to enable Austrade to take a more active role in assisting Australian firms and organisations to secure overseas contacts.

Following a strategic review of factors affecting Australia's ability to win overseas project work and an appropriate role for Austrade, resources to pursue opportunities were put in place. MacAlister mentioned a few of the opportunities available for Australian exporters in a speech to industry in mid-1986[25] which included taking a leadership role in exploring major new power station/port projects in the Middle

---

23 *The Canberra Times*, 12 December 1988, p. 3.
24 Hughes Review, 1989: xix.
25 Address by Lindsay MacAlister to the Australian Mining Industry Council, 1 May 1986.

East. He said at the time that Austrade also may choose to take prime contractor responsibility to ensure the viability of one or more of these multi-billion dollar complexes.

Relationships – ministerial

A Ministerial reshuffle in 1987 saw John Button, Minister for Industry, Technology and Commerce, assume responsibility for Austrade. The former Department of Trade was amalgamated with the Department of Foreign Affairs to form DFAT. MacAlister and Button were apparently not of the same mind regarding the future direction of Austrade, with MacAlister reportedly wanting to take the organisation towards a possible Government Business Enterprise (GBE) and. as such, move further away from government. It is understood that Button did not want this. The issue then became how did Austrade fit into a government framework. It appears there *was* very little communication between MacAlister and Button and no real rapport developed. From MacAlister's point of view, he felt that Button was not all that interested in Austrade, given that he had inherited the initiative from John Dawkins.

Austrade Chairman

In 1985, Ferris chaired the committee report to the Australian Government entitled *Lifting the Performance of Manufacturing and Services Exports*. Its report contained proposals on a range of policies to assist these sectors, including export incentives, overseas aid, government purchasing, offsets and export finance. It also supported the efforts by the government to direct its marketing to those industries and markets with the potential to yield the best results. Some would argue that this report was a blueprint for the creation of Austrade.

Ferris was appointed Deputy Chairman of the Australian Trade Commission (Austrade) in 1986 and was Chairman from 1988 until his retirement from that position in December 1993. As Chairman of Austrade in 1988, he was well equipped to contribute to Austrade's strategies and would prove to be a very different chairman to Christie. He was active and interventionist and this would ultimately lead to deterioration in the relationship between Ferris and MacAlister. In 1990, Ferris was made an Officer of the Order of Australia for his contribution to industry and the export sector.

Government departments – DFAT

Throughout the mandate of MacAlister, Austrade's relationship with the Department of Foreign Affairs was 'testy' at best. The origins of this appeared to lie in DFAT's frustration and annoyance that the trade promotion arm of the Australian government was given to the Industry Department in 1987 and not DFAT. This according to MacAlister occasionally manifested itself through rivalry and the antagonism between DFA and Austrade both domestically but more importantly offshore where Austrade was located in most Australian Embassies. Another example of this friction was over the introduction of new Austrade Head of Post packages introduced by MacAlister. The Secretary of the Department of Foreign Affairs and Trade would in later years be appointed to the Austrade Board and this helped develop a better working relationship between the two organisations.

The McKinsey Review

From early to mid-1990 MacAlister was facing new challenges. He had noticed that some dissatisfaction was starting to emerge within the Board about the direction of Austrade. There was also the perception by some that MacAlister was too focused on the big end of town but any analysis of his industry export strategies would show that they were mostly aimed at assisting small to medium exporters.

Around this time the Austrade Board decided to commission an independent evaluation of Austrade's effectiveness with a view to making improvements. It is understood that Minister Button had agreed to a review of Austrade. McKinsey and Company was selected to complete the review which commenced in August 1990 and delivered the report on 20 December 1990. Somewhere in the Austrade establishment papers there was a provision for such a review after five years though MacAlister may have been unaware of this provision.

On the commissioning of the McKinsey report, MacAlister began thinking that this may be a good time to leave. A week before the last Board meeting for 1990, he resigned his position as Managing Director. As such, he was not present at the last Board meeting which ultimately approved the Review.

The key findings of the McKinsey Review are covered in more detail in another chapter of this book, but in summary they were as follows:

> Australian Companies value Austrade. Companies noted the importance of Austrade in areas such as providing access to key decision makers in overseas markets, providing advice and information on specific overseas markets or particular client related issues.
>
> There is real scope to improve the effectiveness of Austrade. Traditional activities, such as market research and trade promotions, can be made more effective. Resources overseas do not match client needs nor does Austrade's geographic focus match Austrade's ability to have impact. Organisational problems such as the weak link between senior management and field activities, a bureaucratic style and risk averse culture are also limiting Austrade's effectiveness.[26]

Conclusions

Lindsay MacAlister had been given a charter to bring together under one umbrella the export services of three pre-existing statutory authorities and the export services of the Department of Trade into

---

26 Presentation to Austrade Managers on the McKinsey Review, 13 February 1991 (internal document).

a well-oiled machine with a strong commercial focus. He felt he was achieving this objective. Along the way he had to tread the fine line between the commercial imperative and the needs and processes of Government.

In his five years at the helm, MacAlister contributed many significant initiatives, including:

- A more commercial focus.
- Industry based strategies and programs.
- New financial support programs.
- Reorganisation of the offshore network.
- A focus on training and professional development.
- An investment in technology and management systems and business processes.
- Introduction of fee for service to put a value on Austrade's services.

In many ways MacAlister, with his energy, business knowhow and strategic vision, was ahead of his time in seeking to transition a public body into a commercially focused organisation. He may have been "the right person" but the ministerial changes and differing visions for Austrade by others made it difficult for him. Lindsay MacAlister would move on to have a very successful post Austrade career as chairman and executive chairman of Pan Continental (1991-5), Chairman of Orogen Minerals and representation on numerous boards.

7

Austrade before and after the collapse of the USSR

Ian Wing

On returning to Moscow for a second posting in August 1989, the first surprise occurred when driving in from the airport our driver said things about the USSR (Union of Soviet Socialist Republics) and its government unimaginable during the first posting in the early 1980s. Little did we know that the next four years would see political and economic turmoil bringing about the end of the USSR and of the Cold War.

Australia-USSR trade – the 1970s and early 1980s

Australia's exports to the then USSR in the late 1970s and early 1980s were almost entirely commodity based – wool, wheat, mutton and some mineral sands. As a result of the Soviet invasion of Afghanistan in December 1979 Australia imposed "sanctions" limiting the commodity exports to the highest level that had been achieved. Indeed, in 1979 the USSR was Australia's third largest overall export market. A highly inefficient agricultural sector during the years of stagnation under Brezhnev meant that our products continued to be in demand.

Glasnost and Perestroika – Gorbachev the reformer

With the deaths of successive Soviet old guard leaders, Gorbachev emerged as a reformer both politically and economically with the banners of "glasnost" (openness) and "perestroika" (reconstruction).

While some Western observers would see Gorbachev's first steps as relatively small, the shift from the police state which spent enormous resources on the military was dramatic to those of us who had experienced the old regime. Gorbachev had the foresight and courage to see that the command economy was rapidly imploding and that there was no way that the USSR could keep up with the West economically or militarily. With no history of Western style democracy, it was not surprising that there were missteps and resistance in the form of the 1990 coup.

Australia "normalises" trade relations in 1985

It was partly against this background that Australia decided to "normalise" trade relations with the USSR in 1985 with a trade display in Moscow, visit by Trade Minister Dawkins and resumption of "Mixed Commissions" – bilateral trade dialogues on trade. The display was mostly commodity focused but also featured some consumer goods for which scarce hard currency had been made available to the State Foreign Trade Organisations then responsible for all foreign economic engagement . Discussions were beginning about "joint ventures" with foreign companies and the opening of various sectors to foreign direct investment. At the same time, the USSR began importing Western technologies albeit limited by COCOM restrictions.

Austrade and DFAT worked closely together and continued to focus on supporting commodity exports – the USSR was Australia's largest market for wool at a time when world demand was slumping and world markets for grain and meat were being distorted by EU and US export subsidies.

At the same time there were efforts to diversify trade into support of potential exploration projects by major mining houses, telecommunications, and some other joint ventures, enabled by Gorbachev's reforms but all hampered by political uncertainty, an inadequate legal framework and centuries old Russian suspicion of the motives of Westerners in general and Western firms in particular.

Throughout 1989, political upheaval intensified across Eastern Europe culminating with the opening of the Berlin Wall in November and the establishment of non-communist governments in Poland, Czechoslovakia and Hungary. On 3 December 1989 George H.W. Bush and Mikhail Gorbachev declared that the Cold War was "over".

At the time in Moscow, Russians were stunned by how rapidly all of this unfolded but the economic situation in the USSR was becoming increasingly difficult. Gorbachev's reforms had delivered little in terms of daily necessities and Russians faced uncertainty for the first time. During our first posting, arguably the peak of the Cold War, many Russians took the view that, if one stayed out of politics, an apartment, job, education and pension were all guaranteed, and while they might want the West's standard of living, they did not want its way of life – the police state had some benefits. There is much evidence of this thinking in 2014.

Decentralisation of decision making – direct trade promotion to the Soviet Far East

Part of the resumption of trade relations was a focus on direct promotion of Australian products to the Soviet Far east with a trade mission in 1987 followed by a trade display in the then "closed" (to foreigners on security grounds) city of Vladivostok in July 1990. This was based on three factors: the (slight) decentralisation of economic decision making then occurring in the USSR, and a broader Australian geo-political objective of engagement with Russia as a Pacific power; the fact that Vladivostok is closer to Canberra than Moscow (and an entry point for Australian food commodities) and that the region had its own sources of hard currencies (gold, timber and fish).

The Vladivostok Trade Display

The story of the display could be the subject of a book in its own right, but preparations for the display became the focus of the office from the time of my arrival. There were two dimensions to the display:

the logistics, much of which were handled from Australia, our desk under the expert management of Dick Wilson, a former STC Moscow, and the then Trade Display Division in Melbourne with Alan Clarke providing superb planning and support. The post was responsible for local arrangements.

The other dimension was the marketing with Australian participation handled from Australia and with some assistance from the Soviet Trade Ministry and Chambers of Commerce, marketing to regional organisations was managed by the post.

While local organisations all expressed the desire to deal directly with foreign entities, there were still formidable practical barriers – access to a workable banking system and the heavy hand of local and often Moscow bureaucracies – some of whose motives were questionable. Each of these visits involved some "adventures" and surprising insights into life in the remote and climatically hostile parts of the USSR. A lifetime memory of the trip was flying over the treeless tundra to land in Magadan where it was minus 38 degrees centigrade and to receive a "mixed" reception from the local officials – why were Western government officials coming to this remote "closed" location? We were accommodated in what was an NKVD (predecessor of the KGB) facility because there were no hotels able to accept foreigners. I was also detained by KGB border guards on the plane at Yuzhno Sakhalinsk who claimed I did not have permission to be there. Nevertheless, contacts were established and groups from all of these regions came to the display and some business was done.

The local logistics required a lot of creative thinking, patience and risk taking. The starting point was that almost nothing could be sourced locally to the point that we even had to carry bottled water for the 100 or so participants from Moscow. The local authorities, with support from Moscow, did provide as much help as they could.

The first meeting with the Director of the Hotel Vladivostok where the delegation was to stay began with him saying, "Before you start, I'll tell you that the facilities and service level of the hotel are terrible, everyone will be upset and there's no point in complaining to me or anyone else; there won't be enough food so bring as much as you can yourself – and it is still going to cost you!"

Participants were warned beforehand and in good Australian fashion, accepted things as they were (mostly) in a good natured way. A memorable photo of the opening ceremony featured a line-up of officials, including then DPIE Minister Simon Crean, most of whom had wet trouser cuffs – the basins in the hotel bathrooms weren't connected to anything and the water went straight on to the floor and to a drain in the middle of the bathroom.

Getting to Vladivostok was also a challenge as there were no international flights and service even from Moscow could be haphazard. In the end, Austrade chartered two Aeroflot aircraft. One to fly from Moscow via Omsk and Chita to Vladivostok and the other from Tokyo direct to Vladivostok – a first. The former would carry Embassy and some Europe based participants, as well as food, beer and water. The latter would bring participants who travelled from Australia via Japan. While organising the first flight was relatively straightforward, the latter was much more complicated, partly because the Japanese Ministry of Civil Aviation was irritated that the first flight direct from Tokyo to Vladivostok would be carrying Australians and not Japanese – and until I saw the aircraft land in Vladivostok I wasn't convinced the flight would take place!

As an aside, the minister travelled on the twice weekly service from Niigata, Japan, to Khabarovsk. On being seated in the "VIP" first row of the Tupolev 154 from Khabarovsk to Vladivostok he realised that he had only a half of a seat belt and when he pointed this out to the flight attendant, she helpfully responded, "We crash, you die!"

From Moscow, Aeroflot provided a VIP configuration Tupolev 134. When we finally located it at Moscow Vnukovo Airport we were told we had to load the aircraft ourselves as we hadn't paid for "ground services" – we had, but there was little point in arguing. The travellers including Ambassador Ashwin and the Embassy drivers then proceeded to load the plane. I said to the pilot, who seemed most interested in our beer and wine supply, wasn't there some science behind how we loaded the plane? He just shrugged his shoulders and said to do what we wanted. We ended with boxes of water and other supplies occupying the back ten rows of seats. After what seemed to me to be a very long take-off roll, we were off to Omsk. The next day, the Embassy received a call from Aeroflot saying that the plane was dangerously overloaded and not to do this on the return trip! After take-off, we realised that we also had a number of additional Russian passengers who had paid the pilot to get on the plane. On arrival in Omsk in central Siberia, the airport claimed not to have been paid "enough" to refuel us so a deal was negotiated which led them to bring out a number of 44 gallon drums of aviation fuel with a hand pump and the plane was then refuelled – the refuellers all with cigarettes in their mouths while they were doing so.

The Vladivostok branch of the USSR Chamber of Commerce and Industry, in particular, its Deputy Director, Vladimir Gavriliuk, performed miracles as local intermediary. Vladimir subsequently became head of the Austrade office and later, Australian Honorary Consul, from November 1992 until his retirement in 2007.

Subsequent years saw an Australian supermarket and restaurant in Vladivostok, imports of Australian mining equipment by the gold industry, food processing equipment sold to Khabarovsk. BHP and Rio Tinto were also active in the SFE/RFE and were supported by our offices in Moscow and Vladivostok. For a period, Rio had an office in Khabarovsk. The Vladivostok office, described elsewhere as "most needed" in a "really need Austrade" market, continues to support Australian companies.

1990-1 – the breakup of the USSR

Austrade's business plans continued to reflect the transition to a more market-based economy but key commodity imports remained firmly under the control of the centralised Foreign Trade Organisations: Exportljon for wool, Prodintorg for meat and Exportkhleb for wheat.

At this time Australian primary producers were facing difficult market conditions worldwide: a huge wool stockpile and having to compete against EU and US subsidised grain. Against this background, the Australian Government decided in 1991 to extend lines of credit to the USSR to sustain these exports.

In order to foster goodwill and enhance demand for Australian wheat, the Australian Wheat Board decided to establish an Australian bread shop in the centre of Moscow – a similar exercise had been undertaken with success in China. A bakery institute, Moscow City Government and the Russian Ministry of Food were partners in the venture. There were formidable challenges in getting requisite permits, building materials, etc., and the office spent a lot of time lobbying different organisations and making official representations. The AWB (Australian Wheat Board) sent a professional baker and his wife to oversee the installation of equipment, its commissioning and training of staff. The frustrations were constant but in no small measure due to the couple's perseverance and good humour the bakery eventually came into operation and continued for several years.

The winter of 1990 saw major food shortages and I recall a meeting with the Russian Food Minister on bakery issues when he asked me whether I understood what it was like to be minister responsible for ensuring food supply to the population and asked how his Australian counterpart handled this. He was taken aback when I said there was no minister *per se* – it just happened.

The political turmoil continued throughout 1990. In February 1990 the central committee of the Communist Party agreed to Gorbachev's recommendation that it give up its monopoly of political power and this set off a series of elections across the USSR when nationalists and reformers were successful in many republics. Mid-year Boris Yeltsin was elected head of Russia's government and came into conflict with the central government immediately. Local laws were often seen as superseding USSR laws and many local authorities refused to pay taxes to Moscow. Supply chains were disrupted and the economy continued to freefall.

In late 1990 STCs from Vienna, Warsaw, Belgrade and Moscow met in Prague to discuss possible joint activities and broader coordination given the changes underway across Eastern Europe. It was, however, agreed that each country was different and that the situation remained very dynamic. Following that meeting, we did keep in contact but no concrete joint action occurred. 1991 saw several attempts to reform the central government structures. In August 1991 hardliners organised a coup against Gorbachev but it collapsed within days. Boris Yeltsin played a key role in ending the coup and emerged with a much strengthened hand politically. The end of the USSR came on Christmas Day 1991. The next day I took my family to Red Square and experienced a strange silence as Russians stared at the Russian tricolour flag flying over the Kremlin, having replaced the Soviet red banner with hammer and sickle.

Austrade in the post-Soviet period – payment delays and rapid diversification of activities

Payments for Australian wool, wheat and meat were delayed and exports fell dramatically over this period. Then Foreign Minister Gareth Evans visited the USSR the week prior to Christmas 1991 and obtained an undertaking from the Soviet Prime Minister that the accumulating debt would be repaid "shortly". (Russia eventually repaid the debt, which had been in the Paris Club, in August 2006). During the same visit I spent an hour with the Deputy Mayor of St Petersburg waiting for the Minister's arrival at St Petersburg airport. The Deputy Mayor was Vladimir Putin with whom the Minister later had a spirited discussion.

Despite the political chaos, Austrade, was, nevertheless, busy with a considerable number of visitors who saw opportunities emerging from the collapse of the centralised system and there were some small scale successes for items like self-contained brick-making machines, processed foods and consumer goods.

A few Australians were also attracted to the rapidly emerging black economy and one businessman was kidnapped. His kidnapper was known to the Austrade office and was murdered several years later on a street in the Russian Far East town of Ussurisk. The "Mafiosi" became more and more powerful during the Yeltsin years and the office spent much time checking the bona fides of the large numbers of new companies emerging.

There were also some larger scale projects in which we played a significant role, including Telstra/OTC earth stations in Kazakhstan and Sakhalin (both of which subsequently became entangled in political brawls) and the Cape York Space Station which was to use Soviet/Ukrainian Zenit rockets.

Looking for wool in the first weeks of independent Ukraine and Belarus

We experienced firsthand the chaotic beginnings of the post-Soviet period when the office was asked by EFIC in January 1992 to visit woollen mills in Ukraine and Belarus to ascertain whether the Australian wool sold under credit had already been processed and also, from our perspective, to learn whether these mills could emerge longer term as direct customers for our wool. Because of their locations, we had to drive. Our driver, Misha left for Kiev in the Austrade vehicle at midday with documentation authorising him to have the vehicle while Business Development Manager Vildan Zelyatdinov and I took the overnight train to Kiev. Misha turned up several hours after we did having been arrested in Russia for allegedly stealing the Embassy car; and stopped again at the Ukrainian border for not having a visa. Some of the food (and beer) which we had brought with us seemed to have helped solve the problem.

The economic situation in Kiev was grim. We spent a night at the Dnepr Hotel where there was no heat and no hot water – the outside temperature was minus 20 celsius and not much warmer inside. I was given an extra blanket as a foreigner in the hotel but I seriously contemplated taking the curtains down for additional warmth as I was so cold. We were about to leave Kiev for a textile mill in Chernigov when a car arrived with army officers asking me to come straight to the office of the Ukrainian Minister for Defence. I explained my role as a Trade Commissioner but they insisted I come with them. The Minister wanted to make the point that the rockets which were to be used at the Cape York Space Station were Ukrainian (produced at a plant in Dnepropetrovsk, Eastern Ukraine) and we needed to deal directly with the Ministry and plant – and not through the central agency, Glavkosmos. Ambassador Ashwin and I had been the first foreigners allowed to visit the plant in 1991 and were hosted by then General Director Kuchma who went on to become Ukraine's second President and who governed 1994-2005. I told the Minister I would advise the Ambassador and relevant parties.

We were well received by the plant in Chernigov and ascertained that the wool had indeed been processed – the plant was old but well maintained. The drive to Belarus took us along the eastern border of the Chernobyl exclusion zone, a sobering experience. When we arrived at the Belarus border we were met by six or seven young policemen who wanted to see our visas. I explained I was accredited to the USSR and now to its successor states. Vildan suggested that "Fosters" made good visas and we were allowed through. We passed through several Belarussian towns and villages but could find no food shops with anything in them and all of the few cafes were closed. The largest town, Bobruisk, had a tyre factory so we drove there and told the guards we were "the delegation". Vildan found the cafeteria and we lined up with the workers to have cabbage soup and black bread. We got some curious looks but did get fed. On arrival in Minsk we were told that our hotel reservation had been cancelled and that we would stay at the State Guest House and would meet the Prime Minister in the morning! We visited two woollen mills and were again advised that the Australian wool had been processed. The Prime Minister saw us briefly and wanted to encourage Australian investment in the Belarussian textile industry. We returned to Moscow by train and Misha had an uneventful drive back.

Austrade in the Commonwealth of Independent States (CIS) 1992-3

Notwithstanding the collapse in commodity exports, the general view was that Russia and Kazakhstan in particular would present good opportunities for Australian exporters and investors as these countries and other former Soviet republics modernised and their legal frameworks became more open to foreign engagement.

Support for the mining houses continued in Moscow and in the Far East. Remnants of "old thinking" continued in the Russian Duma (parliament) and among many older bureaucrats with discussions along the lines that the role of legislators was to "protect Russia's sacred natural resources" from foreign predators being common. Another dimension was the ongoing tussle between regional authorities and Moscow over which would have final say or derive most benefit from exploitation of resources. Putin shifted the focus very much back to the centre with designation of "strategic" resources, a status that could be declared retroactively. Unsurprisingly, apart from oil and gas, there has been little foreign involvement in Russia's mineral resources industry.

The Cape York Space Project continued during 1992 but eventually collapsed because of difficulties in securing finance, Australian domestic political issues and the complexity of some of the technical issues and export licensing problems. The political and economic problems in Russia and Ukraine added to the difficulties.

The Post also supported an Australian company's efforts to commercialise "Synroc" – an Australian invention which would safely contain high level radioactive waste. The partner was the Ministry of Atomic Energy linked to the Russian military and as they could not visit the Embassy and we could not visit the Ministry we had to meet at various restaurants around Moscow. Unfortunately, this project also failed.

Consistent with Austrade's broad objective of assisting Australian companies deal directly with newly emerging local companies, many of which were not located in Moscow, we continued to travel extensively throughout Russia and to a lesser degree the other Republics. Many of the larger companies were privatised former state enterprises, the origin of many of the oligarchs. In the absence of any form of company reporting, physical visits were often the only way of making judgments about them. This activity was usually in support of an specific Australian company's objectives. There was a lot of activity by other countries, mostly West European and also by multilateral agencies. Trade Commissioner Gerard Seeber participated in a World Economic Forum sponsored mission to all of the "stans" and this enabled us to decide to focus almost entirely on Kazakhstan.

Throughout my posting I was very ably assisted by Trade Commissioner Gerard Seeber and local staff Nina Mitropolskaya, Andrei Knyazhinsky, Vildan Zelyatdinov and our drivers, Alexei and Misha. Additionally our executive assistants, Margaret Binnie, Dorothy Sugden and Teresa Wise, provided very dedicated support. All deserve much credit for their professionalism, perseverance and good humour in their work for Australia. I should also acknowledge the incredible support provided by Ambassadors Ashwin and Hogue and the entire DFAT team in Moscow at the time. It was "team Australia" throughout very challenging times. Vladimir Gavriliuk and his team in Vladivostok likewise performed brilliantly in very difficult circumstances.

Austrade in the Russian Far East

Following the Trade Fair, we entered into an agreement with a small consulting company in which Vladimir Gavriliuk was a partner and they provided assistance to our office in the region and also to companies on the ground. A decision was made mid-1992 to establish an Austrade sub-post in Vladivostok in order to better support the growing number of Australian companies visiting the region. Vladimir Gavriliuk was appointed Manager and he recruited staff who remained with the office long term.

The office was to be opened by then Trade Minister John Kerin who would lead a trade delegation to the region at that time. Again, the lag in legal structures, confusion among local authorities and the physical difficulty of getting an office established required considerable lateral thinking on our part. There was no law allowing an enterprise to lease property to another body and so we negotiated an agreement with a Fisheries institute to provide us with fishing data and use of three rooms at their institute in exchange for a sum of money. One of the legacies of the Soviet era was a great capacity for lateral thinking – under the old regime rarely could any problem be solved by going from "A" to "C" via "B". The solution to our leasing issue was a good example.

The next issue was getting the rooms into a state acceptable for us to use and have the Minister open. A new visa arrangement allowing Russians and Chinese to cross the border near Vladivostok led to huge numbers of Chinese bringing consumer goods to Moscow and it was difficult to get seats on the nine hour flight and almost impossible – and risky – to ship furniture, paint, etc., for the office refurbishment. None of this was available locally which only increased the risk of theft and unwanted attention from some local "businessmen". The solution presented itself when one day a driver told me there was a Russian Air Force Colonel waiting at the Embassy gate who wanted to meet me. This was rather surprising, but in those days in Russia little could surprise so he was invited in. He explained he was taking an Antonov 124 Cargo Plane to the Avalon Air Show and would be carrying Russian helicopters and other aviation related equipment for exhibition in Australia. He asked for assistance in finding some back cargo to bring back to Russia and help finance the fuel cost in Australia. At the time, we were aware of one Australian company which did need to get some goods to Russia quickly. I asked how they would be travelling and he said they would go from Moscow to Ussurisk (not far from Vladivostok) in the Far East and then to Darwin and Melbourne. Calculating the cost of getting our Embassy work crew to Vladivostok and a notional freight cost for the paint, equipment and furniture, I offered him that amount to be paid in Melbourne – if he would take our people and cargo to Ussurisk. After a couple of false starts and some drama at air force bases in Moscow and in Ussurisk, this did take place and the office was ready for the Minister to open.

Kazakhstan

My three-year posting was due to finish at the end of 1992 and Roger James was appointed as my successor. However, because of the rapidly changing environment, it was decided that I would extend for a further year and Roger would come as planned and we would have three A-based in Moscow for a year. Our activities in Kazakhstan were starting to ramp up and I asked Roger to take responsibility for that Republic. Apart from the telecommunications project mentioned earlier, resources companies and some agribusiness consultancies were becoming active. We contracted the Australia-Kazakhstan Association run by two local businessmen to provide services to our office and to Australian visitors and this arrangement worked well. Subsequently, an Embassy was established in Almaty and an A-based Trade Commissioner appointed – Mark Gwizdalla. Our Embassy was closed when the capital of Kazakhstan was moved to Astana and all embassies were required to move there – a move which the Government elected not to make.

Conclusion

The rapid pace of major changes over the period 1989-93 made it almost impossible for Austrade to "plan" in the traditional sense. Essentially, our goals were to find opportunities in sectors of relevance to Australia using traditional – and as outlined above – often "non-traditional" tradecraft. We did provide much "hands on" support to companies which were willing to take the risk of engaging in what was very much an emerging market. Activities in the Far East and Kazakhstan reflected efforts to focus on regions where we had comparative advantage. There were some positive short term commercial outcomes, but fewer medium and long term from this period.

We also had to manage expectations. For example, there were a number of well-intentioned but impractical schemes to restart the wool trade. We had difficulty in getting others to understand that in Soviet times, the wool "market" was the result of decisions by central planners and frequently had little to do with supply or demand. Indeed, Soviet practice was to blend fine Australian wool with much coarser local fibres, to produce a product which a Russian expert once told me was like "making soup out of fine caviar".

By 1993 Russia's rapid embrace of "free market" reforms was starting to have very negative social consequences: huge price increases for basics, loss of savings and purchasing power for pensioners, increasing "mafia" type activity and the emergence of a small but very predatory "nouveau riche". Yeltsin's leadership style was becoming more and more erratic and, combined with the economic problems of the time, formed the basis for the constitutional crisis of September-October 1993 when the Russian White House was attacked.

My family and I left Moscow in June 1993 with mixed emotions. We had experienced first-hand a major event in history. We had also been able to engage with Russians socially as well as officially, and to form some close friendships, which was not possible during the first posting. Despite the often gruff exterior, we found a people of great warmth once trust was established. After living under a totalitarian regime for 60 years when you could not trust anyone, it is not surprising that this took some time. Another element, of course, is Russia's complex and often tragic history, which is why there is a desire for "strong leaders" and a harmful nationalism just below the surface – being skilfully exploited by the current President.

8

The McKinsey Review of Austrade – 1990

Terry Goss

Introduction

I arrived in my office in St Georges Terrace, Perth, in 1990 after my usual early morning swim at the Beatty Park pool just north of the city. A great way to start the day in what was then described as the world's most remote city. It seemed a long way from the headquarters in Canberra of my employer, the Australian Trade Commission.

I had previously spent three years in Perth as Regional Director of the Department of Trade from 1980 to 1983. It was the time when Commonwealth cars, chauffeured by laconic uniformed drivers ferried Commonwealth officers around the city. Heads of Commonwealth agencies were accorded status that in retrospect seems almost quaint. There was a degree of formality in contacts and relationships with public and private sector leaders. Regional Directors were frequently the channel for contact with those sections of the State Government which most closely paralleled the functions of their centrally-located masters. As such they were at an interface that could become disputatious where Commonwealth and State interests diverged. Then, as now, the temptation for State Governments to go to war with the Commonwealth for political advantage could make life difficult.

My return to Perth in 1990 as State Manager was to enter a world which was, superficially at least, markedly different. My previous four years in Canberra had given me exposure to the brave new world of Austrade, a statutory body rather than a department of state. It had been born out of the reforms energetically pursued by the Minister for Trade, John Dawkins, and was conceived as being able to operate in a more flexible, entrepreneurial fashion free from many of the shackles and procedural rigidities of departmental structures.

I had been freshly inducted into the new world in 1986 when the newly appointed Managing Director, Lindsay MacAlister, had generously included me in a meeting of North American trade commissioners in Carmel, California. As a policy officer of the Department of Trade in Ottawa I was being encouraged to work cooperatively with trade-promoting colleagues to pursue Australian commercial interests. The format and style of the meeting was distinctly different, peppered with talk of strategic and operational planning, performance reviews and, significantly, talk of revenue. Previously, services to exporters were delivered free but now, tentatively at first, it would be necessary to charge for those services. This required a complete change of mindset, not least having the confidence to impute a monetary value to specific services and to convince exporters that value for money would be delivered. To begin with there was resistance from some exporters but, as with any change, acceptance was gained over time and charging became entrenched. The new skills required of Austrade staff were unevenly acquired and management was presented with serious challenges in attaining high levels of performance, client satisfaction and, most importantly, export successes for the clients of the organisation.

So, when I arrived in my Perth office in early 1990 I was ready to play my part in leading the staff to pursue corporate goals and to build on the progress achieved by my predecessor Rob O'Donovan. Many of the senior staff whom had worked for me in my earlier incarnation were still on strength and coming to terms, to greater or lesser effect, to the new expectations placed on them.

The invitation from on high

As I arrived in the office on this particular day the telephone rang. Canberra was calling. It was John Bennett, then a senior Austrade corporate administrator, calling to invite me to join a small team that would be working with McKinsey and Co., the prominent US consultancy firm that had been commissioned to undertake a thorough review of Austrade with a view to making it an even better and a more effective trade promotion organisation. Why me? I didn't ask the question at the time but surmised it may have had something to do with my association with regional offices around Australia, including a team heading up the Regional Offices Services Section in Canberra – a job that had me tagged at the time, and subsequently, as Goss the Boss of ROSS.

My response was not long in coming as I had a great commitment to the organisation and was keen to do anything that would strengthen it. I'm in. Little did I know what lay ahead. Thus began a year of intense activity with frequent, and as the year progressed, extended absences on the eastern seaboard. I soon discovered that I would be joined on the team by seasoned Austraders Julia Selby and Michael Johnson who had long careers, including in overseas service as trade commissioners. Other team members for specific periods were David Knoll AM, who liaised with another constituent part of Austrade, the Export Finance and Insurance Corporation (EFIC), and Senior Trade Commissioner Kym Hewett. It became evident over time that the profoundly different character and mission of EFIC meant that it sat oddly with the focus on the trade promotional elements of Austrade. Its focus on finance and risk management meant that it marched to a different drum and it seemed, as time passed, that there was a certain amount of "going through the motions" in the time devoted to studying EFIC's operations.

Getting to know McKinsey

Leaving the Perth office in the capable hands of my deputy, the late Alexander Karas, an experienced Trade Commissioner with a distinguished army background in the Vietnam conflict, it was time to attend my first meeting. We met with the McKinsey members of the team assigned to work with us for the next five months or so until the final report was delivered to the Austrade Board. Ashley Stephenson would be the senior consultant leading the investigation which rested under the imprimatur of the Senior Partner of McKinsey, Terrey Arcus. Ashley was backed up by Michael Masterman and more junior analysts, Alison Watkins and Susan Denham.

How young they all seemed. And how did we seem to them? Experienced sounds better than old. Purposefully conjuring up diagrams on the whiteboard. Friendly but businesslike. As you would hope. And not lacking in confidence or belief in the magical mystery-solving alchemy of the McKinsey model. The legendary (but not to us at the time) framework originally derived from the work of Robert H Waterman Jnr and Tom Peters in the 1980s.

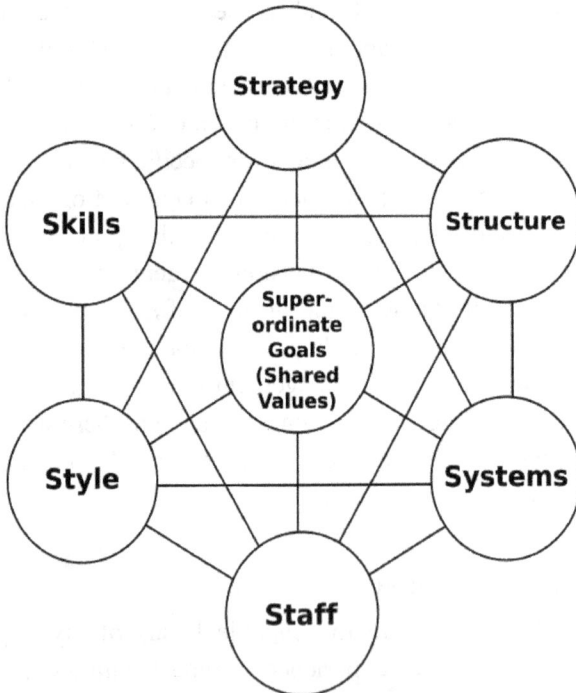

Figure 1: The Seven "S" framework

McKinsey's approach was strongly grounded in the broad principle of fact-based analysis. We came to respect the thoroughly ingrained and disciplined respect for facts that were assiduously and painstakingly gathered by McKinsey staffers for subsequent analysis. This was backed up by the above 7S framework that opened up a framework for digging deep into the organisation and coming to conclusions that would point the way to recommendations for change. In a way the model was going beyond the then conventional approach to organisational renovation of focusing primarily on structure. There is no hierarchy in the seven points of focus – they are all important and there needs to be holistic consideration and coordination to avoid undue weakness in any of them. We received the first "pack" of materials flowing from work conducted to date. It was a series of exhibits with the characteristic McKinsey methodology. We became familiar with these ways of representing lines of argument by setting out logical steps in graphic form running across the page before arriving at a conclusion which was invariably supported by highlighted dot points in the supplementary text.

This was our role. To critically examine the findings based on what we knew from experience, to test the validity of the findings, to identify any traps, and to contribute, creatively, to finding practical lessons to illuminate the way forward.

Even at this early stage we were beginning to enter the curtained-off world of the insider. There was an intense interest in the review within the organisation since Bill Ferris, Chairman of the Board, had announced the independent review (*The Canberra Times,* 31 May 1990). Once it became known that we had been seconded to the review and we became privy to the work being carried out "behind the scenes" we felt the not unpleasant burden of inside knowledge. Discretion was obviously critical but our success would also depend on keeping channels open to our colleagues to maximise the confidence that the review was fair and independent and not a smokescreen for some dastardly plot hatched in Canberra.

Events leading to the review

At around that time rumors began to circulate that the responsible Minister, the late John Button, had commissioned the review following the receipt of adverse opinions on the effectiveness of the organisation from various sources, including from business. He was not happy and wanted change. It also was suggested that he was not satisfied that the Managing Director, Lindsay MacAlister, was the right man for the job. MacAlister had been brought in from the private sector (where he had been most recently CEO of Australian General Electric) to inject more commercial practices into Austrade in 1986. As a newly established statutory authority with a Board including leading private sector figures, it was envisaged Austrade would have much more flexibility and relative freedom from the confining strictures that applied to departments of state.

There were vigorous attempts made in Austrade's early years to adopt a more commercial and contemporary managerial approach. MacAlister was a great believer in investing in training and development and stressing the importance of outcomes. I was a participant in the second Manager Action Program (MAP) in 1988. About 20 people from across the organisation joined an ambitious year-long program of residential courses and live action projects. External consultants (led by Tim Dalmau), supported by internal Austrade trainers, David Faulks and David Crook, worked to raise the skills and self-awareness of the participants (partially via the Myers-Briggs personality assessment tool). I was impressed with this emphasis and investment in people that contrasted with more half-hearted, anemic efforts in the past. In the year of the review some seven per cent of the budget was devoted to training. However, notwithstanding some positives, threatening clouds were gathering.

There was a distinct sense that Austrade had lost its way with exporters and their support needs in international markets. While initially ambitious in its direction, the management of the organisation began to disconnect itself from the operational elements. The introduction of leading-edge commercial practices was occurring slowly. Top management seemed more remote. Job cuts and restructuring took its toll and many of the Austrade staff, especially those who opted for Austrade against remaining in the Department of Trade in 1987 at the time of the Dawkins reforms, were on the whole still civil servants familiar with commercial practices and the needs of companies to a limited degree.

On the other hand MacAlister had had little experience working with government in a structure that, despite its statutory form, was still effectively part of government. A defining aspect of the MacAlister era was his belief that government could be kept at a distance and that this new organisation would be allowed to go its own way and be above politics. This was a fatal error. MacAlister had dramatically communicated his view on where the real action should be by moving large parts of the organisation to Sydney into 201 Kent Street. I can recall my surprise when first visiting the executive 25th floor to encounter what seemed vast spaces and a lavish fit out. The first impression was of large expanses of what appeared to be marble flooring. Welcome to a more commercially oriented Austrade. I admit it – it felt good. But facades hide things and so it came to pass.

In the Austrade Board plans were afoot to tackle the "out of touch" management of Austrade and to do so in an overarching and fundamental manner. There were concerns that MacAlister was out of his depth but what was more concerning to the Board was his inability to balance the fact of Austrade's government status with the injection of business acumen.

Based on McKinsey's meetings with Minister Button it was clear that the minister felt the leadership really didn't have a clear vision of how the organisation was going to add value and that was why he was keen to do something about it. Not surprisingly, as news of the review and its reported origins began to circulate far and wide within Austrade, apprehension grew that there would be a widespread wave of change that would lead to job cuts and dislocation.

Terms of reference

The formal terms of reference were, in large part, as follows:

> To investigate and report to the Board of Austrade on the efficiency and effectiveness of Austrade in meeting its charter – that is, helping to improve the export capability and performance of Australian industry, and assisting to increase the trade and investment links between Australia and its major markets, especially with the economies of the Western Pacific Rim.
>
> In completing this report, the consultants will take as given both the Austrade charter and the strategies enunciated by Austrade in its March 1990 Corporate Plan. The review will examine and report on the effectiveness of Austrade in achieving its charter objectives through the implementation of these strategies, and in particular will examine:
>
> - Organisational and management structure, and operating systems of Austrade.
> - Distribution of resources by Austrade between its overseas, national and State operations and the appropriateness of the resourcing in each of these areas.
> - Effectiveness of Austrade in identifying and providing services to its clients in the private and public sectors.
> - Effectiveness of working relationships with other government departments and agencies, State Governments, industry and other organisations involved directly in export and investment promotion activities for Australian industry.
> - Cost recovery objectives and procedures.
>
> The report will contain recommendations for any changes or improvements in each of these areas of activity.

Early developments in the Review

The time when we joined the review coincided with an offshore foray by some of the McKinsey team to a regional conference of Senior Trade Commissioners in northern Italy. This sort of event was a regular feature of Austrade in those days, providing an opportunity to build collegiality and creating a platform for pronouncements by senior managers flown in from Canberra. For example the Manager International Operations, Andrew Mackintosh, who had the unenviable task of oversighting the global network of Austrade Posts from a desk in Canberra. A task not made easier by the fact that he had been recruited to the 'new" Austrade post-1986 and was required to lead a team of people, some of whom had been in the field since the early 1960s, and who needed to be won over to new ways of doing things.

Ashley Stephenson recalled the occasion in an interview conducted for this book as follow:

> One of the first things we asked when we started was 'what's a good way for us to (meet) as many people in the field as possible without flying around ... to 30 countries?' As it turned out there was this get-together coming up so two of us went to that particular session and I think we were there for about three days and we had meetings lined up with every one of these people and ... we got to spend an hour or two individually with 30+ trade commissioners ... It was a rich and fabulous experience enabling us to hear about the organisation from those in the front line. I could not fail to be very impressed by the commitment of career officers to the organisation (Stephenson 2014).

Reflecting on the value of this form of intelligence collection Stephenson was asked to explore what conclusions were drawn from the exercise:

> The head seemed to be very disconnected from the body ... I think that the answers lay with talking to people in the field and not talking to people in head office. That is often the case in any organisation, public or private. Where do clients benefit and what do they benefit from? And I think those answers became very clear when you spoke to people who were working with clients because they were much more clear (than) when you interviewed the senior executives (Stephenson 2014) .

In addition to researching attitudes of offshore staff McKinsey staff were carrying out an intensive in-depth study of various corporate metrics. Not least the way in which the budget was spent. At team meetings we would be exposed to the progressive findings and invited to discuss their significance. One of the most significant findings that came to light was that 45 per cent of the budget was expended on activities characterised as "administration and support". This was obviously a discovery with enormous implications and would come to provide the *raison d'etre*, post-review, for a raft of measures that would divert more funds towards what may be described as "the pointy end"; in other words diverting monies into client directed purposes. McKinsey felt that reducing the share of administration and support to about 20 per cent of budget was achievable.

Matters arising

One of the more interesting studies was the examination of **how executive time was spent**. This included what at first glance seemed trivial – an in-tray analysis. In other words a snap study of what passed across the desks of various executives (before the mass invasion of electronic communications). It enabled an examination of patterns of delegation (or lack of it) and involvement in minor matters. Indulging in micro-management in other words. This also threw a light on systems issues (one of the 7S factors) as analysis revealed over-complexity in some systems. For example the depth charge finding that revenue collection involved 22 separate steps. I remember looking at the explanatory diagram and saying to myself "Yes that all looks familiar" after I had laboriously followed the trail.

Full analysis of a sample of 11 executives' diaries showed few client meetings, planning meetings were twice those with clients and the bulk of time was spent in Canberra. Links were made to a risk averse culture.

An issue dear to my heart as a State Manager was the question of the **involvement of allies.** Organisations with similar objectives.

Other organisations, both public and private, that dabbled to greater or lesser extent in trade facilitation and promotion. State government departments, Chambers of Commerce, employer organisations, the Australian Institute of Export and industry department programs. A chart demonstrating program coverage revealed enormous overlap, even extending to financial assistance. Trade and investment missions were, and remain, favourites.

McKinsey was offended at the massive duplication of services and waste. They had picked up in interviews with exporters a sense of confusion as to who did what. State governments of various political flavours had, over time, opened offshore offices with trade promotion mandates. Their services, unlike Austrade, which charged, were free. New South Wales had chosen to close theirs, which gave some comfort to McKinsey that others could see the need for rationalisation. I was less sanguine being all too familiar with the political kudos in state politicians getting close to the states' exporters and had little confidence that this one would get anywhere. It gives me no satisfaction to say I was correct.

A key issue was whether the prevailing **global allocation of resources** made sense when considering market potential and where Australian companies needed help the most. Kym Hewett tackled the construction of a matrix that charted market potential on one axis and degree of difference from Australian business practices on the other. This required extensive research to tabulate the necessary data, all conducted at breakneck speed. Thus China and Japan appeared in the top right quadrant and more Western markets such as the UK, where Australian exporters need less assistance, migrated to the left hand side of the matrix at varying heights according to the magnitude of potential for what Australia had to sell. As a tool to guide decisions on where resources should be boosted and where reduced this was very powerful. McKinsey seemed to feel that the steps to reallocate resources were straight forward and massive changes could be made. I was convinced of the need for radical change but knew there would be forces that would temper it to some extent.

And so our work progressed, building towards the climax when our report would be presented to the Board, and our thinking revealed for all to see. It was not lost on us that some of the findings would not be well received by senior management.

At various stages of the project the team outlined the findings to date to the Board. I noticed that at every intervention by the Managing Director, the McKinsey people would take note of his remarks. These remarks would then be quietly fact checked to verify their accuracy. This lack of trust was somewhat disturbing but reflected the tone that had developed of resistance to the new ideas and the falling away of any sense of a shared exploration of the best way forward.

States of mind

Getting towards the end of 1990 and the pressure is telling. I return to Perth occasionally but am spending long periods in Sydney. I position myself in Manly because I relish the trips to and from the city on the Manly Ferry. Particularly the return in the evening after a long day at the office where the team is sequestered away from the troops. The ferry is invariably escorted by a formation of seagulls, dipping and weaving in close support, gliding in and out of the ferry's reflected light and then disappearing into the blackness. I am reminded of Kenneth Slessor's immortal poem *Five Bells*. In stressful times I sometimes take refuge in poetry and this is one of those times.

TEAMWORD BOUND

Goodbye paradise.

I'm off to save the world

The sun smiles on my face from across the Pacific

As I step out hopefully through the bleary Manly morning

Past the Vietnamese youth washing away the mistakes of the night drinkers at the Steyne's bar

Past the banksias, looking uncomfortable amidst the paved

boulevards of take-away commerce,
To the ferry terminal.

Ah, the ferry
Coming, ready or not.

The first bruise of the day as I forego my lovely leisurely slow
boat.
Can't let the team down so I board the menacing hydrofoil.
Noise, rush, frenzy, turmoil,
The destroyer.

I nestle into my moulded plastic seat
It likes me – and may have even known me before
In the cabin the suited cohorts have assembled, shoulder to
shoulder
The *Herald* flaps its banner in my startled face
"US troops land in Saudi"
Laconic deckhands loose the bonds of land
And we're free – and running.

My perch in the after deck sets me apart
From more sensible passengers who stand, backs to the city,
Bathing their faces in the warm flood of the new-born sun.
Eyelids downcast, still nostalgic for sleep's languors.

The wind buffets my face as we set course
Dashing out cheekily into the open mouth of the Harbour.
This destroyer is alive
This destroyer is rushing towards the city
Full of shock troops
Who will crash into its heart and take it
Sparing no one. Without mercy.

A young woman joins me at the rail

Her short fair hair lashed, like mine

by the resisting air

She wraps her jacket to her throat and stares, downcast, at her shoes

Which will soon carry her across the Quay and into the redoubt.

The cool wind of morning has thrashed our exposed skin,

suffusing it with blood.

We are alive!

We are ready!

The denouement

On 12 December 1990 the recommendations from the review were presented to the Austrade Board in the Conference room at 201 Kent Street, Sydney. My memories are sparse. We were there to be seen not heard. Above all I recall the intense focus on the findings by all in the room. Not least the Managing Director who must have felt like Saint Sebastian as each arrow flashed out of the PowerPoint screen as though directed at him. He had achieved much in his time but this was not to be his time. His resignation coincided more or less with the lodgement of the findings of the review.

In McKinsey's final report to the Chairman, Bill Ferris, "Organising to Deliver Export Impact" of 20 December 1990 McKinsey acknowledged the achievements in Austrade's first five years of life including in skills, systems and new product development however its recommendations were far reaching and explicitly called for " a complete change in Austrade". It judged that the return on investment was inadequate but that a quantum improvement was within reach. The caveat was that this would only be achieved if there was complete and enthusiastic implementation of the recommendations.

Recommendations

1. Adopt a market-driven approach, based on yielding better access to overseas customers through utilising government clout and in-depth market know-how and relationships:

- Austrade has an inherently complex task with market and cultural diversity, a broad and complex range of products and the limitations of its advisory role. Focus has been lacking. Part of the reason is a lack on the government's part of a clear strategy to develop exports. There is also a lack of external support for the strategies being followed by Austrade.

- Austrade has a unique role in assisting exporters to reach overseas customers through its international network. The key is to utilise government clout and to cultivate in-depth, in-market relationships. Austrade can cost-effectively help companies, especially those with limited international experience, access and influence foreign governments, overcome language and cultural barriers and obtain low-cost basic information on markets.

- The review warns against Austrade becoming involved in services, such as "solutions consulting", which can be delivered by private sector players.

- Resources are spread too thinly so that some overseas offices (posts) are below critical mass. Resources should be re-directed from domestic operations to markets where the most impact can be achieved – especially the more difficult markets and where Australian companies encounter unfamiliar business practices – Indonesia rather than the US for example.

- Noted that experienced larger exporters ("old hands") use Austrade in markets such as USSR and Iran. Some 90 per cent of revenue for Austrade from the 27 largest exporters came from the "old hands" in the previous year.

2. Restructure the organisation to push more resources and responsibility to the field:

- Strengthen linkages between the Managing Director and the overseas network, including by establishing six new senior positions that would be located in the field. They would have direct responsibility for discrete parts of the network while exercising real authority.

- Concluded that resources are spread evenly with little regard for where there are opportunities to add most value and where the best export opportunities are to be found.

- Austrade's expenditure in the US was nearly seven times that in Indonesia despite exporters, relatively speaking, needing more help to enter the difficult Indonesian market.

- Noted that assistance provided in difficult markets was appreciated and produced results.

- Domestic operations to be managed by a senior manager reporting to the Managing Director.

- Reorganise state offices to separate reactive services and servicing of high potential clients. Rationalise "retail" servicing, preferably having state governments assume this responsibility.

- Raise skills levels in high potential client advice and eliminate fragmentation and overlap of service units.

- Reduce complexity in administrative processes.

- Move resources from Canberra to Sydney to bring staff closer to the business world. Eliminate bureaucratic processes.

- Manage the interface with government through a senior manager still based in Canberra.

- Create two new positions to manage product development quality and evolution and to manage the International Trade Enhancement Scheme (ITES) that provides discretionary funding to exporters.

3. Revitalise and re-engineer the international and domestic network to improve service delivery and impact:

- Concentrate more on delivering services that increase business access to export markets and not mirror management consulting or investment advisory services offered by the private sector.

- More vigorous pursuit of local market opportunities.

- Package and deliver market research services, in-market support and promotion services. Reduce variability in quality of service delivery and raise the quality of advice e.g., in how to gain maximum benefit from an overseas visit.

- Expand use of advanced communications technologies e.g., video conferencing to provide better exposure for the demonstrable expert knowledge of overseas marketing personnel.

4. Change the leadership direction to increase "initiative taking" and change the culture of the organisation:

- Acknowledged that previous few years had required concentration on integrating the disparate organisations that had come together to form Austrade.

- Style and structure were inhibiting initiative. Most of the pivotal field leaders were three to four levels below the Managing Director and were overly taken up in planning meetings and administration rather than being in the field and in client contact. They needed to be more proactive in locating opportunities.

- A less risk-averse culture needed to be established with stronger leadership roles for regional leaders.

- Measurement and incentive systems needed to be restructured to remove internal divisions and to better measure impact.

- Management approaches were driven more by the individual rather than by the specific needs of the markets.

- Regional CEOs needed to drive through best practice more consistently and there needed to be more coaching of staff.

- Clients had commented adversely on the variable quality and effectiveness of staff. Better monitoring of effectiveness and building capability was required.

- A better career path was required for locally engaged staff, who were often of very high quality and cost-effectiveness, and should be given the opportunity to aspire to more senior positions.

- The high priority given by the Board and government to revenue-raising tended to generate conflict and distort priorities. There was a need to refine measurement techniques. The key outcome sought should be trade impact.

- Better internal data systems needed to be introduced, including a simplified client database.

5. Reconfigure its relationship with Government, other trade development bodies (allies) and business:

- Relationships with federal and state government bodies and industry associations influencing trade were sub-optimal. Duplication should be addressed and more effective working arrangements introduced.

- Austrade should be positioned as the central catalyst to leverage and nurture the capabilities of allies.

- Recommended that Austrade remain under government ownership as sovereign government backing or clout was critical to effectiveness.

- Austrade should be more active in involving itself in influencing the trade policy agenda with a bias towards more practical trade-related issues.

- There should be greater efforts to encourage trade commissioners to specialise in markets where language and culture were important factors. More flexibility in remuneration policies was important if staff were to commit to longer-term association with difficult markets in which to operate.

- Duplication of federal and state government offshore representation was a national embarrassment and a waste of resources. Austrade should be the sole trade representative for the Australian government overseas and state instrumentalities involved with trade should focus more on domestic activities.

- With over 50 bodies in Australia involved in trade related activities there was a role for Austrade to act as a catalyst and to coordinate trade support services.

- There was an opportunity to command the central axis and help direct export traffic to specialised organisations.

- Austrade should respond to the wishes of business that it should play a more active role in advocating the removal of impediments to export expansion and generally act more as a spokesperson.

6. Initiate and manage a major program of organisational change:

- Implementation of the changes recommended in the review would require dedication and commitment from the senior management team over two years and would require extensive involvement by many people within the organisation.

- Almost everyone in the organisation would need to do things differently. Partial or adaptive change was not an option.

- The prerequisites for successful change were outlined and it was recommended that a change manager position be created to establish a change vision and to lead a team of dedicated team members.

- It was acknowledged that the reduction of administrative activities to remove waste and to change the culture and style of Austrade would lead to some redundancies.

- The change needed to be led aggressively from the top but ideas and initiatives should develop bottom up.

Making it happen

The complete review report was delivered to the Chairman, Bill Ferris on 20 December 1990. Just what process was followed to brief Minister Button I am unable to say but it would have been expeditious.

There was time to take a breather over Christmas but early in the New Year it was action stations. There had been some press coverage that had inevitably concentrated on the negatives and so there was great unease among staff. Early action was required to generate momentum and the Chairman, Bill Ferris, stepped forward to lead the change process. He did so without seeking financial recompense for the extensive time he spent on implementation issues in the succeeding months. There had been some suggestion that McKinsey would work on to help the change process and indeed they did assist in communicating the results of the review at presentations to staff but then largely stepped aside leaving it to the organisation, led by Bill Ferris, to follow through with a change program.

Four task forces were established:

Australian Operations (Michael Johnson, leader)

International Network (Bob Webb, leader)

Product Development (John Hemphill, leader)

Administrative Review (John Bennett, leader)

Chief of Staff (Ron Maxwell, leader)

HR support was provided by David Richard with Internal Communications being handled by David Faulks.

Staff presentation in Canberra

Although McKinsey had written their report expecting that it would enter the public domain few staff had seen it before presentations were made around the states and internationally. So when we addressed a well-attended meeting of staff in Canberra at a motel on Northbourne Avenue in February 1991 there was a great sense of expectancy.

The presentations were shared between Ashley Stephenson of McKinsey and the team members from Austrade, viz Michael Johnson and Julia Selby and the writer. There was a certain stillness as an attentive audience focused on the many charts and exhibits.

I had been given the responsibility of talking to the matrix which mapped the various countries on the export potential and ability of Austrade to deliver value axes. If you were a pessimist it drew the eye immediately to those markets in the lower left hand quadrant where logically there was less of a case for Austrade's presence. I injected some lightness into proceedings when I complimented Peter Pond on his choice of attire – a safari suit, which would be out of place in some of the markets such as the UK or US, adjudged by the review to be easier for exporters to enter and requiring less resourcing by Austrade compared with some Asian or Middle Eastern markets where a safari suit might pass muster (and promotional prospects be greater). I think there was only one deletion from the video that was taken that day to carry the messages for change to offices (posts) around the world. Goodbye safari suit. I felt a tremendous sense of relief that the findings had been shared with everyone and that we could get on with the task of addressing the implementation issues.

Communications

Issue 1 of the *Review Bulletin* designed to communicate the progress with implementation was circulated on 22 February 1991 (Austrade 1991). The Chairman wrote of the hurtful negative commentary that had appeared in the press but argued that Austrade would be seen as displaying "leadership and sound judgement in holding itself up to the microscope at this time".

Ferris said there had been radical changes to the business environment in the 1990s that necessitated change. It would be necessary to build on strengths and reduce weaknesses and deliver better value to clients. He promised a flatter management structure providing more authority and discretion in the field and, in one of his phrases that would, over the months, become his signature mantra, *"really making a difference* to the export performance of its clients". He did acknowledge there would be reductions in staffing levels but also promised that there would be some new opportunities. It was stressed that proper consultation, including with the unions, would precede any changes.

In what would become a feature of the communications process the Chairman provided detailed answers to the sorts of questions staff were asking and set realistic time frames e.g., that it might take a year before the real benefits of the changes would flow through to clients. In subsequent editions some of the more notable rumours, of which there were many, were frontally addressed.

Task forces

My recollections of the period working on the task force to which I was allocated (Australia Operations) are hazy to say the least, 25 years down the track. The review had been very prescriptive about the shape that state offices should take (break down into retail and impact areas) and so there was a good blueprint to follow. I do recall though one of the team leaders commenting one day, as organisation charts were being discussed, and it came as a sudden realisation, "I may not be able to find a place for myself if this is how it is going to look." And so it came to pass in his case. This highlights the professionalism displayed by some previously very senior managers in working industriously to bring the new vision to reality despite their own job security being in jeopardy.

Considerable work was done to introduce systems that would allow objective measurement of performance. These especially focused on eliciting clients' views on the efficiency and effectiveness of the servicing they received from Austrade and the contribution made to measurable export successes. In my view this resulted in people instinctively knowing the right thing to do and allocating time accordingly – working to see success by clients.

New Appointments

We were aware a vigorous search for a new Managing Director was underway. This took some time but eventually Ralph Evans was appointed. He came to the job from his most recent position as Vice President of The Boston Consulting Group Inc. and took to the reshaping task with enthusiasm. Coincidentally his career included nearly eight years with McKinsey, principally in London and Sydney in the 1970s. Bill Ferris must have been relieved to be able to hand the reins to the experienced newcomer.

One of the main changes in organisational structure came with the placing offshore of Executive General Managers (EGMs) responsible for specific regions. They would live and work in their regions with frequent return visits to Australia. Three of these were to be in Asia, which was a momentous change and shift of resources from the past. These were initially North Asia, East Asia and SE Asia/Oceania. Additionally there were EGMs for the Americas, Europe and what was called Special Markets which covered the USSR, Middle East, Turkey, Africa and the sub-continent – a huge area to be covered. During the review it was thought this latter region would be known as "Difficult Markets" but some clever spin doctor must have decided "Special" would be more polite.

It was significant that the appointments to the regional positions were a mixture of new and existing staff appointments. Other EGM level positions were Australian Operations, Corporate Affairs, International Trade Enhancement Scheme (the discretionary funding scheme) and Product Development. The new leaders met regularly and styled themselves as the G10. A somewhat assertive, not to say brave branding which to the layman had vague UN connotations.

The casualties

As foreshadowed by McKinsey and the Chairman there were indeed staff losses as the organisation was reconfigured. This naturally took quite some time and was at times quite painful for those concerned. I think something like a net 200 jobs were to go when it was all over. Every effort was made to follow fair processes and David Richard, who was HR Manager after a long career as a field trade commissioner, was indefatigable and committed to see it all through. I know from personal experience through my doctor in Yarralumla that a number of people affected (unnamed naturally) required medication for depression during the year.

Epilogue

At the end of 1991 the position of HR Manager became available in Canberra and I was encouraged to take up the position. I insisted the job be advertised as I did not want to be seen to be the beneficiary of preferment but there was only one other applicant. I was soon casually advised, when successful, that I was going to "the worst job in Austrade"! There was still a lot of post-McKinsey activity going on when I arrived in Canberra from Perth. I recall participating in several Achieving Export Impact workshops in South East Asia which were designed to get people on board with some of the new ways of working. Additionally I worked to introduce Austrade's first formal performance management system. A much needed innovation but not one easy to implement as old habits of some managers die hard. I pushed the notion that it should be "I want to help you be successful" not "I am here to judge you". Easier said than done!

The Perth State Manager's job proved hard to fill and after a long period a new appointee reneged at the last minute and it was decided that I should re-join my family in Perth and settle things down there. Thus ended my brief exposure to the "worst job in Austrade". Not true by the way as it is and will always be a vital job.

The McKinsey Review was a fascinating experience and the changes brought about as a result proved to be ground breaking as some international trade promotion agencies showed that imitation was the most sincere form of flattery by copying some of Austrade's innovations.

Bibliography

Austrade, 1991, *Review Bulletin*, No. 1, 22 February 1991, Canberra.

Stephenson A., 2014, Interview with Bruno Mascitelli in May 2014, Melbourne.

The Canberra Times, 1990, Austrade review, 31 May 1990, p. 17, National Library of Australia, http://nla.gov.au/nla.news-article122250664, accessed 13 April 2014.

SECTION THREE

Consolidation of Austrade

9

My years as Managing Director of Austrade

Interview with Ralph Evans

Question: The "one-stop-shop" that represented the creation of Austrade was a merger defined by some as a marriage which did not quite work. Is that your estimation of that merger in your period of Austrade management?

Ralph Evans: The logic was indisputable that there should be a single and highly competent national agency to help Australian companies sell their products and services overseas or establish themselves in foreign markets. This meant having the overseas market intelligence and assistance activities and financial assistance to exporters in the same organisation. They had been separate.

The main parts of the financial assistance to exporters were the long-established Export Market Development Grant (EMDG) Scheme and the less well known International Trade Enhancement Scheme (ITES). ITES was very successful, lending money to outstanding exporters to expand, depending on the assessment of the Austrade Board.

In 1991, the Export Finance and Insurance Corporation (EFIC) was put under the same roof as well. However, I agreed with the government's decision soon after to split it off. EFIC was a financial institution owned by the Commonwealth and worth $3 billion. It had its own quite complex issues. I went on its Board, and EFIC CEO

Graeme Lawless came on the Austrade Board, which I think was a good arrangement.

Question: You entered Austrade in 1991 with the legacy of the previous Managing Director Lindsay MacAlister. Did you need to deal with any loose ends from this legacy?

Ralph Evans: The McKinsey team had looked hard at the old organisation before recommending the new one. My job was to make the new one work. I thought (and I had once been a McKinsey consultant) that their team had done an excellent job. They had understood Austrade's challenges very well and come up with a very good solution.

My task was to make it work. So I looked forward rather than back. I had a wonderful top team: I mean that, 23 years on. They were an outstanding group of executives by any standards. The majority had been chosen before I came on board, so it was a bit like boarding a moving train. It was quite a challenge to get the team and those they managed all working in a coherent way that fulfilled what we all knew Australia needed and what McKinsey had set out in their report. I still see several of members of this team (sadly, two have passed away). We enjoy getting together and swapping yarns about those days. I have met Lindsay MacAlister a few times. I like and respect him, but my job was to look forward rather than back.

Question: One of your key tasks was to implement the McKinsey report and recommendations. How did you go about that and what was done with success and what was not?

Ralph Evans: As I have said, largely before I came on board, Austrade appointed an outstanding group of senior executives who became my team to lead the change. There were six overseas regional Executive General Managers in charge of the Austrade posts in six regions of the world. They included some very strong personalities and very experienced people, like Peter Forsythe, in charge of Greater China, Dieter le Comte, who headed Europe and Charles Jamieson, my eventual successor, who was in charge of less developed markets from Turkey to Bangladesh to South Africa. There was one EGM to run the offices in Australia, one in charge of the Grants and Loans, one to take charge of Administration and Government Relations and one to head Marketing and Business Development. This was an outstanding team which it was my privilege to head. I made only a few changes, for instance bringing in a brilliant man who used to be at McKinsey, Dr Paul Twomey, who helped us re-engineer our service offering (he went on the be the boss of ICANN (*Internet Corporation for Assigned Names and Numbers)*, the international company that supervises the entire Internet).

The second thing was, a great deal of communication had to be done, by the EGMs and by me, to carry the program of change through the organisation and communicate it outside. I used the long-distance phone a lot. I recorded video messages, new tech at the time (I needed some coaching on how to do this). Later, we used e-mail and Intranet a great deal. We got the EGMs together every quarter for a conference. I visited all six of our regions and some of the posts of each region every year. I was away from home many weeks each year. In all of this, we stressed the overall goal of the organisation, to help in the international development of Australian business. One of my tasks was to support this with regular speeches to public forums in Australia and appearances in the Australian business media. I used to say my job was to get us off the front pages and on to the business pages. I think we achieved this, at least up to a point.

Question: Some have defined you as a "game changer" for Austrade in what was still a fragile organisation. What is your view on this observation?

Ralph Evans: Well, it's nice if someone said that, because it was part of what I was supposed to be. I came from a different world from most people in the public sector. I had worked mainly in management consulting. After my MBA at Stanford, I began with McKinsey in London. Later I moved back to their office in Sydney, and I had long periods in East and North Africa and shorter ones in Japan and Europe.

Then with three friends from the same sort of background, we founded an Australian business strategy consulting firm, Pappas, Carter, Evans and Koop. We built this firm up to about 80 professionals in Australia and New Zealand and were then acquired by the Boston Consulting Group, where I became a Vice President. I had spent time in private equity as well. I was used to corporate change and to clients who were reaching for high aspirations, making things work well.

I had a great deal of support. As I have said, we had a fabulous executive team. We had a very supportive minister during my first couple of years in the late John Button. With his help, we found the government (it was the Hawke-Keating era) left us pretty well alone to get on and make the new Austrade work. Then there was the Board, to which I reported. There were some wise heads and some hard drivers there. While they were demanding, they advised and helped me. I was fortunate to have an excellent chairman in Bill Ferris, who knew very well what Austrade should be doing. His successor, the late Robert Johnston, was excellent too.

As for the senior team, I didn't have to drag them along. They were full of energy. The senior team, which we called the "G-10", was a source of tremendous dynamism. I don't want to claim it all myself. You couldn't keep up with Dieter Le Comte. He was a bit of a tyrant in his area. Peter Forsyth was a tremendously imaginative guy and a good leader of his people. So was Greg Dodds in a different way and Charles Jamieson, who ran those Arabian and African places in a style that worked well in that environment. So were each of the others in their own way. I think the overriding goal of helping Australian business in international markets overrode petty issues. We shared this goal and really lived it.

Question: What was uppermost in your mind when you took over from Lindsay MacAlister?

Ralph Evans: Austrade had an important national role, and there had been controversy about it. The Board, I believe pushed by the Minister, John Button, had commissioned a major review by McKinsey.

As a former management consultant, I studied the report closely and thought it was a fine piece of work that provided a framework for a much better Austrade. My goal was to complete implementing the McKinsey review and realise Austrade's potential. The two things uppermost in my mind were: first, getting this high-powered senior team to work together in a coherent way, and second, communication, to get everyone inside the organisation and those who had criticised it to see we were working hard to become a really valuable asset for Australia.

Question: How do you think an organisation like Austrade can measure its performance, does it need to and how important is this?

Ralph Evans: I think measurement is really important to underpin the continuing change I described above and to instil a commercial culture. It can be used as well to adjust resource allocation, for instance between Europe or America and Asia – how else can you do this well? You need to measure what comes out, what Austrade achieves, not what is put in. This is not easy. We developed and implemented a crude system which was a heavy load, but (while some grumbled) it worked reasonably well. Each post had to report its "impact" in the form of business assisted, with the name of the client and a dollar value. We used a third party to aggregate these once a year and survey a sample of the clients, asking them to verify the numbers and assess Austrade's part in each deal, from essential to minimal. They then scaled the aggregates, providing an estimate of impact globally and by region. I am sure you could do this much more efficiently with today's technology.

Performance measurement did not actually come from McKinsey. It was an innovation I introduced. I thought it was necessary to maintain the momentum of change after the people had settled into the new organisation structure. I believe an organisation with a role like Austrade must change continually, forever, to keep ahead of its game. The board gave plenty of support to measurement. I had to keep pushing it against some internal resistance. I know it wasn't very efficient. It was clumsy and labour intensive and annoying to some of the people who were interviewed. However, it gave us some numbers, and even if they were rough numbers they told us we were getting much more bang for the dollar spent in China than in Africa, for instance. So next time we were thinking about budgets, the performance in China needed to be reinforced and maybe we would have to pull back a bit in Africa. I thought this performance measurement was a very useful thing, indeed vital for our further progress. I would think with today's much more sophisticated computer technology you could redesign the process and do something that wouldn't be nearly as cumbersome.

Question: Austrade needs to work with Ministers and ministries. How was your time in this regard and what were the most important aspects of the Austrade-Ministerial relationship.

Ralph Evans: I met the Minister for Trade on a regular basis, generally once a month. All six trade ministers I had were supportive of our efforts, some more than others. None was negative. Peter Langhorne, who headed Austrade's administration and the office in Canberra, set up a regular program for me to call on other ministers and shadow ministers to brief them on what we were doing and to listen to their concerns. This helped mitigate any attacks that developing at a political or bureaucratic level and smoothed the way for our budget. I saw secretaries, deputy secretaries and heads of some agencies too.

Question: Does Austrade benchmark itself against other export facilitators in the world and who would it consider in your day (and today) to be a model to emulate and why?

Ralph Evans: In my last year I was thinking about how to benchmark Austrade against its peers. I was confident we would rate well comparatively. There could be things to learn from others that would allow us to keep pushing our change program. However, the national trade and investment bodies of other countries are very different from each other, reflecting national differences: Japan has its giant trading companies; Singapore has an activist policy of intervention in industry development, and so on. The ones most like us were those of the "anglo" countries such as New Zealand and Canada. We had a good relationship with New Zealand and compared experiences. I think what might work is to have a leading consultant commissioned jointly by several agencies. He or she (or a small team) would visit each and interview some active exporters. They would report back to all the agencies on the things some do better than others and perhaps tell each where they were behind. You would need to keep the latter part confidential or worded in terms of improvement opportunities or it will inevitably lead to headlines like "consultant slams Austrade"!

Question: Would you expect Austrade in an international benchmarking comparison to come out looking good. Are you aware of any such benchmarking and would it be a worthwhile exercise?

Ralph Evans: As far as I know it hasn't been tried. So I think it would be worth commissioning somebody who is neutral to do a comparative high-level look and see what the differences are and see who is better at some things than some others.

Japan's JETRO does things very differently from Austrade because its circumstances are different. France does it differently again. Israel is a special case. I don't know how the Italians do it. I think the most similar are the Anglo-countries like Ireland, Canada, New Zealand and South Africa. I think benchmarking would be a good thing to try. If you can find quantitative things to benchmark then do it!

I can't see any reason why Austrade can't be the best at its job in the world. We are not small like New Zealand who can't possibly afford much presence in Europe for instance or in a specialised place like Silicon Valley. We are big enough to be significant, and important to this country. Going international is quite hard for Australian businesses in services and manufactures. We don't have a nearby larger market that is familiar and the obvious one to start with, as Germany is for Danes or the USA for Canadians. New Zealanders have us to start on. Because of our success in resources, our dollar is strong and costs here are high. A really good agency to help Australian businesses make their way in foreign markets is something Australia needs more than most countries. Some international comparisons might help Austrade to convince its own nation that it is good at what it does and is a key national asset.

Question: Austrade's CEO no longer reports to a business oriented board like you did in your day but directly to the Trade minister. What is your view of this changed scenario and how did you view in your time?

Ralph Evans: I think the board was very valuable and that it is a great shame it has gone. The Board set a standard and stretched me to perform in a management sense up towards their level. Moreover, they provided a cultural separation from the relative lack of results focus in the public service. They did not add much value by advising on trade opportunities; we had our hands on plenty of those. They could and did open some doors for me.

One of the main things on which I think I can have a view was the usefulness of the Board in my time. I felt it was very valuable. I have heard that it didn't work as well at a later time when they had an interventionist chairman who I acted more like a CEO, rather than chairman, but in my time I thought it was very good. As I have outlined, the Board set a standard that I had to measure up to, but it also sent out a signal, a cultural broadcast, that we're there for business and somewhat different from the public service as a whole and particularly DFAT. I was very sad when the Board was abolished. I thought that was a very useful thing and I'm not even sure that the Uhrig report that was cited as source of the recommendation for abolishing it actually said that. I think it said something rather different. But anyway, the Howard Government took that decision. I found the board very relevant. It was expensive, I won't deny that, it had to have a board secretary and the meetings cost money and so forth.

Question: In your day how much did Austrade understand Australian business needs and especially the export side of Australian businesses?

Ralph Evans: We were in constant and intimate contact with lots of exporters. The ITES program was particularly good, because it kept us in close touch with some of the best companies. The name came from Bob Hawke, as PM, who called it the International Trade Enhancement Scheme. It was a loan scheme, and the government supported it to the tune of $50 million a year for several years. The money was lent under contract, subject to guidelines and under quite tough legal terms to fast-moving exporters who were really going places. They had to make a case, and the staff (there were some very good staff doing this under David Oliver, the EGM) filtered them and had a dialogue with the companies. Eventually the staff presented proposals to a committee of the Board, basically the people with a financial background. Bill Ferris was very active in it. There were some fantastic companies there. I think the program would be well worth reviving. One for instance, I remember well, was Austal Ships. You might never think that you could build ships in this country with our high wages and shortages of welders and people like that, particularly in Perth. But Austal has been very successful. They have been innovative and in a niche area with their fast ferries and smaller naval vessels. I would love to see ITES revived to help bring more really good companies like this to the fore. ITES money had to be used for international business development, such as marketing and often establishing an office overseas. It had to be paid back.

When the government changed, the incoming PM John Howard announced a $10 billion "black hole". ITES was one of the things they chopped. Then they put the tail of collectible loans out to tender. A couple of the former ITES staff people who had worked on the scheme formed a company and made a bid. They took over the tail. I believe they collected 100 per cent of the money that had been lent. They have estimated that the ratio of exports assisted to the government cost was the highest ever, much higher than for EMDG, something like 50:1.

So ITES was a really good program for developing exports, but it was good as well because it put the Board and Austrade as a whole in close touch with some of the really hot companies.

Question: The investment promotion portfolio has been with Austrade on and off over the years. How was investment promotion seen within Austrade in your day and did it assist the trade message?

Ralph Evans: The investment program had a separate message: invest in Australia. But it fitted well with the Austrade overseas structure as long as it had an efficient secretariat in Australia. In addition, it gave us the basis for a good dialogue with state governments. This is important because some States keep putting little trade offices all over the place, which usually don't achieve anything very much. I heard Barry O'Farrell, speaking before he was elected premier, saying he was shocked to find when he gave a speech in London that there was somebody there from the Queensland government, somebody from Victoria, from Western Australia, but nobody from NSW. Former premier Nick Greiner had abolished the NSW office because it didn't deliver enough for its cost.

Back to investment. I think it fitted well. To illustrate, once Peter Forsyth phoned from Hong Kong and said they had come across American Express (AMEX) looking for a place to put a multi-lingual call centre for Asia. As he pointed out, we have immigrants in Australia who speak Korean, Chinese and many other Asian languages, and we could do it. Why don't we make a pitch for it? So we did, and it worked, AMEX came here to Sydney. We made a video with pieces spliced in. Prime Minister Keating actually did a one-minute insert addressed specifically to American Express. A separate organisation for investment would probably not have a network big enough to come across opportunities like this; nor would it be likely to have a manager of Peter's calibre to take the initiative and go for it so effectively.

Question: There is talk about Austrade merging back with DFAT. Is this a good idea and what will happen if it were to occur?

Ralph Evans: You can see from what I have said that I see Austrade as a service to business. I think it needs its distinctive business culture, and that this should start with the board and CEO. There should be a number of people at senior levels with strong backgrounds in international business. I do not see merging with DFAT as useful because of these factors.

I often heard from diplomats or deputy secretaries that they fretted that Austrade might somehow do the wrong thing overseas, compromising relationships with foreign countries that had been nurtured carefully. I never had a single complaint of this kind from the embassy network. Trade commissioners are not silly; they know which team they are playing for; and (while it was hardly necessary) we had a document called the Prime Minister's Directive that set out rules for working overseas.

Austrade was transferred from the Department of Industry to the Department of Foreign Affairs and Trade about one-third of the way through my time. I was shocked of course. This was something that happened in the Cabinet, where Gareth Evans outflanked John Button and made this change happen. Shocked though I was I thought it possibly didn't matter much and in fact there were advantages because we had to have contact with DFAT in more than 50 places overseas. In the case of the Department of Industry, we needed to have one main point of contact in Canberra. So in that sense, initially it was probably better. But then the slow process of absorption began to happen. The government abolished the Austrade board and have put people from DFAT in to run Austrade. I the long term, I don't think being in DFAT is a good thing. I think it would be better to keep the board and keep more business people running Austrade, which probably means it should be in the Industry portfolio.

Question: Do you believe there was a process within Austrade of rolling back the McKinsey recommendations?

Ralph Evans: I don't think there was any explicit push of this kind. I was there for five years following McKinsey. The new system got pretty well embedded, and we had moved on to new initiatives. After over five years, many people had either forgotten the review or had never known about it. However, there may have been some inadvertent going back, what I might call reversion to tradition.

One example of a change that undid some of the spirit of what McKinsey recommended was the merging of two regions into one, Japan and Korea plus China, Taiwan and Hong Kong. This was a response after my time to a government demand to reduce costs. However, the super-region this created (which was incidentally the destination of more than half of Australia's exports) had a lot of people in it and a lot of posts. Inevitably, it led to a sub-regional management layer and probably more overhead staff as well. McKinsey had very deliberately recommended a "flat" organisation with minimal layers. Between me and a Chinese member of staff in Guangzhou who dealt with exporter clients every day there were only two layers: the regional EGM and the Senior Trade Commissioner who was manager of the post. Flat organisations are hard work, because you have so many direct reports, but they are responsive and flexible and have more muscle and less fat than more tiered organisations. I would definitely have looked for economies somewhere else and not re-created layers.[1]

Question: How has the staff profile of the Trade Commissioner changed over the years and what do you think the trade commissioners of the future will need to look like?

Ralph Evans: I am out of date here but I advocate having a good proportion or people with strong experience in business. This includes

---

1 [Editorial: This is an important issue and a clear departure from the recommendations of the McKinsey Review but as it turned out not the case for North East Asian region, the amalgam of Japan/Korea and East Asia. The EGM at the time had 17 direct reports and he held onto these until his retirement in 2004 in spite of pressure from some Board members. New management layers was however a problem with the new Europe/Middle east region.]

local staff: I recall one such manager in Russia and one in Vietnam who were both very successful. I think Austrade could offer more medium term positions of three or four years' duration to qualified young business people, giving them overseas experience and training and then releasing them to work in companies.

I had the benefit of the insights of John Allgrove, our most senior GM in years, now retired. When John was first posted to Calcutta in 1962 war broke out with China, which was really frightening. Before he was sent abroad on the P&O ship, John had a private meeting with the Secretary of the Department of Trade, a knight. The great man advised him: "Allgrove, in India, never carry your own briefcase". I think the rate of enquiries then was much lower than now and the pace of them was pretty slow. You would open the mail and there might be a letter from somebody some days, other days not. Now it's e-mail and its on-line and internet and web searches and suchlike. Trade commissioners have to be able to filter, referring enquiries back to Australia which can be better dealt with there. Their job is in a sense like a triage nurse in a hospital emergency department, deluged with people needing attention. Their duty is to assess the importance and urgency of enquiries and either deal with them directly or send them to where they will be dealt with appropriately. It is a demanding job, but I think it is something you can be trained in.

Change happens more quickly today than some people can cope with. Austrade's IT staff in Canberra were grouped to serve an old mainframe computer, which kept a lot of the records. When Dr Paul Twomey wanted to set up a really good website, an Intranet and other systems, he had to set up a separate group in Sydney.

Question: Why has Austrade changed its internal structures many times? What pressures has Austrade sought to address requiring these changes?

Ralph Evans: Some changes may have been needed to adapt to new technology, like the IT example I described. Technology has come a long way since my time and will continue to change, creating new opportunities but throwing up obsolescence.

I still think the 1990 McKinsey report was a good piece of work. An update by someone with comparable sophistication might be good. It is the principles that count, like the principle of a flat organisation that I described.

I really don't know the circumstances now, I'm out of it, but I presume Austrade is under a fair amount of budget pressure. When I was there, I thought having senior managers on the ground overseas dealing closely with the various posts was absolutely right. Now, with Skype and video-conferencing it may be different. It does cost a lot to post someone overseas, to house them and pay for their children's education. However, I don't think you should turn to organisational change to solve every problem. It is disruptive and expensive.

Question: The tension between government and commercial approaches is a constant within Austrade. How did this tension play out in your view in terms of the way Austrade goes about its activities?

Ralph Evans: I would always stress our purpose, what we were there for. We are a government agency but we are there to help business. In more than one city overseas, the regional EGM recommended setting up a "business centre" in an ordinary office away from the embassy. This allowed co-location with allies and avoided the security environment of an embassy which some people, including foreign business people, may find intimidating.

Question: You have observed Austrade over the years from outside as well as inside. What is your impression of the organisation and its direction as best as you can ascertain?

Ralph Evans: Its function will always be needed. It has some wonderful people, dedicated, hard-working and deeply knowledgeable. It should have a business board. Austrade is a great national asset, but it needs a fair go. Benchmarking might be useful: I would bet that an objective observer would find that Austrade stacks up pretty well against its international peers. Australia should be proud of it. Austrade has a fairly high profile and, absent international comparisons, it is vulnerable to occasional attack by commentators or politicians. There is something in our national ethos or political system that leads to it being criticised, often unfairly. Greater clarity of its status would help it with a recurrent problem: state governments setting up offices overseas, often staffed with people trained by Austrade, which are way sub-scale and certainly not subject to effective measurement. Finally, I think it should have a business board, but did I say that?

Question: What are new export challenges for Australian exporters which are different from the past which will be faced by Austrade in the future?

Ralph Evans: More than ever, we have a strong resource sector that sends the dollar soaring at times and a much less internationally competitive manufacturing sector. Our services sector keeps growing and should form an ever-greater part of Austrade's work. Despite these commonplace observations, I am sure there are many little-known businesses in Australia with products or services that should do well in foreign markets, like the businesses I referred to earlier. They need every encouragement and assistance we can give them. Our costs are high and the distances we have to go to markets are long, so these competitive products and services are likely to be based on innovation and high levels of skill. "Me too" offerings are not likely to cut it globally. I expect the Internet, Skype and even social networks have changed the international business environment a lot. I am now deputy chairman of a business in central Africa. It is in constant touch with Australia by e-mail.

Question: How important is language acquisition for Austrade A-Based when sent out on postings?

Ralph Evans: Every week one reads someone saying that too few young Australians are studying foreign languages, Asian ones in particular. I don't know whether this is right: Austrade was always able to attract young Australians who were highly competent in Asian languages. The number of jobs needing them is not huge. What has happened over the last few decades is that Australians have travelled more than ever, to more parts of the world. We are no longer socially awkward in foreign countries, as perhaps we once were.

It is obviously an advantage to be able to speak the language when you are working in a foreign country. But imagine you speak Vietnamese. Are you going to spend your whole career dealing with the one country that speaks it?

Partly because they cost much less, Austrade has for long employed many local staff, who of course speak the local languages (I believe the US Foreign Commercial Service doesn't do this, because of security concerns). Austrade may have 80 or more people in its various offices who speak Chinese.

There are some countries that will always be important, of course one of them being China. Austrade surely needs a number of Chinese speakers among its Australian staff, whom it can rotate from one job to another as they become more senior. The same would apply to Japanese and perhaps Spanish and Arabic, which are spoken in many countries. International savoir-faire and business competence are at least as important as language for trade commissioners.

Question: How important can local employed in Austrade posts be in terms of selling Australia to the world?

Ralph Evans: We employed many local staff because of the economics of it so as to have more presence. They were hard working, often short-term local people: Indians or Chinese and lots of other countries. They were getting experience in international business as part of the deal. But the limit on how far you can go with this is imposed by maintenance of the culture of the organisation and the leadership. So I think it might end up, if you rethought it, a bit like the army where you have actually a relatively small number of people with career progression that will take them all the way to the top and a much larger number of shorter-tem people who turn over including officers. I think if they were to suggest another McKinsey-type review I would look at the personnel policy of the whole place. I think you can work out how many A-based you need, and how many speakers of those key foreign languages. When I finished we had 100 overseas, it's probably more like 70 now.

If you can afford A-based, great! But for communist countries particularly, like China and Vietnam, you have to get local employees from a government agency. You know they're reporting back on you, it's a part of their job. So I think you need probably two A-based people in Vietnam so they can talk to each other without the Vietnamese staff being present. Of course you know that there are some things that are commercial and ought not to go to the host government

Interview conducted in February 2014

10

Some reflections on the Charles Jamieson years

Interview with Peter Langhorne

Question: In which years were you employed by Austrade?

Peter Langhorne: From 1992 until 2001 and arrived when McKinsey had finished the review of the organisation. McKinsey had made a number of recommendations which related to organisational structure and the direction of the organisation along with where the organisation should be focusing its efforts. The McKinsey Review basically said, "Look, you should be focusing more on the larger companies that are going to give the best benefit". In relation to the changes that I saw over that period, I think the focus moved back from large companies to smaller ones and small business. There was also greater emphasis on the Australian end of the organisation. In other words, building up company readiness and working with organisations like AusIndustry to get small business more ready to export. There was certainly a greater use of information systems over that period of time and locally engaged staff were more involved in the front end of the organisation than had been done in the past. And I think also there was a move to specific targeted areas. That was basically, the direction of the organisation.

In regard to the structure itself, I think that it had pretty well settled down after McKinsey had been through the place and the Executive Directors and Managing Director had been appointed. Probably one of the key issues was when the major financial program ITES (International Trade Enhancement Scheme) wound down, I think the role of the Board declined. I simply say that because the Board was very involved with the financial programs as well as the organisation itself. But winding down of ITES, in my view, took a bit of emphasis off the role of the Board compared to the Executive.

In terms of the style of management I would say that both Ralph Evans and Charles Jamieson were ideal for their respective period in which they were Managing Directors. If you look at Ralph Evans, he came from a consultancy background, he was a strategic thinker and he had good organisational skills. He was also from the private sector and he understood where to take Austrade after McKinsey. He found that he could move the organisation that much further. Charles was more of a tactical person who understood politics.

Question: External politics or internal politics or both?

Peter Langhorne: Both. I think that Charles was able to handle the external politics better than Ralph. I think Charles would have had, as any insider would have had, a hell of job, bringing the organisation on from 1992 when McKinsey went through it and there were so many changes. It really needed an outsider and it needed someone who, to be frank, had to have a good strategic view and could think through the issues and can take the Executive with them in that regard. Ralph did that well.

Question: Business acumen wasn't too well known from normal civil servants and some of it needed to come from business itself. Is that a fair statement to make? Or was there, inside the old Department of Trade, people who had a pretty decent knowledge of business?

Peter Langhorne: I would say the latter. I think that there were people within, particularly in Austrade or the Trade Commission, who really did have a good understanding of business, a good knowledge of it and had worked well with it. The issue was really about how to extend the reach of the organisation and how to reorganise it. There were some questions of the MacAlister period. Look MacAlister might have had a good business background and I think that was an advantage.

But effectively he cut the organisation off from the government. And even though it was a statutory organisation, you just can't do that. And I think that led to a lot of the other problems in that there was a need after MacAlister to rebuild that relationship with government after the reorganisation. And of course, Bill Ferris was a major player in that role being chair of the Board, and Bill really saw that need to rebuild the relationship with the government and the relationship with the policy area of the Department of Trade.

Question: The issue is exacerbated by MacAlister's rupture with the Minister John Button. Whether Lindsay would have had the same issue with government if there was another minister, I'm not sure. But the rupture with Button probably looked like a rupture with government.

Peter Langhorne: Yes. Look, you're dead right. I mean, basically I worked with Button when I was at the CSIRO when he was Minister of Industry and Science. Even though we were on the opposite sides of politics Button was a very hard person to get off side. The bottom line simply was that Lindsay just couldn't work with him. And you just can't do that with a senior minister.

Question: On the other hand Lindsay was very warm towards John Dawkins.

Peter Langhorne: Yes I understand that. My view of the two of them was that Dawkins took a short term view of life while Button took the longer term view of life. And when Austrade moved into the Foreign Affairs and Trade portfolio, of course there was Bob McMullan who was an excellent Trade Minister. And Gareth Evans was Minister of Foreign Affairs and Trade. So I doubt that Lindsay wouldn't have survived that.

Just to conclude on the approach of the two managers – Evans and Jamieson – I would be very strong in my view that they were both right for their times.

In relation to landscape changes, I think there were a number of things that were occurring in that period. There was a move from commodities to services and at that stage Information Technology was the magic word. The organisation was moving into things like education, banking, finance, information technology and those sort of new areas. There was certainly quite a bit greater competition in the global business area. The Americans, the Europeans and a number of others, including some of the Asian countries, were getting more and more into trade promotion and pushing products. And China was emerging. There were also economic difficulties in places like Japan with their own economy. So there were quite a few changes on the global front that Austrade had to engage with and really it wasn't a matter of picking winners by any means. It was really a matter of assisting those companies that were emerging, the smaller companies that were coming into the marketplace and try and manage them in stages. For Austrade, areas such as information technology required in markets like the US establishing a presence in San Francisco with people like Peter Lewis. So there were quite a few changes externally as well as dealing with re-organisational changes and issues with budgets and so on. With so much happening internationally there was also the need to try and engage the Prime Minister and Senior Ministers more in trade promotion.

Question: I suppose you couldn't ask for a minister more well placed than Tim Fischer. So what do you remember of his ministership of that period?

Peter Langhorne: On the question of Tim Fischer, I have to have some bias here I think. The advantage for Austrade was that Tim was very keen on trade development and trade promotion. And I would say he was more inclined to be hands on trade promotion stuff rather than the policy.

Question: Why do you think that was the case?

Peter Langhorne: Well, I think he likes a lot of action. He likes things to happen and he certainly likes interfacing and interacting with business people. So the bottom line was that a trade mission was great for Tim because he had business people there, he could be involved on the diplomatic front, he liked to be involved with companies overseas. He could see things happening, whereas trade policy, as you know, it's a life time job. It just goes on forever. So I think the fact that when the government changed in 1996, there was perhaps a new level of enthusiasm. Naturally after a government's been in a place for a long time, there was a mix of bilateral, multilateral trade policy and promotion type activities. And I think that Tim enjoyed the work that Austrade did. He got on well with Allan Jackson who I think was Chairman of the Board then.

Question: He also got on well with Charles Jamieson?

Peter Langhorne: Yes he got on very well with Charles also. Charles was good at facilitating things and facilitating trade missions that would actually achieve something. A lot of that sort of "hands on" type activity was what pleased Tim Fischer.

Question: At the time of the Coalition victory in 1996 there was a bit of fear within Austrade that some Coalition voices such as Alexander Downer which had been extremely critical of Austrade in the press may become heavy handed with Austrade in government. Can you recollect any of that?

Peter Langhorne: Yes. Certainly I do recall it. It was when the Coalition came to power in 1996 and Downer was the Foreign Affairs minister. Downer and Tim Fischer of course were in Cabinet. Downer was very interested and keen in making sure that the Foreign Affairs and the Trade policy part, in other words, the departmental activities were well resourced. I guess Downer may have had some bias in favour of the actual Department of Foreign Affairs and Trade rather than Austrade. Of course there were within DFAT memories of McEwen who set up the Trade Commission Service as a foil to the diplomats because he didn't believe that they were doing what he wanted them to do – specifically working with business. I think both Downer and Andrew Peacock had some negative views about the Australian Trade Commission probably based on a view that it was too close to Labor.

Question: Alexander Downer's concerns about Austrade were quite public. I have never seen Andrew Peacock's public views on Austrade. Were they ever made public?

Peter Langhorne: Not to my knowledge. Look Peacock's views were in my view personal views, except to say that I feel he shared the views of a number of senior ministers at that time. In the changeover in 1996 he thought that Austrade was too close to the Labor Party and there were a number of ex-Labor staffers involved with Austrade. Being from the Coalition side I did feel that Austrade did tend to embrace Labor and that there was some bias there. There's no doubt that Downer saw the need to make changes and encouraged Tim Fischer to do so. But Tim was his own man and I feel he made the changes to the executive and Board that he saw necessary. I said to you before, I think that at the time, for someone like Charles, the time to take over was then.

Question: Yes. But Ralph resigned before any moves were made against him.

Peter Langhorne: The government at the time saw a need for change at the top. Obviously when a government changes there will be some level of bias. I wouldn't want to give the impression that Downer had undue influence over the organisation. I think that anything that happened during that change it was done in mutual agreement between Downer and Fischer. And that it was worked out in regards to the way that the department would actually work and that there's no doubt that Downer saw the need for change. Fortunately the Board and Allan Jackson got on very well with Fischer and of course at that stage, Tim supported my promotion to the position of Deputy Managing Director.

Question: That would have been 1996?

Peter Langhorne: When Ralph Evans left in 1996 I acted in that position for a short period of time, while the replacement was being made. The Board, and with the support of Fischer, appointed me. You could argue that this was more or less a political appointment though I wouldn't say that it was.

On the role that the Sydney Olympic Games in 2000 played for Australia's business opportunities, I think it was very important and in two ways. One is that it brought sport into the international trade area as an export marketing tool from a direct and indirect point of view. It enabled Austrade and Australia to showcase its prowess in building stadiums and running major events. At the same time, it also had some major spinoffs in terms of the effect that sport can be a money making international tool. So I think it really did a lot of good. I think the Games themselves, through the business club, saw a number of Australian companies introduced to buyers and I think the business club was very successful. My memory of it is fading a bit now, but my recollection is that the Olympic Games really did help.

I think the key thing from Austrade's point of view was that the Olympics enabled business people 'the sellers' to get in touch with 'the buyers' and the investors and to entertain them and to follow them up after the Games. Austrade did a lot of that follow up with business and I think a lot of that was productive. It was also used with the Atlanta Games in 1996. And I think there was some testing done in 1996 in Atlanta and I think that worked well. But I think the actual process flowed on, to a number of sporting events including through cricket in the UK and so on. My view is that it had a long term benefit. Certainly it had a medium-term benefit and it's one of those things, as you know that it's up to the business. Once those relationships or once the information is made, to then follow up and keep them going. I've never seen any actual outcomes in terms of how much in millions of dollars of business has done, but I think it was pretty extensive. But I think business was pretty happy with it.

Question: Tim Fischer made the same observation that you just did – I've never seen a dollar figure on the outcome of the games.

Peter Langhorne: Yes. Well, that's right. I mean you don't, because a lot of these things just go on but I'm sure at the end of the day if you were to do a poll of the business people who were there, one would find that a reasonably good percentage of them did get a follow up.

Question: Back to the question of the Austrade management – insider or outsider and different style of management. Is there anything else that you can add to that?

Peter Langhorne: Charles Jamieson was the right person for the job when he took over. He would have had a difficult time doing it back in 1992. I think the timing needs to be right. So my view was that there's a time for insiders and there's a time of outsiders. The time for insiders was after the organisation had been in place for about four or five years. That is when Charles took over. What did he bring to Austrade? Well look, I think Charles had excellent people management skills. He was very good at government relations. He saw the need to maintain a good relationship with ministers but also he was good at using politicians. He was good at using them both in Australia to promote business and particularly overseas. In terms of getting good trade missions, operating he did well with Tim Fischer and Mark Vaile. And he managed to make sure that Austrade got funding – even though in the timing of the budget was difficult, but Austrade wasn't in too much difficulty. He was certainly good up front. Charles was a good speaker and could work a room very well. They both had their strengths but I think Charles particularly was very good in interacting with business because he had a long background based overseas. But look, I think they both understood business very well and I think Charles probably if anything, managed to put in place arrangements while he was managing director that pretty well guaranteed that the organisation would continue well into the future in one form or another. Ralph did the groundwork and put the organisation structure in place and I think Charles built on that pretty strongly and I think that's been shown. The Board's gone now, it's now part of the Department again. But it still maintaining its independence to some extent, which is pretty good when you're in the Department of Foreign Affairs and Trade.

Question: I think Charles commissioned Boris Schedvin to do that trade commission history? You must have been involved in that in some way. Did you attend the launch of that book?

Peter Langhorne: No. I was away unfortunately. But I knew Charles worked with him as a teacher. Charles was also a keen Australian Rules footballer and had a wicked sense of humour too. He was a great entertainer and I think if I remember rightly he had a pretty good voice and he did play a reasonable guitar. But he was the right person for the job he delegated well. He was respected within the organisation and outside. And he only got involved with the day-to-day running of the organisation in terms of the workers, the other senior managers, when it was necessary. He empowered his people very well and I think that his sort of general relaxed management style flowed down through the organisation and it was pretty positive.

Question: In closing you left in 2001, we've just had the Olympic Games and we had the arrival of the New Millennium. What did you see on the horizon that Austrade would have to tackle and deal with as a challenge?

Peter Langhorne: During that period from 1992 to 2001 Austrade had really led the field in trade promotion around the world. We were well respected. I spoke at a number of international conferences and other trade promotions agencies were, to put it mildly, gobsmacked about what we were doing and the way we were empowering people and the support we were getting from government. I think one of the challenges was to keep it that way, which isn't easy. I think on the global horizon if you're looking at it, I think, the key things for Australia were the fact that eventually people in Austrade can see, not necessarily within the period that I was there, but the reliability on commodity trading was increased, that we had to push the agricultural trading, that services would become more and more important but more competitive and that there would be an unstable global picture situation and the need for bilateral trade was more and more important and that the emphasis on multilateral trade and relationship between multilateral trade and bilateral trade had to be built strongly. So the department and Austrade and other trade development areas, trade promotion area had to work closely together. I think that they were the sort of the key issues, I think that the biggest challenge for Austrade was increased competition in an unstable, global situation and you can see that from the global financial crisis just how quickly it can happen and there's a need to shore up the government's side of the business as much as you can. And to keep politicians engaged and business engaged, that's the key thing.

Question: Just a last question related to your comment there. The Abbott government has more or less ignored the national audit commission recommendation about abolishing Austrade. But the smell lingers all the time. Do you think this is a kind of a perennial thing or do you think that to some extent there's always been this threat?

Peter Langhorne: Well I think it's cyclical, but I think the later point is also relevant. With that last question I would say that one of Charles' major legacies, was that he laid the foundations with government for a strong organisation that really assured the organisation of what I believe would be a long life within the Department of Foreign Affairs and Trade. As I said earlier maintaining its independence and an important part of the organisation is continuation of course is that it's got to continue to be seen to be delivering and respected by business and adaptable to change. It obviously needs to be seen to be providing some service to government. Now, having said that and having actually been involved with the government when the decision was taken to abolish the Austrade Board and bring the organisation back into the public service; I think that while at the time that may not have been seen as a forward step for Austrade, I'm sure Ralph Evans would argue strongly that way. The fact that Austrade did come under the umbrella of the Department of Foreign Affairs and Trade more, I think is a real positive, because Foreign Affairs and Trade is a very strong department. The organisation of Foreign Affairs and Trade see more now, that trade promotion is a positive. There is probably more work undertaken by the diplomats now in the trade area than there might have been previously.

Question: As in more economic diplomacy?

Peter Langhorne: Yes, that's right. And of course, heads of missions like to have their names attached to successes. But I think the bottom line simply is that once Foreign Affairs and Trade gets an added function it hates losing it. It might modify, play with it, and the same will happen with AusAid. You can kick it around, but it doesn't like losing functions. And at the end of the day I think that's why there will be some strength there. And look, the Austrade Board in the end was really not adding a great deal of value to the organisation. But I know that a lot of people would disagree with me. The fact that Ralph laid down a strong foundation with business and set the strategic direction and that Charles made the right tactical decisions and worked well with DFAT and government, will make sure that Austrade does continue.

Interview conducted on 8 September 2014

11

Leading from the front

Interview with Tim Fischer

Question: What were some of the highlights of your time as Minister for Trade when you had responsibility for Austrade?

Tim Fischer: It was a great privilege to be covering Austrade for a few years in the first term and a half of the John Howard government. The few standouts were revamping the Export Market Development Grant scheme and pursuing a view that you could run and chew gum at the same time. You could pursue multilateral and bilateral and regional for that matter, concurrently and a raft of meetings – and it got down to persuading the Mexicans to abolish their coal tariff and their wool tariff, so we could get Roger Fletcher's semi-processed wool from Dubbo into Mexico where it was made up into suits and under NAFTA into the US effectively with no tariff. So that was getting right down to – a combination of bilateral and then NAFTA regional – to that level of detail as well as the broader WTO Uruguay Round and all that stuff.

On the Export Market Development Grant scheme, when I became the Minister, there were originally twelve areas of application for subsidies or grants. Six of them were being widely abused. People were driving bloody containers through them and one lady is in jail for lifting half a million dollars out of the scheme without exporting one container. We tightened right down to six simple areas of application in the Export Market Development Grant scheme by a bit of manoeuvring and got that legislation through the senate. It produced a reduction of the pool but it was more streamlined and it worked better. I am always reminded by New Zealand which has quite a tidy export effort and at the same time has zero export market development grant schemes.

Question: What were the landscape changes in Australia and the globe which required Austrade to engage with during the period of your Ministership of Austrade?

Tim Fischer: Emergence of Regional and Bilateral initiatives as the post Uruguay Round multi-lateral stalled and Doha later on jammed.

Question: You seemed to well-liked and appreciated by all in Austrade irrespective of their political views or levels of responsibility. How did you manage to get that appreciation?

Tim Fischer: Well, I was hands on, I was in close contact. I quickly came to give them [Austrade] time when I was in capital X, Y, and Z and not just belt through. Unlike certain other ministers I generally asked 15 minutes to meet all the staff at the Embassies including the local engaged staff. Some staff had been employed by Australia for 30-40 years and never met a Minister once. For me it was normal management and thing to do but it also reflected my interest and motivation.

I was always looking for a few good standout examples of breakthroughs which I would highlight to build the export genre of Australia and the export effort of Australia. When Mick Denigan (Mick's Whips) selling his hand patented web computer to the web, to the world, and wondering why there were so many cattle in San Francisco and Amsterdam requiring his whip. And I said, "Don't worry about it, they're all export items just keep selling them." Or whether it was Roger Fletcher's processed wool from Dubbo to Cuernavaca in Mexico and then into the – NAFTA countries or a raft in between including the difficult negotiations with the USA, USTR over things like Howe Leather, and cattle tariff, meat tariffs. The best way to engage activate your department and your unit in this case Austrade was to outreach to them and not do otherwise and I had to make a whole lot of contact.

Question: The recent announcement of the Audit Commission was a difficult exercise for Austrade to manage especially when there was a recommendation for its closure. What are your thoughts on this matter?

Tim Fischer: Yes with DFAT jamming one way and Treasury the other.

Question: You were still the Minister responsible for Austrade in the lead up to the Olympic Games. What was your estimation of the effect of the Games on business and trade opportunities?

Tim Fischer: It's a bit nebulous though isn't it because they had this Executive Business Club walk in walk out. They had all these CEOs from various companies in the world some of whom may have ended up doing business in Australia but many of them here on a jolly. I kept on asking how do you sort out the wheat from the chaff? I think I had moved on by this time. Actually to this day I query the *Lords of the Rings* template and seriously query whether dollar for value because nobody tipped the bucket on Austrade because they very much enjoyed the Austrade Australian wine, the Austrade lamb, at a marquee somewhere out at Homebush or Darling Harbour. How should I put maybe there were many business deals struck as a direct consequence I am always a bit jaundice about that. But was it a professional effort did they engage with several hundred businessmen, some of whom – I don't think they paid any airfares – so it was a question of catering for event and making a mark. I do not know if anyone has done a subsequent report on the aftermath 12-14 years on from the Sydney Olympics maybe it did lead to extra investments connectivity. It's very hard to know.

Question: It raises another issue on performance measures on an organisation. So how do you know if you are getting value for your organisation which was Tony Shepherd's recommendation?

Tim Fischer: Well his recommendation was closure of Austrade and roll it into DFAT. It comes up from time to time. EFIC could bring about a huge leap in exports of thin-hulled ferries to give you one particular example in Malta and Argentina. I last had lunch with Bruce Gosper six months ago and I will do it again one day but I think once you're an ex, you're an ex. I think he's finding it very tough going. Good man. He knows his stuff and knows the cynicism.

Question: The Coalition came to power in 1996. What changes did you see as a result of this government change? How was your approach different from that of Labor?

Tim Fischer: Pursuit of all openings and opportunities, not just the multi-lateral, so run and chew gum as I mentioned and right down into the detail to obtain breakthroughs like Fletcher International to Mexico and the USA, GMH engines to various outlets and so forth. BHP and other big outfits were generally able to look after themselves but occasionally they also called on Government in terms of getting international access.

Question: What was your view of Charles Jamieson's management of Austrade the only MD/CEO appointed from the "inside", i.e., as an existing Austrader. What are the pluses and minuses of "outside" and "inside" appointments to the top job?

Tim Fischer: I think Charles Jamieson was the best applicant for the job, pure and simple and there can be no hard fast rule on an insider or outsider. Sometimes a good CEO recruitment can work from within and sometimes without. Outsiders can unnecessarily rip the fabric in bringing change that is not thought through but equally can bring new focus. Insiders can be too beholden to mates but equally know that which works well and that which does not and can so act on this.

I was close to Charles in a professional sense and my wife with his wife in a social setting. At one level there was a professional connection and within the scope of horrific schedules we both had there was a little bit more than just a professional perhaps. I thought he was capable, of initiative with determination and helped bring about – you've might have heard – yes, the export of sand to Saudi Arabia and Dubai. Because you can pump Australian sand vertically but you can't pump Saudi sand vertically amongst other things. And we opened up

Lima, Peru and a few other places. Where Austrade should do better is where the natural alignments are lesser. So you do need the prodding of Austrade and the businessmen arriving at midnight on a flight for 48 hours, and if you've got any sense, we'll have the Austrade officer in Lima, Peru set up his room because it'll save him several hours. It's worth paying a couple of thousand dollars to get that much extra done and language and all. So that's happened so well and on occasions and eventually a really good company ended up poaching the Austrade officers in South America for that purpose I thought Charles was a very good CEO. He may have one or two detractors, though I don't remember or of people tipping buckets on him. And I was very sorry to learn of his recent departure.

Question: How did Charles Jamieson operate with you and the Board?

Tim Fischer: Well, at that stage he was still beholden to a Board. Alan Jackson was Chairman of the Board at the time and that was not without its pickles. Because Jackson being Jackson and subsequently blowing up spectacularly if you Google it you will see it all there. I think Charles was hands on. I don't think he was a bombastic manager. I think he tried to reach out and create, aware with all and lead people by example, by extension of his efforts as long serving Trade Commissioner in the Middle East.

Question: What do you think of the role of the Board in Austrade?

Tim Fischer: On the Board I feel that people like Nixon Apple and others made very good contributions to the Board. The problem was having a board that gets in between the Minister, the Chairman and the CEO (and Tourism Australia) and thereby causing some spectacular flare outs at various stages. The Minister needs to respect and deal with a Board and its chairman and its director. It is different from a Minister running a department outright. Comprises of finesse – yes, the Minister will always be listened to and specific directions will be adhered to – some people are better suited for the role of Minister of Trade than others.

Question: One senior trade spokesperson once said that any agency needs to be as close to the PM and Cabinet as possible to have clout. What do you think?

Tim Fischer: Well we could not be much closer than what we were. You needed to get the Prime Minister (PM) focused on trade. The Prime Minister put in a bit of effort with bilateral negotiations on the USFTA but you were never going to get or rarely get – and only where you have a savvy Ambassador working very closely with his Trade Commissioner – two hours in a Prime Minister's program to launch some Australian product in some overseas capital. The PM's schedule were from hell and if it involved two days on a Texas ranch with Bush well that meant there were two less days in the USA to do any promotional activity. But getting that sort of line injected into the schedule was difficult. For that matter, I had to keep an eye on my own schedule. If you drive out of Milan stuck in traffic for an hour, opening up a site on a Saturday morning, related to the wool industry north of Milan. You were probably were with us on that day, and if you asked me what the hell I opened, I have no idea. I remember the morning, I know it took hours in the traffic, I was a bit pissed off.

Question: Being close to the prime Minister and being Deputy Prime Minister must have been useful for the Austrade portfolio.

Tim Fischer: Well, it would help any portfolio. Whether it was transport or trade or science. If I had a particular fixation about something in my 8.30 meeting every parliamentary sitting day with the Prime Minister, a few words of information to the Prime Minister on something I wanted to get across to him that was fast breaking in my portfolio or for that matter with John Moore's portfolio. We were having a huge fight about Howe leather with the yanks. We had a little problem with South Africa the BMW factory. Some of the leather was coming through from Australia with brand marks on it. And so they couldn't use it as a seat for the luxury cars. And surely as a minimum standard you can get the bloody branding right. And – so every other state had branding and that's what goes with the way we put it on the rump, more particularly now. And they didn't get it. They would now need to make seconds of them. They pushed back we've got the right to brand where we want to. I thought well there goes your market. We'll it's your call. I got really angry with them. So a good minister can cut through with the particularity of methods and I called that one particularly well because I hit out because it was a fixable problem and we needed to fix it. But sometimes involving the prime minister for help well ... you might put in a bid for one particular thing you might do in that particular country. Prime ministerial travel might be geared in going to Gallipoli or in doing the South Pacific forum and its not possible to always get this across. The point person for that is for the Trade Commissioner to develop a very good relationship with the Ambassador so that the reconnaissance party for the Prime Minister's office is given two or three ideas that are so interesting and sexy and one of them will get up. They come up maybe a month before the Prime Minister arrives. If they know he's going to visit Rome for the G8, where its two months out, there's a visit one month out. A draft program is made up. He wants to see the Pope and so forth. And then we had another group arrive two days out and then the group on the Prime Minister's plane wanted to change things again. Well do that and you won't get a call on the Pope. The Pope will not change. He's only available or you'll be pushed back to Saturday and you will be lucky and only after Obama sees him on the Friday. You have a perfectly good spot on Thursday morning. I happen to know, your other bilaterals, and G8 commitments don't require the Prime Minister. Your call, but I, as Ambassador to the Holy See, will not accept responsibility for the Prime Minister not seeing the Pope, but that's what you are putting at risk. And so we had a slanging match with the PM's office and then went back to the original time suggested.

Question: Do you think trade commissioners are generally able to handle and work with business?

Tim Fischer: I think there was the odd exchange program for Austrade and different personnel with various business companies and vice versa. It was never meant to permanent. Those who did it always said they'd got a lot out of it. But I mean a capable public service trade commissioner having come through a university and come through a couple of years of junior postings, ought to be able to understand a busy businessman who has clocked into Milan for 40 hours looking for a deal on X Y and Z. It's not rocket science and Goyder of Wesfarmers en route to Davos, was a shrewd businessman and never wasted his time in looking for information that might be helpful for him.

Amanda Vanstone as Ambassador [In Italy] working with Austrade and so forth had an approach from an Australian company which was having an $A18 million problem with the Italian government. It had gone on for a couple of years. She had the right knowledge, made the right contact, submitted the right representation, at the right level and got them into a meeting. 28 days later, they have paid the 18 million Australian dollars owed. The company involved said to her, "What do you want maybe a letter of thanks". I said you bloody fool. She said, "What?" You should have stipulated that they qualify their annual accounts and say our figures for this particular year were 18 million dollars better as a direct consequence of the actions taken by the Australian Ambassador for Italy Amanda Vanstone. Just the one paragraph, it would have come out eight or nine months later. So it wouldn't have caused any trouble and which *The Financial Review* would have picked up on. Part of my beef with DFAT and Austrade is that they are not good at selling and singing their success story. And as a consequence when they get scrutinised they get clobbered.

Question: Austrade can only help a small number of exporters around four per cent. The Commission of Audit would probably see this as adding little value to exports. What is your view on the right balance?

Tim Fischer: Both DFAT and Austrade need to learn how to sell their success stories. And I'll give you a couple of examples. On Friday the night of 13 January 2012, the captain of the Costa Concordia steered his ship on the two rocks, rocks which had on every map of the Mediterranean for the last 500 years. The court case continues and it has just been towed to Genoa for scrap. By 9:45 at night, at least 32 people had drowned. By midnight, we had consular staff, lead Jenny Hobbs, moving up the coast to Porto Stefano where the remaining passengers were expected to come ashore. By 6 am the next day we heard from the deputy harbour master of the manifest in the port of Civitavecchia no ship can sail without a manifest. They hung an Australian flag outside a coffee shop. By lunch time the following day, 21 of the 23 Australians known to be on the boat were accounted for and processing starting for passport replacement to allow return to the airports and emergency loans. Remembering all the passports are in the bursars office of the ship at the bottom of the sea. Two were missing, two 80-year-olds. They knew from the manifest they were 80-year-olds. Four o'clock in the afternoon, they skipped in and said, they just had the most exciting day of their lives. They said "we decided to have a long lunch, we could see the Australian flag straight down the street before we resume our normal life". So 23 out of 23 Australians are accounted for by sunset on the Saturday. DFAT and our Ambassador wanted to head it up. And of course Canberra said, "No, we'll handle it back here." An Ambassador on the spot doing radio interviews on the middle of the weekend would not contradict Canberra would be an enhancement of a bloody good story of a consular reaction on a weekend up the coast of Italy unexpected circumstances and all 23 Australians accounted for. So do we read about that in the DFAT annual report – NO. You'll read about it in my book, *Holy See and Holy Me – One thousand days in Rome*, because I really bang on about it.

On Austrade – we put out a little pamphlet called the, "The Yellow Peril," in Austrade. I wanted 12 sexy examples of trade breakthroughs. The orange growers are complaining bitterly for allowing Brazilians to concentrate into Australia and so forth. Essentially it was Austrade stories and I also implemented an annual statement of trade and export efforts. Again to try and up the profile of some of the great efforts that were being done by business and to encourage a much more export orientated country.

Question: What do you see as Austrade's key defining aspects?

Tim Fischer: An ability to cut through and point to export opportunities that are otherwise under recognised. Their network is Team Australia's vital network and is usually the core of Austrade or should be with information flow et al.

Interview conducted on 24 July 2014

12

"Doubling the number of exporters"

Greg Joffe

This chapter covers a period in the early to mid-2000s when Austrade shifted its focus to a greater emphasis on identifying and assisting potential exporters. It covers the underlying rationale, how the idea was developed and progressed, the public policy issues of setting stretch targets, key strategic initiatives and organisational changes made to align with the doubling objective and the outcomes from the initiative. It examines the outcomes of the strategic initiative and finds that the Bold Hairy Audacious Goal (BHAG) of doubling the number of exporters spurred significant internal and partnership activity to help Australian companies successfully into export.

Background on why Austrade set the target to 'Double the number of exporters'

Where does Austrade make the biggest difference?

A key question for Austrade has always been where it can add the most value. The McKinsey & Company review of December 1990 discussed the need to work in markets where Austrade added more value, whilst highlight the importance of supporting 'old hands' whilst also providing services to high potential and smaller clients and shifting the motivation of non-exporters. This debate about which companies to assist continued through the 1990s. At its simplest there is a spectrum from helping existing (often large) Australian exporters to win large $ deals in existing and new markets through to helping non exporters (usually smaller companies) to become successful exporters. The former deliver bigger $ of export impact, but the latter may over time make a significant difference to Australia's economy and Austrade's contribution may be more critical for these smaller companies.

The Austrade Executive and Strategic Development,[1] wished to better understand how much incremental success was delivered through Austrade's assistance to different companies. If Austrade helped a large existing exporter to continue exporting, were we really making a difference for Australia? One way to better understand our marginal impact was through the use of ratings. Exporters we assisted were asked to fill in forms (Export Impact forms) stating the magnitude of the exports in $ and also to rate the relative impact of Austrade's assistance in relation to achieving the export sale(s).

Understanding the potential exporter and exporter community

In the early 2000s Strategic Development undertook a significant research project to better understand the potential exporters and exporters. We were lucky to have a team of high quality researchers.[2] The research delivered a number of interesting findings including that:

1. There were around 25,000 exporters in 2000-1. This meant that only four per cent of Australian businesses were exporting.

2. The number of Australian small and medium enterprises (SMEs) exporting was relatively low: In European

---

1 The author, Greg Joffe, led Strategic Development in Austrade from 1997 to 2003.
2 Frederique Goy (project manager), Preety Duggal, Belinda Everingham, Tim Harcourt (Chief Economist), Greg Joffe, Yat To Lee, Simon Lees, Declan McCrohan, Robert Samuel, Glenys Schunter, Hala Shash and Bernice Shen.

countries about 30-80 per cent of SMEs exported; Canada's ratio was 15 per cent, and Australia and the US were four per cent and three per cent respectively.[3]

3. There was good evidence that exporting benefitted Australia in a number of ways: both for the individual companies involved and also for the economy as a whole:

- Relative to non-exporters, exporters are more efficient, more innovative, invest more in human capital and provide higher quality jobs and better working conditions. Exporters also apply knowledge and adopt technology faster than non-exporters.[4]

- Exporting enables a higher volume which supports economies of scale.

- Firm level efficiency benefits from exporting flow through to the broader economy, resulting in increased productivity.

- There were also social benefits including impact on living standards through job quality and job creation and knowledge transfer; rural growth; openness to international culture and international relations and linkages.

The research team developed a 90-page report *"Knowing and Growing the Exporter Community"*, which was published in 2002. In developing the report, the Strategic Development team sought to turn the insights into practical guidance setting out what Austrade and others should do. We didn't want to produce an interesting report; we wanted to produce work that made a positive difference for Australian exports and Australian exporters.

---

3 Of course Europe's geography and the EU are the key drivers for these differences.
4 The economic case for exports was set out in an earlier publication, *Why Australia Needs Exports: The Economic Case for Exporting*, Australian Trade Commission, 2000. This work was done by Austrade's Chief Economist Tim Harcourt supported by two analysts.

Developing the BHAG – "Double the number of exporters"

Around the time that the Exporter analyses were being undertaken, a number of senior Austrade personnel participated in the Executive Leadership Forum (ELF) in Katoomba. The attendees analysed Austrade's strategies and direction under the guidance of Roger Collins of the University of NSW and came to the conclusion that Austrade needed a new sense of purpose and direction. The feeling was that Austrade had reached (or even overshot) a *strategic inflection point* and something fairly radical needed to be done if the organisation was to remain relevant to the Australian export and investment community.

One of the business ideas current at that time was the concept of the BHAG – the Bold Hairy Audacious Goal. The term seems to have originated from Stanford University academics Jim Collins and Jerry Porras' 1994 book entitled *Built to Last: Successful Habits of Visionary Companies*. Through these two stands (the search for a new and meaningful purpose and the concept of a BHAG), the idea arose to "double the number of exporters". The idea was to create a "light on the hill" objective that was clear and unambiguous; finding new and potential exporters, working with them to achieve an initial export sale and helping them to become sustainable.

Selling the concept of "doubling"

The next step was to turn the idea into strategy. Austrade's Managing Director, Charles Jamieson, was a supporter of the "Knowing and Growing the Exporter Community" work. Strategic Development had briefed him regularly as it progressed. Obviously having the MD's support was critical to any change in strategy. We briefed him on the insights from the research and also tested with him the idea of setting the "Doubling BHAG". The Managing Director was supportive. He also wanted to ensure the Executive were all on board.

The Executive team at the time was structured geographically, with Regional Directors for different geographies. At our next global Executive meeting, we ran the Executive through the research, the benefits of increasing the number of exporters and the proposed BHAG. The Executive were enthusiastic and strongly supported the proposed BHAG.

The Austrade Board was briefed and also supported the Doubling objective. Finally, we briefed the Trade Minister, Mark Vaile, who was very supportive of the idea. All of these stakeholders understood that the objective was aspirational – it created momentum for significant change, rather than being a concrete target to drive performance for the next few years.

We discussed the risk of not achieving the doubling target with the Minister who understood the risk but also appreciated the political and economic possibilities inherent in the initiative. The objective of Doubling the Number of Exporters over Five Years was built into the storyline for the "Knowing and Growing the Exporter Community" report and Minister Vaile wrote the forward for the report. The report identified an Australian Bureau of Statistics baseline of 25,000 exporters in 2000-1 and the target of 50,000 exporters by 2006-7.

Public policy issue – the interplay between politics and outcomes targets?

There was an interesting public policy issue when we set the specific target of doubling the number of exporters over five years. For politicians and government departments, setting specific outcome[5] targets, especially BHAG targets, can be risky. If the target is achieved – it is a "nice, positive result". If however, the agency fails to meet the

---

5 A key shift in the past two decades in government policy has been the shift from activity or output measures ("what did the agency, deliver?") to outcome measures ("how is Australia better off because of the outputs delivered by the agency?"). Outcome measures are often harder to measure, and many outcomes are influenced by a wide range of economic or societal factors, not just the outputs of the government agency. They can also take longer to become measurable. As an example, it is easy to measure and take responsibility for the number of classes taught in a school (output measure), but harder to impact educational outcomes without also considering a range of social factors such as the socio-economic, cultural and linguistic backgrounds of the students.

target, this leaves the agency open to criticism by other agencies that may seek to grow their own budgets at the expense of the agency in question (for instance by running an argument that "they can't even deliver what they were supposed to"). Not achieving specific targets can also result in questions by Parliamentary and Senate Committees such as Senate Estimates where the agency is asked why the targets were not met. The minister may face similar political risks if she or he sets and then does not achieve the desired targets.

Whilst the doubling strategy was underway, a wide range of views on the pros and cons of BHAG targets were expressed by Austraders and various other stakeholders. These included:

> a. that it was great that the agency was trying to achieve something so significant and that it was okay to aim for big impacts and potentially fall short. As Minister Vaile said (to paraphrase), "it is great to have an aspirational target like this; even if we fall short we will still have created a significant increase in the number of Australian exporters which is a positive outcome for Australia".

> b. Others, including those who may have thought a previous Prime Minister Bob Hawke had been wrong to set the BHAG of "No child shall live in poverty" warned of the folly of setting a hard aspirational target that would be difficult to achieve and that could expose the organisation to criticism.

The target was broken down into key components

The target to double the number of exporters from 25,000 to 50,000 by 2006-7 was broken into three components:

- Direct assistance by Austrade to new or irregular exporters – 9,000.
- Assistance by Austrade allies to new or irregular exporter - 4,000.
- Natural growth in the number of exporters (trend) – 12,000.

There were four key strategic themes to support the doubling objective

A number of initiatives were developed and implemented to support the doubling. These included:

1. **Promotion of the importance of exporting to the general and business community**. Austrade ramped up its promotion of the importance of exporting for Australia and Australian firms. Austrade's Chief Economist, Tim Harcourt, who is an excellent communicator of economics, had previously released a paper on "Why Australia needs exports". Harcourt also wrote a number of further articles and presented in many fora on the importance of exporting. Other Austraders spoke of the importance of exports in presentations throughout Australia. In addition Austrade continued the Australian Export Awards, as well as the Business Club Australia program which encouraged business links connected with major sporting events.

2. **Identifying potential or irregular exporters, analysing what capability building they would need to become successful exporters, and assisting them successfully into export.**

   Austrade developed strong and clear sourcing and servicing approaches:

   Sourcing: Potential and irregular exporters were identified through a range of mechanisms including Direct Marketing tools and data bases. The target companies were contacted with tailored messages to drive a heightened awareness of the benefits of exporting.

   Servicing: The companies' "export readiness" was assessed and tailored support provided to help the company prepare for export. A triage system was used to align support to need. This approach was methodically refined over the years including upskilling and managing TradeStart Advisors, together with Austrade Advisors as one team. The Industry Specialist Units also played their part by providing global industry expertise.

3. **Partnerships with partners including State and Territory export agencies, chambers of commerce and corporates**. The doubling objective required a massive shift in outcomes. To achieve success it was critical to work with a range of partners, including State and Territory export promotion agencies, chambers of commerce and corporate partners to help identify and assist potential exporters. Key initiatives included *TradeStart* where regional offices run by partners were opened around Australia. Austrade provided resources, guidelines, and access to Austrade systems, and jointly hosted presentations by overseas Austraders to engage with businesses. Over time a range of State and Territory agencies, chambers of commerce and others joined *TradeStart*.

There was also a significant *Corporate Partnerships* program. These were partnerships with professional services firms and their respective institutes. Partners included lawyers, bankers and accountants. Austrade provided guides, content and training on internationalisation to partners' staff and to their clients. The objective was to support these existing business relationships and help the corporate partners to support their clients successfully into export. All of the Big 4 accounting firms, the mid-tier accounting firms, all of the Australian Banks, plus some of the Internationals banks and a number of the major law firms became involved with clearly defined objectives under Strategic Alliance Arrangements. These programs have been described as "franchising of Austrade's operations".

Online

Austrade recognised the importance of the role of the internet in facilitating trade. In 1999 we ran a project on the Information Age which resulted in shifts to ensure the organisation fully leveraged the changing environment.[6] During the doubling initiative, online activities included:

- Setting up websites to promote companies direct to buyers – generally themed around a particular product or niche. An early example was Pugglekids, a website promoting Australian children's wear. Austrade sponsored websites proliferated over the course of the doubling project – many posts set them up as well.
- Austrade's point to point (office to office) video conferencing links were also brought into play. Samples would be sent to post, buyers would come into the post, sellers would come into an Austrade office in Australia at an agreed time and make their pitch – and get instant feedback – by video link. Virtual wine tastings were a popular example of this approach.

Changes in KPIs were key to the strategy

Since Ralph Evan's time as Managing Director, Austrade had set and reported on clear Key Performance Indicators (KPIs) and KPI targets. These included measures such as the number of exporters, the $ of export deals where Austrade assisted, $ of inward investment attracted and client satisfaction. KPIs were set for the organisation overall, and then allocated to regions and posts. In a number of cases in the overseas network, KPIs were also allocated to individual Austraders.

6 These included: moving information online that was previously provided by fax and face to face, to free up resources for more value add activities, providing information on how to sell online – directly and via emerging marketplaces and technological enablement of the organization and our staff.

In line with the saying "what gets measured gets done", Austraders focused on their KPIs.

The Executive were keenly aware of the need to adjust the KPIs to focus the organisation on the doubling objective. The Doubling required an increased focus on potential and new exporters, *whilst continuing* to support existing exporters. It made no sense to help new companies into export if they or existing companies did not then receive ongoing support that was needed to successfully remain in export. We spent considerable time developing amended Key Performance Indicators to drive resourcing and focus. Two new measures, "number of new or irregular exporters assisted to an export sale" and "$ of those export sales" were added to the existing KPIs. We debated the relative weightings and agreed on high weightings for the new exporter KPIs to encourage an increased focus on new exporters, whilst retaining the existing exporters KPIs at their existing weightings. Recognising the importance of assisting first time exporters to become consistent exporters 'the overall number of exporters assisted to an export sale' remained as a KPI.

An early issue between the offshore and onshore network was who would be attributed with the export success. This was resolved by giving the offshore the "attribution" for any success on the basis that they were closer to the sale. Australian based exports advisers were noted as "contributors". The KPIs were reviewed and refined as the program progressed.

The structure was aligned with the Strategy[7]

By 2003, a new Managing Director, Peter O'Byrne, was appointed with a clear mandate by Minister Vaile to continue with the doubling strategy and he (the Managing Director) devised, with input from

---

7 I am indebted to Geoff Spears who was Manager, Client Advisory Services and then General Manager (Industry) during the doubling period for much of the content of this chapter, particularly this section and the outcomes achieved section. Also thanks to Leith Doody and Mark Gwizdalla who both worked in senior management roles in Victoria during the doubling period.

Strategic Development, his senior executive team and consultants, a new structure to implement that strategy.

The Australian operations were formed into two divisions: one to **source** clients and build a pipeline of clients (Exporter Development (Sourcing)) and the other to **service** and coach clients in Australia and link them up with posts (Client Services (Servicing)). Two new directors were recruited from the private sector to drive these changes.

The sourcing division comprised three former global industry teams (Food and Beverage, Services and ICT) as it was thought these sectors would deliver the highest number of new exporters and the Austrade Hotline because they would field the incoming requests for assistance arising from the marketing of the new program. State managers were also included in this division due to their links with state government departments and the need to leverage their support for the program.

The servicing division comprised the remaining global industry team members (major projects, infrastructure, mining, agribusiness and consumer products, health, biotechnology, automotive, advanced manufacturing and defence), plus the regional export advisers and the export assistance marketing unit. Within servicing, one group was formed to work exclusively with new and irregular exporters and also to administer the Tradestart program, the delivery of Austrade's services via state and regional governments and industry associations. The other group serviced existing exporters in Australia, the bulk of Austrade's client base.

During the first two to three years of the program there was a great deal of sensitivity and overlap between the sourcing and servicing divisions in Australia due mainly to the fact that many in the sourcing team wanted to continue to work with clients rather than passing them across to the servicing division. This was eventually resolved by the amalgamation of the two divisions under one director (Exporter Services) and a restructuring of the teams. Sourcing a steady flow of quality clients remained an ongoing problem for the organisation and the offshore regions complained they didn't have enough referrals to achieve their targets. Structural change in the offshore offices was less dramatic than in Australia due to the smaller staff numbers involved in each post relative to the overall operations in Australia.

Summary of changes to drive the doubling

Table 1 summarises the key changes put in place to support the doubling objective, using Nous Group's Organisation Architecture pyramid.[8]

Table 1: Summary of changes to support the doubling objective

Component of organisation architecture	Key changes
Purpose	We shifted our purpose to focus more to identifying and supporting potential and irregular exporters and successfully helping them to export, as well as continuing to support existing exporters.
Strategy	We created a new 3 year strategy document, highlighting the increased focus on new and irregular exporters. Key strategic themes included: • Increasing intention to export • Increasing opportunities for accidental exporters • Increasing the success rate of intending exporters • Boosting the number of 'born globals', and • Boosting the number of regular exporters.

---

8 www.nousgroup.com.au

Component of organisation architecture	Key changes
Business/operating model	The core business model remained the same. Australian Operations would identify potential exporters, and pass the exporters to the overseas posts. The overseas posts would endeavour to find purchasers for the goods and services of the Australian companies. The posts would seek out opportunities for offshore sales, and send them to Australia for potential exporters. As discussed above, a key shift in the business model was to work closely with State and Territory government trade promotion agencies and other partners. These agencies sometimes had stronger links with potential exporters and exporters in their jurisdiction through their range of business support programs. The business model therefore relied on strong cooperation so that partners would identify potential exporters, help them assess if they were ready for export, build export capabilities, and then work with Austrade to select markets and successfully find buyers in those markets.
Allies and partners	As above, strong alliances with State and Territory government export agencies and other partners were a critical part of the doubling initiative.

Component of organisation architecture	Key changes
Business processes	Step by step processes for Austrade (in Australia and offshore) and partners were agreed. These built on existing business processes.
	Nous worked with the State and Territory governments to develop screening criteria and tailored training for potential exporters to help businesses establish if they were ready for export. Protocols for what Austrade would do and what partners would do were put in place. The aim was to have a common approach to the journey to export.
Workforce	Austrade needed to deepen two key skills in our own staff:
	1. Negotiating and working effectively with partners including State and Territory export agencies, chambers of commerce and corporate partners to create an integrated system to support companies into export. 2. The ability to work with often underprepared first time exporters. For some posts overseas this was a significant shift, requiring a preparedness to spend time coaching and guiding potential exporters.
	In addition, Export advisers in TradeStart were given extensive training to enable them to better 'coach' new exporters achieve export success. Annual Export Adviser conferences were a catalyst in building knowledge, skills enhancement, and enthusiasm. Up to 180 export and TradeStart advisers throughout Australia plus some offshore representatives, came together to be exposed to new ideas, to train, share best practice and for personal development.

Component of organisation architecture	Key changes
Culture	Austrade in this period had a strong outcomes focus driven by Key Performance Indicators (KPIs). KPIs were changed to shift the organisational focus. Other key mechanisms to shift the culture included: communications from the Managing Director and Executive to the organisation/their divisions, and the increased collaboration by many Austraders with partners.
Physical assets	As part of the shift to support new exporters, Austrade and allies established a network of TradeStart offices around the country.
Organisation design, including roles and responsibilities and collaboration and cooperation mechanisms	Australian Operations was substantially restructured as discussed above.
IT systems	Austrade developed systems to better integrate with TradeStart offices and with other partners. In the course of the doubling program Austrade also developed a better Client Relationship Management System (CRM) to help track the progress of new clients and their likelihood of success.

Challenges during implementation

One key challenge was the need to work with **non 'export ready'** potential and new exporters. Many posts very seriously questioned the ability of potential and new exporters to succeed in their market. They did not believe Austrade should be focusing on these types of exporters, and they thought that allocating resources to export preparation and intensive export coaching was not a good decision. Over time, the organisation focus, KPIs, senior management effort and work by Australian Operations and the rest of the organisation all shifted the organisation to better support potential and new exporters.

Although the target was set as an aspirational target, the year by year **targets** were broken down and allocated to regions, posts and (in some overseas locations) individuals. This was required to focus Austraders on the targets, but it had some adverse consequences, including competition between Austraders for new exporters.

A major issue in the early years was the lack of a **coordination** between offshore and onshore i.e., at times it seemed there were "five little Austrades" (each region) with each running their own race in order to meet the targets they had been given. Some of the adverse behaviours of the offshore post staff included: travelling frequently to Australia looking to directly recruit new clients without advising the key client managers in Australia; and trawling Austrade's Core Business System, (CBS) for records of new clients and approaching them to focus on their region for that important first sale. NEA was the most visible region in this regard; but it should be noted that NEA was also the outstanding performer in achieving and exceeding their target numbers. This issue reduced as the program settled down and the Executive put in place clearer guidelines.

So what happened?

Like most major change programs, doubling the number of exporters had significant supporters and also detractors. Many Austraders enthusiastically shifted their focus to work more closely with partners to identify and support potential exporters and to assist more potential and new exporters. Others considered the doubling objective a distraction and continued to work mainly with medium and large existing exporters who could continue to deliver significant export $. Overall significant energy and effort was exerted on the doubling program, both in Australia and throughout the overseas network.

The targets in the first two years of the program were relatively easier to achieve than in later years because of "the low hanging fruit" factor and also because the target was significantly increased every year. As export advisers and marketing officers were driven by numbers, there was tendency to concentrate on clients in industries which could deliver quick results. For example, education trade shows could provide a quick and easy export sale as new students signed on to study at Australian universities and other educational institutions.

Austrade expended significant additional effort promoting export and working with partners in Australia to target potential exporters. Through this work support for export in the community grew, and the number of companies assisted by Austrade grew significantly.

Number of companies assisted and $ exports by those companies rose significantly

Total number of exporters rose over time as shown in Figure 1. Although the aspirational target of 50,000 exporters was not reached, the actual figures by 2006-7 were just below 45,000, a significant increase from 25,000.

Unfortunately in 2005-6, the ABS changed its methodology for estimating the number of exporters. Therefore, we cannot be sure how successful or unsuccessful Austrade was in achieving its objective to double the number of exporters in five years. Overall though, a clear upward trend can be seen over the five year period. *Other key indicators also improved significantly.* The key areas targeted by Austrade improved significantly as can be seen in Table 2 (page 203).

Figure 1: Number of exporters

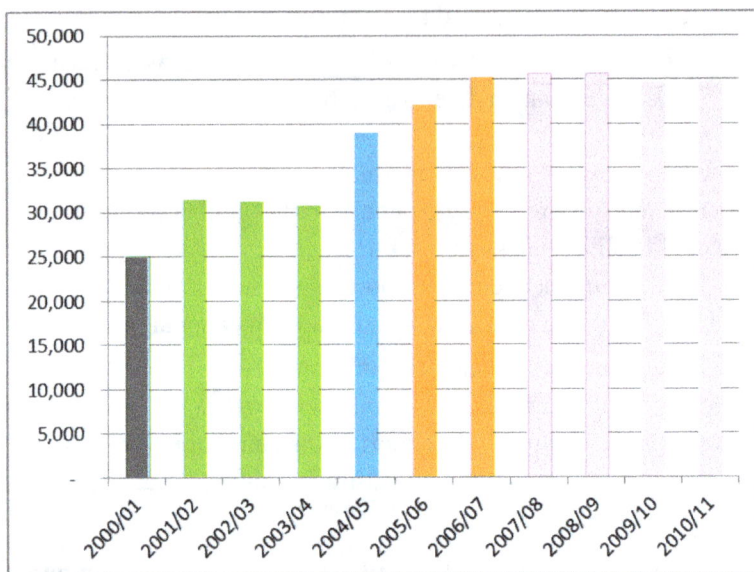

Source: Australian Bureau of Statistics, *Number and characteristics of export-ers* (5368.0.55.006), various years including 2006 and 2012-13; Austrade annual reports including 2006.

As can be seen in the table, there was an 55 per cent growth per annum in new and irregular exporter, growing the figure from 148 to 2041. Existing exporters assisted by Austrade to an export sale also continued to grow strongly over the period.

Although the aspirational target of 50,000 exporters was not met, most Austraders considered that the program had been a success, resulting in a more integrated Commonwealth/State and Territory/ Private sector system to help Australian companies into export, a focus within Austrade on delivering more services to more companies, and a significant increase in the number of exporters.

Table 2: Other Austrade KPIs over time

	New and irregular exporters achieving export success with Austrade's assistance	Existing exporters achieving export success with Austrade's assistance	Total Export impact clients	Export impact $bn
2001/2	148	1358	1506	
2002/3	374	1641	2015	8.8
2003/4	1193	2122	3315	13.5
2004/5	1717	2641	4358	18.4
2005/6	1777	3321	5098	18.4
2006/7	1996	3421	5417	22.4
2007/8	2041	3260	5301	18
Compound annual growth rate (CAGR)	**55%**	**16%**	**23%**	

With the change in government, the program was replaced by new policy directions

With a change of government and a new minister in 2007 the program effectively came to an end. Austrade embarked on a new Journey to International Business initiative and focused on meeting the new Minister's expectations and priorities.

Could the 50,000 exporter target have been met?

On balance, it appears that the doubling target had strong microeconomic underpinnings and was supported by a range of aligned strategies and changes to Austrade business model. Although there were significant improvements in the number of companies assisted into export and the number of companies supported by Austrade, the target of 50,000 exporters by 2006-7 was not achieved.

There is no single reason why the target was not achieved. Some of the reasons put forward by Austraders in discussions included:

1. That the original idea was flawed. This approach argues that Austrade adds the most value helping existing experienced exporters to expand their overseas sales, and that the doubling initiative diverted resources so that Austraders were tied up assisting small, time consuming, companies to achieve small sales, often on a one off basis, instead of focused on more valuable ongoing larger exporters.

2. Other priorities emerged during the period – including the North American Free Trade Agreement, and Austrade was appropriately diverted onto these new priorities

3. A new Austrade Managing Director, Peter O'Byrne, commenced in May 2002, and the Board governance arrangements were changed in 2006 so that the Managing Director no longer reported to the Austrade Board but directly to the Minister for Trade. During 2002 to 2003, many of those on the Executive who had been involved in the original strategy development left Austrade, replaced by a largely new Executive team. The anecdotal evidence is that the new Managing Director and Executive were as committed to the doubling objective as the previous Managing Director and his Executive team. The effort required to recruit and put in place a new Managing Director and Executive team may have been a disruption to the achievement of the target within the time frame.

4. That Austraders gamed the KPIs, focusing on the new exporter KPI as it had the highest weighting, with insufficient focus on the required ongoing support to keep companies successfully in export. The author of this paper has been told more than once of overseas posts helping small companies that were not really ready for exporters to successfully obtain one small sale in order to 'hit' the New Exporter KPI. The posts were cognizant that the sale did not have a significant impact on Australia, particularly if the company was not assisted to successfully remain in export, but considered their efforts appropriate given "the KPIs set by the Executive".[9]

5. That Austrade is a minor factor in the overall number of exporters and couldn't exert sufficient impact on the overall figure to meet the target; for instance that exchange rates and other factors outweighed Austrade's efforts.

6. That the doubling target was always a number that was set as an aspirational target and it was not important whether the exact target was achieved, but rather that it set a direction which drove valuable outcomes for Australia and Australian companies. On this basis the doubling initiative was a major success. This is the author's view. The objective was not to "get to 50,000" so much as to create energy and focus on helping a wide range of new exporters to become successful overseas.

Final reflections on the doubling objective

Following are some of the author's reflection on the doubling target. These points are hopefully useful for others considering a similar initiative.

---

9 Highlighting as always the need to be extremely vigilant when setting KPIs, ensuring one thinks through undesirable behaviours that might arise as a result of the pursuit of the KPI in question.

- It is always important to get key stakeholders on boards. This was a time-consuming, but rewarding process in building engagement and alignment.
- It is very difficult for public sector organisations such as Austrade to set and maintain a major direction:
  - For a public sector organisation to commit to a **stretch target can be risky.**
  - **Key people change.**
  - **National priorities change**. By 2004-5 the Free Trade Agreements with the USA and Thailand were in place and Austrade's focus had partly shifted to these new important opportunities. In that year there are no direct references in the annual report to the doubling objective, although the number of exporters was still outcome measure 1. In the 2006-7 Austrade annual report, the doubling objective is not mentioned and the earlier outcome measure of "number of exporters" is not mentioned. Outcome 1 "awareness raising" and "clients achieving export success" remained, as did a significant program to work with partners, including corporate partners.
- It is challenging to set up and maintain successful partnerships. The partnerships were successful. In the 2007-8 annual report, Austrade reported that 1,648 businesses were assisted to export success through the corporate partnerships program, and a further 1,031 indirectly through traders, consolidators and agents. In discussions, Austraders involved in the partnerships stated that some of the partnerships were very successful, whereas others were challenging. This is aligned with Nous Group's finding in 2014 that collaboration and

partnerships require significant resources and focus and have high failure rates.[10]

- That significant change requires significant ongoing focus and drive from all levels of the organisation.

---

10 *Collaboration between sectors to improve customer outcomes for citizens of NSW,* Nous Group/NSW Public Service Commission, 23 October 2013.

13

Austrade: Winning investment for Australia since 1987

Peter Collens

Introduction

Trade commissioners and Austrade had over many years supported Australian firms investing in foreign markets and this was known as "outward investment". In addition, assistance could be given to foreign firms seeking to invest in Australia, termed "inward investment" through introductions to government agencies and Australian service providers such as banks and accounting firms. Prior to the establishment of a formal program in 1987, these activities were transactional in nature, were based on demand and there was no coordination, guidelines or training of staff. Under its Act, Austrade is required to support and facilitate investment in Australia, particularly where that investment is likely to enhance opportunities for Australian export trade.

The origins of a formal Australian Government program to deliver investment promotion, attraction and facilitation stemmed from the Government industry policies in the 1980s. These policies led to a transition away from protected industries to a more open, competitive and productive economy, refocused on growth through international opportunity. The Australian Government was keen to attract a greater share of Foreign Direct Investment (FDI), which had grown significantly across global markets in those years. According to the

OECD,[1] "FDI" is an investment made with the objective of establishing a lasting interest in an enterprise resident in an economy other than that of the investor. By the mid-1980s many countries (including UK, Ireland and Singapore) were actively competing for investment from multinational corporations with many having specialists working overseas proactively targeting potential investors. As the creation of jobs was a priority for all Australian state and territory governments, their agencies were active in attracting investment internationally necessitating extensive representation overseas to promote their respective state to foreign companies.

Austrade's role in investment changed substantially over the years, and the understanding of terminology also changed over those years. In the early years "Investment Promotion" referred to the full spectrum of investment activities undertaken by Austrade and these roles were defined in an internal report (Investment Task Force report – Austrade, 30 May 1991) as: Image Building, Match-making and Deal-making. In later years (Reform of the Australian Trade Commission, *Maximising Our Value* – May 2011, Austrade 2011) "Investment Promotion" was considered to be the marketing and targeting of foreign firms to influence a decision, "Investment Attraction" related to the focussed and proactive winning of FDI in priorities for government, while "Investment Facilitation" related to activities supporting an investment transaction once the decision to invest had been made.

Investment promotion – 1987-91: Establishment and early years

Program rationale

In June 1987 the Australian Government decided to set up an investment promotion program (IPP) as a joint Commonwealth, states and territories initiative (Charles O'Hanlon). When originally formulated,[2] the rationale for the program rested on three premises:

---

1 OECD 2008, Benchmark Definition of Foreign Direct Investment: Fourth Edition–ISBN 978-92-64-04573-6 – © OECD 2008.

2 Bureau of Industry Economics, 1996, Report 96/4 Evaluation of the Investment Program and Facilitation Program, Australian Government Publishing Service, Canberra

- Foreign investment was important in improving the compet-itiveness and internationalisation of Australian manufacturing and service industries. FDI could increase Australian industrial capacity, enhance transfer of technology and managerial know-how and improve access to overseas markets.

- Australia needed to match intense competition by other countries for FDI, to foster international business collaboration.

- Australia needed to correct misconceptions about its investment policy, industrial relations climate and cost structures, and to publicise the positive aspects of local investment more widely.

Administrative arrangements

Funding of A$2 million per year was provided. The government gave the prime policy role to the then Department of Industry, Technology and Commerce (the Department) as part of its industry development functions. The Department also became responsible for developing suitable promotional material and for overall investment facilitation. Responsibility for program delivery, particularly for overseas operations, was given to Austrade, then also a portfolio responsibility of the Minister for Industry, Technology and Commerce (the portfolio responsibility for Austrade was transferred to the Minister for Trade on 1 November 1991). Initially the IPP was coordinated in Austrade by The Trade and International Development Unit and in late 1987 Charles O'Hanlon was appointed to lead the investment program.

Austrade began appointing investment commissioners (then known as Trade Commissioner (Investment)), preferably with banking or senior corporate management backgrounds, in key overseas financial centres to supplement its existing trade commissioner network. First appointments were Dick Sedden in New York (1988), Sano San as a locally engaged consultant in Tokyo (1988), and Dr Walter Roso in Frankfurt (1988), followed by Kevin Doyle in Paris (1990), The investment commissioners were given the task of offshore investment promotion and publicity, principally using the Department's and other government printed promotional materials.

Early program challenges

In 1987 and through the early 1990s information was transmitted via fax and post. Printed brochures on Australia were used for event marketing and promotional activities, while data/fact sheets were produced to assist Investment Commissioners in one-on-one investment meetings with investors. In the early years of the program the Westpac Bank produced printed fact sheets for Austrade. These covered a wide range of industries and were made available in large ringed binders and forwarded to Austrade offices for reference. These proved of little value as they were always out of date, and being in hard format, were not available to hand out to prospective investors unless photocopied.

Investment Commissioners were given little policy direction for investment attraction and there was a lack of consistency in their approach across markets. For example in Tokyo, much of the work focussed on running image building seminars while in other posts, there was more focus on one on one meetings with targeted companies. Senior trade commissioners were also able to direct IPP staff without regard to the Program's overall objectives. In Paris, for example, Kevin Doyle provided assistance to Australian companies investing in Europe as well as French companies entering Australia. Moreover the level of involvement in investment attraction of posts without dedicated investment staff varied considerably.

In the early days of the Investment Promotion Program and in the absence of any clear guidelines, there was difficulty in establishing what may be productive and valuable investment outcomes for Australia. As a consequence, Austrade found itself supporting many foreign companies who were actually seeking market opportunity with the objective of importing into Australia. State government agencies were called upon to assist by providing detailed information on the Australian market and potential sites for establishment in respective states and territories. They were particularly concerned about the priorities given by Austrade to many foreign visitors who were clearly seeking opportunities to import or acquire Australian businesses.

First Program Review

In 1991-2 the Program had its first review (as noted in the BIE Report 96/4). It identified a number of shortcomings and resulted in 38 specific recommendations including

- adopt best international practice in investment promotion;
- target industries, countries and firms more specifically;
- develop a better research and analytical capability;
- put more emphasis on performance measures and assessment;
- revise the roles of the Department and Austrade; and
- work more closely with the states and territories.

Notwithstanding these issues, it was recommended that the Program be expanded.

During the Review, former Trade Commissioner Tony Baker returned to Austrade in the newly created role of National Manager Investment. Tony had most recently been on a secondment as General Manager in the Victorian Office of Trade and Investment. Tony Baker was instrumental in driving significant changes following the review and developing the Program along the lines of best international practice, as well as bringing about a whole of government approach.

1992-1996: Growing the Program

Developments offshore:

The overseas network was greatly expanded in this period, with new Investment Commissioners appointed in London (David Valentine), Milan (Tony Russo), Hong Kong (Chia Yenon) and Singapore (Mark See), as well as new appointments in the four existing posts. There was a focus on appointing people with corporate banking and/or senior corporate experience in the target market. Dennis Smith in New York and Leonie Muldoon in Tokyo typified the new skills in those markets. Dennis came from Westpac but was a hard-nosed mid-west banker who knew how to focus the team in North America. Dennis implemented a systematic and well researched corporate targeting strategy using a corporate banking sales model. Leonie Muldoon had been a partner in a major Australian law firm and was a fluent Japanese speaker. She brought a new and disciplined approach with targeted one on one business engagement in Japan.

Table 1 – Austrade investment staff September 1995

Post	Full time positions
New York (USA)	7.5
Frankfurt	3
Tokyo	3
Paris	3
Milan	2
London	2.5
Hong Kong (PRC & Taiwan)	6
Singapore	3
Total Offshore Positions	30
Australian Operations	10

Source: BIE Report 96/4

By September 1995 Austrade investment staff had grown to 40 full time positions (see Table 1). Most of the Program's budget was spent on providing dedicated investment promotion resources in Austrade. With the strong support of MD Ralph Evans, reporting arrangements were also changed with Investment Commissioners now having dual reporting to Tony Baker via a "dotted" line as well as to their regional EGM or STC.

Operations and systems

A challenge for the Investment Unit in Australia was to maintain quality control over investment leads generated by posts before they were acted upon and/or circulated to the states and territories. New criteria were developed to ensure consistency regarding leads. Austrade also commenced recording the pipeline of investment activity which was generally shared with state and territory agencies. In 1992 performance measures were established for investment posts as well as a database listing investment successes and the specific role played and value added by Austrade. Independent external assessment of claims was also carried out. This data served Austrade well in later Reviews; providing credibility to claimed outcomes, and consequently refocussed resources in line with recommendations of the first review.

The request by posts for up-to-date data and information was also addressed. By 1993 all staff were using personal computers linked to a network. Although this was before the uptake of the Internet, internal email was possible. This allowed the use of electronic databases and Austrade subscribed to IbisWorld immediately replacing a library of hard copy material. This subscription databases could be installed on investment staff PCs and analysed to meet specific investor and marketing needs. IbisWorld reports could be produced on selected Australian industry sectors and include key statistics, market, industry segmentation, industry conditions and performance, industry participants, key factors and five-year outlook. Tailored reports were also available. In addition ABS data on the Australian economy was used, including trade and investment trends.

Glossy brochures were produced for specific campaigns, trade and investment missions and marketing events. It was not unusual to carry a number of plastic sheets, each with 12 Ektachrome slides ready for the projector. Slide presentations required a lot of preparation and appropriate equipment.

Developments onshore

While specialist investment commissioners had been recruited offshore, the depth of similar experience was lacking in Austrade onshore. In April 1992 Peter Collens was recruited to inject international finance and investment skills into Australian Operations and subsequently the investment office in Melbourne was established, directly reporting to Tony Baker in Sydney. After the review in 1991-2 it was agreed that Austrade would primarily focus its investment work on identified sectors, but still servicing general enquiries. These weren't necessarily areas with competitive strength but were compatible with government policy.

The initial sector targets were:

- Food processing.
- Information technologies and telecommunications.
- Minerals and chemical processing.
- Textiles, fibres and hides processing.
- Waste and environment management.
- Advanced business services.

In 1992 investment opportunities were managed in Australia by industry teams known as Business Development Units (BDU) who held sector knowledge and extensive networks. Some of the BDUs had a dedicated investment person and a number were based in Melbourne. After the Review, a system of dual reporting was instituted with investment staff in the BDUs reporting to the Investment Unit as well as the BDU Manager. Peter Collens, Investment Commissioner Australian Projects in Melbourne took responsibility for the first four sectors and Scott Smiles in Sydney managed both waste and environment management and advanced business services. To provide additional investment skills, Austrade offered to take secondments from some large accounting firms. Four seconded staff came to Austrade in Melbourne with corporate advisory and good analytical skills. Austrade staff with existing industry knowledge complemented the teams in Melbourne and Sydney.

Australian investment briefs

In 1993 a new initiative was developed by the Melbourne office to promote specific investment opportunities in Australia. Australian Investment briefs (AIBs) were used as focused marketing tools by Austrade and resemble a short prospectus to meet the information requirements of prospective overseas investors and highlight the commercial fit of the Australian project with the business of such investors.

Using these briefs commissioners were able to present specific project opportunities to selected potential investors. Access to detailed documentation was restricted to targeted investors who had signed a confidentiality agreement.

Austrade generally initiated an AIB upon becoming aware of an Australian company seeking an overseas partner. Austrade worked with the consulting organisation (such as AIDC) preparing the memorandum, business plan or other basic corporate information to adapt the document's language and layout to the needs of the international marketplace.

The Investment Unit would subject potential AIBs to rigorous quality control checks. It would not accept poorly developed documentation, or market briefs if their soundness was in question. As part of the process Austrade carefully assessed the project and proponent. The "four Cs" was a simple rule developed by the team in Melbourne to describe a rigorous process of evaluating Capability, Credibility, Competitive advantage and Commitment before agreeing to market a corporate or State Agency's proposal through the AIB process. Austrade did not charge for preparing an AIB. Indeed, in some cases, the program supported the cost of an AIB through the Feasibility Study Fund administered by the Department. This fund had a nominal budget of $500,000.

This was a professional and targeted approach resulting in a number of valuable wins, particularly in agriculture/aquaculture (Abalone in Tasmania, Milk in Victoria), mineral processing (Chlor-alkali in WA), forestry (fibreboard in Tasmania) and research collaboration

(Magnesium in Qld). These projects amounted to hundreds of millions in new investment and many new jobs that were particularly valued in regional locations.

Regional Headquarters initiative

In line with the focus on "Advanced Business Services" a strategy was developed to promote Australia as the ideal location for a multinational company (MNC) to establish an Asian Pacific Regional Headquarters (RHQ) or major regional function. This was to be targeted to both foreign and domestic companies. This campaign was very successful in delivering more than 60 new regional headquarters or major regional functions in Australia in its first two years. The RHQ initiative was a key element in the Australian Labour Party Policy[3] running up to the 1993 election. The Special Minister for State, Frank Walker[4] launched the RHQ Campaign in September 1993 with release of the report *Australia: Your Business Location in Asia.*[5] The campaign began as a joint initiative with Telstra and the States and Territories. Specific marketing material was prepared by the Economist Intelligence Unit comparing Australia against other potential RHQ sites across a range of issues important for companies choosing an RHQ. A target list of more than 300 MNCs with operations in Australia and at least three other Asian locations was prepared. (In this pre-internet era, Tony Baker developed this list drawing on Dunn and Bradstreet books sourced from the State Library). Austrade and Departmental staff contacted the Australian office of target MNC to gather information on the location of each company's regional functions and to promote Australia's advantages as an RHQ. Relevant State or Territory agencies were also encouraged to participate. Investment Commissioners then followed up, making contact with decision makers in the parent companies.

---

3 Australian Labour Party 1993, Advancing Australia: Building on Strength, p. 23.
4 Hon Frank Walker, Special Minister of State, 1993, Answer to question in Parliament, Hansard, 1 February 1994, p. 102, question 681.
5 Treasury 1993, Australia, Your Business Location in Asia: A Smart Move, ISBN 0642195447, NLA Bib ID 1387727.

In support of this campaign, Ministers, the Special Trade Envoy and the Special Investment Representative undertook a number of overseas investment missions that were coordinated by Austrade to create high level meetings with target companies. Special sales tax and visa arrangements were put in place by the Commonwealth for companies establishing RHQs.

The program quickly achieved credibility and profile when American Express located a Regional Operations Centre in Sydney in spite of strong Asian competition. This project was initiated in Hong Kong by Austrade's Investment Commissioner Chia Yen On in 1994. He initially identified the opportunity and worked closely with American Express to understand their requirements. Austrade's Sydney office coordinated a whole of government response from Australia, including confidential proposals from a number of States and Territories. This professional response and informed process was highly appreciated by the company and was considered best practice by the State agencies.

The Program was a phenomenal success and by March 1996 had secured about 180 new RHQs or regional services. On 19 December 1994 The Minister for Industry, Science and Technology, Peter Cook, wrote to Ralph Evans[6] highlighting the success of the RHQ Campaign and suggesting its expansion focussing on Technology Research and Multimedia. In September that year it had been announced[7] that Australia had received Corporate Location's (UK Publisher now part of the Financial Times Ltd) *"Best Campaign Award for Excellence 1994"* for the Investment Promotion Program including the RHQ strategy and marketing campaign. In early 1996 Corporate Location awarded Investment Australia as the most effective agency in Asia Pacific Region.[8] In June 1997, Minister Tim Fischer announced that

---

6 Hon Peter Cook, Minister for Industry, Science and Technology, 1994, Letter to Ralph Evans, MD Austrade, dated 19 December 1994,
7 Hon Peter Cook, 1994, Senate Hansard, regional Headquarters Program, 22 September 1994 Parl no 37, p. 1215.
8 Austrade 1996, *Horizons* magazine, November 1996, p. 2, "Investment Australia rated number one."

Investment Australia rated number one

The Investment Promotion and Facilitation Program, jointly managed by Austrade and the Department of Industry, Science and Tourism, has been internationally recognised as the most effective investment promotion agency in the Asia-Pacific region.

Corporate Location Magazine, the world's leading publication on global direct corporate investment, recently presented the prestigious award to Peter Collens of Investment Australia's Melbourne office and Carolyn Walsh, Department of Industry, Science and Tourism Counsellor in London, at the 1996 Annual Convention of Investment Promotion Agencies in Barcelona.

According to Investment Australia General Manager Tony Baker, "This award represents further recognition of the effectiveness of the Investment Australia program in bringing productive investment to Australia: investment which is vital to the expansion of our value-adding industries, the creation of employment opportunities for Australians and the generation of further export earnings.

"The *Corporate Location* award also reinforces the

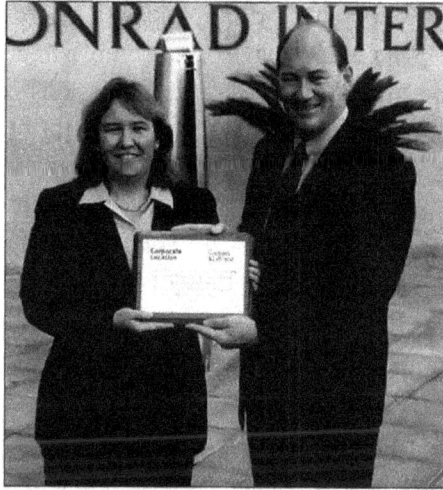

Peter Collens and Carolyn Walsh, Department of Industry, Science and Tourism. The Austrade/DIST-administered Investment Promotion and Facilitation Program has been rated the most effective in the Asia Pacific.

findings of a recent review of the program by the Bureau of Industry Economics.

"The BIE review stated that the program played a significant role in attracting productive investment to Australia by altering misconceptions held by overseas corporations about the suitability of Australia as a strategic investment location."

In 1994, the Investment Australia program received *Corporate Location*'s Best Campaign Award for Excellence for its Regional Headquarters Campaign.

Source: *Horizons*, November 1996

the number of new RHQs or regional services established had grown to nearly 300.

Coordination and planning

In May 1992 the first formal Commonwealth-State-Territory meeting for Investment Promotion was held in Melbourne to coordinate investment activities. It was agreed these meetings would be held twice a year on a rotating basis at senior executive level in Australia.

These were jointly chaired by the First Assistant Secretary from
the Department and the Executive General Manager Australian
Operations, Austrade (then Michael Johnson).

To help coordinate strategy and strengthen the "Australia" brand,
from 1992 annual workshops were held in Asia, Europe and the United
States which brought together investment commissioners, senior
trade commissioners, heads of missions, counsellors (Department)
and local state and territory government representatives. During this
period Austrade hosted annual program management and planning
meetings with Department colleagues. Investment Commissioners
were invited back to Australia to participate. A typical agenda would
review investment promotion performance, look at international best
practice and receive market reports.

Administrative changes

In July 1993 the program was transferred to the Treasurer's portfolio,
where it was brought under the direction of the newly-created National
Investment Council (NIC). Major Project Facilitation (MPF) had been
announced in February 1992 in the *One Nation Statement* and was
initially administered in the Department of Prime Minister and Cabinet.
As part of the reshuffle of portfolio responsibilities, the MPF function
was merged with the IPP to be renamed the Investment Promotion and
Facilitation Program (IPFP). Following a ministerial rearrangement
in March 1994, the IPFP and NIC secretariat returned to the then
Department of Industry, Technology and Regional Development.

In May 1994 as part of the *Working Nation Statement* the Prime
Minister announced that the government would appoint a Special
Investment Representative. The Hon John Dawkins (a Commonwealth
Minister from 1983-93) was the initial appointee. His role was to lead
overseas investment missions, attend key offshore meetings with
potential investors and advise the Minister and NIC on investment
promotion and facilitation matters. During his first year he completed
missions with the support of Austrade to the United States, the
Netherlands, Turkey, Switzerland, Japan, Singapore and Malaysia.

Program review

There was a full independent evaluation of the program in 1995-6 undertaken by the Bureau of Industry Economics (later part of the Productivity Commission). The report[9] was released in March 1996. It found:

> Overall, the BIE considers the IPFP has done much with relatively few resources. The BIE recommends that the Commonwealth government should continue at least the present level of aggregate real budget funding for the program. If the program were to increase its overseas presence modestly with a commensurate increase in Australia to support such an increase, it is likely to continue to yield benefits greater than costs for the short to medium term. Accordingly, a modest expansion of the IPFP appears warranted.

While the review supported the targeted strategy, they also recommended investment commissioners be provided considerable operational flexibility. The BIE also gave support to Austrade developing and promoting AIBs and noted the difficulties that existed in the working relationship between the Department and Austrade. There was uncertainty around roles and responsibilities which arose following the various ministerial changes since 1991 and the merging of the Major Project Facilitation (MPF) role. This led to a Memorandum of Understanding being signed in 1996, clearly spelling out the roles and responsibilities of the Department and Austrade.

At the same time, Coopers and Lybrand UK undertook a benchmarking study of the Program against the leading investment attraction agencies around the world. C and L found that in most respects the Program was operating at the cutting edge of world's best practice and was leading the field in a number of areas including performance management and verification of successes claimed.

---

9 Bureau of Industry Economics, 1996, Report 96/4 Evaluation of the Investment Program and Facilitation Program, Australian Government Publishing Service, Canberra.

1997-2002: New government – new direction

Following the Howard government's election in March 1996, Tim Fischer became Trade Minister and John Moore became Minister for Industry Science and Tourism. There was considerable restructure of Commonwealth departments and scrutiny of budgets in the 1996-7 financial year.

Mortimer Review

In late 1996 a Government-appointed committee headed by David Mortimer commenced a review of Government business programs. On behalf of Austrade, Tony Baker made a presentation to the Committee on investment. In July 1997 the Minister for Industry, Science and Tourism released the Committee's report *Going for Growth: Business Programs for Investment, Innovation and Export.*

Investment was a key part of Mortimer's recommendations being one of five key programs, from the roughly 70 Mortimer reviewed. Mortimer proposed a single agency "Invest Australia" that would be responsible for promoting and attracting investment, and formulating strategies to win investments where there was a net economic benefit.

Creation of Invest Australia

In line with David Mortimer's recommendation the Prime Minister announced in *Investing For Growth*[10] that Australia was to have an "upgraded, high-profile program to promote investment opportunities in Australia. A new body, Invest Australia, was to be established to promote Australia's advantage as a location for investment and an amount of $11 million a year over four years will be provided".

In July 1998 *Invest Australia* was officially launched with the

---

10 Hon John Howard, Prime Minister, 1997, Investing for growth: National Press Club, Canberra, 8 December 1997: address [and] Questions and answers, Parliament of Australia, Citation Id "media/pressrel/MAO30".

opening of the National Investment Response Centre (NIRC) in Bridge St Sydney.[11]

Invest Australia operated as a Division within the Department. A complex partnership arrangement between the Department and Austrade was put in place coordinated by a Steering Committee of the relevant Executive Officer from the Department and the Executive General Manager, Australian Operations, from Austrade.

In 1998, the Austrade Invest Australia staff were relocated from Austrade Offices in Kent Street to the NIRC. Although the Investment team had operated with some autonomy in Austrade, NIRC staff saw their future in Austrade and missed the collegiate atmosphere of Kent Street. Minister Minchin also made use of the NIRC Office and in 1999 AXISS collocated with Invest Australia in Bridge Street.

The Department side of Invest Australia was rapidly growing while Austrade staff numbers (both onshore and offshore) remained at around 30 dedicated investment promotion staff. Of the A$11 million Invest Australia budget in 1998-9, Austrade's share was approximately half.

Branding

Until early 1997 all investment material carried the Austrade logo and design. Business cards had noted the "Investment Australia" unit (as it was then called) but the card was Austrade branding. It was felt that Austrade branding alone did not give the right message to prospective investors. It was clear the Senior Investment Commissioners (as they were then called) used various titles and usually an "Embassy" card rather than an Austrade card in their markets. In early 1997, and prior to Mortimer's recommendation to establish the Invest Australia agency, it was agreed that the name "Invest Australia" would be used on promotional material but with the contact details of both Austrade and the Department. The new website www.investaustralia.gov.au

---

11 Hon John Moore, MP Minister for Industry, Science & Tourism, 30 July 1998, Media Release, Federal Government Fulfils Commitment On Investment In Australia, Parliament Of Australia, Citation Id: "media/pressrel The /HQ705".

was hosted by the Department and launched with the official branding of Invest Australia. This was the website listed on business cards and correspondence of investment staff in Austrade.

Professional training

By 1997 investment promotion in international markets was becoming far more competitive and agencies more professional in their approach. Austrade was concerned that there was no faculty in Australia that provided adequate professional training that prepared staff for investment promotion. There were courses run in the UK (Corporate Location) and the USA but these were expensive. There were some publications on best practice such as World Bank/ International Finance Corporation publication(s) by L.T. Wells and A.G. Wint *Marketing a Country: Promotion as a tool for attracting foreign investment.* The first formal training was initiated by inviting Corporate Location (based in London) to run a short course in Melbourne in 1997 with strong support from State and territory Agencies. However, it was costly (around $90,000) and Austrade was keen to see the course content developed and retained by an Australian institution. There needed to be 4 key elements in a new course: 1) Government Policy and economic fundamentals of "why investment", 2) Marketing and market segmentation, 3) Practical lessons on the key elements to selling, and 4) Global IPA best practice.

After a long search in Melbourne and Sydney, Professor Ian Marsh of AGSM at the University of NSW agreed to collaborate on the development of the course. The first course was held at AGSM in Sydney in 1998. Later when Professor Marsh moved to the ANU, the ANU delivered the program for several more years. Subsequently the contract was given to Greg Joffe of the Nous Group who provided more commercial and practical content. (In 2014 the course "Winning Investment for Australia" is still being sponsored by Austrade and has been adapted for the current skills required by Austrade and the states and territories.)

Key personnel changes

At the beginning of 1999 Tony Baker left Austrade and took on a senior role with AusIndustry in Sydney. Peter Collens acted in the role of GM commuting between Melbourne and Sydney until mid-1999 when Bernd Neubauer the Senior Investment Commissioner Frankfurt returned to Australia and took up the position of GM Investment. Soon after Tony Baker left, Leonie Muldoon (Senior Investment Commissioner, Tokyo), Dennis Smith (Senior Investment Commissioner, NY), Mark Jenkins (Investment Commissioner, London) and Peter Collens (Senior Investment Commissioner, Melbourne) all moved on. These changes had the effect of diluting the senior managerial experience within Austrade involved in investment attraction at a time when the Department was increasingly focussed on investment facilitation.

Change in program focus

Although the Mortimer Report had recommended a One Stop Shop approach to investment promotion and industry programs, there were a number of agencies and departments involved in investment promotion. As result of *Investing For Growth*, a number of new initiatives had been launched and The National Office of the Information Economy (NOIE) was established, as was the Australian Centre for Global Finance (AXISS Australia) in August 1999. NOIE and AXISS would purchase services from Austrade as required to support their offshore visit programs and promotional activities.

Increasingly Invest Australia was taking on additional roles and activities in Canberra. Since 1998 "Action Agendas" had become the cornerstone of the Government's industry policy. In 1999 the government announced a number of industry "action agendas" and, as a result, the Department refocused the marketing and promotional priories of Invest Australia in 2000. The new sector priorities were:

- IT&T
- Automotive

- Petroleum and Gas
- Biotechnology
- Mineral Resources

By 2001 there were 27 Action Agendas including Spatial Inform-ation, Light Metals, Processed Food, Aquaculture, Freight Transport Logistics, Pharmaceuticals, Aerospace, Heavy Engineering, and Infrastructure, Sport and Leisure and Printing Industries. Many of these Action Agendas had investment needs and strategies were developed with Cabinet endorsement to co-ordinate a case by case approach to incentives,

In addition Mr Bob Mansfield was appointed to the new position of Strategic Investment Coordinator (SIC) located within the Prime Minister's portfolio. The SIC was given responsibility for liaising with relevant Departments through a streamlined process and for advising Cabinet on projects which may justify provision of incentives or policy changes.

The Department became more focussed on MPF and coordination as they provided the secretariat and support for the SIC, as well as the necessary ministerial communication.

So although Invest Australia was expanding, all new responsibilities were being created in Canberra and within the Department, while the Austrade sector-focussed teams were constrained by a staff ceiling and budget, and were looking vulnerable as Invest Australia's priorities shifted. In addition, the Department clearly saw Austrade as a service provider rather than a partner at this point.

Investment protocols with States and Territories

In 2000 a set of protocols governing the generation, distribution and management of investment leads was developed as part of a more united approach across Invest Australia and state and territory investment promotion agencies.[12] The protocols were submitted to,

12 Dr Ian Blackburne, 2001, Winning Investment: Strategy, People and Partnerships,

and endorsed by, Industry Ministers at their meeting in Adelaide on 27 April 2001. (The protocols have since been incorporated into "The Operating Guidelines for Commonwealth, States and Territories on Investment Promotion, Attraction and Facilitation" endorsed by NIAB and continue to be used a decade later.)

As part of the implementation of the protocols a new set of Foreign Investment Lead Procedures were introduced to give states and territories early notice of potential investment projects and opportunities to provide information to assist in the marketing of Australia as an investment location.

In addition to the need for standardised inquiry procedures, it was also recognised that there was a need for a systematic process and database for the recording, reporting and management of investment inquiries within the Invest Australia network.

Investment 2000

Another major initiative at this time was Investment 2000 which was a joint venture between Austrade, the NSW government, Westpac and Telstra to use the Sydney Olympics as a platform to promote Australia and the advantages of key sectors and other opportunities in Australia. Initially this program tied up a considerable amount of the overseas investment network time, and indeed that of many trade commissioners and their staff, in arranging general image building/ awareness raising seminars around the world. During the Olympics itself, much use was made of Austrade's "Business Club Australia" and the reception facilities on Darling Harbour were used to entertain many invited international guests as well as existing and prospective foreign investors.

As this was a partnership between Austrade and the NSW government, other states and territories felt excluded and were critical of Austrade directing its global resources to the exclusion of other

A Review of the Commonwealth's investment promotion and attraction efforts, a report to the Prime Minister, August 2001, p. 29.

states. The promotion of the Investment 2000 brand also diluted the Invest Australia brand in international markets.

At the same time Austrade was directing its effort to Investment 2000, the Department was putting resources into its MPF role and there was a view by some states that Invest Australia had lost focus in investment attraction. State agencies in Victoria, Qld, SA and WA viewed the Austrade partnership with NSW as competition to their own efforts to attract investment. In particular, Peter Collens (on secondment to Business Victoria) witnessed that Victoria lacked confidence to share investment leads with Austrade (fearing they would be disclosed to NSW) and as a consequence they started to strengthen their own overseas network with an investment focus.

The changing Austrade role

By 2001, Invest Australia's total budget was $13.4 million of which Austrade was funded $8.2 million.[13] There were 112.5 direct positions of which 28.5 (including 9 part time positions – 4.5 FTE) were Austrade staff in overseas posts. The 84 onshore included 13 Austrade staff located in Sydney and Melbourne and 65 Department staff in Canberra. Investment posts were New York, Chicago, San Francisco, London, Frankfurt, Paris, Milan, Madrid, Stockholm, Tokyo, Hong Kong, Beijing, Taipei and Singapore.

Roles and responsibilities were clearly defined within Austrade and performance targets to deliver export growth meant that senior trade commissioners lacked the incentive to spend time on investment. By 2002 investment activity in Austrade was confined to those staff specifically tasked with the role. Additional support to Invest Australia and other government agencies was seen by Austrade, as a "fee for service role" rather than Austrade delivering an investment outcome, especially when dedicated investment staff were unavailable to

---

13 Dr Ian Blackburne, 2001, Winning Investment: Strategy, people and partnerships, A Review of the Commonwealth's investment promotion and attraction efforts, a report to the Prime Minister, August 2001, p. 28.

provide support. The Department was taking an increasing role in the management of the investment network.

Blackburne Review

In 2001 Dr Ian Blackburne was asked by the Prime Minister to undertake a review of the Commonwealth's investment promotion and attraction efforts. His report *Winning Investment Strategy, People and Partnerships-A Review of the Commonwealth's investment promotion and attraction efforts* was released in August 2001.

His recommendations inter alia were:

- Investment promotion and attraction be delivered through an autonomous, prescribed agency called *Invest Australia* in the industry portfolio.

- The inwards investment promotion and attraction activities of other Commonwealth agencies be incorporated into *Invest Australia.*

Blackburne also commented on the Austrade Act[14] recommending that Section 8 (a) (v) be amended to remove the role of Austrade to promote investment in its own right, but enable Austrade to assist Invest Australia as service delivery agent. Meetings on investment promotion between the Commonwealth, States and Territories had been running since May 1992 and were jointly chaired by Austrade and the Department. He supported the partnership with States and Territories but recommended the Commonwealth, States and Territories have a more formal relationship with regular meetings chaired only by the Department. The government responses to Blackburne's recommendations were detailed in the "Enterprising Australia "Parliamentary report in October 2002.[15]

---

14 Dr Ian Blackburne, 2001, Winning Investment: Strategy, people and partnerships, A Review of the Commonwealth's investment promotion and attraction efforts, a report to the Prime Minister, August 2001, p. 52 & 53.

15 Joint Standing Committee on Foreign Affairs, Defence and Trade, 2002, Enterprising Australia – planning, preparing and profiting from trade and investment, The Parliament of the Commonwealth of Australia, ISBN 0642784191, Appendix D.

2002-7: Austrade out of the picture

On 1 July 2002 the investment resources and investment staff within Austrade were transferred to the new "Invest Australia" that became a division within the Industry Department. Some staff continued to be housed within Austrade but reported to the new Invest Australia.

The new arrangements for offshore promotion were by direct engagement between Invest Australia and DFAT rather than Austrade. There was a significant bank of goodwill and years of knowledge and practical experience across Austrade that was lost. By 2002-3 Invest Australia had a budget of over $20 million but in that year, and subsequent years, had failed to build an effective offshore presence.

Allen Consulting Review

In 2005 the Allen Consulting Group reviewed Invest Australia and it's operations. The July 2005 report, *Evaluation of Invest Australia and its operations,*[16] provided a critique of the proportion of offshore to onshore staff given the objectives of Invest Australia. By this time, Invest Australia staff numbers totalled 119 with 93 onshore and 26 offshore. Over the previous ten years the offshore resourcing of Australia's investment attraction effort had fallen from 30 in 1995 and the onshore resourcing had increased substantially. They were also critical of the lack of administrative support given to offshore staff and recommended co-location with other government agencies. The inability of the Department in Canberra to understand the needs and provide support and motivation for its key sales staff in offshore markets was also seen as a failing of the structure.

2008-13 rebirth

Following the election of the Rudd government in 2007 there was significant portfolio reorganisation and within a few months the decision

---

16 Allen Consulting Group & Invest Australia 2005, Evaluation of Invest Australia and its operations final report, Allen Consulting Group, Melbourne, http://trove.nla. gov.au/work/25804396

had been taken to put investment promotion back into Austrade. This was formalised through the budget process taking effect from 1 July 2008. The initial budget was $10.8 million and included the transfer of 42 staff from Invest Australia.

The integration of investment back into Austrade was directed by Leith Doody who consulted widely in Austrade and with State and Territory governments. Leith had a very good working relationship with Barry Jones the CEO of Invest Australia leading up to the transfer in July 2008. MPF had been a core function of Invest Australia and the Department, but Austrade had no allocated resources for this service.

Peter Osborne had just returned from Beijing and was appointed to National Investment Manager role in Sydney. However, not long after, he resigned to take up a role in the private sector. Nicki Watkinson, returning Senior Investment Commissioner from Frankfurt, was then appointed to take the leadership role during this difficult settling in period.

Simon Crean was Minister for Trade from December 2007 until June 2010 and he was particularly interested in Austrade's investment role, and keen to attract major new investment projects during the Global Financial Crisis. He understood that sometimes incentives were a major competitive factor and was prepared to champion projects to his fellow Ministers. When Nicki Watkinson took up the National Investment Manager position she found a considerable amount of her time was spent servicing the Minister and his office on investment issues.

Integration issues

A key requirement of the integration strategy was for the investment functions to be aligned into Austrade's systems, guidelines and protocols. There was an underlying view that, having reacquired investment promotion, that the functions should be totally embedded within Austrade so it became a natural extension of Austrade's given "Trade and Investment" mandate and operational model. Unfortunately, this was driven by memory of the pain in 2002, when investment was "ripped from Austrade", rather than a practical view of investment processes and best practice. In reality, 42 staff could quickly become lost in an organisation of over 1,000, and it wasn't long before many of the specialist investment staff were transferred to new Austrade roles. Gradually over two years the availability of investment skills started to be lost or diluted across Austrade and there was a lack of readily available experience within Austrade to replace those leaving. Instead of having 100 per cent dedicated staff to deliver investment projects, many staff were tagged with only 10 per cent or 25 per cent. Many of these Austraders had limited training, very little on the job experience and were not always available when demand required resources to sell hard and win the business.

Investment needed a voice and fortunately Kerry Rooney, who was a capable leader, moved across to Austrade with Invest Australia in Canberra. Kerry was initially responsible for the "Cleantech" team globally and through her influence was able to maintain specialist investment skills across the Industry Group and in many of the posts.

Invest Australia personnel were given Austrade titles and positions in various teams, but predominantly onshore in the "Industry Group" and Marketing Team. Offshore, there were some Invest Australia staff that were ex-Austrade returning after six years. Of those, Jean-Baptiste Nithart in Paris and Henry Wang in Shanghai had extensive experience. Overall, the staff that chose to transfer to Austrade retained a high level of commitment to investment and continued to be very effective.

When Nicki Watkinson returned to Melbourne in March 2009 she was given a special task of working on key investment projects, developing training across the Austrade network, managing the investment incentives framework and working on the strategic development of investment attraction. She was subsequently appointed to National Manager Investment in June 2009. Nicki came with excellent credentials having been the Senior Investment Commissioner in Frankfurt for the previous six years.

In July 2009 the Executive were briefed on the progress of Investment after 12 months. Planning was implemented on a regional and industry basis. Trade, Education and Investment strategies flowed from these plans and were resourced accordingly. While plans were market driven there was little consideration given to stakeholder objectives, particularly the states and territories. The exception was Cleantech which received external funding and had clear objectives, and formal structures for communication. The three sectoral priorities for 2009-10 to be supported by Investment resources were Cleantech, Financial Services, and Infrastructure.

Across the regions staff were being trained as Lead Generators in locations and sectors that seemed most prospective, and a number of selected staff who had the appropriate experience and skills undertook fulltime Investment Specialist roles. For example the Americas had 18 staff trained as lead generators and there were 4 investment specialists. By the end of 2009, there were 25 specialist investment staff (those who spent at least 50 per cent of time on investment) across the offshore network.

The Financial Services Industry Group had responsibility for promoting Australia as a centre for Financial Services. It carried on the role established by AXISS in 1999, and which subsequently became a division of Invest Australia in 2003. The promotional material and research produced by this team was highly regarded and used extensively by Austrade, other agencies and stakeholders.

Despite the challenges of re-establishing the Investment Promotion function, Austrade investment services were surveyed by the World Bank Group in 2010 as part of a best practice evaluation of agencies in APEC economies. In its report dated May, 2011 Austrade ranked second after invest in Canada and was rated as "best practice", particularly in on-line promotion and enquiry handling.[17]

Austrade Onshore Review

In early 2010 Peter Collens returned to Austrade to head up the Investment team after 10 years with the Victorian government. The

---

17 Asia-Pacific Economic Cooperation, Investing Across Borders – APEC, May 2011, APEC Publication number: APEC#211-CT-01.3, p. 94.

Investment Unit consisted of seven staff in total located in Canberra, Sydney and Melbourne. He was welcomed with a comment from Michael Abrahams to the effect that the role of National Investment Manager would not be required once "we" succeeded in fully integrating investment into Austrade. Meaning that investment should become a normal service delivered by all Austraders and administered under a single operational structure. This was a common view across Austrade at the time and founded on the belief that investment was a service provided to companies (albeit foreign companies), just like export services are provided to Australian firms. In a practical sense it is true that Investment promotion, attraction and facilitation is about assisting firms with their investment into Australia. However, the purpose of investment attraction is to deliver economic and social benefits to Australians and needs to be in line with the policy objectives of government. Many in Austrade did not see the organisation as a service delivery agency to meet broader policy objectives of the Australian Government and other stakeholders.

In July 2010 Peter Grey, Austrade CEO, initiated the Austrade Onshore Review which provided an opportunity to realign the investment function to meet the policy objectives of governments in Australia. During the review there were two opposing views put forward; one being to manage all service delivery for trade and investment though industry focussed teams, and the other to have separate verticals for export and investment with clear objectives and responsibilities for each function.

Not surprisingly the review coincided with a need to realign resources in offshore markets and an overall reduction in budget.

In May 2011, the conclusions of the review were released in *Reform of the Australian Trade Commission – Maximising Our Value – May 2011*.[18] The new operating model for Austrade was defined and included "sharper investment promotion, attraction, and facilitation priorities". It also called for "a realigned international network – with a different

---

18 Austrade 2011, Australian Trade Commission Annual Report, Appendix B, Canberra.

focus in different markets reflecting the commercial potential as well as the nature and scale of impediments to business in those markets and the optimal role for Government". A key feature of the new structure was "clear lines of responsibility for Austrade's core functions: trade, investment and education and for the EMDG scheme".

Implementation of the new Austrade took effect from 1 July 2011 with the realignment of core functions offshore. Overnight the established markets of Europe and North America shifted their focus heavily towards investment. Combined, their resources amounted to over 70 full time employees focussed on investment. It took another five months before the onshore structure was finalised resulting in an Investment Division of 23 staff headed by a General Manager. Peter Collens assumed this role until his retirement in September 2012.

With many staff newly tasked with investment a heavy responsibility fell upon those experienced investment commissioners such as Chris Knelper (Chicago), Kelly Sims (San Francisco), Nicki Watkinson (Frankfurt) and Leonie Muldoon (Tokyo).

National Investment Advisory Board (NIAB)

NIAB was established by Invest Australia in 2002 and carried on from the Commonwealth-State-Territory meetings which were formalised by Austrade back in 1992. This was a key recommendation of Blackburne, and NIAB was to provide a report to the Industry Ministers Meetings. In 2008 the inaugural meeting of the Ministerial Council on International Trade called for better coordination of inward/outward investment promotion across all levels of government in Australia. The Council also agreed that federal, state and territory inwards investment activity was to be coordinated through NIAB, with NIAB outcomes to be communicated annually to the Council.

Alignment of interests and objectives between agencies can be difficult. Representatives of States and Territories often face each other as competitors for investment, but through the Commonwealth-State-Territory and later NIAB meetings they enthusiastically contributed to "Team Australia" and shared information on best practice. Steve Arnott,

Figure 1: Investment project success by number of projects since 1992

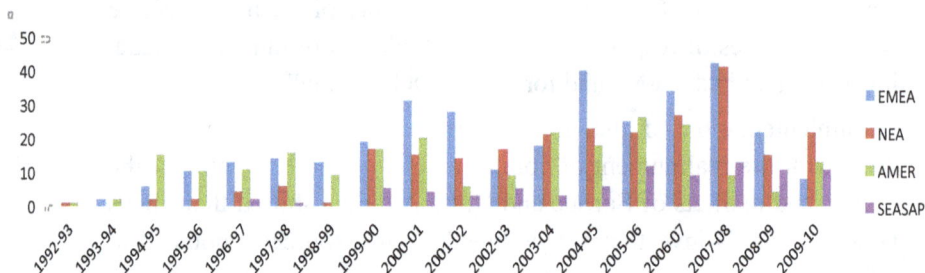

the Western Australian representative on NIAB at his last meeting in 2010, recounted the story of the Commonwealth-State-Territory meeting at Hardy's Reynella Winery in Maclaren Vale SA circa 1995. The meeting was being chaired jointly by Sandra Eccles the FAS from the Industry Department and Mike Johnson the General Manager Australian Operations, Austrade. There was some disagreement between the joint Commonwealth chair on the day which frustrated the meeting. Barry Ferguson the representative from Business Victoria moved a vote of no-confidence in the joint chair. It was seconded by Steve Arnott (Department of Commerce and Trade in WA) and supported by all other state and territory representatives. Subsequently South Australia, the host state, was asked to chair the meeting. The states and territories play an essential role in investment facilitation and need to be treated with respect in the spirit of partnership. There are many examples of states lacking trust in the Commonwealth and also Austrade/Invest Australia subordinating states. Peter Collens, who was also present as an observer at that meeting, chaired the NIAB meeting in 2012.

Investment outcomes

Measurement of success has always been difficult in investment attraction. Winning investment is not just focused on FDI but on what is commonly called "productive investment". Productive investment is that which clearly delivers a positive outcome to Australia and meets the objectives of stakeholders. Objectives such as technology transfer may not be of a capital nature and non-numerical outcomes are not

Figure 2: Inwards Investment Functions

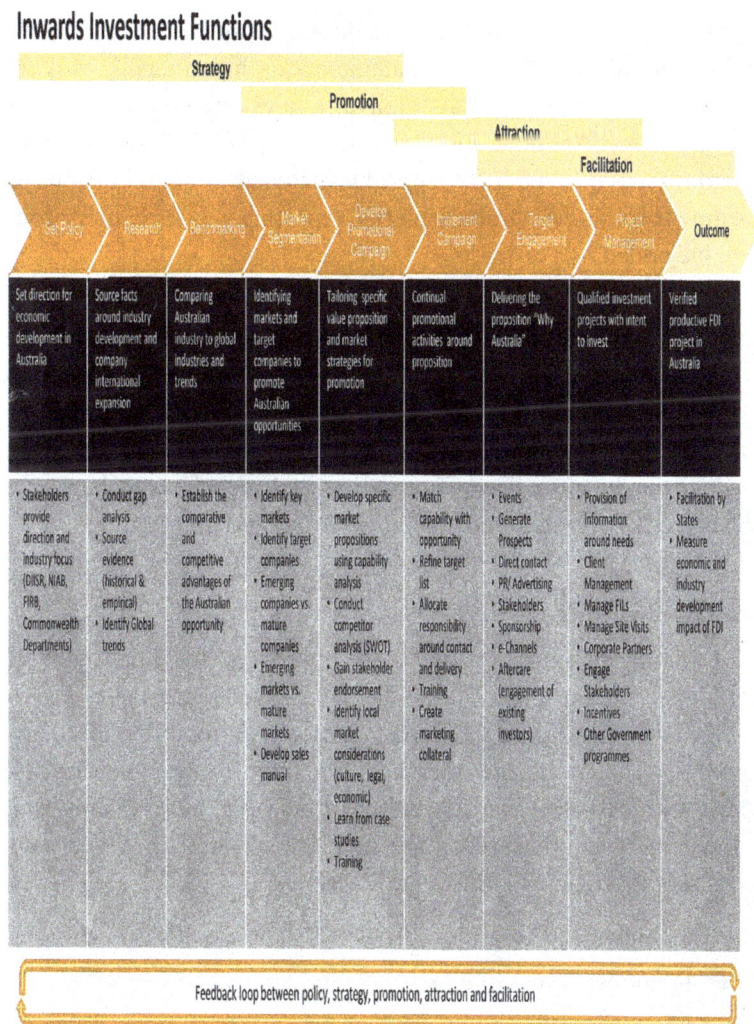

Inwards Investment Functions

Strategy

Promotion

Attraction

Facilitation

Set Policy	Research	Benchmarking	Market Segmentation	Diverse Promotional Campaign	Investment Campaign	Target Engagement	Project Management	Outcome
Set direction for economic development in Australia	Source facts around industry development and company international expansion	Comparing Australian industry to global industries and trends	Identifying markets and target companies to promote Australian opportunities	Tailoring specific value proposition and market strategies for promotion	Continual promotional activities around proposition	Delivering the proposition "Why Australia"	Qualified investment projects with intent to invest	Verified productive FDI project in Australia
• Stakeholders provide direction and industry focus (DIISR, NIAB, FIRB, Commonwealth Departments)	• Conduct gap analysis • Source evidence (historical & empirical) • Identify Global trends	• Establish the comparative and competitive advantages of the Australian opportunity	• Identify key markets • Identify target companies • Emerging companies vs. mature companies • Emerging markets vs. mature markets • Develop sales manual	• Develop specific market propositions using capability analysis • Conduct competitor analysis (SWOT) • Gain stakeholder endorsement • Identify local market considerations (culture, legal, economic) • Learn from case studies • Training	• Match capability with opportunity • Refine target list • Allocate responsibility around contact and delivery • Training • Create marketing collateral	• Events • Generate Prospects • Direct contact • PR/ Advertising • Stakeholders • Sponsorship • e-Channels • Aftercare (engagement of existing investors)	• Provision of information around needs • Client Management • Manage FILs • Manage Site Visits • Corporate Partners • Engage Stakeholders • Incentives • Other Government programmes	• Facilitation by States • Measure economic and industry development impact of FDI

Feedback loop between policy, strategy, promotion, attraction and facilitation

Australia Unlimited

Source: Extract from Austrade and Invest Australia RMS, March 2011.

easy to measure. Creation of employment (a high priority in the early 1990s) is one key outcome sought through investment promotion. Therefore FDI in itself is not the measure.

Further, if success is judged by the dollar amount then a minor engagement in a very large infrastructure project may be seen as a huge win although the value Austrade added may be very minimal. On the other hand a small but strategic research partnership may take years in direct engagement and deliver a keystone investment in line with government policy objectives, although it may have no capital expenditure. While external reporting included numbers of jobs and investment dollars, Austrade's internal reporting was structured around the value added by Austrade.

An investment evaluation model with weightings to signify the value of an investment project was developed in 2009 for use within Austrade. This was applied to all successes claimed by posts in order to direct efforts towards delivering investment outcomes that met strategic goals. As can be seen from the diagram there are many roles and stages in the attraction of investment and at each stage there needs to be effective measurement of the value being delivered.

Investment priorities

In 2011, and in line with the new objectives for investment, an Inter-Departmental Committee (IDC) on Investment Priorities was established to determine a "sharper" investment focus. The IDC was chaired by Austrade and members included representatives from PM&C and Treasury. In all there were 16 Departments and agencies on the IDC. The IDC recommended four Australian Government investment Priorities for Austrade. These were:

- Tourism Infrastructure
- Economic Infrastructure
- Innovation
- Clean Energy

The IDC with the support of Treasury also recommended the downgrading of financial services as a lesser priority and this had a direct impact on the Financial Services Group within Austrade.

In order to have Austrade formally engaged to deliver on these priorities, Craig Emerson, Minister for Trade, together with the relative portfolio minister was required to endorse each priority and strategy. This formality was destined to take time but Tourism Australia and DRET were very active supporters of the Tourism Infrastructure priority and by early 2012 respective ministers Emerson and Ferguson were committing to Tourism Infrastructure as a priority.

In line with *Maximising Our Value* the key role for facilitating investment in Australia was to be transferred to the States and Territories. This was agreed through NIAB and in the spirit of a partnership with the states and territories, Austrade agreed to deliver on three priorities that would be supported by the states and territories. These were:

- Digital Economy, including ICT.
- Agricultural Science, Food Technology and Food Processing.
- Resources Technology, Services and Processing.

Each of these priorities required a formal strategy and signed agreement with stakeholders defining objectives, responsibility, roles, sharing resources and funding.

2013 – Trade and investment

Since joining Austrade in 2011 as Executive Director Australian Operations, Tim Beresford has taken the executive responsibility for investment. Following a reorganisation in June 2014 Tim Beresford continued his responsibility for investment with the position Executive Director: Tourism, Investment, Education and Programs.

In September 2013 the Abbott government was elected and Andrew Robb became Australia's first Minister for Trade and Investment. The

Coalition had outlined in their policy steps to attract investment to Australia by appointing a Minister for Trade and Investment.[19]

Minister Robb has taken this role very seriously and after coming to office had hosted 40 investment round tables in 16 countries by September 2014.[20]

In February 2014 Andrew Robb Minister for Trade and Investment chaired the inaugural meeting of Commonwealth and State and Territory Trade and Investment Ministers and in September he chaired the second meeting in Cairns. In the minister's inaugural annual investment statement to Parliament on 23 September 2014 he reiterated the National Investment Priorities are:

- tourism infrastructure;
- agribusiness and food;
- resources and energy;
- major infrastructure; and
- advanced manufacturing, services and technology.

In addition, the Minister announced the appointment five Senior Investment Specialists[21] from the private sector to work with Austrade to identify inward investment opportunities and to help realise them across these five areas.

Minister Robb went on to state: "Austrade is at the forefront of our efforts to attract new investment" and "Attracting foreign capital is vital if we are to maintain sustainable economic growth and to create additional jobs."[22]

---

19 Liberal Party 2013, The Coalition's Policy: to Boost the Competitiveness of Australian Manufacturing, August 2013.

20 The Hon Andrew Robb, Minister for Trade and Investment, Ministerial Statement on Investment to Parliament, 23 September 2014.

21 The Hon Andrew Robb, Minister for Trade and Investment, Ministerial Statement on Investment to Parliament, 23 September 2014.

22 Ibid.

Conclusion

The government's broad economic reform and deregulation agenda is aimed at making Australia a more competitive location for investment. The government is seeking is to generate growth and jobs following the transition from a resources investment boom to the resources export phase.

There is also a much stronger connection with DFAT than in the past and Heads of Mission in many markets see their main role as being engagement with the major existing investors in Australia in a form of aftercare, as well as directly supporting Austrade investment leads.

Under the current Austrade CEO Bruce Gosper, Austrade is an active contributor to policy development in Canberra. It provides insights about investment barriers and opportunities to policy departments so Australia can maintain a globally competitive investment environment. In 2013-14, examples included a submission to Productivity Commission inquiry into public infrastructure,[23] seconding an officer to the Department of Prime Minister and Cabinet to support the development of the *Industry, Innovation and Competitiveness Agenda* and providing input into the Northern Australia and Agriculture Competitiveness White Papers.[24]

The relationship between Austrade and the Department of Industry remains important and has been formalised through an agency level agreement covering investment priorities as well as trade and international education. There is considerable alignment between the Industry Growth Centres announced in the *Industry, Innovation and Competitiveness Agenda*,[25] and Austrade's investment priorities so further collaboration can be expected to help the Growth Centres achieve their potential.

---

23 Austrade 2014, Australian Trade Commission Annual Report 2013-14, p. 61.
24 Op. cit., p. 78.
25 Department of the Prime Minister and Cabinet 2014, Australian Government Industry Innovation and Competitiveness Agenda Report, 14 October 2014, pp. 72-4.

By 2014, with Australia's first ever minister with investment in his title, Austrade is more actively engaged in investment than ever before. Investment is recognised as a core business and there are more resources focused on Investment Promotion now than at any time since Austrade was established.

Back in 2001 Dr Ian Blackburne's recommendation[26] to amend the *Australian Trade Commission Act*[27] was agreed but never changed. Blackburne's agenda was to establish the independent agency Invest Australia, however, the notion that Section 8 (a) (v) of the Austrade Act was ambiguous has no relevance in 2014. Nevertheless, with Austrade's expanding role in Investment, the Act could now be widened with a separate subsection to confirm the functions of the CEO to facilitate and encourage investment into Australia where that investment is valued by Australian Governments. This would replace "where that investment is likely to enhance opportunities for Australian export trade".

Bibliography

Allen Consulting Group & Invest Australia 2005, Evaluation of Invest Australia and its operations final report, Allen Consulting Group, Melbourne, http://trove.nla.gov.au/work/25804396, Asia-Pacific Economic Cooperation, Investing Across Borders – APEC, May 2011, APEC Publication number: APEC#211-CT-01.3.

Austrade 1996, *Horizons* magazine, November 1996, p. 2, "Investment Australia rated number one."

Austrade 2011, Australian Trade Commission Annual Report 2010-11.

Austrade 2014, Australian Trade Commission Annual Report 2013-14.

Australian Labour Party 1993, Advancing Australia: Building on Strength, policy statement.

---

26 Dr Ian Blackburne, 2001, Winning Investment: Strategy, people and partnerships, A Review of the Commonwealth's investment promotion and attraction efforts, a report to the Prime Minister, August 2001, p. 52-3.

27 Australian Trade Commission Act 1985, including amendments up to Act 46 of 2011, Canberra.

Dr. Ian Blackburne, 2001, Winning Investment: Strategy, people and partnerships, A Review of the Commonwealth's investment promotion and attraction efforts, a report to the Prime Minister, August 2001.

Bureau of Industry Economics 1996, Report 96/4 Evaluation of the Investment Program and Facilitation Program, Australian Government Publishing Service, Canberra. http://www.pc.gov.au/inquiries/completed/96-04/96-04.pdf

Hon Peter Cook, 1994, Senate Hansard, regional Headquarters Program, 22 September 1994 Parl no 37, p. 1215.

Department of the Prime Minister and Cabinet 2014, Australian Government Industry Innovation and Competitiveness Agenda Report, 14 October 2014.

Hon John Howard, Prime Minister, 1997, Investing for growth: National Press Club, Canberra, 8 December 1997: address [and] Questions and answers, Parliament of Australia, Citation Id "media/pressrel/MAO30."

Joint Standing Committee on Foreign Affairs, Defence and Trade, 2002, Enterprising Australia – planning, preparing and profiting from trade and investment, The Parliament of the Commonwealth of Australia, ISBN 0642784191, Appendix D.

Liberal Party 2013, The Coalition's Policy: to Boost the Competitiveness of Australian Manufacturing, August 2013.

Hon John Moore, MP Minister for Industry, Science & Tourism, 30 July 1998, Media Release, Federal Government Fulfils Commitment On Investment In Australia, Parliament Of Australia, Citation Id: "media/pressrel The / HQ705."

OECD 2008, OECD Benchmark Definition of Foreign Direct Investment: Fourth Edition– ISBN 978-92-64-04573-6 – © OECD 2008.

The Hon Andrew Robb, Minister for Trade and Investment, Ministerial Statement on Investment to Parliament, 23 September 2014.

Treasury 1993, Australia, Your Business Location in Asia: A Smart Move, ISBN 0642195447, NLA Bib ID 1387727.

Hon Frank Walker, Special Minister of State, 1993, Answer to question in Parliament, Hansard, 01-02-1994, p. 102, question 681.

14

Austrade's "Special Markets" – A perspective from Russia

Roger James

Background

One of the major outcomes of the restructuring of Austrade following the McKinsey Review in 1990-91, was the implementation of the Regional Area network, whereby groupings of overseas markets were managed by a team of Executive General Managers (EGMs), the majority of whom were located in and responsible for, a specific geographic territory. All reported directly to the Managing Director. The majority of these regions such as Japan/Korea, the Americas and Europe, were easy to identify and understand. Even East Asia and South East Asia were relatively logical and coherent entities. However one overseas region, termed "Special Markets" was at first sight a grab bag of "rest of the world" markets which did not appear to rest comfortably in any of the more conventional territories.

The Special Markets Region initially comprised the Middle East, South Asia (Indian sub-continent), sub-Saharan Africa and the somewhat quaintly named Commonwealth of Independent States (CIS) which had emerged from the wreckage of the former Soviet Union, after its spectacular implosion at the end of 1991. While these markets appeared to have little in common, with considerable differences in political structures, commercial cultures and economic systems, from the perspective of the Australian exporting community, they were all unquestionably difficult places in which to do business. Indeed such were the common problems and issues that they quickly became known as the "really-need-us" markets for Austrade.

Under the leadership of Charles Jamieson (who was subsequently appointed Austrade's third Managing Director 1996-2002), Special Markets Region evolved into a unique body, with many common clients all endeavouring to do business in some of the more challenging parts of the globe. This communality of clients led to a proliferation of cross-linkages and seamless handovers from post to post within the region.

Jamieson was an enthusiastic champion of the Special Markets and was its only EGM throughout its relatively brief history. From its headquarters in Dubai, (assisted by a very effective Regional Support Office in Canberra managed by Richard Wilson), the Region consistently punched above its weight, particularly in terms of client satisfaction. The fact that both men had served as trade commissioners in difficult markets (Saudi Arabia and the Soviet Union respectively) meant that they had a deep understanding of the challenges and issues faced in adverse business situations.

Moscow Post, arguably exceeded only by Vladivostok and Almaty as Austrade's most "really-need-us" offices, was an integral segment of the Special Markets Region from the outset and the gradual turnaround in the fortunes of the Australian exporting community to the former Soviet markets, was due in large part to its inclusion in this region.

The Special Markets

The principal Special Markets posts at the outset were located in Dubai (sub-post Karachi), Riyadh (with Trade Correspondents in Kuwait and Sana'a), Istanbul (sub-post Ankara), New Delhi (sub-posts Colombo and Dhaka), Bombay (later Mumbai), Teheran, Nairobi (sub-post Port Louis) and Moscow (sub-post Vladivostok and Trade Correspondents in Alma-Ata – later Almaty).

These markets all displayed considerable diversity in geography, religion, political systems, culture and economic development. In order to present a coherent strategic market approach, it was considered that a "national coordination of an allied Australian effort would be important to success" (Special Markets Operational Plan 1993-4).[1]

Austrade's "Backgrounder" #24[2] reported that in these markets, the finance of trade and investment was frequently complex. Furthermore, though cultural differences were extreme and political and economic volatility common, in almost all cases government-to-government activity was crucial to business success. Cooperation between ally organisations was critical.

In calendar year 1991, Australia's visible exports to the Special Markets region were worth $3.5 billion or 5.4 per cent of total visible exports. This was down a massive 22 per cent from the previous year because of two critical global issues – the first Gulf War and the break-up of the Soviet Union.

Composition of Australia's exports to the region was traditionally dominated by agricultural products and resources, the key contributors being wheat, livestock, sheep-meat, barley, dairy products, steel and wool. The Special Markets Operational Plan for 1993-4[3] projected increasing opportunities in agriculture, telecommunications, mining/exploration, health, engineering, education and environmental management, which was ahead of its time in the consciousness of the Australian business community. In terms of investment potential, the Arabian Peninsula was considered to be the most likely source of capital from within the region.

Against this background, the following over-arching goals for the region were identified by senior management as the basis for the development of a strategic plan:

---

1 Austrade 1992 Special Markets Operational Plan 1992/93, Austrade Dubai/ Canberra.

2 Austrade 1993 "Backgrounder" #24 (24 February1993), Austrade, Canberra.

3 Austrade 1993 Special Markets Operational Plan 1993/94, Austrade Dubai/ Canberra.

1. To defend and support Australia's existing market share for traditional and commodity exports.
2. To develop new opportunities to expand market share and increase the range of commodities traded.
3. To capture joint-venture and project opportunities for Australian services and capital goods exporters.
4. To expand the range and volume of manufactured goods to selected sectors.
5. To stimulate the flow of investment capital from the region to Australia's export productive sectors.

Before examining how the strategic plan evolved and was implemented in the markets of the former Soviet Union, it is important to understand the impact of its demise and the rationale behind the formation of the Commonwealth of Independent States (CIS).

Commonwealth of Independent States (CIS)

The Commonwealth of Independent States had a difficult birth, complicated by the antipathy between the last Soviet President, Mikhail Gorbachev and the first President of the Russian Federation, Boris Yeltsin. At first they appeared to be in general agreement, with both supporting the concept of a loose confederation, with Russia maintaining control over Soviet property. However, all but two of the remaining republics were swift to declare their own independence.

In early December 1991, Ukraine held a referendum. 84 per cent of the population voted for independence and demanded to keep parts of the armed forces based on its territory. A week later Yeltsin met the Presidents of Ukraine and Belarus and agreed to sign the Belovezha Agreement, which formally dissolved the Soviet Union and created a new Commonwealth of Independent States (CIS).

According to the historian Daniel Triesman:[4]

---

4 Triesman, Daniel 2011:167/172/175/193 *The Return* (Free Press 2011), New York.

the CIS which emerged from the Belovezha meeting satisfied
no-one despite a promising start. In Alma-Ata (Kazakhstan)
two weeks later the heads of eight more republics agreed to
join and in 1993, Georgia signed on as well. Only the Baltics
remained aloof. By late 1991, 58 per cent of Russians supported
an independent Russian state, either within the CIS or outside it.
Yeltsin was probably right that an economic agreement and the
CIS were all that were possible at that time. However, early on,
many Russians in Ukraine and Kazakhstan believed that the CIS
would become a powerful unifying institution integrating most
of the former Soviet Republics.

This initial optimism did not last and subsequent events have led
to the complex and fraught situation which currently exists between
Russia and Ukraine in 2014. Ukraine never formally ratified the CIS
charter which was adopted in January 1993, though until recently
continued to participate in practice. Georgia withdrew from the CIS in
August 2009 after a war with Russia and Turkmenistan downgraded
its status to associate member in 2005.

There is a popular Russian saying also quoted by Triesman which
has been recently been resurrected by President Putin: "Those who do
not regret the end of the Soviet Union have no heart; those who want
to rebuild it have no brain."

It is against this complex and confusing background that the issues
and challenges facing Austrade's Moscow Post in the early 1990s can
be put into context.

1993 – Issues and challenges for Austrade Moscow

As documented in Austrade's "Backgrounder" #24,[5] the disintegration
of the former Soviet Union and emergence of the CIS had a profound
impact on the operation of Moscow Post and the realities of doing
business in the region. Whereas the majority of business negotiations
and decisions were formerly undertaken through a handful of Ministries

---

5 Austrade 1993 "Backgrounder" #24 (24/2/1993), Austrade Canberra.

and Trade Corporations in Moscow, the new scenario meant that Australian businessmen now had to deal with a completely new raft of governmental and commercial organisations, many of whom lacked an even rudimentary appreciation of Western business practices and principles. As the Backgrounder (p. 3) noted at the time "The CIS is the most Special Market of them all."

In this highly volatile political and economic situation, it was quickly realised that Austrade would need to not only support our traditional commodity trade, but also identify and promote emerging opportunities in other sectors during what was predicted to be a rapid transition from command to market economies.

The sectors initially identified by Moscow Post included tele-communications, oil and mineral exploration (including downstream processing), food processing storage and handling, selected capital goods (including mining equipment) and agricultural systems and technology.

More specific initiatives included the provision of intensive in-market support and the production of a regular newsletter providing up-to-date market information to companies and agencies regarding the rapidly changing commercial and trading environment. One early response to the new market conditions was the organisation and management of an Australian government food processing and storage mission to the Russian Far East in May 1992.

Additional resources were also deployed in priority areas. A major initiative was the decision to open a sub-post in Vladivostok to identify and capture opportunities in the Russian Far East – nine hours and seven time zones away from Moscow. Trade Correspondents were also appointed in Alma-Ata (Almaty) to provide support and facilitation to exporters to the emerging Republic of Kazakhstan, which was considered to have the greatest potential (outside of the Russian Federation) for key sectors of the Australian business community.

The addition of a third Trade Commissioner position in Moscow (occupied by Jane Lishman) and increased provision for travel within

the CIS markets placed considerable strain on the post's budget, but
with judicious management of funds and welcome support from the
Special Markets administrative team, an intensive marketing effort
was able to be undertaken.

Austrade Moscow's strategic objectives 1993-4

The basic strategic approach contained a number of radical (and some
controversial) initiatives, which reflected the depth and breadth of the
planning process at the time. These included:

Military Conversion/High Technology. The aim here
was to establish commercial contacts involved in the
conversion process to promote the delivery of Australian
High Technology products. This included the establishment
of a commercial spaceport at Cape York using CIS
launch vehicles. While some of the high ideals were not
forthcoming, there was ongoing cooperation with the
aerospace sector that led to the signing of a number of
lucrative contracts in later years.

**Black Sea Economic Zone (Central Asian Republics
– CARS).** This was designed to take advantage of the
formation of a new economic grouping within the CIS and
neighbouring states. Though the lofty ideals were not fully
accomplished, the concept did enable greater cooperation
between Austrade's posts, particularly Moscow, Teheran
and Istanbul, which enhanced and optimised client service
delivery in those markets.

Trade Correspondent in Kiev. This was aimed to
recognise the emergence of Ukraine as an independent
country and to raise the level of awareness in, and quality
in-market support to, the Australian export community.
However a combination of budgetary constraints and the
poor economic performance of the new republic caused

this proposal to be shelved, which in hindsight and given subsequent events could have been an unfortunate decision. An idea before its time!

Doing business in Russia in 1993

By the early 1990s the Russian economy was in a dire state. *Agence France Presse* (AFP) reported in February 1993 that "the collapse of the Soviet Union and subsequent attempts at reform had caused significant falls in both production and living standards."[6] In an ominous warning, it noted that the gulf between rich and poor was widening markedly. In an attempt to put a brave face on the situation, Russia's then Economics Minister Andrei Nechayev stated, "in examining the situation in 1992, it cannot be said that it was catastrophic or that everything that took place was negative." (ITAR-TASS)[7]

But the facts spoke for themselves. Production had fallen by 18.8 per cent and state revenues by 20 per cent in 1992 over 1991 levels. At least 28 per cent of the population had fallen below the poverty line according to official figures (though 'experts' claimed that the true figure was closer to 80 per cent). Population growth was negative (down by 70,000), a sure indication of economic distress. Paradoxically official unemployment was a mere 0.62 per cent, which demonstrates the paucity of reliable economic data and statistics! Investment in plant and equipment plummeted and it was estimated that 41 per cent of Russian machinery was more than ten years old and only 16 per cent was on a level that it could be said to be competitive with the West.

Against this background, it was hard to paint a positive picture of market opportunities to the Australian exporting community however a modest turnaround in fortunes had already taken place with exports increasing from a rock bottom value of $43 million in 1992, to $187 million in 1993.

The prognosis was generally pessimistic and the then head of the

---

6 *Agence-France-Presse* release dated 11/2/93, AFP Paris/Moscow.
7 ITAR-TASS report (quoted by AFP) dated 11 February 1993, ITAR-TASS Moscow.

European Bank for Reconstruction and Development (EBRD), Jacques
Attali had stated in February 1992 that:

> We anticipate a further decline in production. All former Soviet
> Republics continue to suffer from the haphazard disintegration
> of the old command system of inter-republican cooperation.[8]

The Vice-Chairman of Goldman Sachs, Robert Hormalts added
on a more positive note, "The risks of doing business in Russia are
considerable, but the potential rewards are even greater"[9] and

Sergei Bakarov of the Russian Chamber of Commerce & Industry
stated:

> We want to break this psychology. We want the international
> businessman not to come to the Kremlin to do business, but
> to approach Russian firms, banks, insurance companies, etc.
> directly. This is our goal.[10]

This was a sure sign of the move away from government control
and towards the emerging private sector.

The business environment at the time was extremely fluid and
the advice which was being disseminated by both governments and
organisations such as Chambers of Commerce and foreign banks
was cautious, though relatively optimistic. A consistent line was that
doing business in Russia was not for the weak at heart and required
commitment, persistence and creativity. But for every story of lost
merchandise and corrupt officials upsetting already agreed upon
business deals, there were an equal number of recorded successes. The
most successful and profitable foreign businesses in Russia tended to
keep a low profile to avoid government interference and unwanted
attention from competitors. These were in such diverse sectors as oil-
prospecting, catering, telecommunications, minerals and metals, and

---

8 European Bank for Reconstruction & Development report February 1993, EBRD
Brussels.
9 US Chamber of Commerce Moscow 1993, Goldman Sachs, New York.
10 Russian Chamber of Commerce & Industry 1993, RCCI Moscow.

real estate development. They all shared some common attributes in not entering the market for short-term gain, but a commitment to the long term. Almost all had found reliable Russian partners with good contacts who had the ability to conclude deals and deliver desired outcomes. They also tended to focus on discrete businesses and not spread their activities too thinly.

This business philosophy was relevant to all potential new entrants from the West who were seeking to gain a foothold in this potentially lucrative market

Austrade Moscow in 1995

By the mid-decade, the new Russia and its satellites were beginning to develop into relatively more stable business environments, though serious economic and political issues still had to be faced and overcome.

In a major supplement in Austrade's *Horizons* newspaper in August 1995,[11] the response to the new scenario from the perspectives of Moscow Post and the Special Markets Region were examined in some detail. While previously letters of appointment as trade commissioners to this region were designated to the Soviet Union, by 1992 this entity had ceased to exist. Incoming trade envoys therefore inherited responsibility for not only the Russian Federation, but for twelve former Soviet Republics (excluding the Baltic States which had already been transferred to Europe Region). These were unquestionably Special Markets!

One major issue which had needed immediate attention in 1992 was the $400 million debt incurred by the former Soviet authorities for wool purchased prior to the collapse of the Soviet Union. The new financial authorities initially denied any responsibility for these debts that had been incurred under the previous regime. After many months of wrangling, these debts, together with those of many other Western countries (particularly Europe and the United States), were placed

---

11 Austrade 1995 *Horizons* newspaper (pp. 6-7) August 1995, Austrade Sydney.

under the jurisdiction of the "Paris Club" for eventual restructuring and resolution.

Meanwhile business needed to be regenerated in an environment where strict communism had been replaced by rampant capitalism almost overnight. From a period where Australian exports had exceeded $1 billion in the late Soviet era, business activity hit rock bottom in 1992, when our exports were valued at a paltry $43 million. A modest turnaround to $187 million was achieved in 1993, with a continued improvement to $269 million in 1994. While traditional commodities were still dominant, there were some unlikely new products entering the market. For example, confectionery appeared from nowhere to record $4.4 million in 1993 and $21.1 million in 1994, making Australia the third largest supplier of these products and demonstrating that the Russian population had an appetite for "sweet tooth" goods which had been denied to them for so long under the former regime. The emergence of mobile cellular networks also opened up new opportunities for Australian telecoms, which were quick to investigate and explore this rapidly growing sector.

Moscow Post continued to develop strategies which recognised and adapted to the radically altered business environment. As in every market throughout the world, reliable contacts are essential to successful business and because many of the organisations and agencies under the old system were no longer relevant or functional, a critical task for the Post was to verify the credentials of the "new breed" of entrepreneur who emerged, most of whom were under 35 and many of whom claimed to be related to the President!

Attention was also placed increasingly on projects emerging from the key multilateral agencies such as the World Bank (WB) and European Bank for Reconstruction and Development (EBRD), and though competition for these lucrative contracts was intense, the coordination of Austrade's efforts through the Special Markets Region meant that in-house expertise in dealing with these agencies could be utilised.

It was also realised that in order to capture opportunities arising in the regions, both of the Russian Federation and other republics, it would be necessary to have representation in and the ability to travel extensively to many of the far-flung outposts of the territory. Hence the initial focus on the Russian Far East and Central Asian Republics, with others to follow.

A mid-term report despatched from the Post in April 1995, summarised the situation at that time and provided context to the strategies which were being developed to maximise business opportunities for the Australian export and investment community. Firstly it was recognised that the Russian Federation would continue to dominate activity, taking 95 per cent of Australia's exports, with only small quantities going to Ukraine and Kazakhstan. Some investment interest was evident, particularly in the mining sector. Trade with the other republics was negligible and all faced severe economic problems.

While offering the best prospects, Russia was still experiencing the twin problems of falls in production and high inflation. However it was noted that official statistics largely ignored the burgeoning private sector and by 1995, 50 per cent of business enterprises were held in private hands. The World Bank estimated that the "grey economy" accounted for an extra 25 per cent to 40 per cent of GDP, but in spite of concerns regarding the high level of bankruptcies and increasing unemployment, the doomsday forecasts of widespread civil unrest had not eventuated.

Russia was a difficult, but by no means impossible, market to penetrate. With much new business being conducted through the private sector, exporters were strongly advised to obtain payment up-front, in hard currency and into an offshore bank account if possible. After years of negative assessments, the attitude of Australia's Export Finance Insurance Corporation (EFIC) towards CIS markets appeared to be finally softening.

In 1995, Australia's principal exports comprised alumina, processed foods, confectionery, sugar, butter, meat, beer and wine, telecommunications equipment, plant and machinery and apparel, which already began to signify a healthy diversification from the two or three commodities upon which our traditional trade relied. There were however some warning signs emerging, caused principally by the imposition of a tariff regime in 1994 and supply constraints of certain products from Australia.

In May 1995 the Senior Trade Commissioner Moscow reported that, "Australian interest in the market is high, with 30-40 visitors per month." In response to client requests, a "full-service" suite was offered on a full-fee basis which included meet-and-greet at the airport (greatly appreciated at 3:00 am during the winter months), accommodation bookings, ground transport, provision of interpreters, detailed briefings and introductions to carefully vetted contacts. The success of this initiative was demonstrated by a high level of repeat business and client satisfaction.

Austrade's client base at the time reflected the key industry sectors that had been specifically targeted, ie agriculture (including processed foods), mining (including equipment), telecommunications and multilateral agency funded projects. These were all significant contributors in the Russian Federation and other republics of what became known as the "near abroad". The sub-post in Vladivostok, which had recorded some impressive wins in the processed food sector was continuing to flourish (where competition from Europe was less intense because of distance). A landmark decision was taken to transfer a Moscow-based Trade Commissioner (Mark Gwizdalla) to Almaty, following the establishment of an Australian embassy in Kazakhstan, which displayed a complementarity with Australia, particularly in the mining and agricultural sectors. Linkages with other Central Asian Republics were also strengthened through the Special Markets Region, notably with Iran and Turkey.

Market opportunities were also identified and explored through participation in industry-specific trade displays (processed food and mining equipment) and through a carefully targeted series of seminars and visits to Australia.

Each post/sub-post was encouraged to specialise in specific market sectors with Moscow focusing on processed foods/beverages, mining systems, telecommunications, resources and services. Vladivostok specialised in sugar, meat, dairy products and general foodstuffs, and Almaty concentrated on rural development, livestock, mining equipment and telecommunications.

All of this concerted and targeted effort was designed to defend and promote Australia's market share in this radically altered business environment.

Farewell to the Special Markets

A realignment of the regional structure was foreshadowed in a note from Austrade's Managing Director, Ralph Evans, in February 1995,[12] which announced that as part of the reallocation of territories of the regional EGMs, the CIS posts would be incorporated into Europe Region. As a consequence, the remaining Special Markets would be renamed "Middle East/Indian Ocean Region". It was noted that Austrade's regions, since the reforms of 1991, had implemented an "active and responsive line management system". However it was acknowledged that the organisation needed to respond to the shifting patterns of trade and demands on Austrade's services. The transfer date was set for 1 July 1995.

These intentions were reinforced by the EGM Corporate Affairs Peter Langhorne, in March 1995.[13] While noting that each Austrade region was somewhat diverse, "the sub-regions of Special Markets were based on a communality of clients and management issues, both of which reflect a degree of turbulence that typifies these parts of the globe". It was also noted that some reallocations had already taken place, notably the Baltic States to Warsaw Post. The proposed changes aimed to respond to changes in the patterns of Australian trade and

---

12 Austrade's Managing Director 1995 Cable to overseas posts dated 28 February 1995, Austrade Sydney.
13 Austrade's EGM Corporate Affairs 1995 Cable to overseas posts dated 22 March 1995, Austrade Canberra.

also reflected the good communications links between Frankfurt (HQ of Europe Region) and Moscow.

It was also indicated that, "further changes may occur that cross regional boundaries without weakening accountability to regional EGMs. In future external communications, Austrade will stress trade activities by market as naturally perceived by the community rather than by Austrade region".

The handover

It was agreed that a formal handover of the CIS from Special Markets to Europe Region would be undertaken at the time of a joint visit to Moscow by the respective EGMs, Charles Jamieson and Dieter Le Comte. However this was not without incident as the date chosen, (31 May 1995) coincided with an unprecedented heatwave in the Russian capital which effectively closed Moscow airport for many hours due to the melting of the runway tarmac.

EGM Le Comte had encountered problems with obtaining a Russian visa and after frantic phone calls between Moscow and Frankfurt, it was agreed that he should be free to fly once the airport had reopened, with any lingering issues to be resolved on his eventual arrival in Moscow. EGM Jamieson had decided to fly from Dubai via Europe and was temporarily stranded in Amsterdam while his plane awaited clearance to proceed.

As the day progressed, the prospects of their scheduled arrival became more and more problematic and the Senior Trade Commissioner was reflecting on his career prospects which might be significantly diminished if he managed to lose not one but two EGMs in a single day. The increasing fiasco was further enhanced by the fact that 50+ distinguished senior Russian businessmen had been invited to a reception at the STC's apartment to meet the two distinguished visitors!

After Moscow airport finally reopened very late in the day, EGM Le Comte was the first to arrive and it required considerable diplomacy and negotiation to clear the red tape and finally issue his visa. Meanwhile EGM Jamieson's plane had inexplicably been diverted to St Petersburg and there was little expectancy that he would reach Moscow until mid-evening. They were eventually reunited at a central Moscow hotel prior to continuing to the STC's residence.

The duo finally appeared at the STC's apartment at around 10:00 pm by which time the Russian guests had demolished all the food, most of the drinks and disappeared! Fortunately the STC's ever-vigilant spouse had hidden the last pack of cold beer and a remaining bottle of white wine under the sofa and so the long-awaited handover of the Moscow Post was finally accomplished and could be toasted after a nerve-wracking but memorable day.

Whither the CIS markets?

As the handover from Special Market to Europe was enacted, the Post's aims and objectives were outlined in a briefing provided to the new management in mid-1995 and were subsequently incorporated into the Business Plan for 1995-6. The key strands were designed to achieve the twin objectives of maintaining Austrade's overall market share and developing new market opportunities in response to the rapidly-changing business environment.

These included an expansion in services exports (particularly in the education sector), increased participation in sector-specific trade displays, mission activity and the encouragement of further inter-post linkages in Central and Eastern Europe, which was an enduring legacy of the Special Markets ethos.

The continuing effectiveness of the sub-post in Vladivostok, capably managed by Vladimir Gavriliuk, was demonstrated through initiatives such as the expansion of the market for processed foodstuffs, the long-term provision of Australian sugar to the Ussurijsk refinery and active involvement in the supply of alumina to smelters in Siberia, which became a significant and lucrative business. Vladivostok had long been considered as Austrade's most "really-need-us post" and given the enormous size of the territory, exploratory investigations were made to unearth market opportunities northward into regions such as Magadan, Kamchatka and Yakutia, and westwards to Irkutsk and the heart of Siberia.

There was also a requirement at this time for a longer term view of Australia's business prospects in the CIS and detailed strategies were developed which recognised and acknowledged the possible scenarios which could be foreseen in the still-volatile environment. External factors included political stability, economic growth and the pace of reform, the effectiveness of anti-corruption measures, legislative environments, protectionism, infrastructure (transport, storage and distribution), communications, and the stability of financial systems and institutions.

Internal influences which played a major role in strategic planning, included the necessity of having a strong presence in key locations (e.g., Almaty), a network of influential and reliable customer contacts, enhanced communications, close ally relationships (especially within multilateral agencies) and clear goals and targets.

Five over-arching principles were instrumental in developing business strategies for the late 20th and early 21st centuries. These were:

1. Informing and educating the Australian business community about the dramatic changes since the collapse of the Soviet Union. There are few examples of a major economy transitioning from a centrally-planned command system to raw capitalism overnight. While new opportunities abounded, the pitfalls could not be underestimated.

2. Exploring decentralisation. While Moscow, Vladivostok and Almaty were by then soundly established, plans were developed to establish low-cost "listening posts" in centres such as St Petersburg, Kiev and the Urals, to gather market intelligence and identify potential market opportunities.

3. Expanding regionalisation. The Central Asian Republics (CARS) strategy, which under Special Markets focused on Turkey and Iran, would be extended to encompass the developing economies in Central and Eastern Europe. In Pacific Russia, tentative linkages were to be developed with posts in China, Japan and South Korea.

4. Understanding the competition. The newly emerging "free" markets of the CIS were attracting considerable interest from fierce competitors from Western Europe, the United States and Asia.

5. Adopting globalisation. Exploiting the global opportunities which were emerging, particularly in mining, telecommunications and multi-national projects.

Above all, the strategies which were developed and implemented for the CIS markets at this time recognised that while formidable challenges existed, there were profitable opportunities to be garnered by those Australian firms with the foresight and tenacity to test the market. Austrade's role, as always, was to encourage and facilitate these companies' efforts by providing quality information, support and guidance.

The Special Markets region – a personal reflection

From the perspective of Moscow Post, the inclusion of the CIS in the newly-formed Special Markets Region in 1991, could not have come at a better time. As has been noted, business conditions in Russia and the other republics of the former Soviet Union could hardly have been worse and a major effort was required to help Australian business adapt to the new realities. While this essay has focused on the CIS, many other markets in the region were experiencing considerable problems of their own. The Middle East was recovering from the effects of the first Gulf War, the Indian sub-continent was only in the early stages of its economic resurgence and South Africa was on the verge of transition from the apartheid era to the election of the ANC and presidency of Nelson Mandela.

To bring together such a disparate collection of cultures, economies and political systems, was a major achievement and under the leadership of Charles Jamieson, the Special Markets region consistently punched above its weight, particularly in the critical area of client satisfaction. Jamieson ran a tight ship, but permitted a generous degree of independence in the day-to-day management of his posts. He was always approachable and would offer valuable assistance and advice whenever required.

The Special Markets team comprised an exceptional diversity of Trade Commissioner talent and experience which was harnessed on a regular basis by meetings, conferences and training opportunities all held in Dubai. In those days before instant messaging, Skype and teleconferencing (even email was in its infancy), the importance of these face-to-face encounters should not be underestimated. The opportunity to engage in personal contact with ones colleagues and peers was invaluable in cross-pollinating ideas and best practice and was actively encouraged. On a selfish note it was always gratifying to exchange the rigours of a Moscow winter for the balmy climes of the Gulf, if only for a few days.

The Special Markets conferences were not only important from the work perspective, they were also enjoyable. Charles Jamieson actively organised social programs to complement the serious business of international trade promotion and this was an important element in effective team-building.

On the occasion of the final Special Markets Regional Conference in Dubai in May 1995, which preceded the transfer of the CIS to Europe Region, he penned the following verse, which was sung by the team with gusto to the strains of "Botany Bay".

The Parting of the CIS

Farewell to our pals from Old Moscow
Farewell to Vladivostok as well
Farewell to the Kazakhs in Almaty
Where Gwizdalla is aiming to dwell

Singing: Vodka, beluga and blini cakes
Singing   Bloody cold winters each year
Singing: Aeroflot, Zims and Siberia
And all the pleasures you treasure so dear

Farewell to Roger the maestro
Farewell to Vladimir from the East
Farewell to the Russians and the Tartar
From this region you'll soon be released
(Refrain)

You've had Brezhnev and Gorby, now Yeltsin
What more could a masochist want
You've suffered the tantrums of Jamieson
Now you're safe in the arms of Le Comte
(Refrain).....You'll be sadly missed around here

This reflects the spirit and essence of the unique Special Markets region which made a valuable contribution to the development of Austrade at a critical time in its history. For Moscow and its subsidiary posts, the turbulent years of the mid-1990s, would have been harder to navigate and their contribution to Australia's trade performance would have been considerably diminished.

15

Austrade and the media

Interview with Tim Harcourt

Question – You came into Austrade as a Chief Economist how did Austrade justify the need for such a position and was it something to do with selling the message of Austrade?

Tim Harcourt: I think it was. In my job interview they had people with two PhDs in International trade theory they had all sorts of people who were very highly qualified in econometrics and the like. But they hired me because they said he's a good communicator. So on paper there were people with more degrees and more relevant international trade experience. I mean I was from the ACTU and under a National Party Minister under a Coalition government they hired an ACTU economist to be the Chief Economist, it was quite something.

Question: Given the perception that Austrade was seen as being close to Labor and National Party how was your employment interpreted?

Tim Harcourt: Yes Austrade was seen as being close to Labor and the Nationals. Yes look, not exactly house and commission advocate. I was in some way a unique appointment. When I was at the ACTU I had the job that Bob Hawke had had, Ralph Willis, Jan Marsh and most of those people went on into politics or superannuation or the commission. So when I went to see Bill Kelty to tell him about the job, and he said "no you haven't I can fix one up for you", but I said no I have a real job, I got a job interview, made an offer the real way.

And he said, but Austrade "Why would you want, exports ..." And then he thought about it and said: "Well you had been working on international trade at the ACTU and in many ways your job at the ACTU is about improving wages and improving the standards for Australian workers. Your job at Austrade will be to look for the new jobs in industry around the world that will provide jobs and wages for future generations of workers. So in a way, your job at Austrade is an extension of what you do for the ACTU.

Question: What was the reaction you received when you joined Austrade?

Tim Harcourt: The week I arrived at Austrade *The Australian* wrote every day "What the hell is the Liberal/National Party doing hiring an ACTU economist to be the Chief Economist for Austrade"? Every day there was something in there about it. And I had not met Charles Jamieson or any of the Board and so he came down the corridor and said "You're in the paper again!" I had only met the guy and I thought I've just started a new job here and I'm all over the press and Tim Fischer rang me up and said "Listen, you're going to get a lot of political crap, but you're a good economist, I know you are. I want you to sell the story of trade, backing me up. If I'm the Trade Minister selling exports I need an economist there doing it too. You get any political s**t let me know, I'll fix it up". One thing that I was amazed at was the negativity of the Coalition politicians towards Austrade, particularly in the Liberal Party.

Question: What do you put that down to?

Tim Harcourt: I think there are two reasons for it. One is the Liberals thought it [Austrade] was a Nationals thing. The Nationals thought it was a Labor thing. I think DFAT would say that Austrade are public servants not suited to be with business. I think some business people were hostile towards Austrade as well and they have been as you know since the first Trade Commissioner Shanghai in the early days. And I'll never forget the first time I was on a plane for my Austrade job I bumped into Andrew Peacock and he said "How are you Tim how is the

ACTU? I said well Andrew I'm pretty good, but I've joined Austrade now, I'm the Chief Economist. He said "oh f*****g Austrade, Jesus you'd do more good for the Australian economy working for the ACTU than you would working for Austrade. Why if the likes of Dick Pratt want to go to America, they don't need Austrade do they?" And I said, what about the SMEs that need to start exporting? So there was always that hostility and I think internally most of the people from commercial backgrounds wanted to help clients, customers, they very much talked the language of business, whilst there were a few other people, from public servant backgrounds who wanted to just serve ministers, and didn't want to know about clients.

Question: So you've explained to me what it was like being a chief economist in Austrade, but what is it like being the chief media person of Austrade?

Tim Harcourt: Well, I thought that's what a Chief Economist was at the time, other people probably had a different view of a public servant. But I thought your main role was to publicise your organisation some important information and insights, that wasn't just pure advertising that had a bit of thought behind it. That's the difference, but the others thought the Chief Economist should be behind the scenes and very, very quiet and sending the ministers to make them look good.

Question: There're often jokes and I heard one, but I don't remember it now, that you were the public profile of Austrade and Jokes like – "How you doing, Mr Managing Director, Tim Harcourt". So how did you handle that?

Tim Harcourt: Well, on the record, Peter O'Byrne was initially supportive of it because he thought that I had a comparative advantage in media work. And he was quite happy for me to play that role as were Greg Dodds and a lot of the offshore people.

Question: Did you have to get your script checked, or when you would walk into an interview, would it be pretty much – you knew what you were saying, but did anyone else want to know?

Tim Harcourt: Initially when I first joined Austrade and this from the ACTU and it was under a coalition government, Tim Fischer told me, go off and do the media, he was the Minister at the time. Don't ask permission, because the way the media works, if you asked for permission, it will be next week by the time they'd say yes, and the media would have moved on. So Tim Fischer told me to run the gauntlet. From time to time they wanted to crack down on the process. There was never a time where anything I said was specifically wrong or controversial. But they wanted control over it and complained a bit and at one stage, it became quite unworkable, because I would write a paper and someone would say "Well, that has to come under the Minister's name and if he doesn't want it, it has to come under the Managing Director's name and if he doesn't want it, it's got to come under my manager's name" and I just said, well by the time those three guys have made their decision it will be next week." And true enough, we ended up not doing that. Tim Fischer was good about the media because he too was a good media performer and quite secure in himself. And the people around Mark Vaile were worried about him not getting enough profile and at one stage, Peter Langhorne told me, "I could write whatever I wanted, but I've got to mention Mark Vaile in everything I write." And of course, the media doesn't particularly want to know that. At one time Peter Switzer from *The Australian* wrote an article about one of my export surveys and he quoted me 20 times and his last line was "... And Mark Vaile agrees". And he published it just like that! That put an end to the "compulsory Mark Vaile mentions" in everything I wrote.

Question: Did anyone ever get concerned that maybe some of your message was still too heavily influenced by the ACTU or that was never raised with you in any way and it was never the case?

Tim Harcourt: No, not at all, because my message is pro-trade and investment, very bipartisan, and I always had a view that I would explain economics, I would explain trade, but everything I did was in-line with what the government of the day wanted. Policy wise, I would say, if anything, I think people thought I was a little bit too pro-trade, investment and globalisation critics of both the left and right on free trade. But I didn't have much choice there. I couldn't run my personal views I supported the policy of the day. If the government wanted a free trade agreement with the USA I would explain it and mention companies who may be impacted by it. The same went for Thailand, Singapore or Chile as well. That was my job, whatever I thought of a particular agreement or whether I supported bilateral trade agreements or not.

Question: Did you get on with your managing directors?

Tim Harcourt: Reasonably well. My view was that once the Executive had made the decision, it would have been double the number of exporters or whatever that was. My job was to sell that. Policy differences, there were none publically and my view was – even with the doubling target, even when I had reservations about how it would practically work, I would say so it internally, but never externally. I said in public for a it was a good idea to have a focus on SME's, I think it was a good idea to help the marginal export or the potentially exporter at the margin. But internally I was against the particular target they chose. But once they decided they wanted the target, I sold it because I think that's was my job. So at the big picture level, as far as I'm concerned and if you look at the public record, everything I did was pretty much following the line of the day.

Question: Can you remember how many media commentaries you did make or is that just impossible to number?

Tim Harcourt: I wrote and published three opinion pieces a week. And there was far more TV and radio. But I would make it my own target for up to three a week. At one stage the Austrade board when we had one, my KPI and was how many media mentions I got. So I was getting on a *Better Homes and Gardens*, Kerry-Ann Kennelly, you name it. I was everywhere. That was my KPI at one stage. We had a good run then and built up quite a lot of good profile there.

Question: Did you have a pretty receptive media for that kind of stuff as well?

Tim Harcourt: Fantastic! They were so hungry for it. An example I'll give you – I went to Thailand and this was at Mike Moignard's suggestion and I went round and talked to about the Australian companies, the Port Adelaide Submarine Corporation and so on. And talked about if you had an FTA how would that help you, wrote it up, made it into an article. I get a ring at Bangkok Airport, it's Mark Davis, from *Australian Financial Review*. And he says, "Jesus Christ! John Howard's just announced an FTA with Thailand. Do you know anyone in Thailand?" And I said, "Well, I'm here at Bangkok Airport. I've just written an article about the potential FTA and what it means for Australian companies here," He said, "You bloody beauty!", can you send it to us?" So of cause it was published the next day and for both Austrade and the *AFR* it was awesome because they didn't have anyone in Bangkok. And it gave them copy straightaway from Bangkok Airport like a true airport economist!

Question: How much was your delivery to the media a kind of a hybrid of advertisement as opposed to maybe education?

Tim Harcourt: I think it was more education and awareness. And it was more – I mean, I didn't overtly plug Austrade. What I'd say is, I was in Bangkok and Sean Riley told me this. And so, immediately any exporter who was reading it or watching it, would immediately say, "So that's the guy in Thailand I need to talk to." And I know that the switchboard people told me that if I'm on Kerry-Ann Kennelly, they'd get a lot of home-based businesses ringing, wanting information on EMDG or Austrade services. So I think it was more getting good knowledge out there on the proviso that people will then use our services and so on.

Question: Why do you think Austrade is sometimes misunderstood or undervalued? I'm making reference to the Commission of Audit recommendation. Why do you think that's the case?

Tim Harcourt: It's all political. So I think small businesses go about their daily work, Austrade helps them. But if Andrew Peacock or Ross Adler had a bad experience with Austrade he'll ring up the minister and blow his head off. And I think there was a view that a small number of big business people had a bad view of Austrade and they let people know (particularly their political friends). I think it was a small number of loud voices rather than a large number of smaller ones.

Question: You made quite a few references to SMEs and it probably at some point, there will be some kind of more critical evaluation of how the fact that SMEs are the ones that can least export and get the least help and the ones that have suffered the most. They've got the least capital and all the rest of it. I think what I'm hearing from you is that is still a pretty serious issue.

Tim Harcourt: I think so. I mean, you know from research, that in countries like Italy the SMEs and Germany are feeling the effects of the exporting community in Australia, probably left. And I would have thought that using valuable government resources I think that's probably that's where you probably direct it. And for that reason, whatever you think of the merits of doubling the targeted markets may be wrong but the emphasis on SMEs was right. Because it's the 90:10 rule I mean, 10 per cent of our exporters produced 90 per cent of our revenue and of SME 90 per cent produced 10 per cent of the revenue. So if you take the view that we're not about revenue. We are about growing the numbers and companies and exporting them. And I think to some extent some people like Peter Grey probably prefer being in the policy end, the top end of town and they find it distasteful to be around SMEs. I think, some people don't think it's good for their career. Whilst my view was that SMEs will appreciate that you've got good contacts in government and he didn't. And big business also think it's good that you have a good handle on the SME sector.

Question: Tell me what do you make of the reference towards "economic diplomacy"? Is this some genuine orientation by the current government or is it just parlance and chatter that's been around in foreign affairs for decades?

Tim Harcourt: Well, I think diplomacy's has got to have some sort of economic incentive in it. I think Australia's not punching above its weight, it's a medium power. It's a pretty significant economy and I think it's like the old Jack Lang story that you go to a horse race and back a horse that may never win, but it's always a trier. So, I think to some extent if you have incentives in the game that can be important and Australia's not a military superpower but we are a significant economic player.

Question: But how is it different from what – might have been done 20 years ago, if any?

Tim Harcourt: I don't think it is. I think people want to rebadge things and bring in new language, make it all fresh and new. Look at – I mean, you set example, working nation. Working nation was very, very successful and the new government rebadged it, but they maintained most of the infrastructure and most of the negatives. And I think that's what governments tend to do. You redress things up, but a lot of the things do continue.

Question: Why do you think that Austrade did not hire someone as chief economist in the kind of very public way you were running that area of work?

Tim Harcourt: I think that was just their preference for this kind of person they wanted. Look, I think you've got to make a call on this. I know that a number of government departments decided to create a chief economist based on my role at Austrade. A lot of them have maintained it and a lot of them have changed the role to be very internally focused, and for certain personalities that suits people. Some people do like – they don't like the limelight and they prefer to do stuff behind the scenes. I like to do both, but I think you cannot do a proper role without doing all the number crunching without doing your own writing. But in my new role at university, I've actually spent a lot of my time still promoting Austrade. Even my new book *Trading Places*, in each chapter there's references to the work that Austrade does all around the world. And I give people advice to go and see Austrade in each country. So whether I'm a direct employee or whether I'm here at the University of New South Wales, I'll still be an advocate of what Austrade does. There are some very talented people at Austrade particularly in the offshore network and they make a real difference to Australia, particularly SMEs.

Question: There was significant hostility from the Coalition when they took over under Howard. Do you think the Liberal government warmed up to Austrade after 1996?

Tim Harcourt: I knew Alexander Downer pretty well from South Australia, obviously not his background or politics, but the first time I met Downer I was asked to give him a book I had written. He was at a function and he said: "Thank Christ for that, I'd rather read your stuff, than the shit I get from DFAT." He said this in front of about 10 people. I thought that's nice but don't bag the people who work for you. At a conference he also said: "That's Tim Harcourt from the ACTU, oh no hang on he's joined Austrade. And now I'm his boss. But he's OK really, he's from Adelaide."

I actually liked working with Alexander Downer, and I especially liked Tim Fischer who gave me some great advice on media and in places he knew well like Thailand, and Warren Truss was good to work with. Mark Vaile warmed up too. Tim invited me to the book launch of one of his trains books as we shared publishers at the time (Allen and Unwin).

Question: How was your initiation to the EGM structure.

Tim Harcourt: I quite liked it. One of the first things I did was, no one knew how to measure the number of exporters or what it meant. So I had to deal with Dennis Trewin at the ABS. I knew him well from my ACTU days and he gave me the study at no cost, and we actually measured the exporter community. Which I thought was an interesting piece of work. I sent this thing round to the EGMs saying have a look at this paper there's some new data which shows you where your clients go and shows you where your exporters go. So they all said, they never read stuff I send so I published it in the *Business Review*

Weekly (BRW). Then Greg Dodds sent them a note saying: "Check out this paper by Harcourt, it shows you that North-East Asia is kicking goals and the rest of you are all off the pace." And all of a sudden they got interested in what I was doing. The other thing I noticed was that when I had to talk at Hayman Island about China, I had never gone to China. The real China speaker got sick and they asked me to do it. So I read as much as I could and I gave this talk on China and got invited to China as result of that talk. Alexander Downer was there when I gave it. And Dodds liked it so much he sent me to Korea and Japan and then Mike Moignard invited me to South East Asia and off I went!

Question: What do you think of the performance measurement and measuring the value of Austrade in your day?

Tim Harcourt: Yes. I think it was a bit of a "McKinseyisation" of Austrade and I think it had some benefits to make it activity focused and more commercially measurable. I think the KPI's people were obsessed with measurement and they didn't understand the emotional intelligence of productivity improvement. I think it was better than having nothing and you'll probably ask me about the doubling the number of exporters I thought that the target was wrong, the idea of knowing how many exporters there are out there and how much is you clients growing compared to that I believe is quite a useful exercise, but it should be done holistically. You didn't have to do it with the divide and rule type thing and that was the danger that we had to categorise.

Question: What was your contact with the investment side of the Austrade activity?

Tim Harcourt: In terms of the presentation material and all the investment people were superb whether they were outside or inside, they were good, the education people were good. I used to see it as promoting the Australia economy around the world and tailor it for different markets. I found the investment stuff very interesting, very good, even though I know that the economic case for trade promotion is much stronger than the economic case for investment attraction in terms of Austrade's role.

Question: Did you notice any differences to Austrade after the board was removed?

Tim Harcourt: Oh look I did. It was the pinstripes versus the cardigans. So there were the commercial people who were at Austrade at that time to measure things, commercial like a Ralph Evans, and Peter O'Byrne and Leith Doody and then there were the cardigans who were the hardcore Canberra public servants. Once the board was abolished the cardigans took over and suddenly clients, SMEs, clients, customers all that strategic marketing stuff that they were suspicious of was sidelined and the cardigans; the traditional public servants just said, well we're just there to look after the Minister of Trade, everything else is irrelevant. And I think that's what the tension was and I think towards the end the cardigans won the civil war and the commercial side, you know apart from having an office in Sydney was sort of gone, and that was a great shame because one of the things that attracted me to Austrade was that it wasn't a traditional public service job it was an amalgam of the best of the Australian private and public sectors.

Question: What did you really think Austrade did really well?

Tim Harcourt: Well you would to a yabby farmer in Kukerin and she'd tell me that she got on the internet and then got orders from Hong Kong and Singapore and she didn't know what to do, Austrade helped her to deal with all those market. You'd go to Mendoza in Argentina and you'd meet a few winemakers in McLaren Vale, South Australia and they said that the connections between Austrade and Latin America had got them started. You just met entrepreneurial smart, savvy people who didn't know how to work international connections particularly well, but Austrade gave them that leg-up and gave them that opportunity and also the human capital that we attracted. The fact that you could meet someone in South Korea, Romania, Argentina or the Czech Republic who worked for Austrade for 20 years and were magnificent. They loved Australia and they weren't Australian, you know, they were not even Australian, but they thought that the best thing they could do for their country in South Korea, Romania, Argentine or the Czech Republic was to forge strong links with Australia and help Aussie companies. So I think we said before we went on tape, when I was at the ACTU we had a great set of values about helping the workers, and when I left the ACTU I thought I would lose that, but I didn't because there was Austrade culture and whether you're from, Vladivostok or Western Europe or South America you felt that there was good camaraderie at a certain level.

Question: So what do think Austrade did not do as well?

Tim Harcourt: It's got a good ethos, but I think there were some corporate governance issues. Anything to do with the media it would panic, so when I was at the ACTU we were in the media every day usually negative, the ACTU's ruining the country. If someone said the ACTU's doing a good job we would say "Oh, cut that out!" Some Austrade executives thought that getting no media coverage was a positive. So when I went round doing media stuff, they would panic and they would say "What are you doing? If you write something in the media, someone might criticise it". Well goodness gracious me!

Question: Where does this sense of feeling under siege comes from?

Tim Harcourt: My view was that as Chief Economist is to get in there with the media and to talk about economics. Make things interesting to get the organisation profile and the ethos of what you were doing to attract more exporters. Many times a switchboard would say "Oh we saw you Chief Economist with Kerry Anne Kennelly, how can I export stuff to the Middle-East?" So it was a great way of getting profile for the organisation and for all our clients. The other thing I saw about it was because I was so much in the media – TV, radio, and papers – I could minimise the bad stories because the BRW didn't write anything bad things because I wrote them a column every week and I think what they didn't understand with media engagement, they'd shut up shop, you're not the CIA, you're not the Chinese Communist Party, media engagement you go out there and get your turf and provide useful content to the media and you can minimise the damage.

Question: The mentioned the cardigan versus the pinstripe suits. Will Austrade end up going back to DFAT?

Tim Harcourt: I know the Coalition rolled AusAid into DFAT and they may do the same with Austrade. I don't think they'll do it this time, they might do it next time if they get elected and yes it's been around for a long time, there are a lot of people DFAT in the Coalition, political advisors, always thought Austrade doubling up and was a waste of time, why not just be the commercial part of DFAT that's what it should be. Doing what DFAT does, wearing suits and they've got an office in Sydney and that was the view. I like policy, but you don't need two agencies doing policy. You need one agency doing policy and informing the other and particularly in the free trade negotiations I thought that DFAT could have opened it up because Austrade were good at knowing what clients wanted and I personally found DFAT fantastic in my role. Because whenever I went to China or Brazil, DFAT would give me connections, would give briefings and data, I got articles. Michael L'Estrange, former head of DFAT used to say "We love you coming because say things we possibly can't. Using the Bilateral relationship we ought to be careful being diplomats, but you can do it for us." So the relationships were very good.

Question: How did Austrade stand up in comparison to other trade facilitators in the world?

Tim Harcourt: If looked at these trade organisations, and I visited every one of them in 58 countries, Austrade was probably the best, us and probably the Swedes. The Irish were a bit better, the Kiwis were good, the Kiwis used to brief me in each market. The Pommies got a bit better and the Canadians. So if you look at the institutions of the successful economies you look at the banks, trade unions, trade agencies, Sweden, Canada, Australia are still quite good and that's why our economies are quite successful you know having good labour market institutions and a good central bank and a good trade agency makes a big difference. I've got to say though that we used to win lots of awards for best TPO in Asia, best TPO this and that. It's a bit like that Woody Allen joke, in *Annie Hall* when he goes to California and says: "Everyone goes to award nights in California, there's an award for everything, next thing you'll hear, 'Next we have the award for best fascist dictator, yes the winner is Adolf Hitler, ... Adolf come on down ...'"

One thing about Austrade which I thought was missing, that we had at the ACTU, was that you've got to celebrate wins in life. When we won at the ACTU a large case, Bill Kelty would take us out, when we won the election in 1993 Keating came and said "Go and have two days off" At Austrade there was no celebration of wins. Greg Dodds used to do some in his region, we had the export awards, but you were always like a hamster on a wheel doing KPIs and no one would ever celebrate or say you've done a good job guys. When I had to a book launch I did I would make sure that in every book I wrote I mentioned every Austrader that was involved, they would show their mum, give it to clients. People need a bit of recognition. Tim Fischer taught me one thing, when you go to a market and you are the Minister for Trade and you come back and you're at some function and you say "I was in India last year Mike Moignard, you were there and everybody looks at them". People love it. When you get a personal recognition from someone whether you get it in a book or on TV or at a ministerial speech it makes a big difference and some people forgot those things at Austrade and I think that they don't get it, it's part of your culture.

Question: What did you think of the strategy of doubling the exporters?

Tim Harcourt: Yes. People will talk about doubling the number of exporters. I actually thought that was good idea, not the target, but the fact that we were showing that 66 per cent of exporters who went to Peru used Austrade, but one or two per cent in New Zealand used Austrade. I think what it shows us was that at the margin for the marginal exporter the SME who's trying to get into the market for the first time Austrade makes a big difference. On the ground with an EMDG grant through some sort of connection. Because at the end of the day as much as the free market IPA wants to tell you it's all about business or governments, most of the world trade is done by governments. We all know that whether its wheat deals, health care, education, if you're trying to get a contract in Chengdu and you're an engineer and you want to get into civil government having the Trade Commissioner or the Ambassador, come down with you is a big deal. You know we had an MBA trip to Chengdu recently for a book launch and Jeff Turner launched it. It made a real impact in the local market. The thing about it is don't be ashamed for working for the government. It's a noble thing, public service is a noble thing and you really can add value to the yabby exporting farmer or the winemaker. It's alright you know BHP and Woodside, but at the end of the day they will probably use you. But at the end of the day you're adding value and that's fine. This idea the balance of payments is in crisis is Austrade's fault, then they just don't understand basic economics.

Question: The size of Austrade's posts should be in relation to the difficulties of getting into the market?

Tim Harcourt: Well that's a good idea and the response to your customer base. I met so many people in Russia, Mongolia, and South America with Austrade and they wouldn't have had a snowball in hell's chance of getting anywhere without Austrade and I think we should be proud of that. I think that's a good thing for the country. It's not rocket science, it's a tough old world out there. So every other place in the world entrepreneurs in China use their government so there's no reason why Austrade shouldn't do that as well. Now I've got to say this that the businesses that got up, I spoke to a lot of businesses that would say to me in interviews Austrade did a fantastic good job and I'd quote them, they would get up at conferences and support Austrade, they were very smart businesses. The businesses that said Austrade stuffed me around in public didn't look very gracious or like particularly good businesses. I always advise SME exporters to praise people who have helped you, it makes them feel valued and they will help you again. And you'll have more chance of success.

Interview conducted in September 2014

16

Women in Austrade

Elizabeth Masumune and Pat Evans

Introduction

When Mr. A. R. Taysom penned his memo regarding women as trade commissioners on 13 March 1963, little did he imagine that he would achieve such notoriety for decades to come. The now infamous memo entitled "Women as Trade Commissioners?" opens with the rather ominous statement: "Even after some deliberation, it is difficult to find reasons to support the appointment of women Trade Commissioners."

After highlighting a number of obstacles including limited ability to mix with and engage freely with men, inability to withstand the physical strains of the job, the need to run her household on top of her work, the fact that female appointees would take places otherwise reserved for men, and the likelihood of an older unmarried Trade Commissioner turning into something of a "battleaxe" (on the assumption marriage would automatically end the career of any other women), the memo ends with a simple (if misspelled) conclusion: "It would seem that the noes have it."[1]

Beryl Wilson served as the first ever female Trade Commissioner in 1963 when she was appointed as Assistant Trade Commissioner to the Los Angeles office. She later went on to attain the rank of Deputy

---

1 Commonwealth of Australia, Minute Paper 13 March 1963 – Appendix 1.

Director in the former Department of Trade and Industry.[2] In view of the symbolic nature of her appointment, in 2013 Austrade created a scholarship in Beryl's name to in order to support generations of young women to come.

Over the years countless women in Austrade have received "The Memo" from friends and colleagues as a way of reminding them of how far they have come since 1963 in a somewhat perverse sign of recognition of their achievements as trade commissioners serving offshore and in various professional roles in Australia.

Notwithstanding, the question of "Why have a chapter dedicated to women in Austrade?" springs to mind. Many women have indicated that whilst their career path in Austrade was a personal journey, it was not necessarily defined by their gender. More than 50 years have passed since 1963, and a great deal of progress has been made. This chapter seeks to chart the contribution that women have made since the establishment of the Australian Trade Commission in 1986. It highlights some of the issues which have at times made the experiences of women in Austrade different to those of their male counterparts, looks at how Austrade has changed since its inception in the way in which it has deployed female staff, and provides a snapshot of some of the more recent programs and activities that have been undertaken to support women in Austrade and women in export more broadly.

It should be noted at the outset that this chapter does not represent a definitive history of women in Austrade; rather, it is an essay that will inevitably reflect some of the subjective and personal experiences of the authors. In addition to drawing on archival material and information sourced from Austrade itself, in order to provide a robust and evidentiary basis for the information contained herein, the authors have conducted telephone interviews with a number of individuals, including several women with long careers in Austrade who reviewed this material. In addition, an independent survey was undertaken in November 2014 of 208 former and current female employees of Austrade, receiving 73

2 Australian Trade Commission http://www.austrade.gov.au/about-austrade/
employment/scholarships/beryl-wilson-austrade-scholarship-for-women-in-international-business

responses.[3] Their views have been incorporated wherever possible in the information offered and conclusions drawn here.

Organisational culture

Organisational culture is determined equally by what an organisation does as what it says. In this respect the tone needs to be set at the top and employees need to be able to see it translated into action. As Aristotle said, "We are what we repeatedly do."[4]

Almost all observers of Austrade would agree that since its formation the organisation has made considerable effort to support its employees, both male and female. This has extended to both Australia-based (A-based) staff who work onshore and are posted to overseas offices, as well as to the staff employed locally in the various locations that Austrade is represented around the world (Overseas Engaged Employees – OEE). It has been the foundation for the unique camaraderie that has existed over the years in the "Austrade Family"; so dear to the hearts of former and current employees alike, and one of the cornerstones of organisational culture at Austrade.

This is not to say that organisational sub-cultures have not existed in Austrade. Examples would include the various cultures of the different organisations combining to form the new Austrade in 1986, the very pronounced styles that different offshore regions have chosen to employ to pursue Austrade's mission at various points in time, the ever-present "onshore-offshore" divide, and the predominance of men compared to women in Austrade amongst those seeking to advance into senior management positions, and secure offshore postings.

---

3 Refer to Appendix 2 for summary results.
4 http://en.wikipedia.org/wiki/Aristotle

Chart 1: Women in Austrade

Women in Austrade

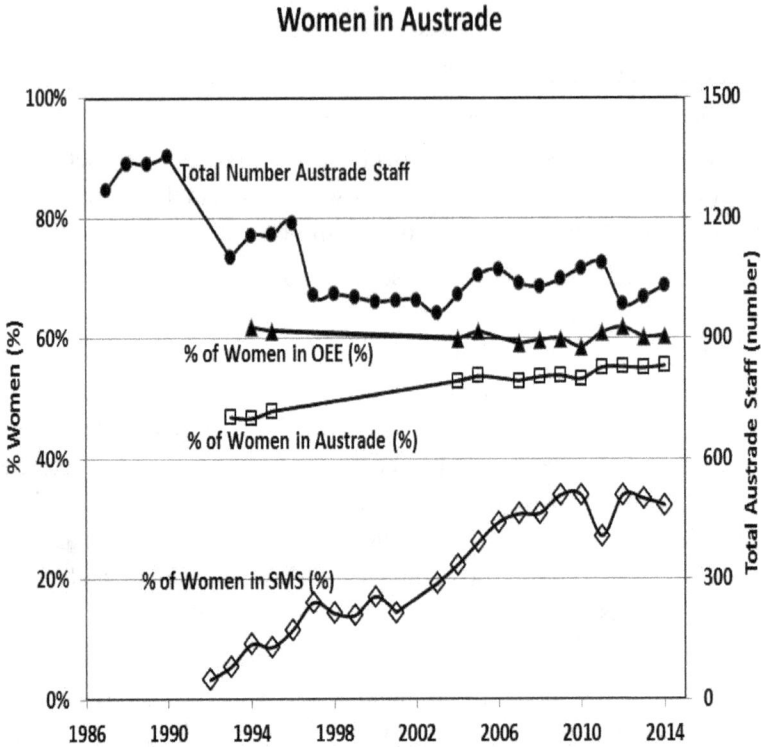

Source: Austrade

Overall, in line with its equitable employment framework, Austrade has employed between 40-50 per cent females over the period for which statistics are available. Chart 1 above[5] provides a breakdown between women in Austrade overall, women engaged as Overseas Engaged Employees, and women in the SMS (Senior Management Service). Now termed SES (Senior Executive Service).

It is interesting to note that whilst the number of staff in Austrade have varied significantly over time, the growth in the proportion of

5 Statistics: Austrade Human Resources Division.

Chart 2: Women in the SES/SMS

Women in SMS/SES

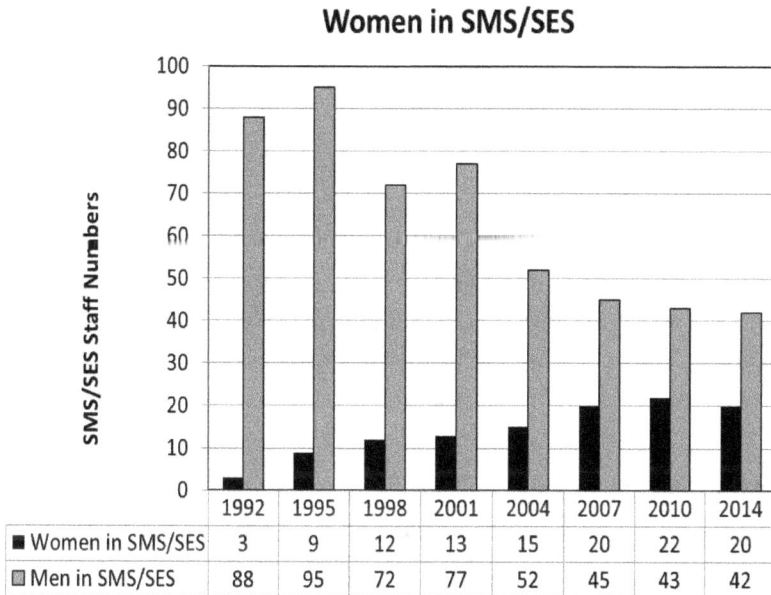

	1992	1995	1998	2001	2004	2007	2010	2014
■ Women in SMS/SES	3	9	12	13	15	20	22	20
☐ Men in SMS/SES	88	95	72	77	52	45	43	42

Y-axis label: SMS/SES Staff Numbers

Source: Austrade

women overall has been more gradual. As of 30 June 2014, Austrade employed just over 50 per cent women in its A-based staff, slightly below the Australian Public Service (APS) average of almost 58 per cent.[6] Across the first three entry level positions at Austrade Performance Level (APL) 1-3, the percentage of women employed was 61 per cent; however, there is a significant decrease in the number of women employed at the first managerial level APL4, where the percentage was 35 per cent women and 65 per cent men.[7]

Similarly, whilst there has been a gradual increase in the numbers of women in the Senior Executive Service (SES), they are still significantly outnumbered by their male colleagues. Chart 2 above

6 Australian Public Service Commission Statistical Bulletin 2013-4.
7 Austrade Gender Statistics, June 2014.

provides an overview of changes to the gender composition of the SES since statistics have been available.[8]

It is clear from Chart 2 that whilst the numbers of SES positions in Austrade have diminished significantly over time, the relative proportion of women in the SES has increased. This is a welcome development, particularly considering the extremely small numbers in the early 1990s. Nevertheless, with women representing 32 per cent of the SES in 2014, there is still a way to go in terms of achieving true equality for female representation at the senior levels of Austrade. The appointment of an experienced female Chief Executive Officer at some point in the future would certainly provide many of Austrade's aspiring female professionals with inspiration to believe that, from small beginnings, all things are possible.

Generations of women in Austrade

The pioneers

There were very few women in positions of responsibility when Austrade was first established in 1986. Several women transitioned into Austrade from the former Department of Trade, the Trade Commissioner Service, and the Export Finance and Insurance Corporation (EFIC). Carol Flanagan was General Counsel for EFIC and assumed this role for Austrade in 1986. Subsequently, Judy Bell, a senior IBM executive, joined Austrade on exchange for an extended period to augment the human resources function and drive the development of a shared corporate culture for the new organisation. Women had domestic roles in Australia as either marketing or administrative and support staff, or were engaged in similar activities offshore, and in some instances, employed locally when their spouse had been sent on a posting.

In the 1960s Beryl Wilson as the first female Trade Commissioner led the way in Los Angeles but did not receive anything like the profile

---

8 Austrade Human Resources Division.

or recognition that she posthumously enjoys today. She was followed by Barbara Higgs who worked in the Department of Trade and joined the Trade Commissioner Service in 1975. Barbara's career as a trade commissioner began with a posting to Hong Kong as assistant trade commissioner in 1976. Some observers have remarked that for a while Barbara seemed to be a lone figure on the horizon amongst an almost exclusively male group. Julie Bayliss and Julia Selby joined her, with another cohort of female trade commissioners to follow several years later in the 1980s. It was not until the 1990s, however, that there was any substantial increase in the numbers of women serving as trade commissioners in what had now become Austrade, or in management positions onshore.

Several of the women who responded to our survey have also had sufficient longevity in their careers to be able to note the changes that have occurred since the pre-Austrade days in the Department of Trade, through the formation of Austrade in 1986 to the present day; their insights have been particularly invaluable. All of them strongly agreed that the environment in for women in Austrade today provides much more opportunity and support than was available in the days when they were starting out as "pioneers".

Survey results from women of this pioneering generation in Austrade indicate that in the days of the Trade Commissioner Service they certainly felt "different"; through sheer lack of numbers they were conspicuous by their very presence. Comments reinforced the perception that the Trade Commissioner Service itself had a male-dominated culture, with performance expectations that were predicated on the way in which a man might approach the job. For example, a young, single female officer would have great difficulty networking on some occasions if denied entry to certain clubs, or without a full-time spouse to regularly host dinner parties and conduct representation at home, as was the "norm" and the purpose of the coveted representation allowance. As one woman said "The biggest challenge early on was overcoming a prejudice/lack of confidence in a woman doing the job. This was both within the organisation and among exporters."

Some of these women remarked on the role of the pre-Austrade culture as it existed in the Trade Commissioner Service in sustaining an unspoken male-dominated sub-culture within Austrade in the early days. "The carryover cultural influence of the 'boys club' Trade Commissioner Service, had a strong early influence. The absence of significant numbers of senior women for a long time reinforced this." Notwithstanding, all agreed that organisationally, Austrade has always adopted an open stance and equitable approach to both men and women since its inception, and that things were better for them as professional women after the formation of Austrade.

This openness was encouraged more broadly through organisational development and training activities in the late 1980s aimed at breaking down the barriers between the separate organisations coalescing to form Austrade, and ensuring equal treatment of all staff, regardless of gender, location or employment status.

In addition to the difficulties encountered by women aspiring to be trade commissioners, women in other roles in the late 1980s have referred in the survey to a culture of separation that existed with "tea ladies and typing pools" and "meetings where my opinions were not valued". There does not seem to be any doubt that women found it more difficult during these times to have their voices heard amongst their male colleagues and to communicate in a way that came more naturally to them. As one individual put it: "Women can be thought less of because they are more honest about their confidence or knowledge, rather than overstating themselves."

Non-gender specific issues shared as common concerns by women from this time include the constant battle that Austrade had even from its earliest days to demonstrate its full value to government and non-government stakeholders alike. The ever-present divide between those who had served overseas and those working in Australia was once again cited. One may speculate that the importation into Austrade of the culture of the Trade Commissioner Service, which was established to focus entirely on offshore activity, could have been a contributing factor.

While women in the 1980s were encouraged to participate in the active training and development program implemented to strengthen the new organisation, they did not have the benefit of programs or initiatives designed to support them as women in their careers. In that sense they did it the hard way, and were pioneers in every sense of the word. In addition to their professional achievements, one of the greatest legacies they left for subsequent generations of women in Austrade was a clear pathway to follow, and a track record attesting to the fact that women could indeed be trade commissioners.

The 1990s

With the 1990s came the emergence of a new generation of female trade commissioners and aspiring professional women in Austrade as the restructured offshore network entered an expansionary phase after the McKinsey Review.[9] Women from the private sector contested and secured roles alongside internal candidates.

The number of women in the Senior Executive Service finally climbed into double digits in 1996.[10] This next generation of women in Austrade were to sustain the growth of female managers into the early-mid 2000s as they went on to develop their own careers.

Amongst the respondents to our survey who served in Austrade during the 1990s, several noted that they did not feel any gender bias and felt it made no difference to their career in Austrade. It would be fair to say that there were significant differences in the way the various offshore regions of Austrade were run at this time, each with its own unique culture influenced heavily by the style of the respective Executive General Managers, some possibly more supportive of women than others.

Other women from this time continued to highlight through our survey the difficulty they felt at times being so heavily outnumbered amongst their peers and within the exporter community more broadly. The only solution in many cases was to "fit in".

---

9 McKinsey Review of Austrade, 1990.
10 Chart 2.

One individual noted that working conditions were very much geared towards a male with a non-working partner. Austrade management reluctance to send females on posting to "difficult" locations was another issue cited, although many would disagree with this comment. The willingness of female applicants themselves to undertake postings in difficult locations may also have been a consideration. In the mid-90s Austrade introduced a number of progressive advances in 'family friendly' policies particularly relating to assistance for partners of staff posted overseas, who were primarily women, as well as working from home conditions for onshore staff.

Women in senior positions still lacked critical mass on the whole, and survey respondents mentioned that they could not draw on other women for mentoring and advice, as in many cases there were no female colleagues close by. On the other hand, virtually all individuals felt supported in their work by their colleagues, regardless of gender.

Our survey indicates that being promoted was certainly a theme that weighed heavily on the minds of women in Austrade during the 1990s (as one may argue it has for all Austrade staff in any era). The introduction of performance assessment processes at posts was cited as patchy, with some male managers failing to treat the process seriously enough. In the view of this author, whilst there was certainly no spoken or official difference to employing either men or women during the 1990s, in reality fewer women emerged from the organisational filter that tended to be applied when making those selections. Perhaps a simple case of the lower numbers of female candidates at this stage, but also a reflection of the advantage held by the incumbents, who were primarily male. As one woman put it: "I certainly had equal access to apply for promotion but I'm not sure I had equal opportunity to promotion. How does someone really assess that in an objective way?" The observation has been frequently made over the years that, in spite of their abilities, women applying for offshore roles that were essentially about marketing often failed to market themselves as effectively or proactively as their male counterparts.

Notwithstanding, the small increment in the number of women in offshore and leadership roles had an impact on changing the culture, empowering the women in Austrade aspiring to future careers and providing more role models to follow. Those women who answered our survey with experience from the 1990s have been emphatic about the positive nature of the change that ensued.

Women on the Executive

Since the formation of Austrade in 1986 there have been relatively few women on the Senior Executive team that has directly supported the Managing Director/CEO. Julia Selby was the first woman to serve on the Executive, having been appointed as the Executive General Manager for Australian Operations in 1998, a position she held until January 2004. There was a significant increase in women on the Executive from 2003 through to 2006, with four women in an executive team of 12 from 2003-5, four out of 11 in 2005-6, and then three out of 10 from 2006-10. Subsequently female representation went down to two out of 10 in 2011 and from 2012 there has been one woman on a streamlined executive team of four to five.

(It should be noted that there were women appointed to the General Manager [SES Band 2] positions created as a result of the *Maximising Our Value* review in 2011.[11] Initially there was one female General Manager appointed out of eight; this has now increased to three out of nine.)

The rather rapid increase in numbers of women on the Executive in 2003 sent a strong signal to the organisation that women could undertake executive roles in Austrade, and provided other women in Austrade with more diversity in their role models. It is instructive to note that women on the executive have held all portfolios excluding that of CEO and Executive Directors with offshore responsibility.

Survey input from some respondents in this group confirms that changes were consciously put in place in the early-mid 2000s to

---

11 Austrade Annual Report 2010-11: Maximizing Our Value, May 2011.

enhance the organisational response to gender issues. These included having a female on all selection panels regardless of whether there were female applicants, improved policies to support part time work and flexible hours, and the recruitment of women to the Executive team and into senior management. Mentor programs for Austrade staff started in the 1990s and continue today. Gender balance remained under discussion at the Executive table as a valid business issue throughout the 2000s. The challenges cited by some of these respondents do not relate to gender but to other business issues such as leading through profound change, lack of recognition of the importance of onshore roles, lack of shared understanding of the roles that made up Austrade and an internal focus on process over outcome.

2000: The new millennium

Survey respondents who worked as female trade commissioners and managers in Austrade during the 2000s cited further progress on gender issues, but some also had challenges related to being a female at Austrade. A few indicated that they experienced no gender discrimination. This group had lots of female role models and support from other women in Austrade. They were very aware of the internal programs for women in Austrade as well as the external programs run by Austrade aimed at assisting female exporters. One individual indicated that Austrade was really helpful in supporting her through the maternity process when she was pregnant on her posting. Another cited the new CEO initiatives for women in 2014 as excellent, but needing more communication.

On the other hand, a substantial number of survey respondents felt that an unspoken male sub-culture was still present in Austrade throughout the early-mid 2000s. Many of these women described a culture favouring masculinity, using words like "boys network moments", "expectations arising from male privilege and expectation", "preferred working styles biased to masculine traits" and "alpha male management culture". A recurring theme seemed to be that these women felt they had to prove their capability twice as much as men.

Different management styles between women and men were also noted with comments that some male managers (with many other exceptions) were poor in delivering performance feedback, or had a sub-conscious or conscious bias and treated female staff like they treated their wives and daughters. Survey responses also highlighted that females on interview panels had a noticeably different approach to communication and interview techniques. Some women flagged the balancing act between not wishing to be too direct and aggressive and still wishing to be considered for opportunities. Others worried about being pigeon-holed in traditional female activities at post like clearing up.

A big issue for many of these women was balancing work and family responsibilities with a sense that interruptions in their work due to childbearing meant it was harder for them to avail themselves of opportunities such as short term assignments offshore, consequently making it harder to get to the top. Many mentioned the difficulties of juggling home, family and work. One cited issues for spouses working in some markets and how this can derail a spouse's career.

Non-gender related challenges cited included a lack of direction in Austrade, ensuring other government departments understood and valued Austrade's contribution, the dilemma of delivering what the government and the minister wanted whilst generating value for Austrade clients, not enough people who were good at detail and fierce internal competition for promotions and postings.

A number of our survey respondents cited the statistics, commenting that A-based representation off-shore and on-shore was still top heavy with men, and that there had been a noticeable drop off in female Senior Trade Commissioner (STC) appointments since the mid-2000s. In support of this observation, it is instructive to consider the impact of the Uhrig Review of 2003[12] and Austrade's transition into the Australian Public Service in 2006. Unlike the previous system where A-based staff offshore were appointed on three year rolling

---

12 http://www.finance.gov.au/archive/financial-framework/governance/review_corporate_governance.html

contracts and assessed strongly on performance, being part of the APS guaranteed them longer-term employment. As current employees needed to be placed in jobs, this generally coincided with a greater focus on promoting internal candidates, in the wake of what some in the Austrade network had come to criticise as a focus on performance leading to a perceived bias towards the "unknown" attraction of external candidates over the "known" limitations of internal candidates.

Whilst this may seem on the surface to have been a good thing, with a corresponding reduction in the number of SES positions onshore and ever-present budgetary constraints, it had become even more difficult to promote younger internal candidates into more senior positions, male or female. In the years leading up to the Maximizing our Value Review of 2011,[13] the vacuum in the talent pipeline became increasingly obvious, and steps have been taken to address it. In 2011 a number of male and female candidates were newly promoted into SES Band 1 positions with a view to achieving workforce renewal and developing the managers of the future.

Women as Overseas Engaged Employees

Austrade has consistently employed a higher proportion of women than men amongst its Overseas Engaged Employees (OEE), around 60 per cent when averaged out across all offshore regions.[14] The observations and comments in this chapter are based input we received from 26 current and former female OEE staff, representing all offshore regions of Austrade, including comments from some who have served as Regional HR Managers.

At the outset it should be noted that the response to our survey from all of the current and former overseas engaged employees was overwhelmingly positive. It is indeed a credit to Austrade as an organisation that it strove to build from its inception a culture which

---

13 Refer footnote 6.
14 Refer Chart 1: "Women in Austrade" Source: Austrade gender statistics, percentage of females varies by market.

values the contribution of overseas engaged employees equally to that of A-based staff. Respondents to our survey all voiced their support for the policies of Austrade as a fair, open and equitable organisation, which empowers and indeed challenges them to develop their capabilities, enhance their knowledge across a broad range of sectors, and take on leadership roles of various kinds.

This translates into a very high degree of job satisfaction amongst the OEE staff in general. Our survey indicates that Austrade is an attractive employer for female OEE staff in many countries, particularly in Asia, as it offers a work environment which is not gender-biased, and in fact gives women more chance to develop themselves professionally than they would encounter elsewhere in their own society. As one respondent noted: "It was quite refreshing for me to join Austrade, where my marital status and relationships did not affect my hiring process. Rather, it was the skills, experience and qualifications that were important." Another added: "Austrade introduced a corporate culture that encourages its women to be more active with their personal development both in business and in their personal lives. This has been made possible with technology." Overall, OEE survey respondents indicated a high degree of appreciation for, and engagement in, the various programs and initiatives that Austrade has implemented in more recent years to support its female staff.[15]

Inevitably, as the roles and responsibilities of OEE staff differ from those of their A-based colleagues, so too do their issues and challenges. In examining the reasons for the larger numbers of female OEE staff in Austrade, nurturing both male and female staff equally has certainly played a role in attracting female applicants. On the other hand, the flat structure and lack of ability to advance significantly, and absence of longer-term superannuation and pension arrangements in some markets have been barriers to attracting quality male candidates to locally-engaged positions. This is particularly the case in Asian markets where life-time employment is still highly valued.

---

15 Refer to later sections of this paper.

Those with experience on Austrade OEE recruitment panels often strike another problem in North and South East Asia: simply that female candidates tend to be of a higher quality and more motivated in many instances. This may be symptomatic of the fact that women in general still feel that they need to work twice as hard to prove themselves in many places around the world.

Maintaining a gender balance across the OEE staff profile, and within the relatively small numbers that apply to specific Austrade offices offshore, can be challenging at times. Experience has shown that too many women in any given office can be just as bad as not enough. There can be a tendency for women to compete too strongly and to judge each other too harshly in the absence of balancing factors. Diversity of thought, action and approaches to the job on the part of OEE staff is best achieved through a mix of both male and female staff. As one interviewee put it: "There is a greater sense of peace and harmony in the office when we have men as well as women in the OEE staff."

By way of contrast, there are different issues to contend with in developed markets such as the United States. Feedback received through our survey and at interview highlighted the litigious nature of the environment, stronger legal protections for women and more conservative approach to political correctness in approaching gender issues, which contrasts with the informal and direct approach common in Australia.

In other markets such as Europe and the Middle East, the observation was made that often women need to be encouraged to push themselves forward and "profile" their achievements. As one individual noted: "Women expect to be recognised and rewarded for their efforts ... which doesn't always happen. Women need to be taught how to manage their careers as well as their projects and families."

The issues raised by the OEE staff who responded to our survey were different in that they tended not to be gender-specific. Rather, they shared a number of common themes that are unique to the OEE staff and primarily relate to the way in which they go about their jobs, their relationships with their A-based managers, and the flat structure that applies to locally engaged staff in Austrade.

There have been numerous examples of women in Austrade over the years, (including Elizabeth Masamune, Julie-Anne Nichols, Nicola Watkinson, Liu Bing, Wendy Haydon, Dianne Zhou, Joanne Lee, Min-joo Sohn, Green Yang and Rika Sasaki), who started their careers in Austrade as OEE staff and made the transition to A-based roles, including that of Trade Commissioner and Senior Trade Commissioner. For those with Australian citizenship, Austrade's policy of considering high-performing OEE candidates for A-based roles has long been a draw card.

For the most part, however, the limited opportunity for advancement and the amount of time that it can take to move through the ranks from a junior to a senior business development manager is a common concern to all OEE staff. Austrade has attempted to compensate for this over the years by offering other forms of personal and professional development to its staff; in particular, short-term overseas assignments to Australia and other markets have been very popular, as has participation in organisation-wide development programs such as AAP (Austrade Advancement Program).

The hierarchical nature of Austrade and dispersed geographical network mean that A-based managers in offshore locations have a great deal of localised power and responsibility, as well as a duty of care to the OEE staff. Ensuring that OEE staff have a way to voice their concerns when rare cases of workplace harassment may occur, and feel well equipped to deal with such pressures is an ongoing issue which Austrade is proactively addressing through its Workplace Health and Safety framework.

The other challenge which has been consistently raised by the OEE survey respondents is the constant changing of the goal posts. As Austrade corporate direction and strategy has changed over the years, a mounting strain has been placed on the OEE staff as they are asked to take on an increasingly large number of tasks of quite a diverse nature. As one respondent most aptly stated: "Austrade is a constant changing organisation. Through the river of changes, the focus of our work could be quite different from time to time. Some changes are good, but some changes are just reinventing the wheels. I feel frustrated when the changes don't make sense." Another added: "My greatest achievement is I am still working for Austrade. Accommodating so many things is now one of my strong skills."

Recent Austrade Programs to Support Women

Internal Programs:

2007: Women's Security Course

In 2007 Austrade offered a personal security course to staff across the network. A female only version of the course came about at the instigation of then Executive Director Pat Evans, who had noticed on visits to posts and offices in Australia that conversations with staff were very different when coincidentally conducted with a group of women only. She considered that it would be good for female staff if a version of the personal security course that Austrade was already providing could be tailor-made just for women. The idea was supported and 15 women from around Australia participated in the two day course. A half-day session on presentation and communication skills was also included as an addition to the security course, specifically designed for women who spent most of their time dealing with male clients.

Many security issues are the same for women and men, but in the female-only group the discussions were quite open and more personal about the issues female staff faced, with a lot of sharing of helpful ideas and tactics. The male program facilitator at the time confirmed that these discussions were very different from those in the mixed gender groups, where women may be more careful about making comments that could expose them as being weak or unsuitable for specific roles. The program received a lot of positive feedback from participants as being designed to meet their specific needs.

2008: The Austrade Women's Network (AWN)

The Austrade Women's Network (AWN) was also started by Pat Evans in 2008 as she believed Austrade had a responsibility to provide more support to the women in its network around the world. She submitted a paper to the Austrade Executive on 1 April 2008 to set out the case for a women's network, citing major corporations and other government departments who had programs in place to develop/mentor their female staff. It outlined how the network would be set up, what the content and communication plan would be, and in true Austrade style there was a steering committee established with a champion from each onshore division and one representative from offshore, with Pat Evans as the Executive Sponsor. Despite some initial hesitance, the business case was signed off by the Austrade Executive, and all members of the Executive allowed their staff to participate.

With the support and energy of a dedicated group of women from all parts of Austrade, a network was developed that surveyed female staff about their interests, reviewed the gender statistics, and set up a virtual AWN communication space. The AWN adopted McKinsey's model "Centred Leadership: How talented women thrive"[16] as the operating model for its network meetings. It introduced and piloted the "My Mentor" program by Emberin[17] and ran four network meetings with over 100 participants at each, breaking new ground in the innovative use of the videoconferencing (VC) technology (i.e., eight VCs, 17 people web streaming and up to 50 attending in the Sydney office), with up to 40 per cent participating from offshore, (including some at home in their pyjamas!)

Guest speakers came from McKinsey, Deloittes, and AON, as well as from the Austrade network and addressed the five dimensions of leadership from McKinsey's Centred Leadership model: Meaning, Managing Energy, Engaging, Positive Framing, and Connecting. Each of the sessions was enthusiastically received by staff around the world. After three years the Austrade Women's Network had

16 Barsh, Cranston and Craske 2008, *The McKinsey Quarterly*, 2008, Number 4:35.
17 Emberin My Mentor program.

made it legitimate for female staff to discuss women's issues in the workplace. The network continued until the departure of Pat Evans from Austrade in September 2011.

2009: My Mentor

The AWN surveyed 118 women in July/August 2008 seeking input on issues of interest to them. The top areas of interest were: leadership skills for women (87 per cent), career planning advice (85 per cent), mentoring programs (78 per cent), and work life balance tips (76 per cent). To address these key areas of interest to Austrade's women, a pilot was launched of the My Mentor program from Emberin. The pilot was an initiative sponsored by the AWN, and Austrade Human Resources provided support in its implementation.

Emberin's My Mentor program is a global research-based educational program especially designed to help women create the careers that they deserve and are capable of, whilst they manage their multiple lives and deal with the pressures of home and family. It is based on global research into the key areas women need to improve in order to move themselves into more senior roles. It has a strong focus on decision-making, personal branding and taking career risks – statistically, women are not as good at taking career risks as men.[18]

The pilot was run over May and June 2009 with 20 women from Australia, North East Asia, South East Asia, South Asia and the Pacific, due to time zone issues. Emberin surveyed participants to assist Austrade evaluate the effectiveness of the program.[19] There was strong support for the program: 100 per cent of participants found the program relevant and effective and have had the opportunity to apply their learnings at work. Key skills learned included: gaining confidence and positive thinking, goal setting, influencing people of different styles, negotiation, communication styles, developing my personal brand, visibility and networking, and planning.

18 Emberin My Mentor program.
19 Emberin My Mentor Pilot Evaluation Report, Program Completion Survey Results Austrade 17 Sept. 2009.

The pilot was deemed successful and enabled the AWN to tailor the program to better suit the needs of Austrade women. The My Mentor program was then handed over to HR and was run a number of times in Europe and the Middle East from April-June 2010 and February-May 2011, and in the Americas and Australia from September-November 2010 for male and female staff alike. The program continues to be run by HR and is well received by female staff. Many have indicated that the program really helped them in their careers.

The insight gained from attending some of the program sessions and My Mentor graduations made it clear that the transformational power of the program was illustrated through the comments from a range of participants. "Not being afraid to speak up", "having 'ah-ha' moments", "telling people about my own successes", "being proud for being a female", "understanding differences in male and female styles", "more confident in dealing with people in the office", "not alone with issues", "aware of personal traits", "moments of discovery through-out", "becoming more proactive and re-evaluating everything in my life" were just several examples of the way in which women felt moved by their experience on the My Mentor program.

External Programs:

Women in Export

Austrade has long been a leader in providing support for women involved in exporting and international business. A "Women in Export" program started sometime in the 1990s, but as interest waned over time it was discontinued. More seminars were trialled in 2002 and 2003, and in 2004-5 Austrade re-launched a formal "Women in Export" program which consisted of an annual national seminar series, publishing and promoting the success stories of women business owners who had achieved export success, export training and education, and overseas missions. This was followed by the formation of the "Women in Global Business" program.

Women in Global Business (WIGB)

The Women in Global Business (WIGB) program[20] is a joint initiative of the Federal, State and Territory Governments, supported by Austrade. It was launched in December 2010. Its objective is to increase female participation in international trade and investment, thereby delivering increased economic benefit and job creation through greater diversity. The program provides information and resources, support, advocacy, connection and communication services to support Australian business women to engage in international trade and investment.

WIGB addresses the barriers women face in doing international business by offering a number of services including:

- information and resources;
- mentoring;
- skills and capacity building;
- workshops and events;
- research into the barriers and motivations of women as they engage with international markets;
- inbound and outbound missions;
- advocacy on the domestic and international stage.

WIGB is the only nationally coordinated joint government program focused on increasing Australian businesswomen's economic empowerment through the expansion of domestic businesses into global markets. The inaugural international WIGB chapter will be launched in Indonesia in March 2015 to build connections between women-owned SMEs in each market and to support capacity building in Indonesia. Other markets are planned to follow in 2015.

International Women's Fora

Austrade and WIGB have been active participants of APEC women's fora, from the initial APEC Women Leaders Network through to

---

20 http://www.wigb.gov.au

the current APEC Policy Partnership on Women and the Economy (PPWE). Austrade organised and Elizabeth Masamune acted as the Delegation Leader for the Australian Delegation to the APEC Womens Leaders Network in Tokyo in 2009. WIGB has presented on multiple occasions at the APEC WEF (Women and the Economy Forum) international conferences. This fora is attended by all APEC countries and involves senior government and private sector women business leaders.

WIGB partnered with the Department of Foreign Affairs and Trade in 2014 to design a workshop under Australia's APEC commitments aimed at developing programs within Trade Promotion Organisations to support women-led SMEs in exporting. The *Promoting SME Development: Assisting Women-Owned SMEs to Access the Global Markets* workshop was delivered over three days in Manila, Philippines in late November 2014. Further stages will be delivered in 2015.

Austrade remains an innovator and through WIGB will continue to engage with international fora such as APEC, IORA (Indian Ocean Rim Association), UN Women and with other international organisations. The objective is to develop interconnectedness with other trade promotion organisations and related agencies.

2013: The Beryl Wilson Scholarship

In 2013 Austrade introduced the Beryl Wilson Austrade Scholarship for Women in International Business in recognition of Mrs Beryl Wilson, the first woman to be appointed as a Trade Commissioner in 1963.[21] The purpose of the scholarship is to encourage, support and advance the involvement of women in international business. The scholarship will also contribute towards building Asia-capable staff and leaders. The award recipient will have the opportunity to contribute to and be supported by the WIGB program and to undertake 6 weeks of paid work experience with Austrade. The value of the one

21 http://www.austrade.gov.au/about-austrade/employment/scholarships/beryl-wil-son-austrade-scholarship-for-women-in-international-business

year scholarship is up to $40,000, which will be applied to tuition fees and texts. Candidates must be female Australian citizens with an Asian language and enrolled full-time in the final year of a master's degree in international business.

Women in Austrade today

Some of the women currently in Austrade are still highlighting issues that were raised by generations before them. Notwithstanding, the comments we received suggest that the situation for women continues to improve at Austrade. Many women responding to our survey commended the current CEO's recent initiatives to support female staff such as inviting two high-potential female officers to participate in executive decision-making, the Beryl Wilson scholarship and his general support for diversity issues, and support of the Women in Global Business program (WIGB). A number of current staff indicated how much they appreciate the flexible approach to parental leave, flexible working hours and part time work for women. Some noted that Austrade promotes on talent and provides a good support network. The mentoring program was consistently mentioned by women as a positive initiative.

It is interesting to note that in response to the question about whether it felt different being a woman in Austrade more of this cohort indicated that it did feel different.[22] On the other hand, they generally seemed aware of the programs available for women and were in most cases supported by female colleagues.

The issue of starting a family continues to be problematic for women with some saying they accept that their career advancement will be limited or on hold for at least five years after they have a child. One woman was asked by a colleague if she was leaving work when she got engaged. Another woman noticed a difference in her interactions with some male managers after she had a child. "Having children is a sacrifice men don't have to make" seems to sum up the

---

22 Refer Appendix 2.

issue. There were also issues raised around the support provided to women on maternity leave to allow them to continue to stay connected to the workplace and changes taking place at Austrade. Women with family responsibilities found it difficult to do short term overseas assignments (STOAs) which help build the experience necessary for postings.

Comments that some men in leadership roles seem more aggressive and 'blokey' in their communication styles contrast with the perception that other respondents equally felt that women in powerful positions are also different in approach or style and can appear threatening or unlikeable. Some women feel they are taken less seriously by external male contacts who defer to male staff rather than the more senior female decision-maker. There seems to be more of a difference for some females posted offshore where there are not as many women, fewer support mechanisms and less recognition that it can be different for women. Often one can be the only woman at the table at representational functions and faces questions on why she is working and her husband is not. Hence, for some of our respondents, cultural differences rank much higher as an issue than gender differences per se.

In terms of challenges for this group, a number cited the lack of women in senior management in the offshore network and the executive. Flexibility for parental carers and a program to transition people to retirement were also nominated. Other challenges were more personal relating to frustrations regarding promotion or lack of recognition for investment, education or tourism skills in an organisation with a culture still dominated by trade.

Outside of gender issues many faced challenges with ongoing budget cuts and lean resources. Some noted a lack of leadership and vison at senior levels or inconsistent core strategy which shifts due to senior management changes and changing governments.

Austrade recently commissioned its own internal research into women's experiences and workplace outcomes.[23] Many of the themes

---

23 Austrade internal research 2014.

from that research were echoed by our survey respondents such as how highly the WIGB program is regarded, the value of mentors, and the importance of women supporting each other. The research found many positive comments about Austrade including participants describing the atmosphere as respectful and non-aggressive, friendly and relaxed with work that is interesting, challenging and always changing. The following themes were highlighted as areas needing attention to help make Austrade an even better place to work: communication, impact of gender on advancement, OEE development and retention, workplace flexibility, recruitment, family responsibilities including maternity leave and return to work, mentors and role models. These align closely with the areas nominated in our survey.

Conclusion

In our survey we asked respondents if it felt different being a woman in Austrade, just as Julia Gillard indicated that gender was one of many reasons why her experience as Prime Minister was different from those who had come before her.[24] The verdict was split squarely down the middle, with half of the respondents indicating that they did not feel different, while the other half did.[25] Notwithstanding the subjective nature of the question, it is clear that for some women, at least, being a woman has posed additional pressures and challenges to their pursuit of a career at Austrade.

For many women who have worked at Austrade in the past and still do today, the open and equitable nature of its employment framework has always been a reassuring and encouraging factor. Some of our interviewees and respondents have noted that this was indeed one of the reasons they chose a career with Austrade, rather than in the private sector where the barriers may have been greater. Austrade has always been a good employer; this is borne out by the results of

24 *Sydney Morning Herald*, 29 April 2014.
25 Refer Appendix 2.

our survey as well as Austrade's own internal research. The efforts of senior female executives who have led the HR team in making Austrade a better place for women to work should be acknowledged here, notably Margaret Ward from 1995 to 2000, and Marcia Kimball from 2000 to 2014.

In concluding this chapter on Women in Austrade we must ask ourselves this fundamental question: to what extent are the issues and challenges for women raised herein specific to Austrade, and to what extent are they symptomatic of Australian society and business circles overall? As Austrade pushes ahead with further programs to support and nurture its female talent and enhance diversity, the Australian business community has also turned its attention to the need for greater participation by women on boards, in senior management, and in the workplace more broadly.

The personal and collective achievements of generations of women in Austrade since its inception to the present day have been an integral part of making the organisation what it is today; sincere thanks to all who have so generously responded to the Women in Austrade survey we conducted and provided input to and information for this chapter.

Women have made a significant contribution to Austrade in a wide variety of roles both onshore and offshore and have made their mark in global business. We trust that Austrade will continue to be a place where women can thrive.

Appendices

Appendix 1: Commonwealth of Australia, Minute Paper, 13 March 1963

COMMONWEALTH OF AUSTRALIA

MINUTE PAPER

THE DIRECTOR:

WOMEN TRADE COMMISSIONERS ?

Even after some deliberation, it is difficult to find reasons to support the appointment of women Trade Commissioners.

In countries where publicity media is well developed, such as North America and England and where there are no other major drawbacks, such as the Islamic attitude towards women, a relatively young attractive woman could operate with some effectiveness, in a subordinate capacity. As she would probably be the only woman Assistant Trade Commissioner in the whole area, as other countries employ women in this capacity hardly at all, she could attract a measure of interest and publicity.

If we had an important trade in women's clothing and accessories, a woman might promote this more effectively than a man.

Even conceding these points, such an appointee would not stay young and attractive for ever and later on could well become a problem.

It is much easier to find difficulties, some of which spring to mind are:-

(i)   Women are not employed, except to an extremely minor degree, as career Trade Commissioners in any known service;

(ii)   It is difficult to visualize them as Trade Commissioners, firstly because they could not mix nearly as freely with businessmen as men do. Most mens clubs, for instance, do not allow women members;

(iii)   Relationships with businessmen would tend to be somewhat formal and guarded on both sides. This would make it more difficult for a woman to obtain information;

(iv)   It is extremely doubtful if a woman could, year after year, under a variety of conditions, stand the fairly severe strains and stresses, mentally and physically, which are part of the life of a Trade Commissioner;

(v)   A man normally has his household run efficiently by his wife, who also looks after much of the entertaining. A woman Trade Commissioner would have all this on top of her normal work;

(vi)   If we engaged single graduates as trainees, most of them would probably marry within five years;

(vii)   If we recruited from the business world, we would have a much smaller field from which to recruit, as the number of women executives in business is quite small;

(viii)   A spinster lady can, and very often does, turn into something of a battleaxe with the passing years. A man usually mellows;

- 2 -

4

(ix) A woman would take the place of a man and preclude us from
giving practical experience to one male officer. She could
marry at any time and be lost to us. She could not be
regarded as a long term investment in the same sense as we
regard a man.

CONCLUSION

It would seem that the noes have it.

ai

(A. R. Taysom)

13th March, 1963.

P.S.
                I have since ascertained the following,
which, it would seem, only serves to support the foregoing
views -

Mr. H.W. Woodruff, U.K. Trade Commissioner:
                They have a few women Trade Commissioners
but only in capital city posts, for they have found that women
cannot operate where contact with businessmen is necessary.
                The women are fairly senior people from the
U.K. Departments and presumably handle trade policy work only.

Mr. N. Parkinson, External Affairs:
                Since their recruitments of trainees are made
under the Public Service Act, there is no way of precluding women
from applying and in fact, many more applications are received
from women than from men. Some are chosen and all appointments
are made on the basis of the quality of their educational achievements. About one woman is appointed to every twelve men. This
year one out of sixteen, last year one out of twelve and the
previous year, none.
                They have to be trained for 18 months before
going to their first post. The average marries within five years.
                It is a very expensive process, but External
Affairs lack courage to slam the door because of parliamentary
opinion, pressure groups and so on.

ai

(A. R. Taysom)

Appendix 2: Women in Austrade Survey, November 2014, selected results summaries

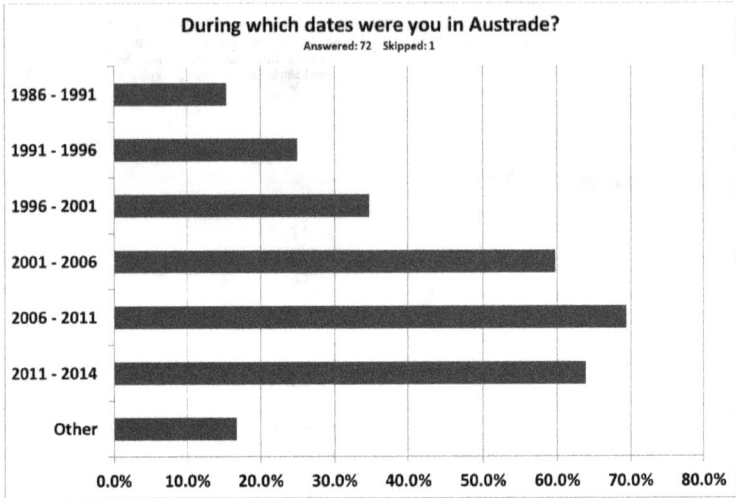

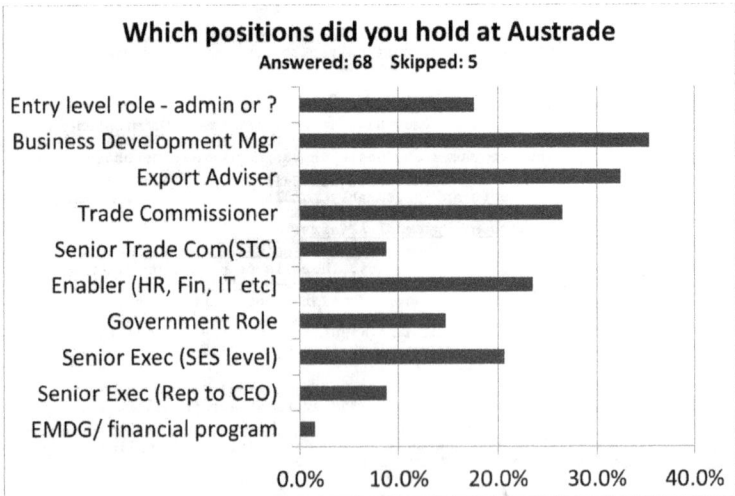

During which dates were you in Austrade?
Answered: 72 Skipped: 1

Period	
1986 - 1991	
1991 - 1996	
1996 - 2001	
2001 - 2006	
2006 - 2011	
2011 - 2014	
Other	

0.0% 10.0% 20.0% 30.0% 40.0% 50.0% 60.0% 70.0% 80.0%

Which positions did you hold at Austrade
Answered: 68 Skipped: 5

Position	
Entry level role - admin or ?	
Business Development Mgr	
Export Adviser	
Trade Commissioner	
Senior Trade Com(STC)	
Enabler (HR, Fin, IT etc]	
Government Role	
Senior Exec (SES level)	
Senior Exec (Rep to CEO)	
EMDG/ financial program	

0.0% 10.0% 20.0% 30.0% 40.0%

Where did you spend most of your career in Austrade

Answered: 72 Skipped: 1

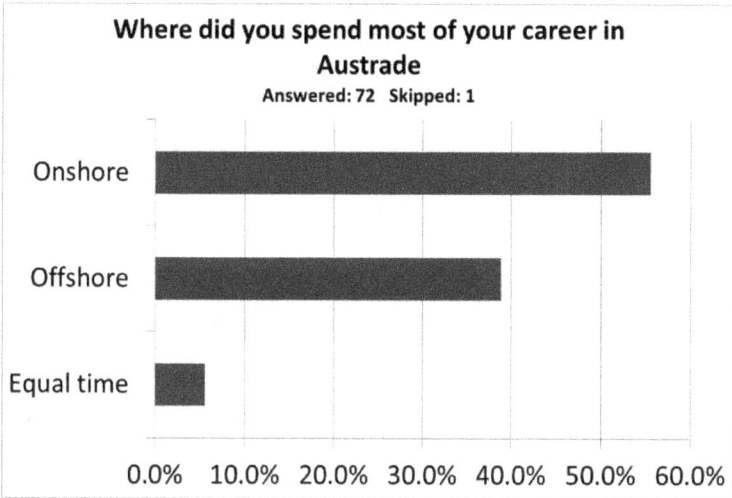

Did you feel your gender made it different for you as a woman in Austrade

Answered: 64 Skipped: 9

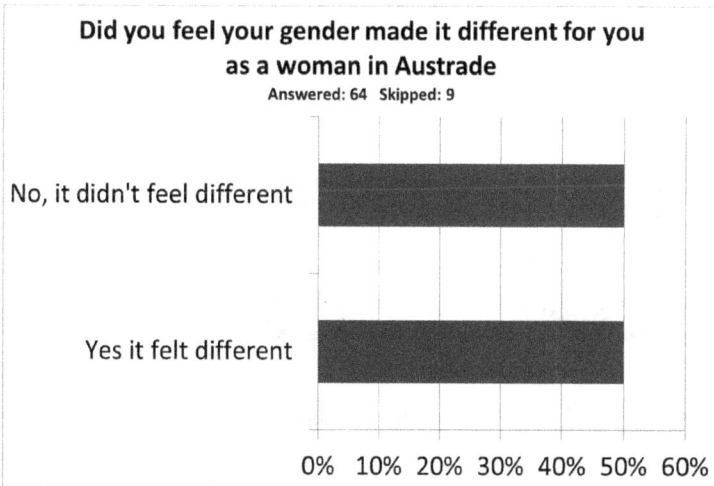

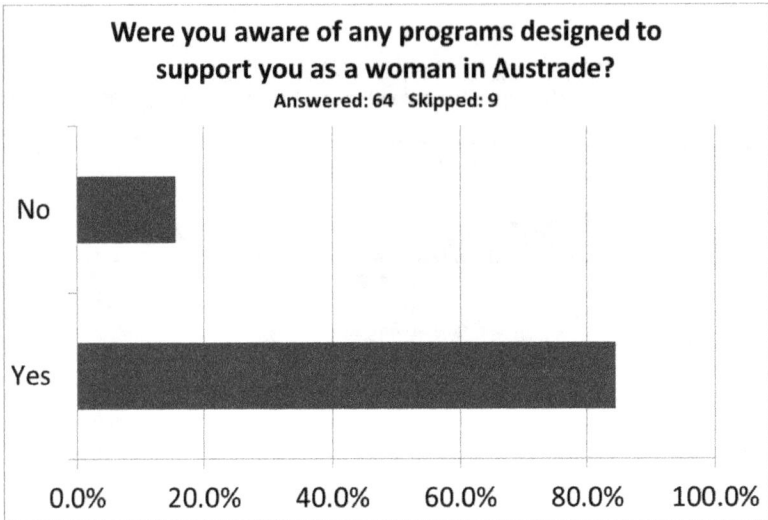
Were you aware of any programs designed to support you as a woman in Austrade?
Answered: 64 Skipped: 9

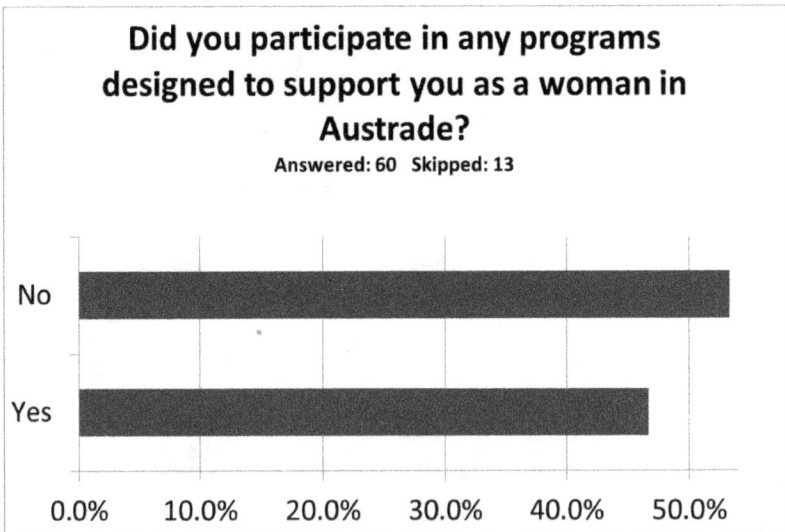
Did you participate in any programs designed to support you as a woman in Austrade?
Answered: 60 Skipped: 13

17

A view from an Austrade local employed manager in Prague, Czech Republic

Petr Vodvarka

Introduction

Smart text books are advising that a male, turning 40, should make a sincere self-assessment of how satisfactory and fulfilling his current job is. This process should be then followed by a decision on what he really would like to do for a living and making appropriate changes, if necessary. Based on that advice, I was carefully looking for my chance. I was employed by quite a reputable consulting company (PA Consulting Group) and was happy there. Except I never received feedback from clients about the usefulness of my work. We esteemed consultants, were not responsible for the implementation of the results of our work. We just delivered our findings and recommendations, got paid and off we went.

An Australian Trade Commission (Austrade) advertisement which I found by chance in the newspapers was a good opportunity to reconsider the above. The Austrade job offer was totally different from other advertisements. It asked for many skills and much experience, it asked for creativeness which would be used within the organisation. My 16 years' experience with Austrade has proven the seriousness and correctness of that offer.

The purpose of this chapter is to inform readers about the Austrade operation in the Czech Republic, as part of Central Europe, and provide an insight into the challenges and benefits from working for this organisation, as well as the function of Austrade, and the position and uniqueness of the Central European market.

Perception of Australia

In the early 1990s, when people from post-communist countries started to take on responsibility for their own lives, freedom in making decisions and returning to a market-driven economy based on capitalist principles, Czechoslovakia opened its borders and let Czechs and Slovaks travel freely abroad. Soon, travellers brought back information about foreign countries, their lifestyles, local communities and opportunities for doing business.

Australia, which was still understood as an exotic country due to its geographic distance, had always experienced a highly positive perception, now confirmed by travellers, businessmen, students and expats returning back home and spreading their positive word. If you asked anybody on the street how he/she would define Australia, the response would be: clean, safe and friendly country taking good care of the living environment and people. Those, who visit Australia, return as Australian ambassadors and would emphasise that the balance between the effective Australian economy and the quality of life of individual people is incredibly precise.

Businessmen appreciate up-to-the point business negotiations and reliability of existing or future partners. Students talk about high quality education courses in modern facilities among the international student community, travellers adore services making Australian cities and the outback absolutely enjoyable. During my 16 years' dealing with Australia I have never heard a single complaint or bad word about the Australian experience, nor about any unpleasant situation in dealing with Australian authorities or individuals.

In light of that, "Made in Australia" is a solid selling message, encouraging Czechs to explore the country as a study or business target, and sensational tourist experience offering everything from shallow tropical seas to the snowy mountains. Australia is an allowed drug for an estimated 7,000 Czechs visiting Australia in 2013, and a number of others, planning or dreaming to visit at some early occasion.

Australian mission in the Czech Republic

The Austrade office was established in 1991-2 in Prague hand-in-hand with the Australian Embassy. Not long after, on 1 January 1993, Czechoslovakia split in two independent countries: Czech Republic and Slovak Republic (Slovakia). As a result the presence of the Australian Embassy in Prague lost its meaning and was soon closed. At the same moment, an Australian Honorary Consulate for the Czech Republic was established, reporting to the Australian Embassy in Warsaw, Poland, while Slovakia came under the responsibility of the Australian Embassy in Vienna (as it was closer to the Slovak capital city Bratislava, than Prague). The Austrade office retained its responsibility over the territory of the two sovereign countries – Czech Republic and Slovakia.

Uniqueness

The combination of Austrade activities on the one hand the business development and on the other the consular service has been a great worldwide strategic decision and is extremely well accepted by local community as a one-stop-shop. Czechs do not make much of a difference between Austrade and the Consulate – they simply see AUSTRALIA and expect high quality service and professionalism.

The fact that there exists an office with a badge of the Australian government, offering trade and investment support, marketing information, as well as a consular advice and service, is very highly valued by the local community and the Australian citizen. At the same time this makes the Prague Post extremely busy. A small team of four supported by onshore and offshore colleagues provides excellent service representing the Australian government.

At the same moment, combining the functions is quite challenging. Emergency consular cases occur in most cases unexpectedly and have priority over all other business and affect the routine performance of the office. According to statistics, provided by the Czech Ministry of Regional Development, 75,000 Australians visited Czech Republic, mostly Prague, in 2013 – and a sizeable percentage require consular service.

Compared with similar foreign in-market business development entities (e.g., Chambers of Commerce), Austrade offers its clients a more complex assistance package and valuable support in properly addressing export/investment requirements, assistance in assessment of readiness to export or investment, providing market insights and industry briefings, positioning clients on the market; and identification of most relevant potential partners and organising direct communication with chosen ones. Without exaggeration, Austrade always goes an extra mile with its clients.

Support to Australian exporters and investors

In the early '90s, the main Australian export item to the Czech Republic was wool and wool tops (demand for Australian wool is traditional, going back more than 70 years). Local demand for new products spun-off Australian export: wine, meat, natural cosmetics, cosmeceuticals and leisure clothing on one side, and information kiosks, horse racing starting gates, telecommunication devices, Cochlear implants and sophisticated medical equipment on the other side. Within the last 20 years, Australian exports has grown almost sevenfold from US$25 million in 1993 to US$170 million 2013 (Businessinfo 2014). During these last 20 years of operation, the Austrade office in Prague has assisted more than 150 Australian companies to find a local distributing partner for their products or services.

Australia spotted Czech and Slovak Republics for investments in the early 1990s. At first, massive outward Australian investment was undertaken by Coca-Cola Amatil (beverage bottler) in 1991, followed by QBE (corporate and retail insurance), Pioneer (ready-mix concrete supply), Anglo-Australian developers Bovis and Lease, Village Cinemas (movie entertainment multiplexes), Mincom (management software for mining industry) and Howe Leather (leather interiors for luxury car). Unfortunately many of those investments left the Czech and Slovak markets as a direct impact of global financial crisis in 2007–9. However, the biggest single Australian investment in Europe ever was completed in the Czech Republic in 2011 was by the Macquarie Group, acquiring Ceske Radiokomunikace (operator of broadcasting and telecommunication tower infrastructure), for €574 million (Macquarie Group, 2010).

Czech imports to Australia

On flip side of the coin, Czech exports to Australia are doing very well also similar to the growth of exports from Australia. Czech imports have grown almost sevenfold within the last 20 years, from US$46 million in 1993 to US$ 668 million in 2013 (Businessinfo, 2014). The main Czech import are passenger vehicles (Skoda brand), toys (Lego, now manufactured in the Czech Republic, and wooden toys) building machinery and machining equipment. Ever since the softening of the global financial crisis in 2010, Czech imports have grown by ten per cent every year.

Czech (and Slovak) investments, on the contrary, are still quite rare and small scale. However, growing interest in investment activities in Australia is visible, *vis-a-vis* the fact that Australia is a gateway to Asia-Pacific region, being at the same time the most developed country in this region.

The Prague Post is also busy promoting Australian education to local students. Quality education traditionally assumes a high position on the prestige ladder. In 2013, there were 2,639 Czech and 1,511 Slovak student enrolments in Australia (Austrade 2014) and the number is a growing trend according to local education agents. Czech and Slovak students target mostly English courses (ELICOS–

English Language Intensive Courses for International Students). However, as the market matures, students' interest will become more focused on higher education. Studying a semester or two in Australia (business, environment, law, medicine, and Asian cultures) belongs to an important part of the student curriculum vitae and is positively accepted by future employees. Australia is, after the UK and the USA, the most favoured study destination for Czech students.

Austrade also assists Australian, Czech and Slovak universities in their mutual collaboration efforts. The number of existing bilateral cooperation agreements, currently at 26 (2014 figures) will be increased soon. Areas of cooperation cover student and teaching staff exchange, sharing curricula, implementation of dual diploma plans and, importantly, cooperation in R&D projects, especially in biotechnology, nanotechnology, telemedicine and innovative materials.

Working for the Australian government is attractive and challenging

With no doubt, working for Australian government is a great opportunity and experience. Austrade constantly develops, reacting to global (and, of course, Australian) economic and business community demands. Like it or not, Austrade staff need to adapt to these changes, should they want to remain capable and respectful to serving the needs of clients and customers.

At the same time, Austraders are constantly exposed to ongoing heavy learning processes. Almost each Australian client deals with a different product or service which they wish to export or find a partner for cooperation. Austrade BDMs (Business Development Managers) are obliged to understand how the product or service works, its features and added value, its benefits to local customers. In other words products or service needs to be "purchased" internally first to be able to be effectively "sold" to local distributors or business partners.

Austrade as an organisation effectively supports its employees and invests much in their education and personal development. Each particular Austrader can access online high quality interactive courses on the Austrade Institute portal. These courses have been developed by reputable providers, ensuring delivery of most up to date information and findings in project development and management, communication and business writing skills, decision making, and negotiation skills. Austrade online courses are a real incentive for all employees.

An important task for all Austraders is to be knowledgeable about corporate procedures and policies. The ever changing situation in Austrade is simply following the dynamic and rapidly changing world, putting demand and requirements on business ethics, work and health safety, self-security, protection of business and personal data.

However, working for Austrade is also rewarding. Just one example for all. One sunny Friday morning I drove to work, and suddenly, a phone call came in. It was a particular wine distributor whom we assisted earlier to establish successful distribution in the Czech Republic. I expected a complaint. Why would you call from overseas otherwise? To my surprise, he told me: "Hi Petr, we are just sitting here on the porch, enjoying Friday evening and sipping wine. And I thought that I would just give you a ring to tell you how much of an excellent job you and your office did for us." Wow, I felt like I was flying after hearing that! That client made me really happy and proud!

Austrade's biggest asset

Austrade's biggest asset is people and the amount and variety of their knowledge, experience and skills they use and share. Working in international teams (nowadays mostly virtual) in combination with onshore colleagues' support, allows exchanging and multiplying this knowledge. It also allows it extension and delivery to newly arrived Austrade employees. This builds Austrade's excellence in high quality service delivery to clients and customers throughout the world.

The engagement of local people in Austrade offshore offices (called OEE = Overseas Engaged Employees) is a great and useful strategy. Applied recruitment system guarantees intake of educated, skilled and motivated people and, importantly, people having full understanding of local business culture and natural gut feeling how to successfully communicate and negotiate with local entities and institutions and businesses. It is a pity that at least some of them – nowadays – cannot become trade (or senior trade) commissioners in order to manage and lead an office. This role is dedicated only to A-based employees. Equipped with knowledge of both local and Australian economic and market trends, as well as business procedures, and using well-developed contact network for developing sound business opportunities for Australian companies, they are better understood and respected by local authorities, key industry players and allies than a foreigner. At times a non-local will have no understanding of the local language, nor its culture, which prevents engagement going any further than just formal and official meetings and negotiations.

When I started in Austrade, I admired how the group of STCs (Senior Trade Commissioners), leading the European posts, would work together supporting each other across-markets. This fact was, in particular, very visible during pan-European meetings where the spirit of collaboration and fellowship was most tangible.

Today, some managers have significant theoretical knowledge based on their education but cannot use it in practical life, lacking enough experience, empathy to accept local culture and adapt to local business culture. As a by-product, internal cross-market cooperation vanishes. I am sure there have been other managers over time that I could draw on as intellectual leaders – gurus. Allow me to mention two of them who had the biggest positive impact on European operations in Austrade.

In the period of the management under Charles Jamieson's (Austrade's Managing Director), the Austrade operation in Europe was managed by Executive General Manager for Europe, Charles O'Hanlon. Charles was exactly the man that any organisation can build on. He was a natural leader with extreme charisma, strategic thinking, and sense of responsibility but also with a sense of humour and deep empathy. European staff meetings, led by him, were always a big learning lesson. He had a clear vision about where the organisation should aim and strategically shifted his team in that direction. He did not hesitate risking and using unusual (now called innovative) ways and solutions. His friendly and open attitude to everybody was legendary.

I remember one staff meeting in Kufstein, Austria. As usual, that kind of meeting included a series of training sessions provided by outsourced specialists. There was a mix of 14 Austraders (some of them were very new to the organisation) sitting in a class room and learning managerial skills. Unexpectedly, Charles entered the room, just to greet the group. Then, he walked from person to person, shook his or her hand, called him or her by first name and said a couple of words of a very personalised character, for example: "How is your dog doing, does he feel any better now after his surgery?" Person by person, the same procedure: unmistakably using names and small personalised case. Then he apologised for disturbing, wished them all good luck and walked away. God only knows how he memorised all those names and where he got that specific information about each of us. Deep silence was interrupted by the presenter who said: "Well, you have just seen a great lesson of management." I am absolutely positive that everybody in the room would never change this boss for the blue sky.

Charles's big plan was to enable all European staff, including administrative and the IT team, to meet in person at one place. We knew each other only through emails and phone hook ups but many of us had never met face to face. It was before there were web cameras and videoconference equipment. That big plan was finally realised in January 2000, and 105 Austraders from all of the European posts met. What a magnificent feeling to see such a great group and be a part of it!

I personally experienced Charles's care and empathy in August 2002 when Prague and one third of the Czech Republic was destroyed by a giant flood. Our office was out of order, we were not even able to reach downtown Prague. Charles called me every day to ask how we were doing. His interest was visibly genuine. And his moral support absolutely priceless.

The other person I wanted to highlight was Charles's successor, Leith Doody. Using leadership tools, he encouraged staff to independently build business case proposals, using their creativity and skills. And then he was there to strongly support if such proposal was meaningful. His method of leadership of going up the pyramid proved its strength. His pyramids were very strong and based on solid ground and motivated staff to build new ones.

I will never forget Leith's invaluable moral support during one of the most difficult times in the Prague Post. Even a director of the worst movie would hesitate to use a horror scenario which happened in reality in Prague. One of my colleagues lost her three children in an accident. She obviously was not able to go to work for some time and during that period, other Prague colleagues quit because she was not able to mentally survive the atmosphere of destruction. Thus, Prague became a one-man operation. All business and consular tasks were on my shoulders and it was a most stressful moment. And it was Leith who kept my head above water, helping me through this difficult moment.

Looking back: What worked well and would be – maybe – worth considering

Austrade's primary role is to serve Australian exporters in overseas markets. In times when one of key performance indicators was generating fee-for-service, most of that fee was collected in the name of the valuable service given to Australian exporters.

In Milan, Italy, an institution Euro Link was established, invented by a great manager Rod Morehouse. For several fruitful years in early 21st century, Euro Link collected Australian potential exporters' inquiries and, where possible, produced samples, and maintained detailed database which was proactively and also reactively used by other posts, following respective markets demand and supply need. Euro link was an excellent and very reputable tool, used by a big number of Australian (potential) exporters.

Austrade has somewhat reduced support to smaller exporters (small and medium enterprises, SMEs), which – as in each developed country – represent the backbone of the economy. Maybe it would be worth devoting some capacity to redeveloping export supporting strategy in relevant European markets?

Expansion of multimedia and communication technologies has resulted in predominantly virtual communication about business, organisational and other topics. Teams meet in person only sporadically which, unfortunately, causes slow depersonalisation of relationships and understanding of other colleagues' thoughts, plans and concerns. I fully understand that saving resources is an imperative, but maybe it would be worth analysing the long-term benefits of meaningful staff meetings and benchmarking against invested financial sources.

Similarly, offshore staff business trips to Australia have almost disappeared. With full understanding of the imperative of scarce financial sources, the truth is that smaller countries from Central Europe, struggle to get on the radar of Australian entities. As such they are losing opportunities of direct interaction with Australian businesses and institutions. I believe that one meeting in person outweighs tens of videoconferences, phone hook ups and emails.

Conclusion

It's been a lifelong experience for me to see "my organisation" developing over time. I am extremely grateful that I have been able to be a humble witness of this fascinating process of growth and maturing, and that I can actively participate in all strategic changes and adopting innovative solutions. I believe that Central Europe is and will be a full-blooded member and integral part of the worldwide Austrade family.

Bibliography

Australian Trade Commission, 2014, International Student Data, http://www. austrade.gov.au-/-Education/Student-Data/2013/Pivot-Table, viewed 14 September 2014.

Businessinfo, 2014, Australia: Trade and Economic Cooperation with Czech Republic, http://www.businessinfo.cz/cs/clanky/australie-obchodni-a-ekonomicka-spoluprace-s-cr-19124.html#sec2, viewed 10 September 2014.

Macquarie Group, 2010, Macquarie-managed funds acquire Ceske Radiokomunikace, http://www.macquarie.co.uk/mgl/uk/about/news/2010/20101206, viewed 10 September 2014.

18

"Crossing the Rainbow": My decade long experience as an OEE with Austrade China

Lucy Luo

Australia-China's economic relations

The seventeenth of November 2014 marks a significant date in the history of Australia-China economic relations. The landmark China-Australia Free Trade Agreement (FTA) has been finally sealed after nearly a decade of intense negotiations. This is an important milestone for the rapidly expanding relationship between the two countries and offered us an opportunity to reflect on the evolution of Australia-China relations and consider new ideas and initiatives to strengthen and deepen our prosperity.

When formal diplomatic relations between Australia and China began 42 years ago in 1972, China's share of the Australian market was only one percent (Au-Yeung 2012). That share has now increased to more than 28 percent in 2014 (DFAT 2014). In 2007, China's exports and imports with Australia surpassed Japan thereby making it Australia's number one trading partner. When Tony Abbott, announced that the landmark China-Australia Free Trade Agreement had been completed, Australian business responded enthusiastically across all industry sectors, indicating the significant impact of the agreement to Australia. According to Trade Minister Andrew Robb, the agreement would unlock substantial new benefits for Australians for years to come (Robb 2014).

Background and Austrade in China

Austrade as the only Australian federal government agency charged with promoting Australian trade and investment internationally, plays an important and unique role in improving economic relations between Australia and China and Austrade's presence on the ground in China is one of the largest and most widespread foreign diplomatic networks. When Austrade was established in 1986, there were just three Australian trade offices while today there are eleven.

As an Australian citizen of Chinese origin, I first came to Australia in 1990 as an international student with little knowledge about this country. It was during one of the worst recessions of the Australian economy since the great depression and also the beginning of the opening of Australian education exports gateway to Chinese nationals. While Australia was going through its recession in the 1990s, China's economic reforms were accelerating and trade opportunities between China and Australia were notably increasing. As I completed my studies in International Business and in Accounting, my passion and desire was to bridge business cooperation between Australia and China. I was hired by Austrade Beijing as a locally engaged Australian employee in 2001. My initial role was as Office Manager. Later I became the Senior Business Development Manager and Trade Advisor in this 10 year career with Austrade in China and Australia respectively. At the time I joined Austrade, it was undergoing an administrative restructure while continuing to expand its footprint in the Chinese market.

Contractual employment arrangements between Austrade and OEE in China

Austrade in China has its main offices located within the Australian Embassy in Beijing and in Australian Consulates throughout China while other additional offices are registered as un-incorporated company representative offices. However, under Chinese legislation, Austrade as a foreign government agency has no legal right to employ local Chinese nationals directly, which produced a certain degree of complexity in the relationship between Austrade and its staff.

Austrade as a foreign government trade and investment agency in China has always been regarded as an ideal organisation to work for. In principle all of its local Chinese employees are hired through an official Chinese Human Resources (HR) agency called Diplomatic Service Bureau (DSB) under the control of the Chinese Ministry of Foreign Affairs. As the Chinese policy towards foreign agencies for employing local staff eased up in 1990s, Austrade accommodated different types of employment arrangements with its OEE staff and each varied in the remuneration and conditions.

During my time as the office manager, there were three different arrangements between Austrade and its OEE staff, based on individual's nationality, town of residence, and channel of employment. These included: 1) Direct Employment Contract for Australian passport holders such as my own case. As Austrade is the contractual employer, all remuneration payment was paid directly by Austrade to the employee but with no reference to any Australian or Chinese labour legislation. 2) Austrade entered into Labour Service Agreement with the Diplomatic Service Bureau (DSB) which manages employment contracts for individual employees that work with Austrade all of whom have local residency status. The majority of Chinese national OEEs are employed through DSB. Austrade pays their remuneration through DSB and then DSB pays the staff after deducting relevant charges as per Chinese labour law. In this case, DSB is the employer and is responsible for complying with Chinese labour law requirements. To compensate for those deductions and management fees that DSB charge from employee's remuneration, Austrade also paid an allowance to staff directly in addition to the agreed remuneration for the DSB deductions. 3) For OEEs that joined the Austrade representative offices outside of the Embassy and the Consulates, their contracts were managed by commercial HR management companies that are certified by Chinese authorities by charging a management fee. Again in this case, Austrade was the ultimate employer but has no direct contractual relationship with its staff.

However, the situation changes over time, both from an Austrade corporate perspective as well as from the Chinese legislative perspective. At one point Austrade was open to being perceived as violating its employer's responsibilities and there were suggestions that it encouraged employees to escape from tax payments by paying direct allowances in addition to the salary payment made to DSB and the commercial HR management companies although employees were advised in writing that they were responsible for their personal income tax liability on this payment. As a result Austrade decided to abolish direct payment to employees in Beijing in 2008. This change caused many complaints from the staff affected, as the total payment to the staff who had not been paying tax resulted in a salary reduction. While the staff understood Austrade's need to protect itself from any accusations of violating Chinese law, it did not give adequate consideration for staff impacted by this action. During this period, the fact was that salary levels in China were rapidly increasing and Austrade was losing its competitiveness in the labour market level. From an Austrade management point view, there was also poor communication. The implicit message to the Chinese staff seemed to be a blunt ultimatum to accept it or leave. Consequently, workplace momentum declined and the relationship between Austrade and its staff became more strained.

The value of Austrade both onshore and offshore

As stated in Austrade's website (2014), Austrade contributes to Australia's economic prosperity by helping Australian businesses develop international markets and win direct investment. Austrade achieves this by generating market information and insight, promoting Australian capabilities, contributing to policy, making connections through an extensive global network of contacts, leveraging the badge of government offshore and providing quality advice and services.

As one of the largest foreign government agency networks in China, Austrade is highly regarded as a trade and investment organisation. It has built very strong connections with both the Chinese government and business community through its extensive network. However connection means relationship and trust in Asian culture, particularly in China. Austrade's fundamental asset is its people. Business Development Managers (BDMs) build relationships with clients through doing projects and events together. They gain business knowledge and collect information through communication and interaction with their contacts. Austrade relies on this valuable information and knowledge to serve its exporters and investors. One BDM from Beijing expert in China's mining industry even became a popular speaker at the annual Diggers and Dealers conference in Kalgoorlie for a couple of years. We all know that nowadays information technology and the use of databases are dominating our world but doing business still largely relies on people and the way people think and act, because business is even more dynamic than ever, as our world becomes more globalised.

In order to stay competitive, and serve its stakeholders more effectively and efficiently, Austrade led the way in implementing its information technology in China systems but not all these projects were successful. Around 2007-8, Austrade rolled out a Client Relationship Management (CRM) tool with the aim of consolidating in its system customer and client contacts and service information. As an organisation, this was a huge investment and a major commitment to implement through its entire global network from a strategic management view. As a frontline practice, this activity required a lot of time and resource allocation for group training, data entry, system review, cross checking of information. Equally it required staff understanding, support and commitment as well. These activities involved huge intangible costs to the organisation and need to be well communicated to staff to ensure it is useful in a practical way. However, while installing and implementing the system, some Austrade managers made it known to the team that the systems which capture information are more useful than its people. Therefore some staff perceived the project intentions of this CRM as that of replacing the people (OEEs) thereby producing a sense of job insecurity within the organisation.

After the system was established and running, in order to enforce the use of the CRM system, a measure was introduced related to its usage which ultimately became a key performance indicator (KPI). However as the system became bigger it also became messier. Important issues emerged: 1) as more data was entered, the system became bigger and bigger. In practice it took more time to find the right information one required than prior to the establishment of the CRM. The reality was that one client or customer may have different contact points in Austrade for different projects or the same project is located in different locations, or at a different stage and/or for different issues and so on. As such the database would be entered into by different colleagues, for different topics and time respectively. So finding the right information became a challenge: 2) once information was entered into the system, it then relied on people to keep it up to date. Despite this time and vigilance requirement, people may change position or job at both ends, either in Austrade or the client company or both. In such cases, as time goes by the information in the system became less relevant or dated, that in turn caused a lot of time wastage and frustration for staff who relied on the system to find useful information: 3) staff need to spend so much time to maintain and update information, not to mention reports and audit, etc. Staff felt they were being distracted from business development tasks to more administrative issues, in turn reducing their productivity and focusing less on generating business opportunities. Due to a combination of factors, which included greater market competition, higher salary levels for staff in the market, lack of acknowledgement of the value of OEE and limited delegation of responsibility, around the period of 2009 to 2011 Austrade China experienced high staff turnover.

The role of A-based versus OEE staff and their contribution to the organisation

Austrade's role is divided into two segments in order to achieve its mission. On the one hand, Austrade generates market information and insight, making connections through an extensive global network of contacts, these require strong experience and knowledge of local culture, businesses and market and ability to make close and continuous relationships with both Chinese and Australian companies. This is the main value that local staff contribute to the organisation. On the other hand, Austrade promotes Australian capabilities, developing policy and leveraging the government badge offshore. This requires extensive understanding of Australian government policies, Australian industry capabilities, political and economic structures and most importantly representing the Australian government with the diplomatic badge. This is the clear value that the A-Based manager brings with them.

In my early years in Austrade, its global network was divided into six key regions. China was part of the North East Asia region under the leadership of Greg Dodds, the regional Executive General Manager. With a regional structure, staff have more opportunities to interact, share and learn experience as well as share information across offices through team building and regional conference opportunities. Staff all loved those opportunities, as that not only helped individuals to improve, also build closer relationships between offices and OEE staff. People had a strong sense of belong to Austrade as an accommodating multinational organisation. During that period, performance was measured with KPIs reflecting Austrade staff contribution to client exports and business successes. Staff were motivated to achieve high results and they were willing to share information and introduce capable clients to colleagues in different markets.

I should also point out here the very different roles of DFAT and Austrade staff. DFAT's principal role was to represent Australia, particularly in policy matters and that required a high ratio of A-Based staff to OEE, usually around 50:50, and most of their OEE were drivers, receptionists or secretaries. Austrade OEE however manned the front line in trade promotion as BDMs and the A-Based officers looked after management, high level business contacts and liaison with DFAT at the post. The ratio here was about one A-Based to seven OEE. This is not a statement about the relative importance of each task – they're both important – but it certainly knocks down the idea that there is any natural affinity between the two organisations.

We admire A-based managers who ought to be a group of talented, experienced and highly capable Australian diplomats bringing rich knowledge and management experience from Australia and often from other markets and regions as well. Like any person going to a new place, they normally will need about 3-6 months to settle into their new position and familiarise with themselves with their team and the market.

OEEs and A-Based generally work in teams, based on an allocated industry, location or project. Such a structure usually works well when all staff demonstrate mutual respect, appreciation of each other's experience, skills and contribution. Trust was the bond of the teamwork. In 2003, in order to reduce overhead cost and help staff to achieve a work-life balance, Austrade North East Asia region implemented a virtual office arrangement, meaning that BDMs and A-Based were allowed to work flexible hours including from home using their computers and mobile phones, so long as they met their agreed KPI targets and outcomes. This arrangement was really beneficial to both the organisation and the staff. The arrangement was highly appreciated by the staff and demonstrated Austrade's ability and integrity and at the same time took into consideration the work life balance for its staff. Though we don't sit in office together most of the time, we had some very happy and highly motivated years with excellent performance outcomes including successfully organising intensive programs for Business Club Australia events during 2008 Beijing Olympic Games.

OEE and A-Based staff work in team structures, and they compliment each other with their unique knowledge, skill sets and experience. I recall one of my STCs would say to the staff: "You are the market experts, you are the professionals with the capability to nurture relationships and make judgements. I am here to support you to do what you need to do. So together we can do something good for Australian businesses". In recent years, language skills have become a key criterion for Austrade when selecting Trade Commissioner positions. Of course, language is a very important attribute when working in China, but I have to say language is only a tool for communication. Chinese culture, especially business culture, is much more complicated than just language. Westerners are no longer being treated differently or privileged as they may have experienced in the early years in China. A-based managers need to be culturally savvy with business and market knowledge to be able to fulfil their role and responsibility.

But this drive for reform and for getting results did not last. After some years of restructuring both onshore and offshore, Austrade has become if anything more like DFAT. In China for example, there are now more Trade Commissioner positions and less BDM positions than before. The current ratio of A-based staff is around 6:1 compared to the earlier ratio of 7:1. Virtual office, meaning working from home with little supervision is no longer allowed. From my discussions with current Austrade OEE staff in China, the workplace is not as happy as when I first worked there. Staff have very limited authorisation to make judgements and work arrangements from their own knowledge and experience in their reports to their line manager. Despite the fact that the salary package is no longer competitive, Austrade still is an attractive organisation because of its government status, its large international network and it provides a good platform for information, for people to learn and accumulate experience for their future career development.

It is sad to see the downscaling and restructuring of Austrade over the past few years. With the new FTA opportunity with China, Austrade should have greater capacity to help Australia maximise the benefit of collaboration with China if it can rectify some of its managerial attitudes and delegate the right people with broader vision and leadership.

Career ceiling of the OEE staff

As mentioned earlier in the chapter, Austrade is not a contractual employer for OEE Chinese nationals, though some Chinese OEE have been working with Austrade for more than 20 years. Because of the nature of Austrade, a foreign government agency and the structure of its operations overseas, there is little opportunity for OEE staff to advance their career with the organisation. Nonetheless training opportunities and short term postings in Australia are highly appreciated by the OEE staff.

There are only very limited opportunities for OEEs to grow and advance their career with Austrade in China. There have been a few success stories of former OEE moving through the organisation and becoming A-Based, even 'though they had the (obviously) necessary Australian citizenship. Dianne Zou, Julie-Ann Nicholls and the current Acting STC of Austrade Shanghai are some examples. Some of these Chinese Australians were given jobs back in Australia that made little use of their China market knowledge and skills.

Retaining talent and knowledge

Besides having a government badge, Austrade is a service organisation where its people's knowledge, skills, and experiences are its most valuable asset in delivering quality service to its stakeholders, differentiating itself from its peer organisations and accountable in the way it expends tax payer funding.

Without doubt, Austrade is a great organisation, and the vast majority of those who have worked with Austrade love it and are proud of having worked in it. It is such a diverse organisation, with talented people and providing enormous opportunities to staff to learn and work with different companies, clients and stakeholders across almost all sectors in the economy. However, in my opinion the weakest part of this great organisation is its talent management, especially for overseas offices. As an organisation, Austrade never seems to care about people leaving the organisation. It seems that Austrade does not have a mechanism that treasures people who stay and grow with the organisation. From an OEE standpoint, staff do not have sufficient opportunity to express their opinions. Especially in recent years, if they want to continue working with the organisation, they can only follow the Australian managers. BDMs, even with expertise in various sectors seem no longer to be respected as professionals valued by the organisation.

Sustaining Austrade's core value in market and competitiveness

With recent restructures, Austrade has seen radical cuts in its onshore operations, with the reasons being that other independent organisations provide similar or better services to Australian businesses than Austrade could in Australia. Austrade is therefore committed to dedicating more resources to enhance its offshore strengths in the emerging markets such as China. Obviously, the rationale behind these restructures is that Austrade's irreplaceable value is its overseas network, knowledge and contacts of international markets. OEEs are the backbone of Austrade's international operations and Austrade can only achieve its best service if it can motivate OEEs to maximise their best potential to contribute to their organisation as respectful professionals.

The balance between the new and the old blood

Austrade in China today has 11 A-based managers plus one investment commissioner, managing 11 offices across mainland China where more than half of the OEEs are new entrants and many are also fresh graduates. Some offices have almost 80 per cent of their staff as new entrants. Certainly, newbies and fresh injections are very important to any organisation in order to keep the organisation active, energetic and dynamic with fresh eyes, minds and ideas. But Austrade as a government service agency, which needs to assist business to succeed, also needs experience, accumulated knowledge about the market, about industries, about policies, about practical challenges and about negotiation and problem solving skills. These attributes do not come from books or the imagination. This intellectual capital sits in people's minds and is accumulated over long periods of work experience. When Austrade loses its long term serving staff, talent and experience are also lost. People come and go within a few years and as a result Austrade becomes a training centre for other more people-oriented organisations.

Organisational culture on-shore and off-shore

My work with Melbourne after being offered a role there following my decision to resign from my role in Beijing and relocate back to Australia was a challenge but equally another memorable learning experience. The work approach and culture in an offshore and onshore office can be very different. Possibly because China has been an engine room for businesses, the work approach in China has always been outcome driven, while in Australia possibly because of its governmental nature, the work approach is mainly process driven. Writing reports, doing presentations seems more valuable than actually servicing and helping companies. Interacting with clients, visiting businesses in China are a major part of tasks of the BDMs, whereas the majority of onshore staff sit in the office doing internal reports and completing organisational processes. In my opinion, because of the difference in work approach it ultimately leads to a difference in value that Austrade staff and office could provide to their clients and stakeholders in the long run.

Transferring knowledge between on-shore and off-shore staff

Ignorance of markets and lacking knowledge of certain country experience is more apparent in the Austrade onshore offices. Work arrangements rather mismatch people's skills, experience with allocation of their work and area. On one hand it is good learning opportunity and experience for individual staff, but on the other hand it's an invisible but big cost to the organisation. Take China as an example. China is Australia's largest trading partner, with that scale reflected in Austrade's business inquiries and workload. Within Austrade onshore offices, there are only a few Chinese speakers in the organisation with limited Chinese market knowledge and experience. As a result this has caused much misunderstanding and difficulties to reach agreement when onshore and offshore teams need to work together. Not only do we see this in China, but also many returned Austrade diplomats are allocated tasks which do not express their best capacities nor in the best interests of the organisation.

Sustaining Austrade's unique value and competitiveness in China

Australia is a relatively small country in international terms. While many of the world's nations set foot in China to share in the growth of the Chinese fast growing economy, Australia should have built on its achievements more strategically. Firstly, with the different layers of government all competing with each other in China, Austrade as the window of trade and investment, should lead with a unified approach and representation for Australia as a nation, avoid duplication by different levels of government and maximise tax payer's resources under one banner. Nowadays, doing business with China is a lot more challenging than before. Austrade can only sustain its competitiveness by nurturing more talented people with rich experience in business, government service, and international environment and be able to adapt to constant changes in the marketplace as well as bilateral relationships.

In conclusion, Austrade in China may be a victim here of bad timing. Its best days during my time may have been the period when OEE were trusted as equal team members and played leading roles in most export development projects, when the Virtual Office system gave them the authority over their daily lives craved by so many modern professionals. The drift back to central control from Canberra evident during the past few years has clogged up this sense of momentum. The Free Trade Agreement and its opportunities however demand the very best we can field and a successful national response to this challenge will need to have Austrade as a key player and it will need to be an Austrade that has committed and enthusiastic OEE in the front line.

Bibliography

Austrade 2014, Australian Trade Commission website, Canberra, http://www. austrade.gov.au, accessed 31 December 2014.

Au-Yeung W., Keys A. and Fischer P., 2012, Australia-China: not just 40 years. *Economic Roundup* Issue 4, 2012. http://www.treasury.gov.au/ PublicationsAndMedia/Publications-/2012/Economic-Roundup-Issue-4/ HTML/article1, accessed 17 December 2014.

DFAT, 2014, China fact sheet, Department of Foreign Affairs and Trade, Canberra, https://www.dfat.gov.au/geo/fs/chin.pdf, accessed 31 December 2014.

Robb A., 2014, Landmark China-Australia Free Trade Agreement; Minister for Trade and Investment, http://trademinister.gov.au/releases/Pages/2014/ ar_mr_141117.aspx, accessed 17 December 2014.

19

Performance Management in Austrade

Greg Dodds

The private sector creates things, the government does things. The private sector earns wealth, the government spends it. And so on. It's like a children's rhyme; every adult Australian, or coalition voter anyway, remembers fragments of it from their childhood. For most, it remains an unexamined idea tucked away up there in the attic for all of their lives.

It might be crude and amusing when trotted out by the simple-minded at a barbecue with all the solemnity of a child reciting a catechism but it is not complete rubbish. Governments may well "do things" and "spend money" but this is supposed to deliver value to the community. How to demonstrate this value and to prove solid performance to the community preys upon the mind of every serious politician, government official and student of public administration, particularly when service delivery, not policy formulation, is involved.

The issue is particularly challenging in Australia where although public servants and public service generally are held in low esteem, there is also a lively expectation that the government will provide a wide range of services and even cash to the "deserving" and not just to the needy. This contradictory attitude is a dilemma to governments from both sides of politics.

How then to convince the community that their taxes are being well spent in the national interest? Performance management is essential: a system where performance is measured and evaluated and actions are taken to improve that performance if necessary. Performance management requires performance measurement and the results of that measurement can provide a credible framework to judge how a public department or agency is travelling. The popular retort that government is incapable of good performance management and the private sector only needs profit as the sole necessary measure of performance is one of those fragments tucked away in the attic that is close to rubbish. Any company that relies solely on a profit and loss statement to demonstrate viability and pays no attention to repeat business figures or client satisfaction will not be around for long.

There is a range of measurable items which indicate the performance of a management unit available to companies and with few exceptions these can be applied to government organisations as well. These items, or Key Performance Indicators (KPIs) vary from organisation to organisation but they all should have the following characteristics:

> **Relevance:** They should be clearly relevant to the mission statement, the main purpose for which the organisation exists. At the same time, they should be goals that are reasonably within reach for the organisation to achieve: no sensible charity for example would task itself with eradicating world poverty within a single reporting year.

> **Able to be measured**: The criteria should be quantifiable and not just a collection of impressions formed by senior managers. Measurement rather than evaluation underpins the idea of fairness, an indispensable quality for the system to be accepted by staff.

> **Be measured objectively:** These criteria should be measured without resort to internal opinion and they must be measured by a professional external agency.

So what might the ideal performance measurement system look

like? Firstly, it should comprise a number of criteria, not just the single profit and loss statement, that tell senior management and stake holders how the organisation is doing. For example, a balanced scorecard measures financial performance, customer satisfaction, internal process performance and innovation and learning. These items can be weighted to produce a single figure that reflects Board priorities or areas where they believe the organisation needs to improve client satisfaction or repeat business, for example

Secondly, the KPIs need to be heavily dependent on external feedback from clients minimising the self-interested musings of management and staff. The results need to count for something, to have consequences within an organisation. Everybody immediately thinks this is a euphemism for sackings which can reduce staff enthusiasm considerably but there are other less draconian and more positive consequences likely, a reallocation of resources among divisions for example. The system needs to be effectively sold, both externally to clients and stakeholders and internally to staff. In government agencies in particular, the idea that this is just another fad to be weathered out can easily catch on.

Then there is the vexed question of measuring activities rather than results. I say vexed because structured activity towards policy objectives is a perfectly legitimate criterion for policy departments. And some service delivery agencies like Centrelink *do* have valid assessment reasons for measuring how many welfare payments they make each month; that's what they do. Other agencies however are expected to deliver results and attempts by them to take refuge in activities – "Look how busy we are" – are transparently self-serving and are quickly exposed by a sound performance measurement system.

Finally, the system has to operate in a structure where the managers and units have a degree of autonomy and authority commensurate with the responsibilities they are being judged against. Corporate KPIs give a courtesy nod to the concept of performance measurement but they are in effect no more than the sum total of results achieved by the major management units. And the results of these management units, in turn, are the sum of their own sub-units' achievements and so on down the line. Managers at each level must have the authority to allocate resources in the way most likely to achieve their targets. Devolution of authority is the *sine qua non* of good performance measurement and without it managers cannot accept the responsibility of reaching targets. They might do their best but they are essentially working in a vacuum. In a world of corporate KPIs, everybody is responsible for everything and thereby, they are also responsible for nothing.

Performance management in Austrade

Performance measurement in the Trade Commissioner Service prior to the founding of Austrade in 1986 was focused on individual trade commissioners, particularly the senior trade commissioners. Feedback from visiting ministers, ambassadors, desks in the head office in Canberra and occasionally from exporters determined whether someone was "doing a good job" or not. No attempt was made to assess the performance of posts: they were a given and like embassies, opened and closed depending upon available funds and policy needs. Local staff (OEE) were seen as beneath Canberra's concern and were managed locally.

For the most part, the Trade Commissioner Service's client base seemed to consist of the commodities exporters, particularly the major agricultural marketing boards. These exporters were more than capable of looking after themselves in markets but the existence of export controls and government to government contracts gave trade commissioners an important but limited role at posts. Small and medium enterprises or attempts to export processed or manufactured products received little attention beyond participating in trade missions and trade fairs and most marketing activities by posts were decided in Canberra anyway with little discussion with the posts involved.

The Trade Commission had several unique characteristics that would largely continue beyond the looming government reforms. Most officers were located in the local embassy and had to participate in routine embassy activities that had nothing to do with trade promotion. In exchange, they had diplomatic passports which gave them access to local officials and agencies that was impossible for most private sector operations. In command economies like Japan or China, this was a vital advantage and in spite of several internal discussions about the attractions of moving out, Austrade remained inside the Embassy walls. Finally the trade commissioners had to accept all comers, serious or not; a rejection could trigger a complaint to the minister and an angry rebuke from Canberra. Skilfully handling these "tyre kickers" became an important albeit worthless skill for ambitious trade commissioners.

In 1986, the Hawke government established Austrade, the main purpose being to separate formally the policy and trade promotion functions of the Department of Trade. Policy formulation and advice remained with the Department of Trade (to be joined with the Department of Foreign Affairs to form DFAT the following year). Austrade was given its own discrete budget and was to be directed by a Board mostly comprising senior executives from successful exporters. The Act also enabled the Minister to direct Austrade towards industries whose growth was desirable from a national interest point of view such as food processing or computer software. There was the unformed but strong expectation in government ranks that Austrade would deliver results in these sectors.

The government was in for a disappointment. By and large, it was business as usual in Austrade. Senior trade commissioners still reported to junior clerks in Canberra, budgets were still tightly controlled in the Head Office and performance assessment remained a subjective and limited process.

And these changes were not welcome to some of the senior officers who seemed to feel that their privileges and entitlements had been earned by years of service rather than results achieved. John Dawkins became involved in a public spat with some trade commissioners over this question, galling enough for any minister but made all the more so by the fact that his opponents seemed unaware that the Austrade Act now made it impossible for the minister to sack an Austrade employee. That became the prerogative of the Board. In the big scheme of things, these incidents were insignificant but they did slow down the momentum of reform and soak up valuable time and effort. *The Austrade Act* was necessary to get serious reform under way but it was obviously not sufficient and some further measure was needed.

The Minister at the time, John Button, agreed to commission a report from McKinsey and Co. in 1990 to review Austrade's performance as a trade promotion agency and to recommend changes. The report did not disappoint. Considerable executive authority was to be placed offshore in six major regions headed by an Executive General Manager and important financial authorities were to go with them. This great increase in authority offshore was accompanied by an understanding that greater accountability would be levelled against executive general managers and their senior trade commissioners. It was no longer enough to carry out other people's bad ideas well. Now any bad ideas would squarely belong to them and there needed to be a corporate system to measure results fairly in the different regions. And these results would matter.

But which results and how would they be measured? The annual Balance of Trade figures published by the Treasury each year seemed the obvious answer. Everyone knew what they were and Austrade could easily demonstrate its worth through these figures to the government and the community. But that thought didn't last very long. There were too many key variables (exchange rates, international commodity prices, etc) over which Austrade had no control and everyone knew that Austrade played little or no role anyway in annual negotiations with major buyers of our commodities like the Japanese power companies for example. Better to pick sectors like food processing, manufacturing and information-based service companies which really did need a hand in markets like Japan or China. And both the government and the wider community understood the importance of reducing our heavy dependence on commodity exports. This was not an imbalance that would automatically be corrected by the market. This was how Austrade could really make a difference.

This is not to say this crucial challenge was overlooked in the established bureaucracy. In the early 1980s, the Chief Economist of the Department of Trade, Denis Gastin, set up the China Action Plan and the Japan Market Strategy to promote the exports of processed and manufactured products to those two key markets. Crucially he used the long established bilateral business councils as the key vehicles for the programs and the responses were generous, particularly in Japan where the CEO of Itohchu one of the leading trading companies, was chosen to spearhead Japan's support for the idea. But the key question remained: how could we demonstrate that this strong commercial support and Austrade's promotional activities were producing results?

Given the scale of reform and restructuring introduced by Ralph Evans, the new Managing Director, it's probably not surprising that it was 1993 before a rudimentary performance measurement system for posts was introduced. Proposed by Peter Forsythe, the EGM for China, it simply measured the number of cases where assistance to a company from Austrade staff in, say, Shanghai resulted in an export sale. Even at this basic level, the system was immediately valuable in helping the Board review and reallocate staff and resources across the global network. Forsyth and the EGM for Strategic Planning, Paul Twomey, quickly developed other criteria so that by the end of 1994 we had a full suite of KPIs that satisfied the three principles of relevance, objectivity and ability to be measured.

These KPIs were:

_ Number of companies serviced.[1]

_ Number of companies achieving an export sale as a result.

---

1 The number of companies serviced was indeed a measure of activity but it was necessary to establish a base line to measure success in converting mere contact into export success, revenue from service fees and so on. This would capture companies which had received vital support from Austrade after a sale had been made, the facilitation of quarantine clearance for example.

_ The dollar value of these sales.

_ Client Satisfaction Survey results.

_ Fee for Service revenue.

_ 360 Degree Survey results.[2]

The overall KPI results quickly became the principal, if not the only, element in the senior trade commissioners' performance assessment and they were encouraged to cascade that process down to their staff. The date each year therefore when the final annual results for individual posts of this process were released, depending on your prospects, had all the joy and excitement of a dentist making his annual visit to a medieval village!

Performance management works

The system was then left to operate unchanged for several years and staff came to realise that it was not a management fad and it was here to stay. It drew special potency from its transparency. Everyone across the global network knew how posts were performing and the sense of embarrassment over a poor result reached even the most recalcitrant heart among senior trade commissioners. The time framework for performance measurement was the calendar year and the financial year (both were used by the government). This framework was familiar to business and to the general community and fitted in with other regular requirements like annual reports and annual performance assessments. But it overlooked results for helping companies bidding for work on large projects, projects that might take several years to produce commercial results. Posts usually established their own milestones and internal registers with clients to ensure that this important business stream was not ignored.

---

2 The 360 Degree survey provided staff feedback at posts on how the Austrade staff judged the effectiveness of their own senior staff as managers and leaders. Initially derided by some DFAT staff as a popularity contest, the 360 Degree Survey turned out to be a testament to the perceptiveness and integrity of OEE staff. It was also a great help to STCs in improving their own performance.

The results for each KPI were potent enough by themselves but they were turbocharged when related to each other. Simon Watson, the senior financial officer for North East Asia showed endless ingenuity in highlighting aspects of post performance through interrelating the figures. How much did each post cost? How many staff did it have? Factor these figures against the number and value of export successes and you had the cost of earning an export dollar and the per capita achievement at each post. This enabled a comparison of region and post performances across the global network. It also enabled productivity assessments, an idea that put Austrade miles ahead of most government agencies at the time.

But not all. Performance measurement systems had been in use, albeit unevenly, in the private sector for years but were also introduced, again unevenly, in the 1990s at all levels of government in Australia. Kloot and Martin (2000) tracked performance measurement in local councils in Victoria, Halachmi (2002) reviewed performance measurement in the US and OECD governments and the Australian Public Service held senior management seminars on the subject in the late 1990s. Austrade invested much time and effort in developing its own systems but it was not the only interested party. It was developing an idea whose time had definitely come.

In 2000 the Managing Director, Charles Jamieson, introduced a new KPI, achieving export sales for new exporters and among other things, this decision validated the KPI system. The response was immediate as staff went in search of companies that had never exported before but their conduct was not always as professional as it should have been. Apart from the fact that Austrade events in Australia came to look like visits by the naval press gangs of the 18th century, a prominent expert on trade with Asia also pointed out to me that staff were recruiting all sorts of companies as one-time exporters, not first-time continuing exporters and that this could be a negative outcome for all parties further down the track. For the most part, these small companies were not equipped to make good choices of foreign markets and handle the demands of exporting. On the other hand, there was always the chronic danger of Austrade presiding over a gentleman's club of exporters where new members were not welcome. The New Exporter Program could be seen as a revolutionary drive to upset and revitalise the established order of things, akin to the Red Guard in China in the early 1970s as one wag suggested.

The Head of Strategic Development, Greg Joffe, came up with the solution of measuring repeat sales by these first timers and while some aspects of the problem resurfaced from time to time, the situation had stabilised in eighteen months or so. The underlying and more important message here 'though was the point that the system could be extended and then corrected if problems emerged. In North East Asia, individual performance agreements included a substantial section on the achievement of KPI targets and the results determined the payment of individual and group bonuses. Placing a proportion of salary or salary increases at risk in this process was never implemented but was certainly discussed, albeit with some pretty unenthusiastic staff.

The downside of performance management for Austrade

Inevitably, competition between regions, competition within regions and even competition within posts became a defining feature of the performance measurement system. The competition was for the esteem that comes from success and not for material benefit for the individual, at the beginning anyway. This was a terrific way of getting staff engagement that few managers could have resisted. The devil certainly had a good tune here but like most of his wares, it came at a price. Management texts great and small enjoin us to develop teamwork and few measures more corrosive to teamwork could be imagined than one which celebrated ultimately individual achievement and vanity. This was particularly true in North East Asia where group harmony and interests are stressed above those of the individual in most of the local cultures.

As mentioned above, this problem was initially worsened by the need to get early results under the New Exporter Program and some post managers were content to look the other way while their staff manipulated the system. Good STCs however were able to ameliorate this potential damage and stay focused on the big picture but this spirit of relentless competition remained a troubling element throughout the life of the system.

Akin to competition among posts was the fractured relationship between the overseas regions and Australian Operations. According to traditional procedure, staff in the State Offices would find companies interested in export and then do a round robin of overseas posts to find possible buyers. Alternately, overseas posts might come across a local company wanting to buy certain materials or products and then contact state offices to see if they had likely suppliers on their books.

All this changed radically with the implementation of the McKinsey review. Overseas posts now had a locally-based Executive General Manager (EGM) who greatly outranked nearly all managers based in Australia and was someone "on their side". The introduction of the KPI system and the exhortation on overseas staff to demonstrate "initiative", unleashed a torrent of activity on Australian Operations that it was unable to deal with. In response to an enquiry from a local Chinese company, staff in Austrade's Shanghai Office could easily contact possible Australian suppliers directly or through a State Government agency without resort to Austrade. For Austrade staff in Australia with an anxious company wishing to export to China, direct access to Chinese industry associations or companies in Shanghai on the other hand was next to impossible without local assistance.

The cards were stacked against Australian Operations from the start. The staff in Australia felt that they were being put aside and locked away from access to that most valuable corporate currency, credit for export sales.[3] Some of the bad feeling could have been assuaged if effort had been made towards developing a separate set of KPIs that measured the valuable work done by staff in State Offices and other parts of the network but all the effort went into refining the

---

3 Based on anecdotal evidence and discussions between senior Austrade management.

KPIs that applied to overseas posts and these KPIs were just twisted and distorted to accommodate the circumstances of state offices.

The situation improved later in the life of the KPI system when teams comprising staff from state offices and from posts were formed, in particular to manage the New Exporter Program, and KPIs were awarded to the team rather than to posts or to individuals. One of North East Asia's most sensible STCs implemented a system of Goals and Assists that rewarded collaboration from other posts and from Australian Operations. Furthermore, the Journey to Export Program in 2010 was enormously valuable in identifying the different points along the way where Austrade staff might contribute to an export success and therefore where staff should be given KPI credit for their work.

All this constitutes progress but it was uneven, late in the day and caused ongoing organisational trauma. It was probably the most serious deficiency in the Austrade Executive's management of the export development process.

Thirdly, awareness and understanding of the KPI system outside Austrade was for the most part poor. In part, this came from rejection, or at the very least disinterest, from within Austrade itself. Many individuals within Australia-based units were lukewarm towards the system and this was not without impact on outsiders who were encouraged to see it all as a crackpot public service fad that would soon disappear. The rumoured comment by a senior Austrade executive that "No one has been sent home (from overseas) for failing to meet KPI targets" while true at the time, confirmed the impression that the system need not be taken too seriously.

In truth, I never sacked anyone in North East Asia for failing to reach their KPI targets but I didn't have to; they sacked themselves. Life in a highly competitive environment was uncomfortable to say the least when your post was consistently at the bottom of performance charts. Better to jump before you were pushed.

Austrade had put together a system of performance management over several years that was certainly the equal of any other agency in the public service and could have served as a useful model for others. Instead, Austrade was chosen by the National Audit Office to be the object of a performance audit on client satisfaction surveys. Our humiliation at being singled out for this was only exceeded by theirs on discovering that we had been operating such an annual survey for several years. They harrumphed off into the sunset in search of new dragons to slay.

Austrade and government

Looking in at outside Austrade, one comes firstly across ministers and their offices. According to Australian popular mythology, one need go no further than politicians in search of the villain in government stuff ups, along with a retinue of rheumy eyed public servants of course. "Bloody politicians" are routinely blamed by the public for every problem starting with a misplaced cat. However the truth was quite different. Trade Ministers of the Hawke-Keating governments and well into the Howard government were unfailingly supportive of performance management. Tim Fischer even introduced an annual Trade Outcomes and Outlook Statement (TOOS) into Parliament, thereby inter alia extending Austrade's idea into the very highest level of government. Parliamentary committees and backbenchers were similarly positive on both sides of the House and the Senate.

State governments and other departments and agencies in the federal public service constituted the next level of engagement within government for Austrade. The notion of claiming demonstrable credit for export and investment promotion struck an immediate chord with state government departments and their representative offices overseas. Working through the collection of state bureaucracies could be hard work at times but apart from tiresome behaviour by one or two individuals who wanted to claim credit for export successes, this was not a serious problem. The federal and state political audiences were quite different and therefore credit could be shared comfortably.

This was not automatically true of the federal departments where the political audience was the same and zero sum rules applied. Austrade claiming credit for developing an export market for sea urchin, for example, might be seen as an incursion on the responsibilities of the department looking after fisheries and could have caused serious problems. Furthermore, the entire Australian public service was engaged in developing performance management systems at that time to demonstrate the delivery of value and outcomes to the community and departments could have been tetchy about letting Austrade take credit for work "on their turf". But in fact, nearly all of these encounters turned out well. Export development was highly desirable and Austrade knew the overseas markets while the departments knew their client industries.

The most significant point of contact with the Australian public service was with the Department of Foreign Affairs and Trade, Austrade's "parent" department and this is also the only area where serious and consistent problems arose. Engagement between Austrade and DFAT took place both in Canberra and in the various overseas posts. In Canberra, the main game was policy advice to ministers on trade policy and this was the sole reserve of DFAT and an area where Austrade never trespassed to my knowledge. Whether DFAT officers were similarly reticent in discussing Austrade issues with the minister was another matter.

Overseas posts, the area where the KPI system was most keenly felt was also the area where the interests of Austrade and DFAT could easily clash. For DFAT, visits by ministers to a post were the high points of a year and the main activity would usually be meetings with counterpart ministers and progressing government to government issues with that country. If Austrade featured at all in the DFAT program, it would be to provide a "light relief" element like a so-called Australian Fair in a supermarket for example. For the Austrade staff at the post, the imperative to get results made these bread and circus activities a waste of time and they usually countered with proposals for selling products and services that could well benefit from the minister's involvement.

Most ambassadors incorporated these into a visiting minister's program without demur.

But not all of them. One ambassador having insisted that Austrade arrange an Australian Fair at a supermarket to be part of a visiting minister's program, immediately launched into musings about Austrade's judgement and real value when it became clear that the exercise was worthless and the minister himself had doubt about its commercial value and the value of his involvement.

The ambassador was undoubtedly the key figure at any post, "extraordinary and plenipotentiary" who enjoyed an almost feudal span of authority enjoyed by few other senior executives in the modern world. For the most part they delivered the stature and gravitas as well as the advice necessary to help Austrade do its job in their posts. Their personal involvement in promotions could bring great force to bear behind Australian promotions and ambassadors like Ric Smith, a former Ambassador to China and the late Ashton Calvert provide outstanding local leadership and support in this regard. Others however seemed to view their job as an ongoing Game of Thrones in which all that was good and worthy was due to them and them alone. They were most difficult to deal with and one could sympathies with the exasperation often expressed by business people about the waste of government time and money surrounding embassy events.

Finally we come to the reaction of exporters themselves. Unsurprisingly, this depended very much on the quality of the established relationship. Where it was good, clients readily understood the purpose of a performance management system and were happy to participate in order to benefit a helpful trade commissioner or local staff member. Even when fees for service were introduced, most clients while unenthusiastic, accepted that some form of payment beyond taxes was appropriate.

And these links with clients sometimes had unexpected benefits. The polling company doing the annual client survey would sometimes invite companies to be surveyed who would ask questions such as

"Austrade claims they helped you sell your auto components to Daewoo in Korea. That can't be true, can it?" Expecting a chummy, blokey response, they were startled when the companies bridled and reported these questions verbatim to Austrade staff at the post.

Where the relationship was not so strong however, the performance management system brought pressure to bear on both sides, particularly when service fees were to be paid. Clients would not express satisfaction in surveys when they were paying substantial fees but not getting sales. Austrade staff would not waste time and resources on companies that never took advice and could not make a sale

This pressure helped get rid of the aptly named "tyre kickers", individuals and companies that hung around Austrade posts and events simply because it was free (Yes Private Sector enthusiasts: there is such wasteful and pointless behaviour in your ranks too).The appearance of fees cleared them out quickly.

There were also stories of collusion between companies and individual staff members to "fix" survey results in exchange for free services. Whether this ever took place is doubtful but the discrepancy between high satisfaction levels and hardly any fees paid would have become glaringly obvious to Austrade management. It was simpler for all parties just to pay the fees and get on with building the export market.

Performance management in Austrade *quo vadit*?

With the departure of Charles Jamieson, Austrade undertook no more major export development initiatives. The New Exporter Program was allowed to run for a few more years but was then quietly shelved. The change of government in 2007, normally an event that invites new proposals and invigoration among government agencies, drew no such response from Austrade which seemed content to sit quietly in the corner. The Labor governments repaid the compliment by appointing a series of ministers who had little or no interest in trade promotion.

The Uhrig report had disposed of the Austrade Board in 2006 and while its departure was lamented by few within Austrade itself, a small number of executives realised that this left us fully exposed to the direction of the government. This of course was no bad thing in itself but with Labor ministers being uninterested and largely unaware of Austrade's activities, government direction meant direction by DFAT which resumed a process of takeover that had probably been on their books forever. The departure of Peter O'Byrne in 2009 allowed them to provide the successful candidate to replace him as CEO, a former Deputy Secretary with a background in trade policy.

As one should expect from Canberra, the centralisation of authority away from posts and back into the Head Office in Australia was high on the list. The new CEO set about dismantling some of the reforms from the McKinsey report, principally the downgrading of the positions and authorities of the executive general managers overseas. This of course compromised the autonomy necessary for the performance management system to work so the watering down of the KPIs was hardly necessary. Pleasingly (for the McKinsey enthusiasts anyway) this "Back to the Future" policy was firmly resisted by many mid-level managers who had grown up in the KPI environment and were deeply suspicious of the subjectivity underlying the traditional DFAT system. The current CEO while also from the same area of DFAT, has shown some awareness of the value of a system of objective and measurable criteria. And he isn't the only one. The Treasurer has apparently (re) discovered the merit of fees for service for government agencies like Austrade and fee collection has suddenly acquired importance within Austrade itself during the past few months.

In 2014, the Commission of Audit apparently identified Austrade as performing a role better undertaken by the private sector and Austrade was apparently due for the chop but it managed to survive, in 2014 anyway (NCOA 2014). Strong advocacy in Cabinet by the Minister Andrew Robb and firm supportive editorial articles in the Australian seems to have made the abolition of Austrade a "bridge too far" in a very ambitious campaign of cutbacks on government activity.

Commissions of audit, razor gangs; everyone understands their political purpose but their intellectual quality is less obvious and the Tony Shepherd exercise in 2014 was no exception. It gets to Performance Management on page 36 of a 400 plus page report and quickly descends into dry nostrums about the *Public Service Act* (NCOA 2014: 36). It makes only a passing reference to increasing productivity and seems unaware that at least one government agency (ironically one under threat of abolition by the Commission) had already developed a performance measurement system which could deliver solid productivity figures and be used as a base for comparing different departments and agencies.

"On reflection, we should have ..."

The problems caused by competition for good KPI results have already been examined in detail but in one important respect, the first response to a call for what we should have done differently will be very short: not much. The Performance Management system animated staff within Austrade to a high level of commitment and effort over a long period of time that was unthinkable under earlier management arrangements. In this context, Performance Management was both valuable and sound.

The second point was to have sold the idea better within the Public Service, particularly at a time when the APS itself was in search of appropriate performance management systems. Engaging the National Audit Office to undertake the annual measurement of Austrade's performance criteria could have led to a much higher status as a "Best Practice" leader in Canberra.

Allied to this was the failure to find and develop alliances within the business world. Managing better productivity is a topic of keen interest in the world of business and strategic alliances with several major firms like banks and the leading accountancy companies as well as business associations could have delivered support and publicity when needed. And the interest shown by the private sector in the subject of Performance Measurement remains strong. In mid-

2014, the Macquarie Bank issued a report demonstrating the value of staff feedback surveys in achieving high performance levels against standard market measures (Macquarie Bank 2014).

Both "if we had our time again" items here concern the externals and I place less importance on our internal mistakes and failings. While they were real and I think I have been honest in identifying them throughout the chapter, I also think that in an environment of unrelenting pressure such as Austrade throughout the 1990s, internal problems have a way of resolving themselves. People change their minds, others try harder, some quit, compromises are worked out. This all takes time but perhaps just one very good idea at the beginning is enough; beyond that a good management team stands back and lets the idea grow and evolve naturally with minimum interference. The KPI system continually evolved and was undoubtedly a much better system in 2002 than it had been in 1993.

Austrade should continue as an independent agency for the next few years at least and it may continue with its notional independence indefinitely. DFAT already has the CEOs job in hand and is unlikely to lose it: directives from the CEO can ensure greater collaboration with DFAT in financial controls and HR matters. Why struggle for absolute control (and responsibility) when you already have such a high degree of influence? As for exporters, their interests feature little in this calculus and perhaps it will take another severe crisis in our balance of payments or the appearance of another government with the glittering array of talent seen in the Hawke-Keating years to restore their voice and to give trade and investment promotion the priority it needs in a country like Australia.

Bibliography

Halachmi A. 2002, performance measurement and government productivity, Public Performance and Management review, Vol. 25, Number 4, 370-374, http://www.jstor.org/discover/10.2307/3381131?uid=35776&uid=3 737536&uid=2&uid=3&uid=67&uid=35775&uid=62&uid=5909656&si d=21104400383131, accessed 22 October 2014.

Kloot L. & Martin J., 2000, Strategic performance management: A balanced approach to performance management issues in local government, *Management Accounting Research*, Vol. 11, Issue 2, 231-251, http://www.sciencedirect.com/science/article/pii/-S1044500500901306, accessed 22 October 2014.

Macquarie Bank, 2014, Employee Engagement Survey 2014, 15 April 2014, Sydney.

NCOA (National Commission of Audit) 2014, Towards responsible government, The Report of the National Commission of Audit, http://www.ncoa.gov.au/report/index.htm, accessed 23 October 2014.

SECTION FOUR

Austrade today and tomorrow

20

The architecture of trade promotion

Bruce Nicholls

Introduction

Having served through the transition to Austrade, and led a small team working on its formative structure, I was delighted to contribute this chapter. Its observations are tempered by a continuing involvement with trade, observing it more often through a private sector prism. It attempts to answer the question: *"If we were to set out today, with a fresh sheet of paper, to design a trade agency uniquely tailored to Australia's needs, how might it look?"*

In 1984, Trade Minister John Dawkins decided to restructure the long-serving Trade Commissioner Service. His questioning of that revered institution evoked an immediate, indignant response, confirming that the passage of years had produced a strongly entrenched culture. Organisational theory asserts that it is not just healthy to question institutional values, but critical to institutional survival, for institutions *must* change over time, or risk irrelevance.

This contribution stands on the fundament of that unassailable logic. Beginning with a 'fresh sheet of paper' liberates the analysis from historical prejudices and enables an objective view. Many questions arise which are rarely explored because they are mired in controversy. What drives trade? Is the invisible hand of the market greater than government? Should governments direct trade or grease the tracks and get out of the way? Does the cost of trade promotion deliver a dividend or is it a fiscal drag? How do we measure those things?

Do governments have a role?

Free trade and the *invisible hand of the market* are utopian ideas which require that everyone plays by the rules, in a world without subsidies, duties or confected barriers. That world does not exist. In their theories of free trade, Adam Smith and Ricardo held that, to win trade, one needed a comparative advantage; a genuine, or perhaps a cleverly confected one. A scarce resource, like oil; a unique technology; a 'first-to-market' advantage or, quite simply, a price advantage. In considering the architecture of trade promotion, it is therefore important to ask whether comparative advantage can be influenced by government. The answer is an emphatic "yes". The removal of trade barriers, the opening of markets and the publication of critical economic data all lie solely within the province of government to secure on our behalf. Innovation feeds off government R & D policy. Resource projects depend upon foreign investment, making foreign investment policy a critical determinant of trade. The movement of goods and services requires good transport infrastructure and bold public investments.
Moreover, public trade architecture extends beyond Foreign Affairs and Trade (DFAT) and Austrade to less obvious areas – Treasury and Finance, Education and Training, Research and Development, Regional and Rural Development, Law and Justice – and other government portfolios which, often unwittingly, provide important platforms for trade. One must therefore conclude that governments are central to a nation's trade architecture. If they get things right, trade will flow, just as surely as water flows down a well-constructed canal.

Policy versus promotion

In fostering export growth, governments have three economic levers at their disposal; a trade policy lever, a trade promotional lever and an investment attraction lever. Each is fundamentally different and requires different resourcing. Trade policy finds its voice in multilateral forums, like the WTO, where processes are slow and ponderous. The Doha round trudged on for years. Recent governments have sought speedier, bi-lateral solutions. Trade Minister Andrew Robb found a circuit breaker in his bilateral Trade Agreements with South Korea and Japan and will hopefully sign another one with China. However, while bi-lateral arrangements are easier to achieve than multilateral consensus, they happen at a macro-economic level, remote from the real-time challenges faced by businesses. Businesses are driven by more urgent realities, like cash flow and overheads. If governments will assist them, they must offer "just-in-time solutions" and a nimble response to win new markets.

While trade policy is a fundamental plank in Australia's trade architecture, policy work is delivered by a small, elite team, working in a closed environment and directing representations to a few, select forums. Policy work and the imprimatur of a trade minister are critical. However, they happen remotely and constitute unnecessary *clutter* in the search for a business-oriented export role, operating closer to the pavement and meeting "just-in-time" business needs. If the ponderous policy lever has no place in a 'just-in-time' agency, only two other levers remain – the trade promotion lever, and the investment lever.

Which sectors need help?

To fairly answer this question, one must examine Australia's trade composition, strip out the non-promotable items (i.e., those driven by market or other forces beyond a government's influence or control) and attempt to isolate the remaining, "promotable" categories. In 2012-3, almost 61.1 per cent of Australia's product and service exports were contributed by just 10 product categories (ABS 2012-2013):

Table 1: Composition of Exports – Major Ten Categories

Iron Ore & Concentrates	$57	bill	18.9%
Coal	$38.6	bill	12.8%
Gold	$15.3	bill	5.1%
Education related travel	$14.5	bill	4.8%
Natural gas	$14.2	bill	4.7%
Personal travel services			4.0%
Crude Petroleum			3.8%
Wheat			3.0%
Aluminium (& derivatives)			2.0%
Copper (& derivatives)			2.0%
			61.1%

Source: ABS 2012-13.

Over a century ago, Australia's exports were dominated by a dozen or so primary products, challenging the architects of our nascent economy to "diversify" its exports. Over the intervening century or so, one might have hoped for much greater diversification. Once a colonial "warehouse of supply" for a distant Empire, Australia remains, it seems, a "quarry of supply" for newly emerging ones. Its comparative advantage remains "primary product-based", just as it was when, as a fledgling nation, it exported wool, wheat and mutton tallow.

Moreover, if the top ten categories are assessed for their promotability, many of them are seen to be controlled by global oligopolies, using investment instruments to create vertical and horizontal inter-dependence and control markets. Iron ore, coal, oil, nickel, aluminium and gas all stand well beyond the promotional horizon of even the most zealous public servants, while the rest of the Australian economy looks like an emperor without clothes.

Is the residual 40 per cent of Australia's exports the part we need to grow, or just the top 60 per cent, which provides the biggest dividend? Exporting is not just about shipping minerals. Its river has many tributaries, embracing a miscellany of other employment and forex generating sectors, including tourism, educational services, consultancy and others.

Moreover, exports in the bottom 40 percentile, worth $125 billion, largely emanate from our cities. That miscellany of products and services makes a higher contribution to national employment than the fewer, more remote primary projects. The $180 million annual cost of Austrade (Austrade 2014: 161) comprising appropriations, non-appropriated revenues and the operating deficit, represents just 0.07 per cent of the $125 billion contributed by the bottom 40 percentile. Moreover, the $22 m in "user-pays" revenues is not transparent (i.e., not reduced by the costs of administering and collecting payments) and represents just 12 per cent of that 0.07 per cent (0.0084 per cent). This raises real concerns about the user-pays system, which I explore in the following paragraph. Why have it at all?

User-pays and getting the best bang for our buck

Most of Australia's competitors support exporters or protect their markets in ways which are prohibited by the WTO, including the use of tariff and non-tariff barriers to trade, production subsidies and other trade distorting measures. Indeed, the only way a nation can legitimately assist its exporters, within WTO rules, is by funding a government department or public sector agency created for the purpose. Despite this fact, Australia rails at the practices of others, while cutting funding to this one, permitted area of government assistance. That, it seems to me, is pure folly, and trivialises the economic contribution made by our exports. Every nation assists its exporters. Whether that assistance amounts to a *subsidy* depends how generous it is and whether it *distorts*. By any standard, Australia is a very clean player.

When Austrade introduced its user-pays principle, it made export support *conditional* rather than a *strategic tool of public policy*. In doing so, it made two errors. It failed to exploit the one avenue of support permitted under WTO rules and possibly alienated a clientele which had enjoyed a free service, albeit one they already paid for through company taxes. Has the "user-pays" formula worked? Did it deliver higher efficiency? Better services? Reduced costs? Did it provide a better performance measure for employees? In serving only those who could pay, did it fail to support those who most needed support? These questions require honest, objective analysis to establish, once and for all, whether the user-pays model has delivered a real, quantifiable efficiency dividend. I suspect the dividend is illusionary.

If we compare the value of promotable trade with total agency costs, it appears that agency costs are dwarfed by the larger, macroeconomic returns available from a well-constructed national trade effort. It may be time to ask whether removal of the user-pays formula might encourage a closer interface with the private sector and a more collegiate business relationship, with compensating trade dividends. In the final analysis, what matters most is that the trade agency model we choose delivers an *incremental return* for each public dollar spent on export development and that it *grows and diversifies* its client base each year.

Integrating federal and state efforts

All levels of government promote trade and commerce, but geopolitical factors tend to fragment, rather than harmonise, those efforts. Could governments, by some better synthesis of efforts, overcome duplication and vertical fiscal imbalance? That would improve the return on each dollar invested in export development, but it would require a national approach; one reaching across geo-political divides to pool resources. While that goal has always seemed a bridge too far, on 18 August, 2014, the Abbott government took a bold step in that direction, when Trade Minister, Andrew Robb, and Foreign Minister Julie Bishop announced a new approach to economic diplomacy (Lowy Institute 2014).

The government's new economic diplomacy agenda outlined four key principles: (i) Promoting Trade; (ii) Encouraging Growth; (iii) Attracting Investment and (iv) Supporting Australian Businesses. The mechanism for delivering the new, Economic Diplomacy was outlined in: (i) a Business Charter, outlining twelve key commitments, and (ii) a State and Territory Government Charter, outlining a coordinated Commonwealth approach, based upon all states sharing information and other resources. Importantly, both Charters contained input from 95 ambassadors, high commissioners and consuls general and from 72 trade commissioners, and will operate to integrate their trade and investment efforts.

This new strategy reflects many of the ideal traits posited in this contribution and represents an important change in our trade architecture. (Further information on the initiative is available from business@dfat.gov.au). It thus deserves special mention in this narrative.

Investment as a locomotive for trade

When the present government appointed a "Minister for Trade and Investment", it gave a voice in Cabinet to that important relationship. Trade is increasingly driven by investments in source markets, to the point that trade without investment is like a horse without a carriage. Indeed, Australia must now compete as vigorously for capital as it does for markets. In 2013, while Chinese global investments continued to rise, Chinese investment in Australia *fell* by 10 per cent (KPMG 2014). Trade-linked investments give the foreign investor "skin in the game" (something to lose) and thus lock-in long-term market access. The investment nexus is even more critical at the capital-starved, SME level, so policies which encourage capital into small, export-oriented ventures (for example, through a revamped Business Migration program) are integral to effective trade promotion. Investment is a hand-maiden of trade promotion and the two must work together to multiply trade.

A "supply-push" or a "demand-pull" strategy?

When an exporter thrusts a home-grown product (say vegemite) down the throat of an unwilling foreign consumer, simply because he has a surplus for export that is a "supply-push" export strategy. In stark contrast, a "demand-pull" strategy researches what the foreign market needs, calculates what market share the exporter might hope to capture and tailors the export strategy to meet these dictates. The successful "China Action Plan" (Department of Overseas Trade 1982) resolved this tension with a strategy of *market interface and threshold inquiry*.

Demand-pull strategies sound good in theory, but most requests for export assistance begin at the door of a government agency at home, resulting in a "supply-push" response. An ideal export agency will understand this tension and require a well-researched market, a good product fit and a capacity to manage export risks. It will encourage exporters to start their journey in the international marketplace, identify demand and build a case for an investment in meeting demand. In proving its "demand-pull" business case, the exporter will be alerted to other, market-critical factors, like taste, packaging, labeling and branding (e.g., use of Chinese characters on packs, meeting local regulations, using familiar local branding totems, etc.)

Which exporters should we assist?

Multinational corporations are often bigger than governments. In Australia, for example, vehicle manufacturers demanded a minimum 58,000 units per annum to sustain production and threatened to pull out if that critical mass was not supported (Ford Australia 2013). At that level of the game, a trade promotion agency is dancing with elephants and stands a good chance of being trampled. If it hopes to make a difference at the enterprise level, a trade promotion agency has no seat at the multinational's table. However, that does not mean that it should focus solely upon SMEs. That strategy simply limits the rewards that might flow from bolder initiatives. Nor should it pick winners. In our egalitarian society, it would be undemocratic and politically unwise to favour any particular product or industry group. How, then, should efforts be targeted?

This vexing question resolves itself if we proceed from the assumption that only those in need of export assistance will seek it out. If that is so, the ideal agency will focus on the suite of export services required to win markets and let its clients evolve from that. If those services include lending a government imprimatur to support an Australian consortium's bid for a major global tender, that service will be seductive, even for a major corporation. At the other end of the scale, an introduction to an import agent may be the ideal solution for a small, first time exporter. It follows that trade priorities should not be driven by the size of the client, but rather by the mix of services needed to win markets. Moreover, those services should be delivered by a market-nimble agency, ready to go where it is called to go.

Which markets should we target?

Should governments "direct traffic", by targeting markets, or let trade grow organically? Should they respond opportunistically, when a once in a lifetime opportunity emerges? In 2012-3, just three markets – China, Japan and the Republic of Korea – accounted for some 60 per cent of our total exports (ABS 2012-3), highlighting an unhealthy market dependence and a need for diversification. If diversification is the strategic goal, efforts might logically concentrate upon developing new markets. Ranking markets by their export contribution is an unworthy strategy, since it fails to respect those markets which deliver the highest value-adding. New frontiers of trade always provide the highest value-adding, or return on each export promotional dollar, since they start from a low or zero base.

Another way to view the issue of matching resources with markets is to decide which markets require the *least* support. By this logic, markets which closely mirror our own – USA, UK, Canada, New Zealand, Germany, etc. – should be accorded low priority. Assistance in these 'easy' markets might be constrained to providing market

The Austrade Story

intelligence (a service which should probably be provided to all exporters on a fee basis) and local, logistical support.

The penalty-costs associated with posting Australian officers to 'easy', Western markets must also be considered, since those markets tend to have the highest economic rents (and costs are multiplied by the cost of co-locating the officer's family). In these 'familiar' markets, costs will be greatly reduced if support services are provided by locally-employed staff. Australian expats could be recruited to provide "just-in-time" intelligence on trade and investment opportunities, commercial support services (including submitting tenders, finding local agents, etc.) and logistical support (for trade missions, etc.). They would need security vetting and management supervision by a Regional Trade and Investment Commissioner.

"Perfect information" and "just-in-time" intelligence

Camel trains once traversed deserts and mountain passes to deliver tribute to emperors. Nowadays, trades which took months to transact, happen instantly. No contemporary trade agency could hope to be effective without a "just-in-time" information highway. In today's frenetic marketplace, this should be the single, most important function of any export agency. The Austrade website is excellent, but it stops short of providing one, vital feature – a "call to action". It provides background on markets, a directory of suppliers, a calendar of events and information about grants. However, there is no "just-in-time" intelligence enabling an exporter to submit a commercial offer; no function supporting a "first to market" advantage.

Moreover, the present website's orientation is confusing. The "directory of suppliers" contemplates that foreigner buyers will visit the site while advice on grants contemplates, instead, that Australian exporters are the main visitors. Secure access to market intelligence would require engineering of downstream services, to farm intelligence from the agency's partners and stakeholders. If Austrade hopes to build a close relationship with businesses, providing intelligence on business opportunity, is the way to do so. Like feeding time at a zoo, a regular feed of commercial intelligence will drive habitual behavior and repeat visits. This rational favours the development of a more functional, "just-in-time" web portal (refer Section (v) – (v.iv) – Divisional Structure), to replace the existing web site.

A just-in-time web portal may be a difficult concept for a government agency, since it requires "letting go" of bureaucratic controls and trusting technology. In a trade context, the uploading of back end content must ensure that the source is trusted and the information accurate, but the portal might also permit Australian businessmen and women, who see trade opportunities on their travels, to make that information available to other Australian exporters. This would reinforce a "Team Australia" approach across our export community.

How might an ideal agency look?

(i) Culture

If the positive features identified are the bricks for an agency's construction, the mortar must surely be a strong business culture. Rightly or wrongly, government agencies are perceived as bureaucratic, remote and slow to react. Overcoming these perceptions is a challenge best met by giving *all* stakeholders "skin in the game", to encourage a shared culture across the public-private divide, in partnership with national and state agencies, businesses and governments.

In seeking to change the cultural paradigm, there is much to be learned from business models designed to shape business behaviour. National franchises maintain high, uniform standards across their networks, with staff training regimes to shape behaviour. "Optus World", Bendigo Bank and other *customer-focussed* agencies train staff to ask "open" questions (to determine wants and needs), rather than "closed" ones (which assume the answer). A business-like, service-attuned, open agency will quickly enhance its reputation. Removing red tape will make it more responsive. Functional technology, including online and web-based solutions, will extend market reach, improve service delivery and lower costs.

(ii) Duplication

Efficiency will be greatly improved and costs lowered if duplication is removed, not just across state borders, but within the agency itself. (This issue is addressed in more detail below and in the earlier outline of the Coalition's new Economic Diplomacy strategy).

(iii) Funding, and vertical fiscal imbalance

The recently announced "new strategy for Trade Diplomacy" seeks to integrate efforts across all levels of business and government. However, it does not quantify cost-sharing or the national dividend such an approach might deliver. How, then, might an ideal agency, seeking to harmonise national efforts, be funded? To achieve equity, it would have to achieve acceptance of a joint funding model across the geopolitical divide, requiring states and business organisations to contribute funding or operational support. This ideal relies upon the dubious assumption that governments are capable of acting in the broader national interest. In this joint funding model, the federal government might retain a 51 per cent stake, to reflect its sunk investment in Austrade and federally-owned infrastructure (e.g., embassies, support agency offices, etc.) That would leave the states with a 49 per cent stake. Let us assume an agency budget of $A200 million p.a. (roughly equivalent to Austrade's present budget). Equity accounting each state's share of exports yields the following funding model:

Table 2: Equity-accounted Funding of National Export Agency Costs

Total Agency Cost / Annual Budget (2012-13)	100%	$200.0 m
Federal contribution	51%	$102.0 m
State contributions	49%	$ 98.0 m
(based upon an equity accounted share of total national exports)		

State % of Total Exports		Annual equity-accounted share of agency cost
WA	40%	$ 40.0 m
NSW	21%	$ 21.0 m
QLD	18%	$ 19.0 m
VIC	12%	$ 12.0 m
SA	4%	$ 4.0 m
NT	2%	$ 2.0 m
ACT	(funded under Federal umbrella)	$ 0.0 m
TOTAL		$ 98.0 m

When these numbers are unpacked and compared with State revenues from export-related activities (e.g., from mining royalties, tourism, education services, etc.) they represent a small outlay relative to the Gross State Product (GSP), while making a relatively large contribution to State commerce and industry and, most importantly, to State employment.

Source: Author 2014, based upon ABS 2013 export statistics, by value and State.

(iv) Leadership

A more business-oriented agency would ideally be seriously corporatised, not just in name but in nature, and chaired by a charismatic business leader, able to win the support of peak business councils. It would be led by a CEO recruited by executive search process.

Table 3: Proposed Leadership Structure

Chairman	**Charismatic Business Leader** – international experience; casting vote
Dep. Chair	Secretary of Trade, (as Minister's delegate)
Director 1	Minerals & Energy sector business leader
Director 2	Agriculture and Ag Sciences sector leader
Director 3	Tourism / Education / Other Services sector Leader
Director 4	Transformed products sector
Director 5	Aust. Chamber of Commerce & Industry Rep (as mouthpiece for respective national Chambers of Commerce)
CEO	**Appointed by private search process with a clear business mandate and corporate mission, measure by KPIs.**
Source: Author 2014	

To ensure equal representation for all states over time, there should be no more than two board members from any one State and any new vacancy should be filled by a state nominee not already represented on the outgoing board,

(v) Divisional structure

The head office team would ideally be located in a major capital city (probably Sydney, as is now the case) and comprise the CEO, the core functions which support him (human resources, administration, I.T. support, etc.) and divisional heads, as follows:

(a) Investment Division.

(b) Export Growth Division.

(c\ International Markets Division.

(d) E-Commerce Division (managing a *Trade Hub* , or export web portal).

Table 4: Conceptual organisation Structure (Note name change – 'Corporation')

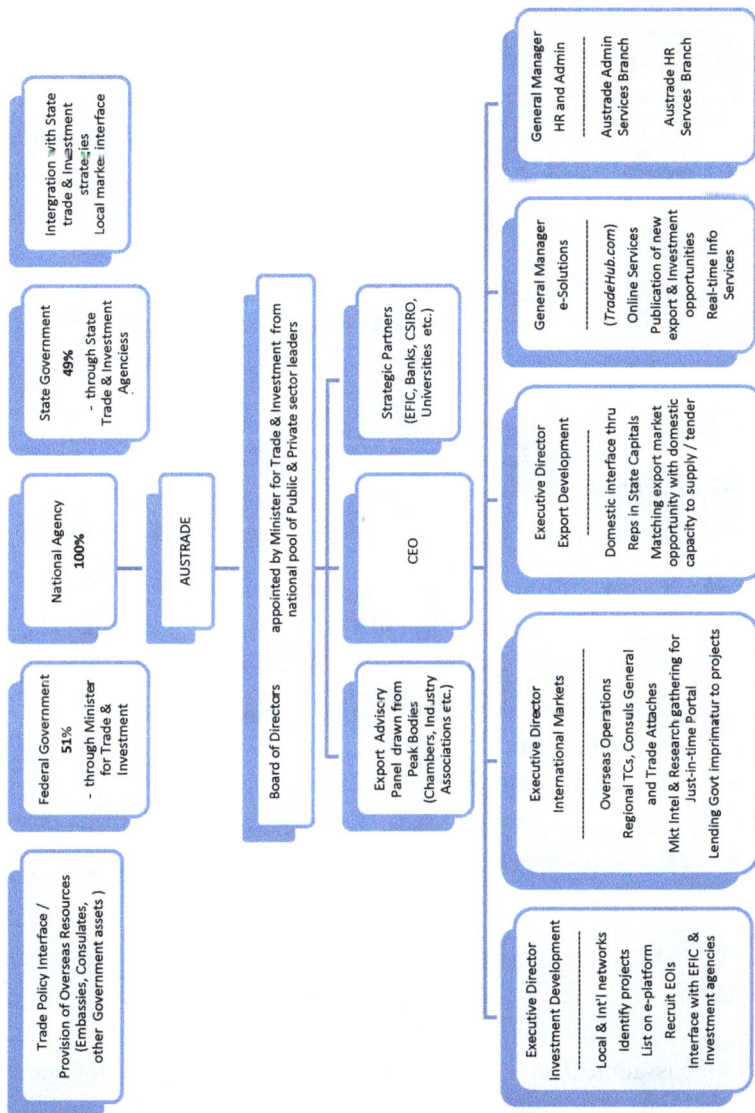

(v.i) Investment Division

A small cell, literate in financial services, FIRB/Treasury rules and project planning and approval issues with a mission to develop investment networks and links, including with the states, with chambers of commerce, the banking and finance sector and other multiplier agencies at home and abroad able to inform new investment capture initiatives. This division would gather data from state partners and overseas posts on investment and joint venture opportunities, including requests for venture capital from bona fide businesses. It would publish opportunities (e.g., "Investment Partners sought") on the agency's web portal, inviting expressions of interest, with a legal disclaimer requiring respondents to make their own further inquiries. Expressions of interest would be screened and passed back to the source.

(v.ii) International Markets Division

This Division would support market-based field assets, comprising:

1. Regional Commissioners for Trade & Investment (Ministers Commercial) with responsibility for driving regional efforts (e.g., in North Asia, South East Asia, etc.)
2. Trade Commissioners (Consuls General) in major commercial centres or markets designated as support-dependent/unfamiliar business cultures, and ...
3. Trade Attachés, providing basic market research, trade assistance and logistical support in familiar business cultures/commercial centres.

In posts where our trade interests have primacy over international relations, the trade commissioner should fill the consul general post (to improve business access). Trade consuls general would defer to ambassadors (on non-trade matters) and to regional trade and investment commissioners (on trade and investment functions). In familiar, western markets, trade support staff would ideally be recruited locally and attached to consulates general. This strategy would significantly reduce overseas salary and support costs.

Field assets deployed by International Markets Division will ideally have commercial skills which distinguish them from home-based, support staff (language skills, market familiarity, negotiating experience, etc.). Those skills ought to be highly valued, targeted by an elite recruitment and training process, and developed in a separate, overseas career stream (e.g., by contract appointment, perhaps, rather than giving permanent public service status).

A separate, overseas career stream would ideally permit the short-term attachment of experts from the business sector (e.g., to manage a bid for an aerospace contract or support a consortium bid for a major project) and the short-term attachment of Austrade staff to businesses requiring special assistance (e.g., to set up local operations in difficult language environments or provide a liaison function, if the project requires a government interface). Commissioners might also be recruited from the private sector on term contracts; e.g., a recently-retired mining executive, or a well-travelled global commodity trader. A capacity for public-private sector interchanges of this kind would do much to foster a business culture within the agency and a more collegiate relationship with the agency's business clients.

(v.iii) Export Growth Division

Reflecting a vertical integration model, a State Commissioner for Trade and Investment would be appointed by the Federal Minister on the recommendation of a State Minister, to lead export development initiatives in that state and feed those into national initiatives. This division would integrate state and national efforts, matching export capability with identified market opportunities, administering requests for assistance, processing EMDG grants, and coordinating participation at fairs and exhibitions or in trade missions. It would feed information on export capability and investment opportunity into the web portal and provide the regional interface between Austrade and trade and investment clients around Australia.

(v.iv) *TradeHub.com* – A just-in-time, trade portal

A small unit with I.T skills would manage a new web portal, with an executive team editing and approving content. Ideally, the portal would be separately branded – something like *TradeHub.com* – to give it wide reach, visibility to search engines and attract inquiries from around the world. Each area of agency activity would supply, refresh and remove trade and investment data. The portal would allow access to public content, but restrict access to commercially sensitive or valuable information to those paying an annual subscription fee and using a user name and password (ideally, the client's email address and ABN).

The portal would ideally include links to state partner agencies; to banks (for venture capital or business loans); freight forwarders, shippers; insurers and other export-service providers. Commercial content typically attracts referral fees or trailing commissions and may provide a source of revenue for the agency. Functionality would support on-line transactions and payments (e.g., applications for grants, booking of space at fairs and exhibitions, applications to join trade missions, inquiries for agents and distributors, etc.) Functionality will seek to remove red tape and bureaucratic process and to reduce overheads.

The *TradeHub* portal would ideally include an area where Australian business representatives, who see trade or investment opportunities during their travels abroad, can pass information back to other exporters. The portal should also include a "Partners Sought" area, with a legal disclaimer, directing inquirers to investment or joint venture opportunities.

Restricted content would include protected, or commercially sensitive, information only available to bona fide Australian companies subscribing to the service. Content would include new product or service opportunities or new investment or joint venture opportunities, up-loaded to the back end of the site after vetting for accuracy / suitability. Charging a fee to access this content makes sense, since it has real, commercial value.

Conclusion and recommendations

In exploiting a licence to innovate and reconstruct Australia's trade architecture, this chapter glosses recklessly over inconvenient truths about practical implementation. Happily, many of the desirable features canvassed in this essay exist in the current architecture of Austrade. However, the following elements, I suggest, provide fertile soil for further growth:

Recommendations:

- Inculcating a *real* corporate culture and changing the name of the agency from "Commission" to "Corporation", to strengthen business ties.
- Removing red tape, duplication and fiscal imbalances.
- Integrating national efforts (one agency; one mission; one culture; one budget).
- Up-grading technology to deliver new functionality, including …

  Online processing and delivery of requests for services.

  'Call to action' content on new trade and investment opportunities.

  A range of "just-in-time" business solutions, with links to partner providers.
- Abolishing the "user-pays" formula and introducing collateral, online revenues.
- A leaner support structure at home and abroad, with attendant savings.
- Creating a separate, overseas career stream, with recruitment of expat staff in Western markets, short-term attachments from the private sector and short-term attachments of Austrade staff to businesses (to assist with special projects or challenges.

In the final analysis, there is no perfect model. Achieving that ideal is, at best, a work in progress and, at worst, a relentless journey in pursuit of excellence. If the ideas presented in this chapter stimulate further discussion and debate, they will have served a useful purpose.

Bibliography

ABS 20012-13, Australian Bureau of Statistics, Canberra.

Austrade 2014, Austrade Annual Report 2013-14, Australian Trade Commission, Canberra.

Department of Overseas Trade, 1982, China Action Plan, Department of Overseas Trade, Canberra.

Ford Australia, 2013, Submission to Victorian State Government, November 2013.

KPMG 2014, Demystifying Chinese investment in Australia, A KPMG-Sydney University Study, March 2014, http://www.kpmg.com/au/en/issuesandinsights/articlespublications-/china-insights/pages/default.aspx, accessed 31 July 2014.

Lowy Institute 2014, Launch of the Australian Government's economic diplomacy agenda- Foreign Minister Julie Bishop and Trade Minister Andrew Robb, 18 August 2014, http://www.lowyinstitute.org/news-and-media/audio/launch-australian-gover1nments-economic-diplomacy-agenda-foreign-minister-julie-bishop-and-trade, accessed 31 July 2014.

21

The future role of Austrade
in a globalised trade market

Peter Wilton

Wherein lies the future of Austrade? Since previous chapters have so insightfully described the history and evolution of Austrade, it is fitting to turn our attention to the question of Austrade's future role in an ever evolving global marketplace.

Like most trade promotion organisations, Austrade has its origins in the world of export development and promotion. This focus upon export facilitation as the core purpose of Austrade in turn draws upon the well-articulated economic theory of national comparative advantage which suggests that each nation should leverage its own unique advantage, whether natural factor-based (e.g., low-order advantages such as mineral deposits, low labour costs, etc.), or knowledge-based (e.g., high-order advantages such as education and technology). These advantages in turn may be generalised, applicable in a wide range of industries and markets, or specialised, based upon specific characteristics of a particular industry, market, or firm.

Under the national comparative advantage model, nations are assumed to be self-sufficient and superior in their respective trade domains, leading to surpluses which can be exported at a comparative advantage. Whilst evidence of this type of advantage clearly remains in Australia (e.g., minerals, natural gas, education), in other sectors of the Australian economy (e.g., car manufacturing) it has become increasingly apparent that Australia lacks the relevant combination of natural and supporting factors to sustain such sectors in a global trade environment.

One often posited reason for Australia's lack of global competitiveness in many sectors is the limited population size of the country (23 million). This has frequently been cited as an inhibitor to economies of scale, and sustained investment into technology, infrastructure and innovation. However, in terms of international trade, this argument is largely spurious. Witness leading global firms from Scandinavian countries whose populations range between five and ten million inhabitants. Nokia and Ikea are two very familiar examples of firms that recognised the opportunity to design offerings that were relevant to a global marketplace, thereby bypassing the limitations of domestic scale. Cochlear, of course, represents the Australian equivalent of such success stories. These examples indicate clearly that population base should not serve as the limiting factor in Australia's global competitiveness. Rather the focus of the debate should be directed to the lack of global mind-set and orientation driving the value-creation process of many Australian enterprises.

The traditional view of export-oriented trade has enormous political appeal. The underlying economic logic is job-creation. "Exports create jobs" is the mantra. Again, this is an oversimplification of the economic development process. The core enabler of all job creation is capital. Given this, the more important question is whether exports are a productive or unproductive use of the nation's private capital? In many instances, it is likely that Australian small and medium size enterprises (SMEs) attempting to export are ill-equipped to compete globally, thereby tying up capital in unproductive use. In a recent study of Australian SMEs involved in the defence industry, only two percent (65 out of a total SME defence industry population of approximately 3,000) had been able to successfully win international business from global prime defence contractors on the basis of competitive merit.[1]

---

1 A Review of the Global Supply Chain Program of the Defence Materiel Program, report prepared by ORBIS Associates, for the Defence Materiel Organization, October, 2013.

The profile of this small sample of globally successful SMEs in many cases is markedly different from the typical Australian SME attempting to export from a purely domestic-based value chain, as will be seen in a later part of this chapter.

In a separate multi-country study conducted by this author for Austrade,[2] international buyers and distributors of Australian exports indicated a strong desire to see fewer, but more competitive, Australian exporters. In order of preference, these global marketing and channel partners were seeking Australian SMEs offering superior quality, highly differentiated/unique products, lowest cost pricing, strong merchandising and promotion support, access to a continuous stream of new products/innovations, and an ability to meet short lead times. SMEs that were incapable of meeting these requirements were considered to be damaging to "Brand Australia", and negatively impacting buyer interest in future Australian sourcing opportunities. In short, to the extent that Australian SMEs are attempting to export without the capabilities, expertise, and commitment to compete globally, export activity may in fact destroy productive capital, leading to fewer jobs, not more.

Putting the exporter competency question aside, a more relevant question for the "job-creation" discussion is how to attract sustainable, long-term capital inflow into Australia to build new economic sectors (or reinvigorate existing ones) that will sustain the country as the resources boom tapers off. This is a much more important structural opportunity facing Australia than driving further exports in the short- to medium-term.

Reliance upon exports to drive economic development, and specifically job creation, is limiting. First, comparative advantage in key economic sectors can shift. Natural resources are depleted, labor cost advantages disappear (witness the current migration of labour-intensive manufacturing from China to south and central Asia), and

2 Strategic Partnering for Global Success: The Customer/Ally Perspective, report prepared by ORBIS Associates, for Austrade, October 2008.

competition in knowledge-based sectors can increase and create dislocations in leadership (witness the shift in the mobile handset leadership from Scandinavia to Korea, China and North America). Moreover, the perennial problem of exchange rate volatility can erode (or enhance) competitiveness virtually overnight, rendering exports at the mercy of global capital markets.

For these and other reasons, the central focus of the discussion of Austrade's role in the emerging global economy is twofold:

i.   *What can/should Austrade do to enhance the global competitiveness of Australian SMEs?*

ii. *What can/should Austrade do to attract private capital into Australia to strengthen existing economic sectors and build new ones?*

The answers to both these questions are interrelated, but collectively should address the goal of job-creation, and more importantly, job and enterprise value.

In his seminal work "Comparative Advantage of Nations",[3] based upon extensive research into firms in multiple industries in multiple countries, Michael Porter advances a very simple premise underlying success in global markets.

> Around the world, companies that have achieved international leadership employ strategies that differ from each other in every respect. But while every successful company will employ its own particular strategy, the underlying mode of operation— the character and trajectory of all successful companies— is fundamentally the same. Companies achieve competitive advantage through **acts of innovation**.

Herein lies the answer to the first question regarding the role of Austrade in the emerging global economy: *what can/should Austrade do to enhance the global competitiveness of Australian SMEs?*

---

3 Porter, Michael, "The Comparative Advantage of Nations", *Harvard Business Review*, March-April 1990, pp. 74-91.

Austrade needs play a more proactive role in assisting Australian SMEs to gain access to innovation that drives global competitiveness. This is a significant shift in Austrade's role within the Austrade export community.

Historically, Austrade has, through a variety of direct and indirect assistance programs, focused upon building export readiness among new exporters and market selection and entry assistance for SMEs beginning or growing their export activities. By and large, like many similar organisations, Austrade's activity focus has been around the traditional trade promotion model, with an emphasis on trade missions and international trade shows and events. This format aims to connect a broad audience of buyers and sellers around a concentrated, one-time, event. The activities of SME innovation and capability building, however, are generally much more targeted, aiming to connect a specific buyer to a specific seller around a specifically matched long-term demand/capability opportunity, usually as a result of much more intensive opportunity analysis.

Whilst the traditional broadly focused trade promotion format may have value for SMEs with less experience in international trade, comments from SMEs highly experienced and successful in global business (obtained by this author in various reviews) indicates a clear preference for more highly targeted assistance to establish and demonstrate advantage in specific competitive contexts. This goal of proactively driving innovation and global competitiveness of Austrade SMEs has not in the past been a specific direct mandate for the organisation.

Proactively supporting innovation and global competitiveness throughout the value chain of an SME is commercially and ideologically very distinct from traditional export activity. In particular, building SME innovation and global competitiveness is uniquely aligned around:

- the identification and realisation of highly targeted long-term international demand/capability opportunities, requiring intensive analysis, support and collaboration

between specific international customers and the
individual SME (see discussion of anchor customers
below);

- the optimal positioning of Australian SME capability
within the value chain of the right global customer;
- the growth and development of the SME's value chain
contributions over time;
- The development of globally competitive SME firm- and
industry-level capabilities over time.

Given these distinctions, how can Austrade meaningfully contribute to the level of innovation and global competitiveness among Australian SMEs?

First, Austrade can become an active participant and collaborator in the many federal, state, regional and industry innovation initiatives, both public and private, that are already in place throughout Australia. As an example, within the defence industry in Australia, the portfolio of current or recent assistance programs and capability building frameworks designed to assist SMEs within the industry is vast, including:

- The Defence Industry Policy Statement, including the:
  1. Strategic Industry Capabilities (SICs).
  2. Priority Industry Capabilities (PICs).
- The Capability Technology Demonstration (CTD) Program.
- The Defence Materials Technology Centre (DMTC).
- The Defence Capability Plan (DCP).
- The Australian Industry Capability Plan (AIC).
- The Priority Industry Capabilities (PIC) Innovation Program.
- The Australian Military Sales Office, comprising:
  1. The Global Supply Chain (GSC) Program.
  2. The Defence Export Unit (DEU).
  3. The International Materiel Cooperation (IMC) Program.

- The Skilling Australia's Defence Industry (SADI) initiative.
- The Industry Skilling Program Enhancement (ISPE) initiative.
- The Defence Industry Innovation Centre (DIIC).
- The Defence Industry Skilling Taskforce (DIST).

These and other programs can be grouped into four major classes of assistance:

- Domestic Competitive Efficiency Programs.

  Developing business, technical and other capabilities that deliver superior value relative to other businesses within the Australian domestic market, independent of industry (i.e., generalised skill and capability across all core business functions: – strategy, finance, R&D, (lean) manufacturing, marketing, human resources, performance measurement, risk management, etc.).

- Global Competitive Efficiency Programs:

  Developing business, technical and other capabilities that deliver superior value relative to other businesses within a global market, independent of industry, both generalised skill and capability (knowledge of core international business functions) plus specialised skill and capability over the global business life cycle (transitioning from simple export to a true global enterprise).

- Sector Readiness Programs:

  Developing business, technical and other capabilities that deliver superior value to customers in a particular industry (e.g., mining, financial services, education, health care, etc.). These are specialised advantages, requiring in-depth knowledge of the requirements of the specific industry.

- Customer-Specific Readiness Programs:

  Developing business, technical and other capabilities

that deliver superior value to a specific anchor customer
or class of anchor customers (e.g., global prime defence
contractors and the defence agencies they serve). These
are specialised advantages, requiring in-depth knowledge
of the requirements of the specific customer or class
of customers, matters such as procurement processes,
supply chain configurations, supplier benchmarks,
product portfolio strategies, technology strategies,
regulatory requirements, security requirements, etc.).

Similar portfolios of innovation and capability-building initiatives
can be described for other sectors within Australia and abroad. In
all such cases, the goal is to increase the level of innovation and
competitiveness among one or more SMEs within the sector. Many
of these programs have a direct focus upon the transfer of Australian
technology into international markets, as well as the development of
specific commercial export opportunities. Clearly, the role for Austrade
would not be to duplicate or assume primary responsibility for such
programs. However, the opportunity for Austrade to coordinate and
align its support to such programs to build globally competitive
SMEs, particularly in the areas of "Global Competitive Efficiency"
and "Customer-Specific Readiness", is significant.

Second, Austrade can assist Australian SMEs in identifying and
establishing meaningful relationships with one or more core *anchor
customers*, either internationally or domestically, that will drive
innovation within the SME, and the industry to which the SME
belongs. Studies of the development of world class clusters, conducted
separately by this author,[4] have highlighted the importance of a strong
anchor customer that drives innovation within the cluster by constantly
demanding new approaches to the challenges and opportunities
that customer is facing. The existence of this anchor customer has
historically been shown to have far greater impact on the emergence

---

4 Building a World-Class Entrepreneurial ICT Cluster: A Ten-Year Strategic Plan
for the Panama ICT Sector, report prepared by Dr. Peter C. Wilton for the National
Secretariat of Science, Technology & Innovation, Panama. December 2008.

and growth of industry clusters than any portfolio of private or public sector supporting capability development initiatives.

An example of this approach is the Global Supply Chain initiative of the Australian Defence Materiel Organisation. This program has targeted global prime defence contractors as anchor customers for Australian defence SME's, with the aim of embedding Australian SME's into the supply chains of the defence primes on the basis of globally competitive capability within specific anchor customer needs. This experience has shown the power of the anchor customer to stimulate and bootstrap innovation within the responsive SME. Given Austrade's extensive global network of international customers and allies, a similar opportunity exists for Austrade to deliberately match capable Australian SME's against known anchor customers to drive innovation within the SME, or their respective sector.

Thirdly, and perhaps more importantly, Austrade can more proactively encourage and support the migration of Australian exporters through the global business life cycle, depicted in Figure 1. As suggested by this cycle, the longer and more successful the presence of the SME in international markets, the greater the likelihood the enterprise will begin to disperse key activities in its value chain outside of the domestic market in search of new advantage. The reason for this is simple. Innovation across the key activities within the firm's value chain is globally distributed: it is not concentrated within one domestic market. In order to capture this innovation and build global competitiveness, the firm must build presence at the source of innovation, either through direct investment or the creation and leveraging of an open innovation network.[5] The key decision is not whether to distribute critical value chain activities abroad, but which ones, when, and how soon?

This is not simply a search for lower cost. It is a search for innovation and insight into critical activities within the value chain. As

---

5 For a discussion of open innovation networks and their role in global markets, see Henry Chesbrough, *Open Innovation: the New Imperative for Creating & Profiting from Technology*, Harvard Business Scholl Press, 2003.

Figure 1: The Global Business Life Cycle

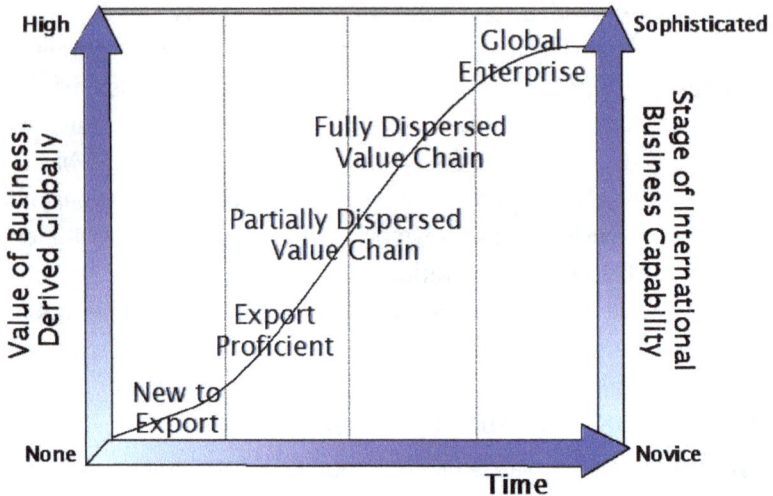

such, "getting smarter" in each value chain activity can be decoupled from where the activity is physically performed. As a simple example, the SME learns how to improve manufacturing in Germany, but then performs actual manufacturing in China.

The pattern by which this migration occurs is depicted in Figure 2. The firm starts with a competitive advantage in a proprietary value chain within its domestic market. This is referred to as the core formula strategy. Through greater exposure to global markets, the firm builds scope advantage: i.e., understanding of a broader mix of approaches to managing the value chain. In an attempt to capture and leverage these advantages, the firm begins to disperse the learning and innovation component of critical value chain activities, looking for opportunities to improve R&D, product design, marketing, sourcing, manufacturing, customer service, finance, HR, etc., but still retaining proprietary control and ownership of advantage.

The rationale for this dispersion is to increase competitive advantage, either by lowering the cost of inputs, providing greater proximity to international customers, or by accessing new sources of innovation, learning and other advantages not available in the home market. Regardless of motivation, the result is a deconstruction of the firm's vertically integrated domestic value chain. This deconstruction is essential if the firm is to become globally competitive, and is normally considered evidence of a successful international presence.

In a parallel path of the migration to global enterprise, the firm acknowledges that it is not fully capturing advantages created by others, specifically by lead countries in their sector (the countries generating the bulk of the innovation in the industry due to cluster effects), or by other international partners who possess complementary skills and assets which might benefit the firm. To capture these advantages, the firm will begin to make direct investments off-shore.

Figure 2: Capturing Advantage Globally – The Sources of Advantage

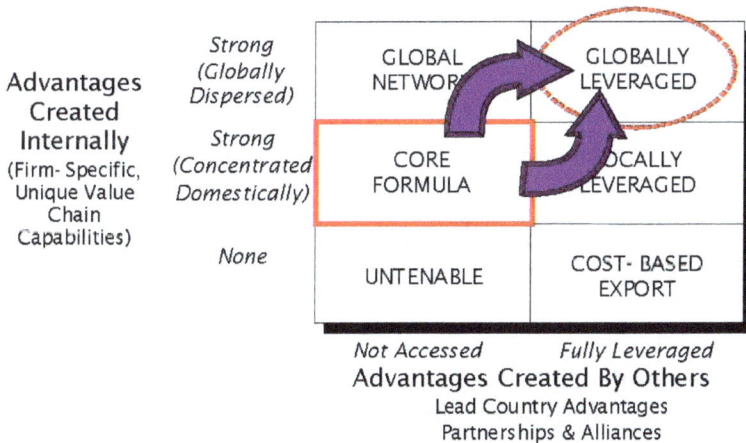

Advantages Created Internally (Firm-Specific, Unique Value Chain Capabilities)	Strong (Globally Dispersed)	GLOBAL NETWORK	GLOBALLY LEVERAGED
	Strong (Concentrated Domestically)	CORE FORMULA	LOCALLY LEVERAGED
	None	UNTENABLE	COST-BASED EXPORT
		Not Accessed	Fully Leveraged

Advantages Created By Others
Lead Country Advantages
Partnerships & Alliances

This migration pattern has been extensively documented in the global business literature,[6] and so will not be elaborated upon further here. Suffice it to note that the consequences for the export-based model of economic development are significant. In short, the business

6 Christopher Bartlett and Sumantra Ghoshal, *Managing Across Borders: The Transnational Solution*, Harvard Business School Press, 2002.

that began as an exporter is now a globally distributed network, with multiple locations for the design and implementation of key value chain activities. In the extreme case, the SME may no longer export from its home country. This is a natural outcome of its success as an exporter. Indeed, it is one of the primary factors underlying the reluctance of nations to punish trade partners for alleged infractions of global trade rules. Any sanctions imposed on the trade partner may equally hurt domestic firms who have located value chain activities in the domicile of the trade partner.

Examples of this migration can be found in two Australian SMEs with strong track records of global performance in the defence industry, Lovitt Technologies and Ferra. In the case of Lovitt, the dispersion has been driven by the need to access scale capabilities which could not be found within Australia, despite attempts to aggregate scale across multiple SMEs within Australia (resisted by potential partners due to the fear of competition among like competitors). In the case of Ferra, the dispersion has been driven by the need to access both lower cost manufacturing and learning and innovation advantages.

From a policy perspective, encouraging the global dispersion of SME value chains to build greater global competitiveness, as and when appropriate, is likely to build greater long-term national prosperity than encouraging a purely domestically focused vertically integrated export base that relies on only a domestic pool of innovation and competitive advantage opportunities. In light of this, Austrade has the opportunity to realign both its policy frameworks and core trade support mechanisms to provide direct proactive assistance in the design and implementation of globally distributed value chains and innovation networks for carefully selected Australian SMEs to accelerate their migration through the global business cycle.

Lastly, no discussion of the future role of Austrade in the emerging global marketplace would be complete without reference to ways of aligning and focusing the organisation to effectively support SMEs in the search for innovation and global competitiveness. Historically, and even today, Austrade has embraced a macro-level view of market opportunity which has been geographic region- or country-based. Whilst there have been various shifts over time in the specific regional/ country priorities, the view of relevant opportunity and corresponding support models has been heavily macro-economic focused: i.e., country-opportunity based. Unfortunately, this view does not neatly correspond to the distribution of innovation and competitive advantage opportunities globally

If the goal is to help Australian SMEs to first increase the level of innovation and global competitiveness, as a precursor to specific commercial opportunities that flow as a result of that competitiveness, then the structural and support focus of Austrade needs to be aligned around the sources of innovation and competitiveness globally. From numerous examples of successful global enterprises, these sources are widely distributed and are not concentrated in one or two regions or countries. Hence, the focus upon regional or country priorities is not likely to be helpful to Australian SMEs in the long-run.

Even if the primary Austrade focus remains upon facilitating exports (rather than global SME competitiveness), studies of global market participation have identified very differing models of identifying and managing such opportunities, as follows:

o Multi-domestic opportunities, in which international markets are treated as distinct and unrelated to each other, requiring significant tailoring of one or more aspects of the firm's offerings or other elements of its strategy; and;

o Global opportunities, in which sufficient similarities exist across markets to allow for consistent product development, positioning and customer support.

The differences between these two types of commercial opportunity are summarised in Figure 3. Regional or country-based structures are an example of the former (multi-domestic) approach, whilst global business segments (which focus upon common segment needs across regions) are an example of the latter (global) approach. Global business segments are more likely to describe the true nature of the export opportunity whenever there are:

- global customers (customers who search globally for the best solution and coordinate their purchases and support requirements globally, a typical anchor customer in industries such as defence, aerospace, manufacturing, pharmaceuticals, etc.);

- global competitors (i.e., competitors who face each other in multiple international markets);

- common customer needs, which allow the exporter to aggregate customers across markets to create and serve a uniform market segment with a uniform marketing mix; and;

- cost structures which favor economies of scale and consistency.

Identifying global business segments allows for both reduced risk and greater efficiencies in international export activity. This is because the SME faces less uncertainty (conditions are similar across markets), and strategies and operations require less tailoring. From the perspective of an aspiring Australian exporter, globally structured export opportunities are highly appealing, since they rapidly enable economies of scale, international growth, and diversification of country risk.

If such opportunities exist (and trends point in this direction in many industries), then Austrade's current regional priority structure is likely to inhibit the identification of global business segments for Australian exporters, since the structure quarantines resources, customer focus, and opportunity analysis by region, not globally. For Australian SMEs, this is likely to result in both under-scaled opportunities and increased redundancies in their export and capability development activities.

Let us now turn to the second question relating to the role of Austrade

Figure 3: The Structure of Commercial Export Opportunities

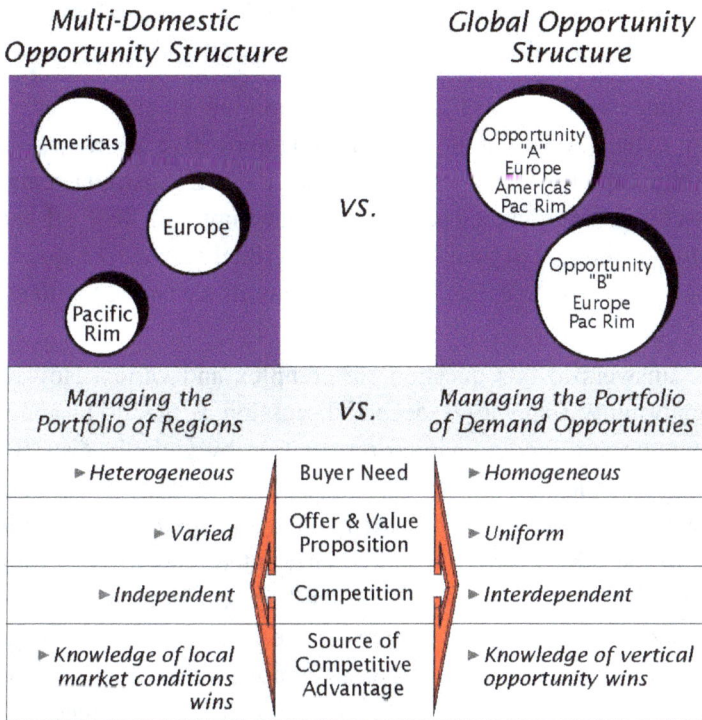

Multi-Domestic Opportunity Structure		Global Opportunity Structure
Managing the Portfolio of Regions	*vs.*	*Managing the Portfolio of Demand Opportunties*
▸ *Heterogeneous*	Buyer Need	▸ *Homogeneous*
▸ *Varied*	Offer & Value Proposition	▸ *Uniform*
▸ *Independent*	Competition	▸ *Interdependent*
▸ *Knowledge of local market conditions wins*	Source of Competitive Advantage	▸ *Knowledge of vertical opportunity wins*

in the emerging global marketplace: *What can/should Austrade do to attract private capital into Australia to strengthen existing economic sectors and build new ones?*

Imagine a world of no domestic exports, only a collection of highly successful globally dispersed enterprises of Australian origins (e.g., News Corporation). Would this necessarily be bad for Australia? The answer to this depends upon three things:

1 The fiscal policy and taxation environment surrounding repatriation of capital generated outside of Australia;

2 The potential for the Australian operations of the global
enterprise to add unique value in one or more elements
of the value chain;

3 The potential for the emergence of a domestically-based
cluster or industry lead country.

As suggested previously, the key to all job creation is capital.
To the extent Australia is globally uncompetitive as a base for
exporting, capital outflows will increase. Even if Australia remains
export-competitive, capital and investment may still flow off-shore
by virtue of the global business cycle described above. The question
then becomes how to offset the loss of benefits associated with such
capital flows?

The answers to this question are complex and varied. However,
one opportunity that merits deeper discussion is the fiscal and tax
environment surrounding capital repatriation by globally distributed
enterprises. In the United States, for example, current tax rules penalise
firms with overseas operations heavily upon the repatriation of foreign
profits to the US, thereby incenting such enterprises to keep capital
off-shore. Imagine a situation in which the tax treatment of globally
distributed enterprises was reversed: i.e., repatriation of capital
generated overseas was taxed more favourably, rather than at standard
(or punitive) tax rates. Such enterprises would likely be incented to
return capital to Australia.

While the mechanics of such incentives would require considerable
thought and consultation, the debate between export-driven economic
development and the creation of globally distributed and competitive
enterprises would become moot. So long as, on balance, the pool of
available capital for future investment within Australia was increasing,
national economic prosperity would ultimately improve. Indeed,
providing long-term public assistance for export-based industries
that are not structurally competitive (e.g., motor vehicles) is likely to
produce the reverse outcome. A more productive use of such assistance
would be to direct it to enterprises that are successfully assuming the
risks of innovation and global growth.

An important opportunity exists for Austrade to begin this policy discussion and shape the framework for how such mechanisms can be put in place. Many interesting possibilities can be envisioned, including (for example) linking the favourable tax treatment of repatriated capital to the development of new or existing innovation clusters or to further direct investment into firm-specific innovation within Australia. Notwithstanding the specific nature of such incentives, if nothing is done to address the opportunity, the national prosperity benefits of the globally distributed competitive enterprise will remain elusive.

A second opportunity for capturing a "natural" share of the capital generated by a globally distributed enterprise is for Australia to continue to play a meaningful role in one or more of the activities in the globally distributed value chain of the enterprise based upon its unique value-adding contributions and capabilities. Australia could, for example, remain the locus of innovation in technology/R&D or product development, whilst innovation in other value chain activities is located elsewhere.

Figures 4 and 5 depict a typical universe of value-creation opportunities and associated advantages for a manufacturer of component products being integrated into a broader solution for an end customer. In a vertically integrated export chain, the bulk of these activities are concentrated in the home market, with perhaps limited customisation for selected international markets. In a globally distributed competitor, any one or a combination of these activities will be dispersed internationally. In order to capture a significant share of the value created in such a chain, activities performed in the home market will ideally be focused around the high-order advantages that cannot easily be replicated elsewehere.

A key role for Austrade is to work closely with SMEs that are globally dispersing their value chains to identify and strengthen a set of "high-order" activities that will be retained domestically and drive the leadership reputation of the SME internationally. Hand-in-hand with this role, Austrade would be actively encouraging the

Figure 4: The Value-Creation Opportunity

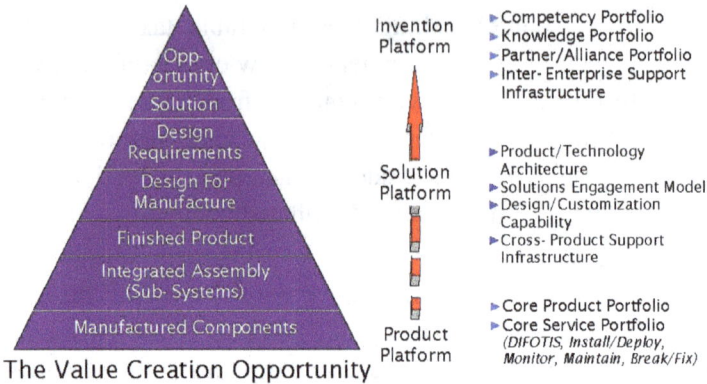

Invention Platform	► Competency Portfolio	
	► Knowledge Portfolio	
	► Partner/Alliance Portfolio	
	► Inter-Enterprise Support Infrastructure	

Pyramid layers (top to bottom):
Opportunity
Solution
Design Requirements
Design For Manufacture
Finished Product
Integrated Assembly (Sub-Systems)
Manufactured Components

The Value Creation Opportunity

Solution Platform
► Product/Technology Architecture
► Solutions Engagement Model
► Design/Customization Capability
► Cross-Product Support Infrastructure

Product Platform
► Core Product Portfolio
► Core Service Portfolio
(DIFOTIS, Install/Deploy, Monitor, Maintain, Break/Fix)

Figure 5: The Nature of Advantage

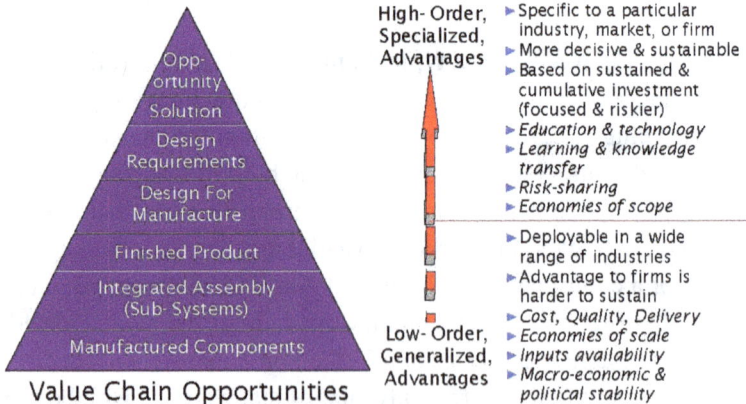

Pyramid layers (top to bottom):
Opportunity
Solution
Design Requirements
Design For Manufacture
Finished Product
Integrated Assembly (Sub-Systems)
Manufactured Components

Value Chain Opportunities

High-Order, Specialized, Advantages
► Specific to a particular industry, market, or firm
► More decisive & sustainable
► Based on sustained & cumulative investment (focused & riskier)
► Education & technology
► Learning & knowledge transfer
► Risk-sharing
► Economies of scope

Low-Order, Generalized, Advantages
► Deployable in a wide range of industries
► Advantage to firms is harder to sustain
► Cost, Quality, Delivery
► Economies of scale
► Inputs availability
► Macro-economic & political stability

global dispersion of other activities to international locations where innovation and advantage can be maximised.

A third opportunity for Austrade to play a meaningful role in attracting capital into Australia is to support the development of "clusters of innovation" or lead country reputations for one or more economic sectors. Clusters are a sub-set of firms within an industry that collectively produce a disproportionate share of innovation within their industry. Lead countries are those countries or regions that generate the bulk of the innovation in a key economic sector (e.g., Silicon Valley for computing and health sciences technology, Japan and Korea for consumer electronics, Germany and Japan for automobiles, etc.).

The forces underlying the creation and development of innovation clusters have been studied extensively in the literature, and so will not be detailed here. Suffice it to say that market forces trump government policy and support as critical success factors in the emergence and growth of such clusters. These market forces (demanding and sophisticated customers, intense competition, related and supporting industries, factor conditions, etc.), create the underlying pressure for firms within the cluster to innovate.

It is important to distinguish "cluster" development from development initiatives that target an entire industry. Clusters are always a sub-set of enterprises within an industry that behave more competitively than others in their industry: i.e., are more responsive to the pressure to innovate than others in the same industry. For this reason, attempts to stimulate industry-level capability are not always successful.

Austrade, as a globally distributed knowledge organisation, has significant opportunity to directly enhance the level of innovation within key sectors of the Australian economy, and so drive the development of clusters of globally competitive firms. Ways in which this can be achieved include:

- Identification and targeting of anchor customers (either domestically or internationally) who will drive innovation within their supplier base.

- For those anchor customers not present in Australia, encouraging and facilitating opportunities for direct investment into Australia (already part of Austrade's mandate).

- Identification and targeting of Australian SME's with a higher propensity (willingness and capability) to innovate.
- Assisting in the design and creation of global open innovation networks for specific SMEs or clusters.
- Facilitating knowledge exchanges and collaboration between innovative SMEs who share a common market interest.
- Facilitating the development of related and supporting partners/allies necessary for development of a cluster eco-system.

These actions are entirely consistent with the views of international buyers noted earlier in this chapter, expressing the desire to see fewer, but more competitive Australian SMEs offering a constant stream of new innovation. The opportunities are also consistent with the existing policy framework governing the organisation's purpose and scope.

In closing, Austrade, like all other trade promotion organisations seeking relevance in an ever changing global marketplace, faces many specific opportunities for building and sustaining the leadership of the organisation, and the Australian enterprises it serves. To summarise:

- First and foremost, focus on building the long-term global competitiveness of carefully selected Australian SMEs as the enabler of, and precursor to, sustainable export capability. Transition from tactical, opportunistic, event-related activity, towards activity that enhances the drivers of long-term, sustainable, export performance.
- Second, proactively assist Australian SMEs to gain access to innovation that drives global competitiveness. Assume a lead role in developing and supporting open global innovation networks and domestic innovation clusters.
- Third, proactively support and enable the migration of successful SMEs from export-driven domestic businesses to

globally distributed enterprises in search of innovation and global competitiveness;

- Fourth, facilitate the development and growth of fewer, more differentiated SMEs capable of supporting their international presence in a competitive and sustainable way.

- Fifth, assume a leadership position in proactively managing and influencing the trade and investment environment, specifically through the development of a collaboration framework that engages industry, service providers, state, territory and federal governments in stimulating innovation and international competitiveness. Among the key policy outcomes to target is fiscal and taxation policy that encourages repatriation of capital generated by trade and investment activities outside of Australia.

Given these opportunities, the future for Australian businesses operating in a changing global marketplace is indeed bright.

22

Austrade today and tomorrow

Interview with Bruce Gosper

Question: What were your impressions of Austrade from the outside in your previous responsibilities in government?

Bruce Gosper: I have worked on trade policy and negotiations for over 30 years, and most of that time alongside colleagues from Austrade. Usually that contact was at post overseas or in conjunction with some ministerial visit, some particular event or some mission of some sort. While our different worlds – trade policy, and trade promotion – bumped up against each other there was not a lot of deep collaboration or interaction however. That said, my appreciation of the people in Austrade has always been pretty positive. I'm talking here of the trade commissioners. They are people who are out and about in the business world, who are busy and well-connected and who are good at finding something positive to contribute. And they are terrific at getting things done, whether trade shows or missions or events of one sort or another.

I had less of an appreciation over those years of the quality of Austrade's overseas engaged staff, our Business Development Managers, who make up about half of our staff. Seeing them much closer has been something of a revelation. The understanding of local culture and language they bring is obvious, but I'm talking more particularly of their knowledge and expertise in particular industry sectors and how that can connect with Australian business. The best ones are really very impressive.

Nor did I see or appreciate the way in which Austrade had developed and the extent to which its management had benefitted from the infusion of business management systems and practices. It's a much leaner organisation than many other public sector organisations because of that, which is a good thing – and puts us in a good position in the tougher budget environment which we now face.

Question; How do you navigate your way around the government now that is no Board, how do you ensure your line of communication with the government?

Bruce Gosper: It's pretty simple really, I report directly to the Minister for Trade and Investment. I'm not in a position to say what a particular board may have brought to the organisation in the past. We are a relatively small organisation of only 1,000 people. We have some clear directions and a minister who is actually engaged and talking to business day in and day out, and quite connected to the things that you are doing. I think it was a mistake to think that we are not government but private sector in nature – our only core value-add comes from the way we can use our insight and contacts together with the badge of government. We recruit heavily from the private sector, but we are a government agency working directly to a minister. I meet regularly with him on the key issues and he is engaged with our people every day. The minister has high quality people in his office and they give great support to our work. The minister has also convened a good trade policy council comprised of people with direct business experience, which he uses as counsel across all trade priorities. So we have very good business input.

Question: You mentioned Tourism and Education becoming new portfolios for Austrade to take on. Can you elaborate?

Bruce Gosper: We must be doing something right because we keep being given new functions. Over the last few years we have taken on additional functions: investment attraction, education promotion, and now tourism policy. It's startled some that a policy function like tourism would be placed in a small agency like Austrade but it reflects the role of tourism as an export sector, the linkages with other things we do, in particular investment, and most importantly the interest of our current minister to make a difference in this sector of the economy. It's a potentially big driver of jobs growth but faces significant challenges around cost and quality.

Tourism Australia is currently running a campaign around tourism related to the gourmet food experience in Australia. It's focused on the attractiveness of food as part of the tourism experience Australia offers. But we have other, related interests – exporting food, attracting investment from offshore into Australia's agribusiness sector, and providing training and skills for the food and hospitality sectors. So there is an opportunity for us to make some linkages across all parts of Austrade's work.

We've taken on these new functions but our overall resources have decreased. We're only 1,000 people. We've been about 1,000 people for 15 years, and have lost quite a bit of money over that time. We've grown less than 1 per cent over 15 years at the same time that staff numbers in the Australian public service have grown 39 per cent. We're going to have to take another $20 million out of the budget over the next three years, at a minimum, due to budget cuts. So we are running a leaner mix – not a complaint, just an explanation of why we have to be clear about where our value-add is found and make sure we focus there and not elsewhere.

Question: I was baffled by the policy side – Austrade has an international footprint that is enviable.

Bruce Gosper: We do have a significant international footprint. It's declined in recent years, down from about 112 locations to some 80-odd. About half of our offshore offices are in places where there is no other diplomatic presence, no DFAT presence. We've used the criterion of market failure to decide where we need to be – in other words if the private market can easily provide a service, then a government agency doesn't need to be there or needs to only provide particular services. Even SME exporters don't need us much in the developed markets with sophisticated economies and the rule of law. So we've pulled back from those places. What the government wants from us now is increasingly also to bring the insight we have developed to inform policy development, particularly around investment facilitation.

Question: Do you feel confident that your connection to business is as strong as it has ever been?

Bruce Gosper: Yes I believe so – it's as strong as ever even if we don't perhaps deal with as many businesses. We are not seeking to be all things for all people. Because of resource constraints and the growth of capability elsewhere we have stepped back from a lot of things we used to do. We no longer run export readiness training, for instance. Services of one sort or another that are relevant to export are provided by the state and territory governments, industry associations, banks, the big four, some of the law firms, and others. They're all sort doing something in the export space. And there's no point in us trying to compete with that or duplicate it. But we still deal with 6,000 or more exporters in a year providing some specific support or service. What we seek to do now is to partner with firms or associations for specific projects or around particular markets or opportunities. For instance we are working now with Austmine to map out opportunities for Australian businesses to link with the global oil value chain. There are many other examples of this sort of well-targeted, collaborative work. I think this is much more valuable than getting locked in some numbers game around transactional opportunities or increasing the number of exporters – whatever the merit of such approaches in previous times.

The doubling of exporters episode was not all bad. It had some useful results. But it produced a lot of errant behaviour which drove the organisation into a cul-de-sac. I'm not interested in too much effort going into low value, quick transaction type work.

Question: How should staffing, heads of trade posts, trade commissioners and others need to be equipped today with their respective responsibilities and targets as opposed to yesterday?

Bruce Gosper: First and foremost our people have to have some meaningful experience or understanding of the commercial world. Our people work for a government agency that seeks to assist business. We recruit heavily from the private sector – there probably aren't any others who do this as much as we do. Two-thirds of our senior and middle management have worked in the private sector. Our people need to be at that intersection of the commercial world and government – to be able to talk convincingly to both a senior government representative and a commercial board. Two things give us some value for business, the contacts and networks we create in business and government in a market, and how we use the badge of government to leverage that. Our trade commissioners should be the "most connected" Australians in the country we put them. They are an important part of our overall Australian effort, working closely with the Head of Mission and the rest of the Embassy team. So when I talk to our Ambassadors they all say they need our people to be able to tell them what a major company is thinking at the board level, but also to be engaged with very senior government figures, talking to them about how they're dealing with an Australian interest.

Question: You have been in the position only for a short time but have you had the time to examine other country agencies like Austrade?

Bruce Gosper: They're all different and there is no one agency that is the same as us in terms of how it's structured or what it looks after. They all have their strengths but respond to different needs and objectives. I look at JETRO and see their research capability and I would love to have that. We recruited a new chief economist in Mark Thirlwell, from Lowy Institute, and he has enabled us to increase our analysis around issues such as global value chains and investment in particular..

Question: A little bit like Tim Harcourt did?

Bruce Gosper: Yes. Austrade used Tim heavily for surveys and analysis and the promotion of export, telling the story of the importance of exports and export successes, all good for the time. We are using Mark mostly for detailed analysis, supporting a complex trade and investment agenda.

Question: How about benchmarking Austrade internationally?

Bruce Gosper: I admire the Singapore Development Board, but you know they're doing that in a unique, corporatist state. The Koreans are quite good and have recently taken on investment. The Norwegians have been able to put 90 per cent of their resource into offshore and to keep a very modest onshore foot-print. New Zealand Trade & Enterprise are doing some quite innovative things very tailored to individual firms. The UK Trade & Investment set-up is quite interesting and we've taken some leads from them. The British do public diplomacy in parts that work quite well and have quite well integrated with both foreign and trade. So those are the ones that come to mind and each of them has got something interesting or something that you would like to be able to do here, but there is no particular one match. How do we rank against them? I'd say pretty well.

We don't have the network that some of them have. And you know we've come down from 112 to about 80-odd offices overseas. Our footprint in some of the key Asian markets is pretty good, compared to others. Not many can do what we do in China, Indonesia or other parts of South East Asia. Some of them are much better represented in Latin America and Africa than we are. So the Canadians are much better in Latin America than us, the Japanese much better in Africa than us, the British much better in the Middle East than us, at least in terms of reach. I think in terms of effectiveness, probably rank pretty well against most of those.

Question: The focus on China if you think where Austrade was and where it is now 11 offices spread throughout China. Do you it needs more attention?

Bruce Gosper: I'd look at fine-tuning the resources we've got in China in the next couple of years. I think a little bit more on the investment side in that market and maybe we should look a bit harder at North China and somewhere like Chongqing a little bit more. Within the total resources we've got, no I wouldn't be suggesting we invest a lot more in China. On the other hand if we conclude an FTA with China that will drive a lot of our work. There are other demands for our time and effort. I think if I had a marginal dollar I would put it in the oil sector – in particular Houston – perhaps other investment areas like Zurich. Then although we've got a sort of sizeable office in Jakarta we should think about outside Jakarta and Java; there's some interesting things happening in eastern Indonesia, particularly Makassar. The story about ASEAN I think is quite promising in a number of places, so we should be focusing a bit more on ASEAN. East Africa looks promising. There is a lot of work to do around skills training in ASEAN and India. Our investment network can be strengthened. New resources in these places means we will have to downsize or close elsewhere, but this is not the time or place to discuss what that might mean.

Question: The investment portfolio on and off over the last 30 years with Austrade and it has it back again. Are you able to make it part of the portfolio of trade commissioners in such a way that it can positively influence the trade sell?

Bruce Gosper: It requires particular expertise, so we've brought in the last few years different sorts of people in the organisation, people like David Campbell in Frankfurt and Richard Leather in New York. People who have investment bank type background. And we're going to be bringing some more people into the organisation in the next 6 months, onshore, with that sort of background to help the investment work. They will be termed senior investment specialists and their job will be to work with the states and territories and help individual investors or investment opportunities – so investment facilitation and after care, in addition to promotion and attraction.

If you talk to the Indonesians about infrastructure, they'll talk about access to financing, about public private partnerships, about construction work, but also about education and training for the local population. I want to do a little bit better in making the links across those silos so that we can do that sort of work more effectively. Often others want to talk to Australia because we can talk across a number of sectors or capabilities – so for instance we can talk about good health policy, health management practice, hospital construction, medical training, medical devices manufacturing.

Question: The structure of Austrade today and the global network of Austrade reporting to Sydney – a change from the original reporting lines. Does this work?

Bruce Gosper: Yes it is working and it was the right thing to do. The previous model was becoming a bit distant, a bit remote from Australia. It's more securely linked to what governments want us to do and what businesses are really thinking about their overseas interests. It's working much better and that's not going to change.

Question: I hear from ex-trade commissioners of Austrade going back into DFAT? Is this a possible prospect?

Bruce Gosper: There's a big drive across government to really look at whether small agencies are the right things, whether there should be simpler and more cost-effective structures of government, whether there should be more joining up of agencies in a portfolio. And at the same time of course there's a big push which I fully support to improve the economic diplomacy of Australia's total international network and make DFAT more supportive of economic interests. So this is part of the context for that sort of speculation. That's all understandable.

My perspective is that we should just worry about the only thing that is in our control, and that's how well we do our job. I'm confident that we are demonstrating the value of what we do and how we do it. What we have that others do not is an international network in places that matter for business, our onshore people in business centres (rather than Canberra), and people with commercial experience. I'd hate to see a change for narrow budget reasons that lost any of those strengths.

Question: What do you think is in store for the future of Austrade?

Bruce Gosper: Well I'm going to be making some changes in the organisation because we're really driving more to that sort of high value add, to strengthen the quality of our advice and market insight, around difficult markets and complex opportunities. We're going to have to reallocate resources accordingly, and probably thin out what we do onshore a little more. Our bureaucracy is still too heavy and we need to do some serious weeding. Our people are good but we need to do more capability development. We need to do better in getting women into senior roles in the organisation – but we have made some progress. Our IT is good but we have to deal with limited resources and demands for greater mobility and interactivity.

At the moment we have the confidence of our minister and government, they're asking us to do a whole lot of new things, investment, tourism policy, big business missions and opening new posts.

Importantly business is responding. The number of businesses we are providing services to has increased 30 per cent in the last 12 months. Our business satisfaction rate is up for the second successive year, to 89 per cent. 75 per cent of those we help say we make a real difference to their commercial outcome. Our net promoter score is up to +25. We're in good shape and there's plenty of work to do.

Interview conducted in February 2014

23

Austrade's greatest asset:
Our people shine through

Laurie Smith

These days, we see ourselves as having less independence than
in the 1990s and early 2000s when we had a very strong focus
on our mission to service the corporate client base and deliver
on our KPIs. In recent years, we have felt the need to stay closer
to Canberra and government priorities and be well wired in
there. That means that trade commissioners at post have to be
represented at, but not exhausted by, inter-agency forums that
link us into to broader whole of government work. That said, I
think the art lies in the A-based also preserving the vast majority
of the time of the BDMs to work with clients and deliver the
outcomes of the day. It is BDMs who do the heavy lifting. We
strike a reasonable balance at present and I think that contributes
to our current good standing.

Kym Hewett, STC Jakarta

I joined Austrade in 2004 after 20 years working on China and other
Asian markets in government and for small and large companies. I spent
seven years as Austrade's Regional Director for North East Asia based
in Shanghai and returned to Sydney in 2011 to lead the International
Operations Group created as a result of Austrade's 2011 review:
Maximising Our Value (Austrade 2011). However my exposure to
Austrade actually goes back to a brief stint in the Department of Trade
in the mid-1980s when I met and worked closely with colleagues in the

new organisation located in the adjoining wing of the Edward Barton Building in Canberra. I had later exposure as a portfolio colleague, occasional client, acquaintance and friend of various "Austraders". Like other contributors and most Austrade alumni, I have always had an opinion about Austrade. During this last decade, I have been proud to have a chance to contribute directly to its work.

Throughout this time, I have seen budgets wax and wane, and government priorities, corporate strategies and structures shift. In the 1980s, Austrade began with a focus on making the biggest possible difference to the trade account by focusing on sizable exporters with strong growth potential. In the 1990s, as the effects of tariff reductions continued to sweep through the economy, the organisation made a decisive shift of resources towards Asia. Initiatives to double the number of exporters and better understand the "Journey to Export" were followed by the 2011 Review which emphasised a narrower focus on investment in established markets in North America and Western Europe and expanding our export promotion and facilitation in Asian and other growth and emerging markets.

Through all these shifts in strategy, Austrade has played a vital role in promoting Australia as a place to do business and invest in and supporting Australian companies competing in international markets. And a constant strength of Austrade throughout has been its people and their culture. They are talented and passionate about our work and doing it as well as possible.

As this book shows, Austraders, current and former, can be critical of perceived weaknesses in strategies, systems, processes and management. And they come at issues from a very wide range of perspectives that often reflect their role and unique experience. So, strong and sometimes divergent opinions are hardly surprising. But for all this, our people invariably remain fiercely committed to the organisation, its improvement and the contribution it can and/or should make to Australian success in international markets. This high level of commitment continues to sustain the organisation.

Our trade commissioners

> Versatility and flexibility are vital traits. You never completely know what a given day will bring as Austrade is a service delivery agency that needs to be responsive to multiple stakeholders across government, Australian business and local market contacts. We deal with everyone from the highest echelons of government and big business to SMEs who may be exporting for the first time.
>
> We live in a globally connected world with a lot of information readily available. A trade commissioner needs to be on top of the issues that are front of mind for business people in Australia and in our local markets, as well as understanding the drivers and dynamics of the government arena.

Dan Tebbutt, STC Hong Kong

Austrade's trade commissioners have always been a diverse group of professionals and remain so. But our best trade commissioners do possess or develop a unique set of skills. Trade commissioners join us at different stages in their careers from many industries and sectors. Recent appointees have backgrounds in investment and commercial banking, the law, public relations, journalism, wealth management, management consulting, automotive manufacturing, recruitment, education and government.

Veterans of 30 plus years such as Kym Hewett and Martin Walsh now in Jakarta and Taipei respectively, joined us young and now provide valuable continuity, bringing deep corporate knowledge to our network. Others join Austrade with 5-10 years experience in the private sector and spend a decade or more with us, often on several postings. Amanda Hodges, for example, joined us from a consulting firm after experience working in Korea. Following a number of postings, most recently in Dubai, she has just returned to lead a key team that liaises across government in Canberra. Pat Kearins came to us with a background in the building materials and food sectors and has just returned to Adelaide as State Director where he will draw on the experience of postings in Jakarta and Mumbai.

Yet others have successful single postings contributing much to the organisation but return to the private sector in more senior roles, enriched by the experience. Chris Wright who was in Shanghai from 2006-11 and James Casey in Seoul in the late 1990s exemplify this pattern. In 2012, the then CEO of Austrade Peter Grey, re-introduced an annual Trade Commissioner Development Program to attract outstanding young recruits to Austrade. The third intake of assistant trade commissioners under this program is due to be posted in mid-2015. This more structured program provides an additional pathway for entry to the organisation and a first posting opportunity for promising staff. The first intake, for example, included an onshore Trade Adviser, a Business Development Manager from Ho Chi Minh City and two outstanding external candidates with deep experience in China and Indonesia respectively. In-market and at home, Austrade works at the intersection of government and international business.

Trade commissioners need to understand the setting for Austrade's work: the Australian political system, government policy and federal and state relationships and domestic business trends and interpret its implications for their offshore teams and their work.

An understanding of the Australian business scene and the dynamics of the markets in which they operate enables trade commissioners to provide insight and advice on doing business in their market that is relevant and valuable to companies. International experience, knowledge of local markets, and language proficiency, where relevant and available, remain important attributes of a successful trade commissioner.

As representatives of Australia, trade commissioners are part of the official 'face' of Australia. They have to be able to communicate with people from diverse backgrounds and places, and are expected to be able to motivate and lead teams of locally engaged staff. Trade commissioners are expected to develop strong relationships at a senior level across business and government in their host country. They need to maintain productive professional and supportive relationships with the local Australian business community, other federal and state representatives and key industry associations active in the market. Austrade's teams also need to work productively with the ambassadors, high commissioners and consuls-general who lead the official Australian presence in most markets.

Changes in government priorities, Australia's economic circumstances and the trade policy environment have shaped and re-shaped Austrade's work over the years. Communications between Australia and the world have also been transformed, reducing the isolation and thus, to some extent, the independence of trade commissioners. There is now much more information in the public domain for Australian business, placing a greater premium on interpretation and insight versus information *per se* as might once have been the case. The scope of Austrade's responsibilities now includes investment promotion (again) and international education as well as international tourism policy. And Austrade has tightened its governance and security arrangements in recent years to provide greater accountability and better protect our people.

As at 30 June 2014, Austrade had 72 trade commissioners (Austrade 2014) in place across its international network, down from 102 in 1995.

Despite these changes in the settings for our work, the value of well-connected trade commissioners who can lead teams effectively and provide good advice to Australian business on local conditions and issues remains high. As at 30 June 2014, Austrade had 72 trade commissioners (Austrade 2014) in place across its international network, down from 102 in 1995.

Overseas-engaged employees or local staff

Six out of every seven members of our offshore team are local hires, most of whom come to us with private sector experience. These 'overseas-engaged employees' numbered 486 at 30 June 2014. In most markets, the majority of staff are local nationals. But there are also a good number of third country nationals, dual nationals or Australian citizens with family and other ties to the market who all add "hybrid vigour" to our teams. The market knowledge and networks that our local staff bring to Austrade and continue to develop with us are unique assets for Australian business.

I have often felt that Australia, the Australian business community and Austrade don't always know how lucky we are to have local staff of the calibre we do. Under the current government, we have worked on very large missions to China and India led by our current Trade and Investment Minister, Andrew Robb, smaller missions to a host of other markets as well as targeted investment roundtables in a range of key cities. We have also had the opportunity support business missions led by Prime Minister to numerous markets.

Without our capable local staff, we could not deliver these programs or our other ongoing market development work and tailored service to companies. Our strong 'footprint' across all segments of Australia's internationally-oriented business community and the international education sector, solid client satisfaction ratings for our posts (averaging 87 per cent since 2007 and rising to 90 and 91 per cent in the past two years), strong advocacy among the client base and significant client outcomes provide good measures of the quality of their work.

Staff development, career enrichment and its limits

Even before joining Austrade, I could see that following the McKinsey Review, it invested very heavily in staff development. We still do. Austrade continues to fund study and professional development programs. In recent years we have also increased the number of short term assignments offered to our local staff – typically of 6-12 weeks but sometimes longer. Recent examples include Julianne Davis from London helping the USA team develop a stronger referrals network and methodology to support Australian exporters in that market and Jay Hu from Shanghai seconded to the investment team in Melbourne to work with inbound Chinese investors and broaden his knowledge of Australia. Not long ago, Anna Plawinska from Warsaw spent several months in Johannesburg creating new systems and processes for that office. We also promote secondments of similar duration for our offshore staff to industry associations such as recent assignments to Meat and Livestock Australia and the Australian Industry Group. In early 2015, we deployed a multinational team of Austrade staff to India from Saudi Arabia, Kuwait, Germany, China and Australia to support the South Asia team with Australian Business Week in India. These opportunities are welcomed by local staff as challenging and enriching.

For those who are Australian citizens, there is also a fairly well-trodden path into the trade commissioner ranks dating back at least to John Tinney in the 70s[1] followed by Liz Masamune and many others during the Austrade era. But we otherwise have a fairly flat structure offshore, so ultimately there are limits to the promotion opportunities available to even the best local staff.

Nonetheless, many staff still enjoy very long and productive careers with us enjoying the wide diversity of industries we work across, opportunities for development and mobility, constant new challenges in the market environment, changes in Australia and our organisational strategies and priorities. They mentor younger colleagues and provide good advice to enthusiastic trade commissioners on 3-5 year postings. Kumar Sreekumar who retired after 35 years with us in Riyadh and the UAE and Haesook Chung who has been with us in Seoul for 20 years are just two examples of long-serving – and outstanding – local staff who fit this pattern.

The consular work currently done by our teams in 16 locations is often not fully recognised. It is demanding but rewarding for our staff. Our Honorary Consuls in Prague, Vancouver and Vladivostok have particularly heavy responsibilities in this regard. Some other local staff excel in their roles but decide to move on to other opportunities after a shorter time with us. The positive thing is that the vast majority of our former staff comprise a valuable and constructive alumni network that retain affection for the organisation and continue to contribute to our success in whatever ways they can.

---

1 John Tinney former Senior Trade Commissioner started his distinguished career with the Department of Trade (and then Austrade) as an 'LES' in Paris from 1964-6.

How are we doing and what are does the future hold?

I referred above to the changes of strategy and emphasis for Austrade's work over the years. These have been in response to macro-challenges and opportunities for Australia, assessments of the needs of business at the firm-level as well as judgements about the capacity and appropriateness of government to assist. Some have been internally generated, others have reflected the explicit priorities of ministers.

So, when was Austrade at its peak? Who was Austrade's best leader? How are we doing now? Did things go to the dogs with the last change of leadership? Or will that happen with next minister? Austrade's clients in the business community in Australia and overseas are best placed to answer these questions. Ministers also have expectations and form judgements on our capabilities, relevance, achievements and alignment with their government's priorities. Because yes, we are and always have been a government-funded body and no, we never have been a for-profit consultancy.

As much as we wish to manage ourselves and our work in a business-like way, using tools and practices drawn from the corporate world, distance from ministers and government – which fund us – on the premise that we are totally client-focused has been proven to be bad for our health.

Suffice to say that there are at least as many views about Austrade as there are current and former Austrade staff, leaders and ministers. As I know this book will show, there is strong debate about what we have been and have done, what we do now and what the outlook is and should be. Amidst the contention on these issues, the passion and quality of our people and our shared collaborative culture, noisy but productive, continues to shine through.

Bibliography

Austrade 2011, Reform of the Australian Trade commission – *Maximising Our Value*, May 2011, Australian Trade Commission, Sydney.

Austrade 2014, Austrade Annual Report 2013-14, Australian Trade Commission, Sydney.

24

Austrade seen from the outside: Views from within the Department of Foreign Affairs and Trade[1]

Mike Adams and Nicolas Brown

Trade matters because economies, however large, never have all of the resources and skills they need to produce all the things they want. Trade policy matters because borders impede markets, and trade promotion matters because markets do not always work efficiently enough to allow companies to respond to market opening opportunities. And all three matter for their contributions to growth, jobs and living standards and for building links and understanding between nations and cultures.

Introduction

Department of Foreign Affairs and Trade (DFAT) views on Austrade centre around mostly informal perceptions of the importance of working cooperatively to combine the different skills of trade policy and trade promotion in the national interest. There has never really been an enduring single or dominant DFAT view of Austrade – how the agency is perceived or how the relationship works. Rather, there are many different, and highly personalised, views based on officers' often intermittent interactions with Austrade in Australia and at

1 The authors would like to thank Dr. Ron Wickes of Trading Nation Consulting for comments on earlier drafts of this paper. We also would like to thank former colleagues in DFAT and Austrade. Their insights have added greatly to this chapter.

overseas posts, and memories of how individual relationships worked or didn't. We also suspect that many DFAT officers have had sketchy views at best about Austrade. Traditionally, much of DFAT has had no trade or economic role. Marketing and access issues have been the primary 'crossover' or intersect in the DFAT-Austrade working relationship and, even then, trade policy and trade promotion have often occupied separate universes, particularly within Australia.

This chapter is based on our experiences of DFAT-Austrade relations, in Australia and at posts, bolstered by the reflections of many former colleagues over numerous cups of coffee. Our views should be seen principally as a personal statement on attitudes and policies and on the personality-driven nature of much of the relationship, though we hope they capture wider sentiments that exist, or have existed at one time or another, in DFAT.

A key observation is that DFAT perspectives on Austrade are different in Australia and at overseas posts. In Australia, DFAT officers, even senior ones in the trade divisions, typically spend relatively little time interacting with Austrade because the agencies' roles have traditionally been distinct. DFAT is responsible for trade negotiations and most of the policy work associated with the World Trade Organization, the Asia-Pacific Economic Cooperation (APEC) forum, other regional meetings, bilateral ministerial forums, joint trade commissions, implementation issues associated with concluded trade agreements and so forth. Austrade is responsible for trade promotion and now the foreign investment agenda, trade in education and tourism.

At posts with busy trade agendas and where there are large trade and investment relationships between Australia and the host country, heads of mission and many DFAT officers spend considerable time with Austrade trade commissioners and their staff. Distinctions between trade policy and trade promotion blur. This blurring is partly because both DFAT and Austrade officials deal directly with the business sector. Visiting Australian trade delegations want good advice about particular markets and perhaps assistance with access to host-country ministers and business leaders: they care little about the differences between the agencies providing that assistance. And it is partly because some access issues or projects are highly political and require the active involvement of both agencies and, in some cases, of attached agencies with responsibilities for issues like agriculture/ quarantine, defence, education, finance, and immigration.

The chapter is organised around four propositions:

• Establishing Austrade was a good thing in commercial terms. It also helped to pave the way for the creation of DFAT.

• The distinct roles of DFAT and Austrade have limited the scope for interaction over the years in Australia, though the points of intersection have broadened, particularly over the last decade or so, with the growing prominence of FTAs, the shifting focus of trade policy from tariffs to behind-the-border regulatory barriers to trade and investment, and the growing role of services and investment in international trade.

• The DFAT-Austrade relationship is closest at posts with a strong trade focus.

• Changing regional and global economic and trading conditions, in particular the growing prominence of value chains with their often intricate combinations of imports and exports and outward and inward direct investment, provides an opportunity for DFAT-Austrade links to deepen on issues ranging from understanding structural change to trade intelligence to injecting trade perspectives into domestic economic reform.

Establishing Austrade

The earth must literally have moved for the old Department of Trade (DoT) when Austrade was established in January 1986. By that time the Department's glory days of power and influence under Trade

Minister Sir John McEwen and Secretaries Sir John Crawford and Sir Alan Westerman were over. Losing the Trade Commissioner Service and the divisions and regional offices that provided outreach to Australia's business community was a major body blow that confirmed the Department's reduced status. For some DoT officials, this was a disaster: careers were impeded and expectations perhaps dashed. For others, new career opportunities were perceived in a new political and business environment. And for all, perspectives on Austrade's creation were probably coloured to some extent by politics.

Trade Minister John Dawkins, as the architect of this organisational re-structure, was predictably demonised or lauded as either a 'wrecker' of the old DoT or as a public sector reformer trying to achieve better policy and commercial outcomes. That debate still goes on among old trade warriors. For what it's worth, we believe that setting up Austrade was entirely sensible for two reasons. First, creating a more professional, business-oriented agency responded to business wishes and was consistent with the reform ethos of the time. It provided an opportunity for inter-generational change, including through recruiting more officers with relevant business experience. And second, and very importantly from a DFAT perspective, it helped to pave the way the following year for merging the Departments of Trade and Foreign Affairs and therefore the creation of DFAT.

There was nothing inevitable about this merger. DoT could have survived the departure of what was to become Austrade by transforming into something like the United States Trade Representative office – a small agency focusing on international trade negotiations and coordinating market access issues and broader aspects of trade policy across government. But instead it merged with the Department of Foreign Affairs as part of a wider restructuring of federal government administration that introduced two-tier ministries and drastically reduced the number of government departments (Nethercote 1999, pp. 2-12).

Merging the Foreign Affairs and Trade Departments was an inspired decision, though difficult for all concerned at the time. It was inspired because it gave each element a stronger constituency and a better and more broadly focused overseas network: the DFA had a commercial arm that increased its relevance domestically; the underweight trade policy rump of DoT had a readymade international network. Suddenly old "tradies" could expect that their trade agenda would get full attention at all posts instead of at just a handful of "trade posts". It also was inspired because it facilitated the integration of political and economic views about the region and world in the new amalgamated entity. In these senses, Austrade's creation benefited both foreign and trade policy.

But the merger was difficult because there were inevitable cultural issues. For a time there was a Team A (Foreign Affairs) and Team B (Trade). The old DFA had operated remotely from most trade and commercial bilateral and regional relationships. This approach lingered, including at senior levels. And the trade side of DFAT became preoccupied with the GATT Uruguay Round of Multilateral Trade Negotiations (1986-94) and building pressure for agricultural reform through bodies like the Cairns Group – priorities that remained a black box for most Foreign Affairs officials.

Eventually these disconnections washed through the system: people at the top of the department made the merger work, more integrated processes permeated through the department and the passage of time made revisiting old structures and old cultural battles somewhat ridiculous. Bit by bit, a new entity emerged where officers, regardless of their previous affiliations, understood the importance of trade in bilateral and regional relationships and of putting their shoulders to the wheel in advancing broad industry interests. In our judgement, this transformation stands out as one of the key highlights of economic diplomacy in Australia in the past 30 years. It helped in establishing the professionalism and "trade craft" that underpinned much of Australia's engagement with the Asia-Pacific region.[2] It also laid the foundations

2 Australia's trade with Asia was already substantial prior to the Second World War, but trade and investment with the United Kingdom dominated into the 1950s and 1960s. Up to this time, "Australia saw itself – and was seen by others – to be on the periphery of an Anglo-centric world" (Adams, Brown & Wickes 2013, p. 56).

within Australia for a close DFAT-Austrade relationship (albeit after many years) and for a highly interactive relationship at posts with a big trade agenda from the outset.

Relations in Australia

In McEwen's day, trade policy and trade promotion worked together with industry policy, albeit for protectionist purposes. But in the decade or so following the organisational changes of the mid-1980s, DFAT rarely thought deeply about Austrade, trade promotion and the links between trade policy and trade promotion, and we suspect that it was much the same in Austrade.

The two agencies obviously had a great deal of contact and many good personal relationships were forged. The DFAT Secretary (or the Department's senior trade official) sat on the old Austrade Board; there were formal discussions, often about process, between the agencies at deputy secretary level; the trade divisions interacted on various bilateral, regional and multilateral initiatives; the geographical divisions interacted on everything from fire blight in New Zealand apples to the political and economic consequences of the breakup of the Soviet Union to the risks and opportunities associated with opening up China's economy; and there were projects galore and associated meetings on a range of topics. From time to time there were also informal discussions within DFAT, perhaps over a bottle of red wine, on issues like the merits of Export Market Development Grants, Austrade's attachment to quantitative targets and the policy of charging for services.

These contacts and discussions were interesting in part and useful up to a point, but they were not a priority for either agency. For example, DFAT involvement in Austrade Board meetings was valued largely for networking opportunities with senior business representatives rather than as a basis for coordinating trade policy and trade promotion strategies. Issues raised at these meetings were rarely injected into DFAT policy processes judging from weekly discussions at Division

Heads meetings, and there were probably few "strategic" discussions of Austrade at the level of DFAT's Senior Executive during these years.

There are two key reasons for the disconnection – or partial disconnection – between DFAT and Austrade at this time. The first is that both agencies were busy building their own identities and advancing their different priority issues. The second, and more important reason, is that, in Australia at least, there was no solid point of intersection on which to build the relationship between trade policy and trade promotion.

On the first point, DFAT was wrestling with integrating trade and foreign policy perspectives across a broad range of issues. DFAT culture may not have embraced trade promotion, but embracing trade policy proved to be a stretch in some quarters, especially in the geographical divisions. In the case of Austrade, Dawkins saw a clear separation of trade policy and trade promotion functions, emphasising Austrade's commercial charter and the independence of its personnel: staff were not employed under the *Public Service Act*. Austrade was a statutory body responsible for its own destiny through its Board and later through the Chief Executive Officer reporting to the Minister for Trade. In line with the Dawkins' reforms, Austrade was led by powerful business personalities who did not want to get too close to public service processes, but did want to achieve results more in line with business expectations. Establishing a headquarters in Sydney was a tangible symbol of this aspiration, as were the various reviews into its international operations, programs and management and Austrade's focus on narrow, but quantifiable, key performance indicators. Staff were hired from the private sector. Staff inter-change with agencies like DFAT was sporadic at best. And all of this, understandably, contributed to Austrade's sense of identity and defined the turf to be defended and the priorities to be pursued.

DFAT and Austrade must have struggled at times to work together as equals and partners in Australia, juggling DFAT's policy role and the quasi-business/quango nature of Austrade. DFAT appreciated the role for a savvy government organisation promoting trade and no doubt would have liked Austrade to operate more closely with other government agencies. Austrade wanted to operate more as a commercial entity. And the right balance between these positions probably was never struck in these years, and relations must have been strained further by periodic financial constraints that kept senior managers in both agencies focused on their own patch. Once Austrade returned to the Foreign Affairs and Trade Portfolio in 1994.[3] competition for funding was inevitable. When push came to shove, both agencies defended their financial base and eyed each other's new policy proposals warily out of concern that generosity to one would come at a cost to the other.

On the second point, there were few areas of solid ground where DFAT and Austrade could build a relationship based on integrating trade policy and trade promotion. In theory there are close links between trade policy and trade promotion, particularly through Austrade identifying barriers to trade and investment in markets of interest to Australia and DFAT then targeting those barriers in trade negotiations. But theory didn't work out in practice through the 1980s and 1990s.

This is not a negative judgement about either agency. It is simply a statement of fact that they had different objectives and serviced different clients. DFAT's main trade policy preoccupations in these years were the Uruguay Round, building momentum for a new round of multilateral trade negotiations – the less than illustrious Doha Round – and using processes like APEC to encourage unilateral economic reform and facilitate close engagement of officials, business and academia on regulatory reform and governance issues (Adams, Brown & Wickes 2013, p. 314). These were not the preoccupations of Austrade. Multilateral trade negotiations, for example, take generic, industry-wide perspectives on issues like agriculture, tariffs, services, intellectual property and government procurement that are of interest

---

3 As part of administrative changes introduced in 1987 by the Hawke government, trade promotion responsibilities were transferred to the industry portfolio.

to major companies and some business associations, but are not directly relevant to Australia's small and medium sized enterprises (SMEs). Their focus was accessing particular overseas markets, they were Austrade's core clients, and Austrade was not set up to provide input to multilateral rounds and had no role in these negotiations.

We are not in a position to assess whether these types of disconnects have entirely disappeared from the DFAT-Austrade relationship in Australia, but we are confident that the relationship has strengthened considerably over the last decade or so, that the agencies are more useful to each other, and that DFAT and Austrade officials spend more time working together on issues of common interest.

To some extent, the closer engagement must reflect evolving approaches within government to governance arrangements for public institutions. The Uhrig Report (2003) resulted in Austrade being assessed and restructured as a budget-funded service delivery organisation subject to ministerial oversight rather than as a predominantly commercial organisation. In 2006, Austrade was brought back into the public service: the old Board was replaced by a chief executive officer reporting directly to the Minister for Trade. This was followed, from 2010, by appointments of CEOs from the ranks of senior career public servants – DFAT Deputy Secretaries Peter Grey and Bruce Gosper – along with other senior appointments from DFAT and elsewhere in the federal bureaucracy.

But what else drove these changes within government that led to new high level appointments to Austrade from within the federal bureaucracy and to key recent decisions to place tourism, foreign direct investment attraction and aspects of investment policy under the Austrade umbrella? In our view, a major driver of the increasingly valuable DFAT-Austrade relationship goes back to changes in international trade and investment – especially the increasing connections between trade and investment in value chains and the growing role of services trade – and how these changes have played into trade policy, trade negotiations and available opportunities for useful, and well-regarded, collaboration across the trade agenda.

Over the last 20 years, a new wave of globalisation has transformed the business environment: international trade has risen from less than 20 per cent as a share of world GDP to more than 25 per cent, and more than half of world manufacturing imports are now intermediate goods and more than 70 per cent of world services imports are intermediate services (Kelly & La Cava 2014). These changes have in turn transformed business expectations about what a modern trade policy agenda should deliver. The agenda has broadened to include services, investment, protection of intellectual property, competition, and trade facilitation, as well as staples like market access for agriculture and manufactures. In turn, this broadening has shifted the focus of trade policy from transparent border issues like tariffs and import quotas to removing or lessening often ill-defined behind-the-border regulatory measures that are central to trade in services, establishing commercial presence and trade in many goods such as food and high-value manufacturing components. Tackling behind-the-border barriers is key to coming to terms with trade along global value chains and is especially relevant to understanding and addressing practical commercial issues in our region. Struggling multilateral trade negotiations have provided both the incentive and policy space for countries wanting to move further and hopefully faster on the new trade agenda to pursue high-quality FTAs. Australia's transformation from firm opponent to supporter of bilateral and multi-party FTAs ranks as the biggest shift in our trade policy in recent years (Adams, Brown & Wickes 2013, pp. 113-19).

FTAs, the behind-the-border regulatory agenda, the expansion of services trade and the increasingly close nexus between trade and investment have emerged as a major – arguably *the* major – intersect of the Austrade-DFAT relationship, creating more scope and opportunity for the agencies to interact. Austrade officers with a business background probably understand the commercial implications of particular regulatory measures more readily than their DFAT colleagues. Austrade is an obvious source of information on commercial issues and barriers to trade and investment that can be folded into FTA negotiations as negotiators delve deeper into the weeds of countries' economic and commercial relations. Austrade-hosted events increase awareness of FTAs and the generic and specific opportunities they can offer to businesses, large and small. Austrade's skills in putting together business delegations headed by the Prime Minister and the Trade Minister variously build on opportunities provided by FTAs or inject additional political and commercial momentum for concluding them. And Austrade's "one-stop-shop" approach to business has predictably led it to offering services to assist companies in utilising FTAs.

Not everything in these relationships works perfectly. The core issues – globalisation and how it impacts on the pursuit of mutually beneficial commercial relationships – are new and fast changing. The mindsets required to address these issues effectively are still in the early stages of becoming ingrained in institutional cultures – so personalities inevitably affect the level and quality of inter-agency interaction. And the various components of trade policy and trade promotion (and foreign policy more generally) are very segmented: DFAT negotiators have overall responsibility for concluding trade negotiations; others within DFAT may have responsibilities for implementing and reviewing agreements to improve them over time; and Austrade puts together marketing strategies for concluded agreements. There is a great deal of time pressure and competing priorities that may result in inadequate follow through. But this shouldn't disguise a basic fact: DFAT and Austrade work collaboratively on substantive issues on a scale that would have been unimaginable half a generation ago.[4] They are useful to each other, deliver solid results but could do more.

Relations at posts

The extent to which DFAT and Austrade are useful to each other and the scale and complexity of their interaction seems to peak at posts with a substantial trade agenda. Posts are wonderful examples of

---

4 In this context, DFAT secondments to Austrade, as well as to the Business Council of Australia and prospectively to other areas of business, are welcome developments. They provide additional, and potentially important, networking opportunities. If sustained over time, they also should help more DFAT officers to gain first hand knowledge and experience of the international needs and priorities of Australian business.

social engineering. Officers are appointed from various government departments and agencies for their professional skills – typically scant attention is paid to how they will fit into a group. Officers often arrive with formed views about how certain relationships work – Austrade adds real value or doesn't, DFAT works hand in glove with Austrade or is too bureaucratic and remote from business realities. Officers may or may not be accompanied by families and may or not live in compounds but, one way or another, family issues at times add to the social and business complexity of life of posts. New officers arrive and others depart: posts are always in a state of flux. And the personalities and interests of ambassadors, senior trade commissioners and other senior officers may not align at times. But in this often personality-driven environment, we have no hesitation in suggesting that the Austrade-DFAT relationship can soar to heights at posts that would be hard to match in Australia.

This observation does not apply to all posts. In some, markets are reasonably open in the host country and there is not enough trade and investment activity to make close interaction between DFAT and Austrade especially meaningful: over the last few years, Austrade has closed down many such posts[5] or has downgraded them to outfits run by often highly impressive locally engaged staff. At other posts, the combination of multiple market failures, significant state intervention and perhaps endemic corruption in the host country greatly politicises international trade and investment. If big companies need to talk about new regulatory changes or potentially important new trade and investment projects, they are more likely to talk to DFAT and heads of mission about the political, economic and security environment and try to enlist Australian government support to their cause. In these posts, DFAT involvement with Austrade might go no further than providing occasional embassy cover for relatively minor Austrade initiatives.

It is very different at posts where there are robust trade and investment relationships with frequent visits by Australian ministers and companies and where perhaps there is an established Australian

---

5 This applies specifically to offices outside national capitals.

business presence. Ambassadors support Australian commercial interests through frequent calls on ministers and senior officials of host governments and regional and provincial governments; by facilitating high level business-to-business meetings and making it a priority; and by opening big trade promotion events – rightly or wrongly, ambassadors tend to encourage higher level representation from host governments than senior trade commissioners. Major commercial projects are often backed up by teams involving DFAT and Austrade officials. Market access issues are a signature "DFAT" issue but may involve Austrade in several ways. As indicated in the previous section, Austrade is involved in identifying impediments to trade and investment and much of this work is done at posts. Austrade officers also become involved in access issues because they often understand better than their DFAT colleagues the commercial realities of having products tied up at ports because of quarantine or other regulatory issues: Austrade talks the language of frustrated Australian exporters more readily than DFAT.

Depending on the post, trade-related work increasingly involves trade in education services, inward and outward investment and things like trade displays and business missions. Policy and promotion aspects of trade in education aspects are drawing closer together, at times producing some creative tensions between agencies. DFAT works with Treasury and others on the policy context of foreign direct investment flows in FTAs and negotiations for bilateral investment agreements. Austrade works on investment attraction and has quickly warmed to this task, especially the deal making aspects of state asset sales and big infrastructure projects. Heads of missions in turn add value to this work through their geopolitical and whole-of-government insights and by drawing on their wider government networks in host countries, and on the resources of the economic and political sections of embassies. The strongest internal links of embassies' economic sections are often with the political sections, Austrade and immigration sections – visas for official and business delegations visiting Australia are the lifeblood of commercial relationships.

This sub-set of posts, often located in emerging countries, buzz
with energy. Synergies between trade policy and trade and investment
promotion are driven fundamentally by the mass and quality of the
trade work. There is a great deal of it, it is interesting, and it keeps on
increasing and changing in response to broader economic, technical
and policy changes in host economies and in the global and regional
economies. Synergies also are driven by the quality of working
relationships between the agencies. Relationships matter more at posts
than in Australia because a relatively small number of officers are stuck
with each other for several years and have to pull together to make
things work. At the end of the day, relationships are driven more by
personalities than policies or administrative circulars that try to define
what a particular relationship should be. There can be gaps between
the approaches of Austrade officers – often private sector-recruited
– and more conventionally bureaucratic DFAT officers. There can
be tensions if the media target very senior Austrade representatives
rather than ambassadors on subjects where the latter may have a more
'whole-of-government' view. There can be budget-related tensions:
differences over 'fair' payment from attached agencies for common
services provided by the embassy can get the blood running at times.
But, as a broad generalisation, so long as both DFAT and Austrade
officers are sensible and corporate-minded, it is not too difficult to
work through these sorts of challenges.

Proximity and less hierarchy than in Australia help in this process.
The two agencies are often co-located. Heads of mission, senior trade
commissioners and their staffs usually get to know each other very
well and come to understand posts' overarching objectives. Less
formality, coupled with less proximity to ministers or secretaries/
chief executive officers or the Australian media, also creates space
in a hands-on environment for more interaction, personal initiative
and reaching common sense arrangements in pursuing inter-agency
goals. But however it works, the bottom line is this: close cooperation
between DFAT and Austrade at a number of posts has delivered notable
successes from supporting national efforts to win supply contracts

for liquefied natural gas, to securing banking and insurance licences in China, to participating in Hong Kong's Rapid Transit Railway system, to securing access for mining and mining services companies in Asia and South America, to attracting foreign direct investment into Australia, to pulling together for prime ministerial and other high level visits.

DFAT-Austrade relations: possibilities for the next few years

Looking out to the next few years, it seems reasonable to expect that the DFAT-Austrade relationship will continue to evolve and become closer. This has possible institutional dimensions – the National Commission of Audit (2014) has recently recommended merging DFAT and Austrade – and more fundamental dimensions based on how threads of trade policy might combine more effectively with trade promotion strategies, as well as with foreign and economic policies, to steer Australia through a potentially difficult period in the international economy.

We have no sense of the outcome. We do, however, see that the federal government's budget pressures and claims of duplication within the bureaucracy will encourage moves to rationalise and consolidate departments and agencies. We also see that, possible 'easy' portfolio savings apart,[6] incorporating Austrade into a new commercial arm of DFAT could well turn out to be a bad idea.

DFAT already has enough problems integrating the former AusAID without adding to them by incorporating Austrade with its own distinctive and separate culture. More importantly from the broader perspective of the government's trade and investment agenda, a commercially focused Austrade is doing good work, particularly in emerging and difficult markets and in established markets in relation to investment attraction. Quite plausibly Austrade's commercial culture

---

6 So-called 'easy' options for portfolio savings, like closing the head office in Sydney and moving trade teams to Canberra, could turn out to be costly if they weakened Austrade's links to international business and reduced its access to private sector talent. Around two-thirds of Austrade's senior staff have private sector experience. Persuading them to move to Canberra would be challenging.

would gradually weaken by being too close to DFAT. Austrade's standing in the business community certainly would be damaged: a statutory authority headed by a secretary-equivalent officer has more status than the commercial arm of a large policy department. And, crucially, Austrade's capacity to 'polish' the trade minister's profile in the business community and reinforce the minister's own links with that community would be weakened: depending on the extent of any weakening, this could have negative implications for advancing domestic and international elements of the government's trade and investment agenda.

Irrespective of institutional outcomes – DFAT and Austrade remaining distinct and separate institutions or merging or even trade policy and trade and investment promotion functions being merged within a re-created DoT – the trade policy and trade and investment promotion agendas will need to draw closer together over the next decade in response to difficult and fast changing regional and global economic and trading conditions (Adams, Brown & Wickes 2013, especially Ch. 5). The following trends in world trade and trade policy stand out:

- Relatively slow growth in advanced economies has the potential to retard growth in emerging and developing economies and stoke protectionist pressures.

- Economies in East and South Asia are likely to become more important. China, in particular, should become a key partner in bilateral trade relations with more countries. South-South trade and investment should increase in significance but is not "de-coupled" from growth in advanced economies A key implication is that Australia has a big stake in supporting access for Chinese/Asian products into US and European markets through actions that reinforce the centrality of the global trading system.

- Technological change and competitive pressures will

lead to more unbundling of functions in manufacturing and services. More trade in intermediate products and services will involve more countries. And more supply chain trade will occur not only within large multinational companies anchored in advanced economies but also in multinational companies anchored in emerging economies, especially China. All of this will increase the importance of understanding the links between imports, exports and inward and outward investment in these chains, how to access these chains and how to extract more value from them. It also will increase the importance of sound domestic economic settings and efficient regulatory systems that facilitate trade and investment.

- There will be more bilateral and regional trade agreements that will delve deeper into behind-the-border regulatory issues and focus more on economic cooperation and issues like trade and investment facilitation.

- And the conduct of international trade and investment will become more complex with more prominent countries wanting to play a role, more issues and more politics as countries trade more of their economies across national borders. With their different histories and priorities, leading developed and emerging countries will struggle at times to manage their relationships on trade and other matters.

Closer DFAT-Austrade coordination across the range of trade issues in response to these and other challenges raises the obvious question: what does closer coordination mean in practice beyond vague statements like doing more to improve trade performance across all sectors and doing more to capture the synergies between good trade policy and trade promotion? (For expositional purposes, we assume that DFAT and Austrade remain as separate agencies and retain their current core points of focus – the former on broad international policy and diplomacy, the latter on providing trade intelligence and support to SMEs and facilitating inward investment – but our comments apply equally to other institutional possibilities.)

At one level, closer coordination means building on what is already in train. Examples include:

- Assisting Australian businesses – large and small, and across a wide range of sectors – to identify and capitalise on opportunities expected to flow from the recently agreed FTAs with China, Japan and South Korea (Australia's first, second and fourth largest trading partners respectively). This work could be enhanced by DFAT and Austrade collaborating on why Australian SMEs are less involved in regional value chains than some of their counterparts overseas, and on the policies that might encourage greater involvement.

- Tasking DFAT and Austrade with making FTAs "living agreements" by fully utilising the built-in agendas of high-quality FTAs to pursue reform over time. The Australia-New Zealand Closer Economic Relations Trade Agreement is the classic example of the commercial and wider economic benefits that can flow from driving ongoing commitments within trade agreements. The Australia-China FTA may be the latest example with more negotiations foreshadowed in three years time on agriculture and foreign direct investment.

- Regular government-to-government reviews of agreements, preferably at ministerial level, can inject a sense of ambition into taking agreements further. But the effectiveness of reviews depends on DFAT and Austrade being tasked, as a priority, to monitor the implementation of agreements. This encompasses identifying barriers and other regulatory impediments to full access that could be taken up in various consultations and other processes created by trade agreements. It also could include developing strategies to update agreements in line with evolving business requirements.[7]

- Building on Austrade's "one-stop-shop" approach on FTAs. An Austrade group with expertise in the complexities of FTAs could be set up to provide advice directly to companies or to its geographical divisions to reinforce their discussions with business. To be effective, the group would need critical mass and some stability: senior officers in Austrade, as elsewhere in the Australian Public Service, tend to move jobs fairly frequently. Close links with DFAT negotiators also would be essential in building expertise.

- Complementing DFAT's broad policy interests in investment, education and tourism. Austrade's role on foreign direct investment includes promotion, attraction and facilitation, and is supported through the recruitment of specialist skills (from banks and investment firms). Similarly, Austrade has particular skills and policy roles in relation to education and tourism – Australia's third and fourth largest exports respectively.

- Setting out the scope for more systematic engagement between ambassadors and senior trade commissioners at posts. To some extent this is already done through ambassadors' appointment letters but these letters tend to be very general and are not distributed widely, even at posts. Generic codification by head offices would be needlessly bureaucratic and perhaps counter productive. But arrangements worked out by heads of missions and

---

7 Progress has been patchy to date in transforming interest in to action in making FTAs "living agreements". In part, this reflects the different circumstances and priorities of our FTA partners. But, arguably, it also reflects "uneven oversight and direction of review processes within DFAT" (Adams Brown & Wickes 2013, pp. 325-6).

trade commissioners to meet unique requirements at individual posts, regularly reviewed by them to remain relevant and endorsed by head offices might add value, especially where embassies and Austrade offices are not co-located.

At another level, closer coordination means having the vision to build new areas of cooperation that focus more on achieving quality medium-term outcomes for Australia's trade and investment performance. Four ideas are considered here. The first can loosely be described as more cooperation at the level of strategic thinking. This could take a variety of forms. An important one would be joint cabinet submissions on topics like what FTAs Australia should consider negotiating and how existing and prospective FTAs might impact on value chains. Joint work, whether for cabinet or other purposes, also would be useful on topics like offshore opportunities in regional car components value chains, aspects of international education and tourism, and the links between trade and investment – there is still no refined understanding of trade and investment patterns in Asia and what drives them. Similarly, it could be useful on topics like how services (testing, design, engineering, research and development, etc.) can be leveraged internationally in their own right and in supporting manufacturing, resources and Australia's technological leadership in agriculture, and how administrative and regulatory reform and changes in markets of interest to Australia may impact on Australian companies and the options available to the Australian government to keep markets open.

Second, information is ubiquitous because of massive advances in communications technology over recent decades. Large companies have their own contacts and systems to get information on market opportunities, impediments and risks, and SMEs can assemble a great deal of information about particular markets from online sources. The dynamics of providing trade intelligence are therefore vastly different from when Austrade was set up nearly 30 years ago. But a major challenge has emerged: commercial information may be ubiquitous but commercially valuable information is not. This creates potential opportunities for new and improved management of trade-related information:

> Government agencies working overseas – DFAT, Austrade, Treasury, Defence, Immigration, Agriculture and so on – collect an enormous amount of information on economic and trade issues in the course of their day-to-day work. Some of it is similar to information in specialist newspapers and journals. Some is more sensitive being based on privileged access to political leaders, policy makers and business leaders. The latter can be accessed by government departments in Australia through the diplomatic cable network and a sub-set of that is occasionally made available to business in a sanitised form. But much of the gathered information – classified and unclassified – stays within defined administrative silos at a considerable opportunity cost. Even in an information-rich world, clever collating, slicing and dicing of information and targeted dissemination of tailored 'products' to clients – industry associations, companies and government clients – would be valuable (Adams, Brown & Wickes 2013, p.273).

Third, understanding business needs and capabilities by staying close to companies and business associations, international trade negotiations, government-to-government consultations, and trade commissioners networking in foreign lands to open doors to commerce are instantly recognisable as core aspects of trade policy and trade promotion. What is not so recognisable, though it is important and is notionally part of the trade armoury, is the value that could be added to the efficiency of domestic regulation, and therefore to Australian industry's international competitiveness, if DFAT and Austrade's perspectives and priorities could be injected more readily into regulation and policy on issues that feed in to business costs and competitiveness. This is an old issue that has perplexed liberalising trade ministers since at least the time of Peter Cook in the mid-1990s.

There are obvious reasons why trade agencies will never play a big role. They lack the resources and scale of domestic agencies. But this is no reason why they shouldn't play more of a role on a carefully selected set of issues or on aspects of those issues – examples are infrastructure development, energy costs and the links between trade, inward and outward direct investment and the long term development of Australia's domestic economic capability – because international competitiveness understandably is not the principal focus of domestic regulatory agencies.

Take for example the question: how can Australian manufacturing companies fit more effectively into global or regional value chains? Answering it clearly requires an understanding of domestic supply capabilities and the dynamics of modern manufacturing: about half the gross value of Australia's manufacturing exports comes from either imported inputs or the inputs of other domestic sectors. It also requires having a good working knowledge of the domestic regulatory environment. But actually assisting companies to link into value chains requires having internationally competitive regulatory systems. An important priority for DFAT and Austrade should be to gear up to play a more influential role in developing a domestic regulatory framework that reinforces links to value chains. Without it, trade negotiators and trade commissioners will have a much harder job in opening doors to Australian commerce and their labours might generate fewer benefits for the national economy.

And fourth, the Australian government needs to develop and articulate a consistent view about trade, investment and trade policy and their contributions to Australia's future. DFAT and Austrade can add value to work on the international economy and trade by drawing on their global networks and telling stories that link into good policy analysis, add a human dimension and reach out to a broader audience than Treasury's more technical analyses. This audience prospectively includes business, civil society and state and territory governments. DFAT and Austrade also can add value by acknowledging that distinctions between trade policy and trade promotion are narrowing given changes in value chains and investment relationships. This means that definitions of an Australian company, product and interest are blurring. It also means, for example, that DFAT has an opportunity to complement Austrade's work on investment attraction through significant and sustained outreach strategies targeted at improving the Australian community's awareness of the benefits of foreign direct investment. There is a great deal of misinformation about the economic implications of Asian/Chinese direct investment in particular. To have any chance of resonating with the wider community, positive messaging would have to be backed up by real life and 'fresh' examples of the benefits flowing from overseas invested projects.

In the more fluid relationship that has evolved between trade policy and trade promotion, ministerial statements that extol the value of exports and inward investment and ignore or downplay imports and outward investment miss the point about what makes successful international companies in the 21st century. Successful exporters are often successful importers and have to be to keep their costs competitive. Similarly, successful companies might be simultaneously both importers and exporters of capital, ideas and strategies, and again have to be to remain competitive. It is perfectly understandable why ministers and agencies stick with old stories and formulations. They are easy to explain to the public: they side step the creative destruction that is part and parcel of trade-induced structural change, and ignore the fact that imports from more efficient sources are the principal way that trade contributes to rising welfare. They also provide guidance to officials: attract investment into priority sectors of the Australian economy, work with business to increase exports of a particular product or service and so on. But these approaches are out of date and too mercantilist. The mercantilist mindset has been degraded over the years in Australia but it needs to be buried across government and replaced by a narrative that properly, and consistently, links trade and investment, imports and exports, goods and services, and emphasises the centrality of unilateral economic reform and trade liberalisation if Australia is to remain a successful, confident country that can continue to deliver growth, jobs and higher living standards.

For any of these four suggestions to be taken seriously, they would have to be a priority for portfolio ministers, have the support of the DFAT and Austrade leaderships, and be backed up with appropriate funding either through new budget allocations (which would seem unlikely in present circumstances) or through some agreed re-prioritising (which is always contentious even if it occurs at the margin).

Some initiatives, like on trade intelligence and being credible contributors to domestic reform, would be expensive and require good staff with deep knowledge and a willingness to specialise. If they were to be implemented, progress would probably be made incrementally through a series of small steps rather than through one or two leaps. But budget constraints aside, the single biggest challenge to implementing these types of initiatives is that ministers and the senior executives of both agencies would need to recognise more – and act on – the limitations imposed by short-termism and policy segmentation, and consciously want to look for synergies at all levels between trade policy and trade promotion (and foreign policy). The odd inter-departmental committee meeting would not suffice. But recognising these limitations is very hard. Immediate issues have to be addressed. And the importance of trade (even buttressed by the priority accorded to economic diplomacy) will, and must, wax and wane relative to other issues like security, defence and geo-strategic issues as international circumstances change. Ministers quickly become obsessed by new issues and transmit their obsessions to their departments and agencies. Taking a medium term view on trade in this situation is not for the faint hearted.

Conclusion

From time to time trade ministers must have wondered why DFAT and Austrade weren't working more closely together. By and large they have worked closely at posts, but the record is more mixed in Australia. For some time, relations in Australia have been getting closer. At one level this growing closeness is a response to changes in international trade and investment that are blurring the distinction between trade policy and trade promotion and increasing the scope for interaction. At another level it is a response to Austrade operating more easily in the policy space.

The two agencies naturally have their own priorities. Everyone is busy. Officers get together as needed. But the relationship should desirably become closer still if trade policy and trade promotion are to work in harness in meeting challenges thrown up by structural change in world trade and investment. Just how the agencies might manage this transition institutionally and through adjustments to their priorities requires serious thought and commitment. Senior managers and portfolio ministers can't be too busy with other things. It must be one of the priorities for the government's economic diplomacy initiative. The initiative would make a solid contribution if it leads to more strategic vision and serious policy analysis on trade and investment issues, encourages ministers to abandon mercantilist rhetoric and recognise the implications of international supply chains, and gets more people into key positions with a remit to institutionalise changes that might outlast them.

Bibliography

Adams, M., Brown, N. & Wickes, R. 2013, *Trading Nation: Advancing Australia's interests in world markets*, UNSW Press, Sydney.

Kelly, G & La Cava, G 2014, International Trade Costs, Global Supply Chains and Value-added Trade in Australia, Reserve Bank of Australia, Research Discussion Paper RDP 2014-07, Sydney.

National Commission of Audit 2014, *Towards Responsible Government*, Commonwealth of Australia, Canberra.

Nethercote, J. 1999, *Departmental Machinery of Government Since 1987*, Research Paper No 24, Department of Parliamentary Library, Commonwealth of Australia, Canberra.

Uhrig, J. 2003, *Review of the Corporate Governance of Statutory Authorities and Office Holders*, Commonwealth of Australia, Canberra.

25

Quo vadit Austrade?

Bruno Mascitelli

Austrade today

With fewer than 1,000 staff of whom 75 per cent are based overseas and operating in 82 offices in 48 countries, Austrade's challenges are bigger than ever before. Since 1986, Austrade has had six managing directors (CEOs since 2006) and 10 ministers from both sides of politics. In 2013 added to the Austrade portfolio of export and investment promotion education was tourism policy, programs and research. A significant 60 per cent of overseas staff are based in Asia and at last count Austrade was in 12 locations in China, plus 10 across India. Besides its trade functions, Austrade is also the manager of 17 consulates across the world providing consular services which in 2013 assisted over 100,000 Australians.

The Austrade of today operates under very different conditions from those at the time of its establishment. The changes in technology, internet, social media and other forms of marketing out-reach make the task of helping exporters and trade promotion more challenging. Today the exporter is better equipped and informed when embarking on new markets so the Austrade value adding has had to adjust to these new conditions.

The 2014 budget deliberations were preceded by the Abbott government appointment of a National Commission of Audit which made more than 65 recommendations. Amongst these recommendations was one for Austrade to be absorbed into DFAT. Many were shocked that such a recommendation be splashed all over the newspapers and done so publicly. Others in and around Austrade were surprised, but not entirely. The following days saw a number of pundits come to the defence of Austrade including Greg Sheridan in *The Australian*, whose editorial piece was titled "To slash Austrade a mistake" (Sheridan 2014). Sheridan noted the importance of an organisation like Austrade to Australian exporters and its elimination would be harmful to the Australian economy. Equally he acknowledged the disciplined and collected response of the Austrade management to the news from the Audit Commission. He aptly noted:

> In response, the head of Austrade, Bruce Gosper, quietly sent out an email to Austrade staff around the world telling them this was a report to government, not by government, and that the best thing Austrade could do would be to continue to do its work as well as possible (Sheridan 2014).

Despite this bombshell announcement from the National Commission of Audit one week before the national budget, the Abbott government made no reference to Austrade in the budget or in any of the budget narrative. Nor was Austrade in the 150 agencies destined for closure and restructure announced in December 2014. It was a close shave yet again.

The events of 1985-86 which saw the establishment of Austrade in a grand "one-stop-shop", providing a user-friendly, externally focused and consolidated export facilitation operation seem almost unrepeatable in the context of the modern Australian political economy. Governments of today are relatively lackluster in terms of visionary scenarios, especially considering the tighter control of fiscal purse strings. As such, grandiose plans for government expansion – leave aside those of the 1973-75 Whitlam period – and those like the Dawkins plan for Austrade – are almost unimaginable today and governments on both sides. Equally today more than ever,

Australian governments of both persuasions are coming to the view that government activities should interfere in the economy as little as possible. This is notwithstanding the benefit of "seeding" initiatives, especially where it may reduce the time, cost and risk of business trying to establish new markets.

Austrade has been Australia's primary and indeed preeminent government export facilitator since it was established. Austrade arose out of a merger of five disparate segments of export related activities within various government portfolios. But since its establishment it has lived a rather precarious existence. At the behest of each change of government, or government policy and each financial budgetary cycle, plus government's obsession with reining in excess government expenditure in the economy – making Austrade operate effectively has become even more difficult. Why after almost 30 years of existence is Austrade still vulnerable and insecure? Why can it still find itself targeted for removal as a government export and international business facilitator as was witnessed in 2014?

The collection of chapters and interviews presented in this book provides ample evidence of an organisation which has worked hard at achieving its mission – improving Australia's export and investment performance and thereby contributing to Australia's ongoing prosperity. The theme of this book has been to put Austrade under the microscope. Some of the accounts in the front of the book provide a historic overview, prior to the advent of Austrade. Fletcher's journey from the Commissioner Service to the establishment of Austrade is one such account. The beginning of Austrade clearly required the ministerial architect John Dawkins to provide the political leadership and narrative for the need for an organisation of this kind. The chapter addressing the first years of the new Austrade under the direction of Lindsay MacAlister reminds many of the difficult task of establishment and finding its feet on the journey to a new approach towards export facilitation. Investment attraction was added to the Austrade portfolio in the late 1980s. This is articulated extensively and in detail by Peter Collens in his chapter. The demise of MacAlister and the first review of Austrade, by McKinsey & Co was certainly historic and defining. This is meticulously brought back to life by one of the managers assigned to the Review team, Terry Goss. The 1990s saw an expansion of Austrade under Ralph Evans and Charles Jamieson both explained through interviews (Jamieson through the eyes of his deputy, Peter Langhorne). Working in Eastern Europe, before and after the fall of the Berlin Wall and the end of the USSR is sometimes overlooked. Fortunately Ian Wing and Roger James in their respective periods bring these markets to life and explain how Austrade operated in them. During the early Howard government years, Austrade ended up in the arms of Ex-Minister Fischer who relished both the trade policy as well as the Austrade trade promotion through his most original style and approach. The long O'Byrne stewardship of Austrade saw many important developments which covered the "doubling the number of exporters" initiative, greater media exposure, opening up more key senior management positions to women, re-absorbing Invest Australia, galvanising the benefits of a growing number of free trade agreements, capitalising on major events through the Business Club Australia, plus starting the integration of the international education promotion portfolio. Throughout Austrade's period of operation measuring the performance of the organisation has routinely come up for scrutiny. Greg Dodds tackles this thorny question in this book in a measured and retrospective manner. The final section of the book addresses the Austrade of today and tomorrow. Bruce Nicholls suggests there might be better ways to carry out export facilitation while Peter Wilton examines what is around the corner in terms of future international business developments and how Austrade will be part of this scenario. The chapters by Bruce Gosper and Laurie Smith seek in part to address many issues about the Austrade they know and work in today with forthright responses to many dilemmas and challenges they are faced with. The chapter by Mike Adams and Nicolas Brown provides a most balanced view of the real relationship between DFAT and Austrade as they see it and lived it. The chapters in their totality address the almost thirty years of persistent activities which an export facilitator faces on a daily basis. Sometimes with experiments, untried formulae and novel approaches all to further Australian exports. Being an agency of government there was also the balancing act of addressing a multitude of stakeholders, needs and desires. The experience established highs such as that of its establishment, a business board to oversee and guide it, the evolution of an organisation seeking to promote trade and investment.

At its zenith Austrade could claim to have one of the largest and most extensive global footprints of any government agency, including its senior portfolio partner, DFAT. Equally Austrade was not new to innovative approaches towards new export channels. One such activity, in concert with New Zealand's Tradenz, involved developing sectorally segmented business development units (BDUs), which reached right back into industry development, through the creation of "joint action groups" (JAGs), networks and consortia to capture targeted initiatives. These were so popular with Senator Peter Cook, the then Trade Minister, in the Keating government, who when asked to become Industry Minister, reputedly requested to have the BDUs transferred with him! Suffice it to say this didn't happen. Instead and unfortunately they were disbanded under the incoming Conservative government. Moreover Austrade with all its government monitoring and mentoring was very much the product of the initiative of individuals and leaders innovating and thinking for what was unavailable as a blueprint. This is an organisation with a pioneering, innovative and independent spirit quite rare in most of government, which is to some extent envied. On the other hand Austrade also experienced difficult moments such as being caught in the ethical traps of international business and judged by the recent National Commission of Audit as not worthy of an independent existence.

The changing external environment: new challenge or opportunity for Austrade?

The 30 years that have passed has witnessed a staggering change in the external geopolitical, technological and economic environment, much of which directly impacted Austrade and the way international business is being conducted. Domestically this has included the perennial reviews, government and ministerial changes, and not forgetting the yearly financial and budgeting difficulties, plus the increasing desire of Australian state and territory governments to install their own representation overseas, thereby fracturing the "Australia Inc." message. Some domestic changes have been welcoming, including 20 years of strong economic growth, the commodities and resources boom, the rise of the services sector, albeit alongside the regrettable decline of manufacturing, as the MNCs in particular chase production bases with the lowest point on the cost curve and economies of scale. But this has meant greater dominance of "price taker" sectors – for example resources and agriculture, versus "price maker" sectors which are more differentiated, with lower dollar sales volumes, but higher sustainable returns like hitec and services, including education and tourism.

Internationally we have seen in the last 30 years, the end of the Cold War; two serious economic crises (Asian and GFC); upheaval in the Middle East; plus the staggering rise of China and other Asian economies, right on Australia's door step and time zone. As such we are reminded by the prospect of moving from Geoffrey Blainey's concern at "The Tyranny of Distance", to Tim Harcourt's "Power of Proximity", all within a context of the so-called "Asian Century". Markets have changed each with its own features and each with a trade narrative requiring solutions not only at the multilateral level, but equally at the bilateral, regional and even pluri-lateral level. The rise of technological and digital economies alongside greater levels of accessible travel and global people movement, plus the use of social and other media, allowing for easier spread of information, means there is now a markedly changed world in which business is operating. Many of these changes have provided greater commercial opportunities while others can equally provide uncertainty in the market place. Within the thinking of many economies we have witnessed important political movements rise to prominence, many having economic implications, including the assertion of desired self-sufficiency creating in some countries a reversion to protectionism and even nationalism. These are new challenges to contend with when doing business internationally.

Domestically the changes have been just as profound. Awareness of international markets and understanding their characteristics has raised expectations on Austrade service delivery. The differentiation and therefore different approach required towards the "born globals" (as McKinsey coined them), multi-domestics and multinationals as well as the need for accessibility to integrated global supply and value chains makes the tasks of trade facilitators that much more complex. Equally we are witnessing the blurring of domestic and international markets, two-way interaction between exports and imports, plus inwards and outwards investment (including the establishment of strategic alliances, partnerships and joint ventures) and how these relationships can provide greater leverage for growing international business. These developments have necessitated the need for Austrade to provide a more sophisticated, streamlined and valued service, especially as companies have greater access to market intelligence. This in turn changes the nature of the desired service delivery both at desk and in country requiring not only the need, for "concierge", but also "trusted advisor" type services (especially in developing nations).

The last three decades for Austrade have also witnessed a number of internal changes which have been as defining as they have been structurally significant. The McKinsey Review changed the *modus operandi* of the organisation, the most significant impact being decentralised senior management out into the field. The government's Uhrig Review of Statutory Agencies lead to the removal of the Board, change from a Managing Director to CEO and transition from being under the Trade Commission Act, to the Financial Management and Accountability (FMA) Act, and therefore fully integrating within the Public Service machine. The Peter Grey "Reform of the Australian Trade Commission – *Maximising Our Value*" of May 2011 equally reaffirmed what Austrade uniquely provided to the Australian business community and how its internal operations would need to be in line with a more strategic approach. Not being all things to all people in short. Much of the current Austrade global approach remains wedded to this this reform and may do so for some time.

The National Commission of Audit: More than just a bleeding of Austrade?

For decades funding for Austrade has been declining in real terms, under the administration of both sides of politics and government. The exception to this was when funding was injected for specifically defined new initiatives or programs (such as TradeStart, or Business Club Australia). As a prelude to the delivery of the first Abbott government budget, news spread that the government had appointed a Commission of Audit, designed to investigate Australia's government expenditure. The Commission was headed by Business Council leader Tony Shepherd and the findings were released in early May 2014. Austrade was amongst an extensive list of agencies singled out by the Commission "for being wasteful". According to the Audit Commission, Austrade's $335 million per annum budget didn't appear to represent 'value for money'" (Janda 2014). The Commission also recommended to "significantly reduce the activities of Austrade and incorporate any residual functions into a commercial arm of the Department of Foreign Affairs and Trade" (NCOA 2014). The Commission of Audit also called for the scrapping of the Export Market Developments Grants and as well as the Export Finance Insurance Corporation (EFIC). The Commission found that Austrade should be reduced as it was assisting in a relatively small level of export sales. The National Commission of Audit recommendation under the category of "Assistance to Exporters item number 33" reads as follows:

> As the benefits of exporting accrue primarily to the business undertaking the activity, the Commission considers that there is scope to reduce current Commonwealth assistance for exports by:

> Abolishing EFIC, ceasing funding for Export Market Develop-
> ment Grants, tourism industry grants and the Asian Business
> Engagement plan, halving funding for Tourism Australia and
> significantly reducing the activities of Austrade: and moving
> residual functions of Tourism Australia and Austrade into a
> commercial arm of the Department of Foreign Affairs and Trade,
> with existing loan book of the Export Finance and Insurance
> Corporation also transferred to DFAT to investigate options to
> on-sell or wind up the loans (NCOA 2014).

Speculation about Austrade's survival has rarely been off the
agenda over the years though rarely publicly presented by the
government of the day as it did with findings of the Commission of
Audit. Suddenly Austrade found itself at the centre of an identity and
functional crisis asking itself why this poor appreciation of its role and
function? What is different from the past with this declaration is that
it was no longer just whispering and innuendo circulating about what
might or might not happen to Austrade. This time it was commissioned
by government and placed in the public domain. Moreover it is a
conservative, seemingly "pro business" Coalition government which
has declared war on "business welfare". Whichever way one seeks
to look at this even Austrade is, as the preamble to the report asserts,
"business welfare". To make the point further the report stated that
export benefits "accrue to the business undertaking the activity". That
is, the Commission of Audit questioned why government support
should be provided when the benefit goes to the individual company.

Austrade's relevance in the bigger picture of global trade?

Free Trade Agreements (FTAs) have dominated the trade policy space
for over a decade. No doubt some of this is due to the failure of the
multilateral (WTO Doha Round) as well as the desire for quicker
results of medium benefit, be they bilateral, regional or pluri-lateral
agreements. The current Abbott government has been even more
effective in this area with the signing of three FTAs (South Korea,
Japan and China) in one year alone, albeit after many years of

negotiation, including under the prior government. Some might say that the numbers game of more FTAs has become an obsession by governments, with too much emphasis on the political impact of these agreements than the real long term substance and outcome. But what do these extra FTAs mean for Austrade? In actual fact they provide the means for business to export (and import) or invest with fewer obstacles with specifically agreed FTA partners. But how does business undertake this task? Is the policy and regulatory liberalisation of an FTA sufficient to encourage Australian business to export? What of the smaller companies – how do they leverage these FTA outcomes to export? While government feels it has carried out its obligation of removing obstacles to market entry, in certain markets the hard yards of actually exporting remain the domain of business. Will businesses act on these FTA changes? Should businesses be entitled to assistance in order to benefit from these new opportunities, as happened with the FTA with the USA? These are some of the questions querying the need or otherwise for the continuation of a government funded export facilitation agency. Notwithstanding the gradual removal of some regulatory constraints, often business is not aware of the opportunities they may now enjoy, plus other obstacles still remain to growing sustainable international business. With opportunities come the need, for example for market intelligence, export preparation, advice on international risk minimisation, supply and sustainability of exports, market search for importers, distributors end users and partners, investment opportunities and promotion. The trade promotion side of exports will become more intense with more agreements.

There is much rhetoric on Australian trade and exports heard daily, broadcast from government and media channels. Research shows that in the past decade, the number of Australian companies actually exporting has grown from about 25,000 to some 45,000 equating to an increase from four to six per cent. While the number of companies that export is at least increasing, the question that must be asked is if and to what extent should government play a role in assisting them to expand internationally?

Over the years a number of services have been refined and perfected to accommodate each step in the journey to export and international business. These were "in house", or by establishing formal relationships with clearly defined objectives with allies (other federal agencies, state and local government, industry associations, chambers of commerce and bilateral chambers), or corporate partners (professional service providers such as accountants, lawyers, bankers, insurance and logistics houses and their institutes) to achieve a "power of one" or multiplier effect. In addition to raising awareness about the benefits of going international (including, for example developing and administering a program across secondary schools with a national take up of over 95 per cent in business or economic related curricula), Austrade's ability to impact on the number of exporters appears to be around 4,500-6,000 of those companies that are export ready and that Austrade can work with on a yearly basis. The debate which has been at the forefront of the role of government is equally relevant to the role and future of Austrade. While much rhetoric is consumed on the benefits of trade, the concern expressed by government of the costs involved in providing this service is equally as strong.

Another key aspect relating to the relevance and value that Austrade can provide, is the issue of measuring the value of government agencies and specifically in this context Austrade. Throughout the 1980s and 1990s measuring the performance of government agencies took hold. In some cases it became an obsession. More recent times there has been an easing of this necessity as efficiency measures have reached extreme proportions, invariably decided by budgetary restrictions. Key performance indicators, as widespread as they might be, remain in certain scenarios a blunt instrument. In the Austrade case they certainly were less helpful than expected. In fact measuring client satisfaction for future intentions and referring services to other companies and entities ("the net promoter" score, as Peter Wilton calls it) has proven a more beneficial barometer.

The risks of being a government agency in dealing with international business

Austrade was struck by publicly broadcast scandals throughout the first decade of this century, the extent of which it had not seen previously. This was despite the fact that the organisation had in place an active and diligent Audit and Risk Committee and Probity regime. The three events included the Australian Wheat Board (AWB) scandal over the Iraq food for oil program; the Firepower fraud reputed as being "the most spectacular fraud in Australian history" (Ryle 2009); and Securency, the subsidiary of the Reserve Bank of Australia seeking to win a tender for the provision of new bank note technology with the Vietnamese government. Each of these events has been heavily investigated for the public record. Authors such as Overington (2007), Bartos (2006) have covered the AWB and Ryle has published on Firepower (2009). Each issue involved senior levels of Austrade but in different ways and each left their mark.

The question asked by many is whether there is any meaning or significance to these events in terms of the integrity, character and functioning of Austrade? Touching these issues in this Austrade book was probably the most delicate part of this study and yet in some respects the least important. It was essential to treat these issues so as to demonstrate there was no defensiveness in this project despite its embarrassment for Austrade. On the other hand over stating the significance of these events would at the same time provide a distorted view of what makes Austrade tick.

The risk of assisting in international business, be it for Austrade or any other business or government agency are a constant concern. Commercial due diligence in an international environment can be a full time task and is easier said than done. This is no excuse but a statement of fact. Doing this along with other more central activities in an environment of ongoing and declining resources might be a recipe for concern. In the case of the AWB investigative journalist Overington duly noted that "More than 50 of Australia's diplomats, officials and bureaucrats in New York, Washington and Canberra had now been made aware of the 'allegations' or 'irregularities in AWB's contracts" (Overington 2009: 42). This included Austrade in the US. But Austrade was one of the government crowd and according to both Bartos and Overington, was quite peripheral to the events and was more a party to indirect information than directly involved in dealings with either the company or the Iraqi government. The fact that it was John Finnin that met the Iraqi trucking company, Alias (Baker 2007), is both ironical and the continuation of bad luck for Austrade.

Selling the message

In an interview recorded with Tim Fischer, former Trade Minister and Deputy Prime Minister (and latterly Ambassador to the Holy See in Rome) (see Chapter 11), he was asked precisely why a valuable organisation like Austrade can come under the knife of the Commission of Audit? Besides underscoring that there may have been some prejudicial views from Treasury, Fischer felt that Austrade and other government departments – he also pointed out DFAT – shared a strong weakness in their inability to sell their good work and results. He believed they failed to realise the value they were adding and how it impacted on Australian trade outcomes. He indicated that these organisations seem to shy away from glare and attention and thought being back room staunch loyal civil servants was sufficient. Fischer may have a point here but is it really simply a matter of lack of self-publicity and promotion?

Government departments and agencies rarely are in the game of high profile and media attention. The manner in which former Austrade Chief Economist Tim Harcourt managed the media while at Austrade raises precisely these dilemmas but also the success in doing so. Harcourt provided a profile for Austrade never seen before. He ensured that he had two to three press releases per week, sold the story that exports produced more and better paid jobs, relatively better company returns, improved living standards and thereby contributed to the economy and not just exporters. Arguably this was the right thing for Austrade to be doing. Harcourt gives the impression it was "tolerated" within Austrade though there was some resentment in the back rooms.

Working with DFAT

The Bartos study (2006) on the Australian Wheat Board (AWB) scandal of 2004, besides tackling in succinct terms the events surrounding the AWB scandal, made some illuminating commentary on the relationship between Foreign Affairs and Trade – I.e., DFAT and Austrade. He acknowledges that the 1987 merger between Foreign Affairs and Trade while hesitant and uncertain at the beginning ended with greater coordination. He states:

> The rationale for the amalgamation was that both the trade and diplomatic/consular functions involved representing Australian interests internationally, and should be brought together (Bartos 2006: 61-62).

However the divide in the foreign affairs and trade area remains at the operational level with the separate existence of Austrade. According to Bartos, parts of DFAT still look down on Austrade because "they are all cowboys" ... because of the applied, operational nature of its business" (Bartos 2006: 62). A more measured DFAT view is available in the chapter by former DFAT colleagues in this book.

This raises the question of "economic diplomacy" which has become a standard part of the discourse of the current Abbott government and especially of the Foreign Affairs portfolio as well as the Trade and Investment portfolio. In the websites of both Foreign Affairs and Trade and Investment, the two ministers have eloquently defined their understanding of "economic diplomacy". Minister Robb says:

> Our economic diplomacy drive is intrinsically linked to the Coalition's aggressive trade and investment agenda. Better outcomes from our economic engagement with the world result in stronger economic growth, more jobs and greater prosperity for Australians" (Robb, Trade and Investment website, 2014 website).

Equally as engaging is Julie Bishop, Minister for Foreign Affairs, who states:

> Economic diplomacy is a collaborative process, beyond government. Australia's business community, our think tanks, our NGOs and our community are an integral part of our economic diplomacy efforts. We look forward to working together to pursue shared opportunities to drive economic prosperity, in Australia and in our region (Bishop, DFAT website, 2014).

In some respects the merger of Foreign Affairs and Trade in 1987 was the first act of "Economic Diplomacy" in the pure sense. Foreign Affairs and Trade working together on key national interest activities at home and abroad. But some healthy skepticism has to be part of this narrative. What does it really mean? Besides ambassadors and high commissioners being briefed by the Foreign Affairs Minister before going to a post, are their KPIs now based on economic returns to Australia as well as the smooth relations with the host country? Is it a first step in the re-alignment of the two separate areas of foreign affairs and trade whereby it is now time for Austrade and trade promotion to close the separateness bringing foreign affairs, trade policy and trade promotion all under the single umbrella?

In conversations with former DFAT personnel the response was somewhat inconclusive. One colleague referred to it as "new parlance" for old tasks. Another commentary was:

> it might be trying to convey the view that the Abbott government's foreign and trade policy has a hard economic edge. This hard edge must come as no surprise to those who have been negotiating FTAs over the last few years or negotiating closer economic and political engagement with the region over many more years (Adams 2014).[1]

Is Austrade a part of this "economic diplomacy"?

---

[1] Personal email communication with DFAT colleagues taking an active interest in Trade Policy, 2014.

Conclusion

Ultimately government, more so than business, will have the final word on what form, if any, Austrade should continue to provide the role of the export and international business facilitator. The political argument for having an organisation like Austrade would, it seems, be the decisive factor in justifying this commitment more so than the economic one – though it too is important. The decision to maintain, renew or remodel an Austrade will come down to its value as an organisation and its ultimate value adding rather than a bottom line "bean counting" monetary justification. If it is seen as being indispensable, adding value and improving the scenario for growing exports, investment and internationalisation, hence contributing to the ongoing prosperity of the nation, then more than likely it will have a future. Though what that might mean as can be evidenced from the chapters in this book, is less clear.

The separation of Austrade from trade policy within the Department of Trade in 1986 was not appreciated by all. The following year, 1987, when Trade and Foreign Affairs merged, the irritation was in some quarters, even greater. Foreign Affairs from within remained constantly concerned that Austrade needed to be with DFAT. Total absorption under the management of DFAT, as recommended by the National Commission of Audit is a possible scenario. The fact that the last two CEOs have emerged from the Trade Policy and FTA negotiation side of Foreign Affairs and Trade provides a greater bridge to this hypothesis. But the last four years might also signal "peace talks" that together is better especially when abroad and especially when the government wants a stronger Australian Inc "Economic Diplomacy" approach. It would in effect represent the return of Trade Promotion to the same department as Trade Policy which some feel is its natural home.

From one angle, many of the issues raised in this book connect to the great debate between those who scorn support for exporters as business welfare and those who believe that government plays the key role in nation Building. Our very heavy dependence on the export of raw materials is obvious and even the most fervent barbecue catechist does not quite believe breezy assurances that the "market will fix it" if international markets for these items collapse. The government is expected to plan (and protect) against adversity and Austrade's programs can be seen as one of those measures, helping diversify the trade mix and increase the high value add exports. Nevertheless, the debate continues and the turbulence of Austrade's short history is due in part to the intersection of these two powerful rivers of opinion in our public life.

John Dawkins indicated at the 80th Anniversary of the Trade Commission Service, celebrated in the Old Parliament House, Canberra, in February 2014, that Australian trade policy and approach has essentially been a bipartisan one and has sought to pursue free trade, in whatever form, against protectionism, for this is seen as in the best interests of all. Austrade, yesterday and today, has played a role in pursuing this objective.

Austrade faces a pivotal moment in its future. Not a scenario of its choosing but one imposed by changing governments and the limitations of the public purse which is unforgiving. Historically there has been much anger directed at Treasury as being the fiscal dries and even in some quarters as the "hidden Tea Party" faction of the government. While humorous on the surface, the discourse on the government purse is one that will not tolerate major government expenditure. The governments of both sides are convinced that lower taxation is good for all and as a result so too lower government spending, in order to hopefully maintain budgetary balances and maybe later budgetary surpluses. In this context the future of Austrade is a difficult one and as such one which covers a spectrum of possibilities. Will it remain as it is, will it be totally integrated into DFAT (or say the Industry Department) or could it simply disappear? A series of questions few will admit to knowing the answer to.

In all likelihood Austrade will remain a feature of the international business landscape in the short term. Beyond that it is difficult to tell. The presence and influence of certain government ministers appears to be a decisive feature of how Austrade is seen. The activism and effectiveness of Minister Andrew Robb has postponed any pessimistic scenario and highlighted Austrade's invaluable features in enhancing international business. The content of this book has also sought to highlight what these traits were and are and how they played out to promote Australian trade. It would be a worthy thought that before other reviews are undertaken of Austrade, that there is some familiarisation of the content of these pages which may provide some deeper understanding of this organisation, of how it has travelled in the last 30 years and what its role should be in the next 30 years.

Bibliography

Adams, M., 2014, Personal communication with Mike Adams, Canberra.

Baker, R., 2007, Downer 'knew' about AWB kickbacks, *The Age*, 7 November 2007, http://www.theage.com.au/news/federal-election-2007-news/downer-knew-about-awb-kickbacks/2007/11/19/1195321 695303.html, accessed 16 December 2014.

Bartos, S., 2006, *Against the Grain: The AWB Scandal and Why it Happened*, UNSW Press, Sydney.

Bishop, J., 2014, What is economic diplomacy? Adams M., Department of Foreign Affairs and Trade, Canberra, http://www.dfat.gov.au/trade/economic-diplomacy/, accessed 10 January 2015.

Janda, M., (2014), Commission of Audit: Industry assistance and support for exporters targeted, 2 May 2014, http://www.abc.net.au/news/2014-05-01/hold-implications-for-business-of-commission-of-audit-report/5423572, viewed 15 May 2014.

NCOA National Commission of Audit, 2014, Towards Responsible Government, The Report of the National Commission of Audit – Phase One, http://www.ncoa.gov.au/report/phase-one/index.html, accessed 3 November 2014.

Overington, C., 2009, *Kickback: Inside the Australian Wheat Board Scandal*, Allen & Unwin, NSW.

Robb, A., 2014, What is economic diplomacy?, Department of Foreign Affairs and Trade, Canberra, http://www.dfat.gov.au/trade/economic-diplomacy/, accessed 10 January 2015.

Ryle, G., 2009, *Firepower: The Most Spectacular Fraud in Australian History*, Allen & Unwin, NSW.

Sheridan, G., (2014), To slash Austrade a mistake, *The Australian*, 3-4 May 2014, News Limited, Sydney.

Appendices

Appendix 1 – Austrade Board: Chairmen and Secretaries 1986-2006

Date	Austrade Chair	Board Secretary
1986-1988	Vern Christie (Bill Ferris)	Geoff Spears
1988-1993	Bill Ferris	Mike Moignard – starting in 1992 Alan Hartigan
1993-1995	Robert Johnston	Alan Hartigan
1995	Roger Allen (acting)	Alan Hartigan
1995-2001	Alan Jackson	Stefan Trofimovs
2001-2006	Ross Adler	Stefan Trofimovs

Appendix 2 – Managing Directors and CEOs of Austrade 1986-2015

Years	Managing Director/CEO
1986-1990	Lindsay MacAlister
1991-1996	Ralph Evans
1996-2002	Charles Jamieson
2002-2009	Peter O'Byrne
2010-2012	Peter Grey
2013-present	Bruce Gosper

Appendix 3 – Austrade Staff by Group or Division – 30 June 2014

Group/Division	Aus	Overseas-engaged employees	Total staff 30 June 2014	Total staff 30 June 2013
Established Markets	24	154	178	155
East Asian Growth Markets	30	180	210	228
Growth and Emerging Markets	25	128	153	149
Australian Operations	139	0	139	167
Tourism, Education and Corporate Operations	234	18	252	207
International Operations Australia	15	0	15	13
Human Resources	37	6	43	40
Office of the CEO	19	0	19	12
Inoperative	23	0	23	32
Total	546	486	1,032	1,003

Source: – Austrade Annual Report 2013-14.

Appendix 4 – Senior Executive Service by gender 30 June 2014

Category	Female	Male	Total 30 June 2014	Total 30 June 2013
SES 1	14	27	41	39
SES 2	6	11	17	17
SES 3	0	3	3	3
Total	20	41	61	59

Source: – Austrade Annual Report 2013-14

Appendix 5 – Austrade locations as of 30 June 2014

Australia	East Asian Growth Markets	Established Markets	Growth and Emerging Markets
Adelaide	Bandar Seri Begawan	Auckland	Abu Dhabi
Brisbane	Bangkok	Chicago	Accra
Canberra	Beijing	Frankfurt	Ahmedabad
Darwin	Chengdu	Fukuoka	Bangalore
Hobart	Guangzhou	Istanbul	Bogota
Melbourne	Hangzhou	London	Buenos Aires
Newcastle	Hanoi	Madrid	Chandigarh
Perth	Ho Chi Minh City	Milan	Chennai
Sydney	Hong Kong	New York	Colombo
Townsville	Jakarta	Osaka	Dhaka
Wollongong	Kaohsiung	Paris	Dubai
	Kuala Lumpur	Port Moresby	Hyderabad
	Kunming	Prague	Islamabad
	Manila	San Francisco	Jaipur
	Nanjing	Sapporo	Jeddah
	Qingdao	Seoul	Johannesburg
	Shanghai	Stockholm	KarachKochi
	Shenyang	Suva	Kolkata
	Shenzhen	Tel Aviv	Kuwait
	Singapore	Tokyo	Lahore
	Taipei	Toronto	Lima
	Ulaanbaatar	Vancouver	Mexico City
	Wuhan	Warsaw	Moscow
	Yangoningdao	Washington DC	Mumbai
			Nairobi
			New Delhi
			Port Louis
			Pune
			Rabat
			Riyadh
			Santiago
			Sao Paulo
			Vladivostok

Appendix 6 – Ministerial Trade portfolio 1972-2015

Dates	Name of Trade Ministry	Minister	Date of Ministerial tenure
19 December 1972 20 December 1977	Department of Overseas Trade	Jim Cairns Frank Crean Doug Anthony	19 December 1972-11 December 1974 11 December 1974 – 11 November 1975 12 November 1975 – 20 December 1977
20 December 1977 11 March 1983	Department of Trade and Resources	Doug Anthony Special Minister for Trade negotiations – John Howard Minister for Special Trade Representations Ransley Garland Doug Scott Ian Sinclair	20 December 1977- 11 March 1983 20 December 1977 – 11 March 1983 20 December 1977 – 8 December 1979 8 December 1979-19 August 1980 19 August 1980-3 November 1980
11 March 1983 24 July 1987	Department of Trade	Lionel Bowen John Dawkins	11 March 1983-13 December 1984 13 December 1984-24 July 1987
24 July 1987 Present	Department of Foreign Affairs and Trade	Bill Hayden Michael Duffy Gareth Evans Minister for Trade Negotiations Michael Duffy Neal Blewett Ministers for Trade and Overseas development Neal Blewett John Kerin Ministers for Trade Peter Cook Bob McMullan New Howard Government Tim Fischer Mark Vaile Warren Truss New Rudd government Simon Crean New Gillard government Stephen Smith Craig Emerson Ministry of Trade and Competitiveness Craig Emerson New Rudd government Richard Marles New Abbott government Trade and Investment Andrew Robb	24 July 1987-7 August 1988 18 August 1988-31 August 1988 2 September 1988-24 March 1983 24 July 1987-4 April 1990 4 April 1990-27 December 1991 1 February 1991-27 December 1991 27 December 1991-24 march 1993 24 March 1993-30 January 1994 30 January 1994-11 march 1996 11 March 1996—20 July 1999 20 July 1999-29 September 2006 29 September 2006-3 December 2007 3 December 2007-28 June 2010 28 June 2010-14 September 2010 14 September 2010-5 March 2012 5 March 2012-27 June 2013 27 June 2013-18 September 2013 18 September 2013-incumbent

Appendix 7 – Austrade's Brandmark – A history

AUSTRADE BRANDMARK
HISTORY
28 JANUARY 2015

Brandmark	Implemented	Notes
	1986	Original brandmark Introduced at the establishment of Austrade
	1991	Green and gold brandmark with black text › Modifications: reduced text size relative to map, fully justified text, text colour changed to black, increased angle and length of stripes and amended top and bottom of map
	1994	Kangaroo and swish brandmark › New Austrade brandmark and colour scheme introduced (1994-95). › Annual report first appeared in – 1994-95.

	2003	Agency Coat of Arms
		Two variations:
		1. Australian Trade Commission
		  a) Annual report first appeared in – 2002-03.
		2. Austrade
		  a) Annual report first appeared in – 2003-04.
		  b) NB: Austrade means the Australian Trade Commission [as referenced in the Export Market Development Grants Act 1997].
		The Australian Government decided in June 2003 common branding would apply to all Australian Government departments and agencies (and this branding policy continues to apply under the current government).

	2010	Agency Coat of Arms lock-up with Australia Unlimited brandmark Two variations (Austrade and Australian Trade Commission). › Annual report first appeared in – 2009-10. › Brandmark continues to be in use to this day.

Footnote: The Australian Trade Commission version of the brandmark is generally used offshore.

Appendix 8 - Business Club Australia

Capitalising on major events through Business Club Australia

In the late 1990s, the scale and profile of major international sporting events was growing and amidst the media-friendly spectacle of sporting competition, the world's focus and interest was also drawn to the characteristics, culture, business strengths and capabilities of host nations. No structured program existed to convert the accompanying profile into a platform showcasing Australia as a sophisticated supplier of goods and services, or as an attractive investment destination.

The impending 2000 Olympics to be hosted in Sydney provided the imperative for the Federal Government to task Austrade to create an innovative program leveraging the international excitement of the Olympics into business results. *Business Club Australia* was launched, and an exciting new era in corporate networking began. And the Club started with the iconic 98m, 5-story Incat moored alongside the Australian national Maritime Museum in Sydney's Darling Harbour.

The outcomes

From 2000 until 2010, *Business Club Australia* transformed into a continuous multi-year, multi-market and multi-sport platform to facilitate international business across a range of industries. It was endorsed by the Australian Government as its official business networking program around global sporting events. During this time, *Business Club Australia* engaged 38,990 high-level international business executives and senior government ministers through targeted networking activities. 329 business-networking events were delivered around the world. The program is accredited with facilitating over A\$2 billion in international business.

The program

Business Club Australia leveraged the excitement and international media attention around major sporting events to showcase Australia as a preferred trade, investment and education destination, and to boost opportunities for Australian firms to build productive international business connections. It provided a genuine and forensic platform for a range of Ministers, Federal and State, to have a meaningful role in a national business program.

A typical program had a dedicated venue and included a mix of business and industry networking events, business missions, an integrated marketing and media campaign plus high level sporting and business Ambassadors. It incorporated public and private partnerships, corporate hospitality at sporting events and high-level government and business involvement. Importantly, it also carried the endorsement from the respective peak sporting body such as the Australian Olympic Committee.

Business Club Australia programs were delivered for:

Sydney 2000 Olympic Games

Rugby World Cup 2003 (Australia)

Melbourne 2006 Commonwealth Games

Rugby World Cup 2007 (France and Wales)

Melbourne Cup Spring Racing Carnival (2006-2008)

Beijing 2008 Olympic Games

Vancouver 2010 Winter Olympics

FIFA 2010 World Cup South Africa

New Delhi 2010 Commonwealth Games.

The shift came with the London 2012 Olympics where a different approach was executed to solely showcase Australian expertise and capability in delivering major sporting events to the decision makers from countries hosting major sporting events until 2022, including Japan, Qatar, Russia, Brazil and the Republic of Korea.

Legacy

Created and managed by Austrade, *Business Club Australia* was the first program of its kind in the world. Following the program's success over the years, *Business Club Australia* was replicated by numerous countries including the UK, India, Canada, New Zealand and Scotland. In all instances, Austrade assisted relevant TPOs and Organising Committees to create their Business Club. In 2008, the International Olympic Committee (IOC) also produced a case study on *Business Club Australia* to help future Olympic bidding cities in their submission. In 2005, the program won the Australian Marketing Institute National Award for Innovation in Marketing Excellence, a first by an Australian government agency.

~~~~~~~~~~~~~~

Words by Ashley White. Ashley was Business Club Australia Manager from 2003-2010 before heading up the Major Sporting Events section for Austrade until his departure in 2013. Prior to then, he designed the business strategy for the AFC Asian Cup and the Cricket World Cup 2015 in Australia. He is now the General Manager International at Bastion S+GO, a consultancy firm which designs and deliver high-level business development, engagement and stakeholder relations strategies for a range of business, government, community, cultural and sporting organisations.

Index

www.ingramcontent.com/pod-product-compliance
Lightning Source LLC
Chambersburg PA
CBHW060126280326
41932CB00012B/1437